Y0-BCD-360

THE LIFE OF
THOMAS HUTCHINSON

A Da Capo Press Reprint Series

THE AMERICAN SCENE
Comments and Commentators

GENERAL EDITOR: WALLACE D. FARNHAM
University of Illinois

THE LIFE OF
THOMAS HUTCHINSON

ROYAL GOVERNOR OF THE PROVINCE
OF MASSACHUSETTS BAY

BY

JAMES K. HOSMER

DA CAPO PRESS • NEW YORK • 1972

0269079

98839

Library of Congress Cataloging in Publication Data

Hosmer, James Kendall, 1834-1927.
  The life of Thomas Hutchinson.
  (The American scene: comments and commentators)
  Reprint of the 1896 ed.
  1. Hutchinson, Thomas, 1711-1780. I. Massa-
chusetts (Colony). Governor, 1770-1774 (Thomas
Hutchinson). II. Massachusetts (Colony). General
Court, 1773.
F67.H9806   1972   974.4'02'0924 [B]   70-124926
ISBN 0-306-71038-2

This Da Capo Press edition of *The Life of Thomas Hutchinson*
is an unabridged republication of the first edition published in
Boston and New York in 1896.

Da Capo Press, Inc.
A Subsidiary of Plenum Publishing Corporation
227 West 17th Street, New York, N.Y. 10011

All Rights Reserved

Manufactured in the United States of America

THE LIFE OF
THOMAS HUTCHINSON

From a painting by Copley

THE LIFE OF

THOMAS HUTCHINSON

ROYAL GOVERNOR OF THE PROVINCE OF MASSACHUSETTS BAY

BY

JAMES K. HOSMER

AUTHOR OF "SAMUEL ADAMS," IN "AMERICAN STATESMEN" SERIES
"A LIFE OF YOUNG SIR HENRY VANE" ETC.

BOSTON AND NEW YORK
HOUGHTON, MIFFLIN AND COMPANY
The Riverside Press, Cambridge
1896

Copyright, 1896,
By JAMES K. HOSMER.

All rights reserved.

The Riverside Press, Cambridge, Mass., U. S. A.
Electrotyped and Printed by H. O. Houghton & Co.

TO

JOHN FISKE

LONG MY FRIEND

IN RECOGNITION OF A SPECIAL SERVICE

GENEROUSLY RENDERED

Surrexit clypei dominus septemplicis Ajax;
Et nostræ valuere preces.   Si quæritis ejus
Fortunam pugnæ non sum superatus in illa.
Opposuit molem clypei, texitque jacentem.
                    OVID : Metamor. XIII. 89, etc.

CONTENTS.

CHAPTER I.

YOUNG MANHOOD AND ENVIRONMENT.

1711–1737.

CHAPTER II.

FINANCIAL SERVICES.

1737–1749.

CHAPTER III.

THE CHIEF JUSTICESHIP.

1749–1762.

0269079

98839

CHAPTER IV.

THE STAMP-ACT TUMULTS.

1762–1765.

CHAPTER V.

THE REPEAL OF THE STAMP ACT.

1765–1766.

CHAPTER VI

THE END OF BERNARD.

1766–1769.

CHAPTER VII.

HUTCHINSON AT THE FRONT.

1769–1770.

CHAPTER VIII.

ACCESSION TO THE GOVERNORSHIP.

1770–1771.

CHAPTER IX.

ROYAL INSTRUCTIONS.

1771–1772.

CHAPTER X.

THE COMMITTEE OF CORRESPONDENCE.

1772–1773.

CHAPTER XI.

CHAPTER XIV.

THE YEARS OF EXILE.

1774–1780.

NOTE ON THE ILLUSTRATIONS.

The portrait of Governor Hutchinson used as a frontispiece is from a painting by John Singleton Copley, now in the possession of the Massachusetts Historical Society.

The Hutchinson House, facing page 24, was situated on Garden Court Street, Boston, and destroyed by the mob on the night of August 26, 1765. The reproduction is from The American Magazine of Useful and Entertaining Knowledge, February, 1836.

The original letter from Governor Hutchinson to Samuel Swift, a facsimile of which faces page 304, is in the Massachusetts Archives, Boston State House.

INTRODUCTION.

LESSING once projected a series of papers to which he purposed to give the name *Rettungen* (Rescues), his design being to vindicate from obloquy great men of the past to whom harsh measure had been dealt out. It was a generous thought of a most just and courageous mind, and deserves imitation in every age. The history of America, like that of every land, has its *bêtes noires*, characters remembered, for the most part, only to be execrated, some of whom certainly do not deserve their bad fame ; and of these there is no more pathetic example than Thomas Hutchinson, the last royal Governor of Massachusetts Bay before the futile effort of England to divide with the sword the perplexities of the on-coming Revolution.

Says Lecky of the American Loyalists : " They comprised some of the best and ablest men America has ever produced, and they were contending for an idea which was at least as worthy as that for which Washington fought. The maintenance of one free, industrial, and pacific empire, comprising the whole English-speaking race, may have been a dream, but it was at least a noble one." [1] Such a declaration sounds in American ears very British and extravagant, but it is certainly right that the characters and principles of the Tories should be restudied. The number of those

---

[1] *Hist. of XVIIIth Century*, vol. iii., p. 454.

who took the Tory side in the American Revolution and were driven into exile, it has been claimed, was relatively to the full as large as the number of Huguenots expatriated from France by the Revocation of the Edict of Nantes. There were no better people in the country for intelligence and general worth, — none who, up to the time of their mistaken and unfortunate choice of sides in that last crisis, had served their country better. That one error has canceled in the minds of their countrymen all their excellence. Where their meed has not been utter oblivion, it has been ignominy. Scarcely more than one Tory can be mentioned who has been made the subject of a respectful biography, Benjamin Thompson Count Rumford, whose scientific note and romantic career it was impossible to overlook. Ought this neglect and misappreciation to continue always?

Among Tories there was no one so illustrious through his position and abilities as Thomas Hutchinson. His historical writings give him a respectable place in the literature of his century. They are in fact declared to have " the highest value, proving his mind to have been a judicial one, full of candor, moderation and a desire for truth." [1] To his ability as a judge the following testimony may be cited from one of his successors in the governorship of Massachusetts, himself an eminent jurist, who says, speaking of Hutchinson as Chief Justice : —

" Few who sat upon the bench in the last century were more deserving of commendation than Judge Hutchinson. His character in this capacity was irre-

---

[1] Hon. Charles Deane : *Proceedings of Mass. Hist. Soc.*, vol. iii.

proachable. His learning, even in the science of the law, was highly respectable, and, when we consider his early education, was indeed remarkable. He possessed great clearness of thought, and excelled in that most difficult property of a good judge, a clear and intelligible statement of the case upon which he was to pass. It is a traditionary anecdote that, after listening to the charges given by his associates, juries were in the habit of remarking when Hutchinson rose to address them, 'Now we shall have something which we can understand.' . . . In his official character he had great readiness and capacity for business, and was faithful and laborious in the performance of his duties. He was a fluent and graceful speaker, a vigorous writer, and a respectable scholar. . . . Had he lived at almost any other period of our history, with the same industry and application of his powers, his fame would have survived as that of an useful, honorable, and honored man."[1]

As a financier John Adams celebrated Hutchinson thus thirty years after his death : —

"If I was the witch of Endor, I would wake the ghost of Hutchinson, and give him absolute power over the currency of the United States and every part of it, provided always that he should meddle with nothing but the currency. As little as I revere his memory, I will acknowledge that he understood the subject of coin and commerce better than any man I ever knew in this country."[2]

In the time before John Adams became Hutchinson's

[1] Emory Washburn : *Judicial Hist. of Massachusetts*, pp. 304, 305.

[2] Given in Curwen's *Journal*, p. 456, from " an unpublished letter to Joseph Ward," October 24, 1809. The letter, though not included in John Adams's Works, has indisputable internal marks of genuineness.

bitter enemy he wrote thus of the general estimation in which Hutchinson was held: "Has not his merit been sounded very high by his countrymen for twenty years? Have not his countrymen loved, admired, revered, rewarded, nay, almost adored him? Have not ninety-nine in a hundred of them really thought him the greatest and best man in America? Has not the perpetual language of many members of both Houses and of a majority of his brother-counselors been, that Mr. Hutchinson is a great man, a pious, a wise, a learned, a good man, an eminent saint, a philosopher, etc.? Nay, have not the affection and admiration of his countrymen arisen so high as often to style him the greatest and best man in the world; that they never saw, nor heard, nor read of such a man, — a sort of apotheosis like that of Alexander and that of Cæsar, while they lived?" [1] Hutchinson in fact pervaded the life of his time in a remarkable way, standing out as a leading figure in the most various spheres. The chapters which follow will, it is believed, show that for a quarter of a century, from before the fall of Louisburg up to the year 1774, when his exile began, there was no more eminent personage in the western hemisphere than he. How it has come about that a fame once so brilliant has passed to such an extent from the memories of men, the reader will come to know, and find reason, it is hoped, for kinder thoughts of the discredited chief magistrate of those stormy times.

The position of the writer of this book needs to be distinctly defined at the outset. He believes that in

---

[1] John Adams' *Diary*, March 17, 1766.

any Anglo-Saxon community Abraham Lincoln's "plain people" can be trusted to govern themselves, and that power to do so should belong to the masses, each man having his vote. "Some men are fools all the time; all men are fools sometimes; but all men are not fools all the time." Our great Abraham leaves us but a narrow margin; it will suffice, however, in any English-speaking land, for the basis of a stable polity. Undoubtedly such a democracy is often unlovely in its manifestations. Emerson quoted approvingly Fisher Ames, as saying that "a monarchy is a merchantman which sails well, but will sometimes strike on a rock and go to the bottom; whilst a republic is a raft which would never sink, but then your feet are always in the water." [1] The discomforts of the raft are indeed great, and the feet of those who are embarked upon it have never been wetter probably than at the present hour. Many who until now have floated upon the raft confidently begin to feel that it must be forsaken. When such a leader as Herbert Spencer declares that his faith in democracy is gone and that we are on the high road to military despotism, believing apparently that it will be a better consummation than a continuance of present conditions, ordinary men cannot be blamed for feeling some doubt about institutions heretofore cherished and implicitly trusted. We are, however, on the raft for good and all. We must make the best of it; whatever defections may occur, it is unmanly for Americans to be faint-hearted. When all is said that can be said, democracy exhibits no disad-

[1] *Essays*, 2d series; "Politics."

vantages which cannot at once be paralleled or surpassed in the experiences of aristocracies and monarchies. In an Anglo-Saxon community, inheriting as it does the traditions of two thousand years of self-government, the people can and ought to take care of themselves; and it is culpable faint-heartedness to believe that the elements other than Anglo-Saxon which have flowed in upon us have so far canceled or emasculated Anglo-Saxon strength that we need to be taken in hand by a master.

As to the "Anglo-Saxon Schism," as Goldwin Smith calls it,—the splitting apart of the race which took place when the Thirteen Colonies broke away,—a schism which some lament as a calamity, what is the wise view to take at the present moment? The writer of this book believes that there should be a cordial fraternization of the whole great English-speaking world, to-day 130,000,000 strong, and really in all substantial respects one and the same as regards tongue, literature, institutions, and social usages, whether settled in South Africa, in Australasia, in the primitive home, or in the United States.[1] Old prejudices should be cast aside; the English-speaking states, recognizing their kinship, should knit bonds together around the world, forming a kingly brotherhood inspired for beneficence, to which supreme dominion in the earth would be sure to fall. According to Gladstone's couplet: —

> "When love unites wide space divides in vain,
> And hands may clasp across the flowing main."

[1] For a detailed presentation of this idea, see the writer's *Short History of Anglo-Saxon Freedom.*

If love would but once unite, the seas could not sever. Earth has never beheld a commingling of men so impressive, so likely to be fraught with noble advantages through ages to come, as would be the coming together of English-speaking men into one cordial bond.

Yet, with all that, it was not a calamity when the men of '76 broke the empire apart. We have made no mistake in doing them honor; it was well that the schism came. To use a figure no homelier, perhaps, than that of the raft which Emerson takes so approvingly from Fisher Ames, — a political construction should be after the model of the *bob-sled* of the lumberman of the Northwest. If the vehicle were in one frame, the load pressing from above and the inequalities of the road beneath would rack it to pieces at once; let there be runners, however, before and behind, each pair distinct and independent, yet linked by appliances always flexible but never parting, all immediately goes well. Among the stumps and gullies of the rough track, the contrivance, readily yielding yet never disconnected, easily bears on its weight of timber; the shortest corners are turned, the ugliest drifts surmounted. That Anglo-Saxondom was sundered is not a subject for regret. In one frame, so to speak, it could not do its work. That its burden might be well and safely borne the division into two was salutary, indeed inevitable. What is to be regretted is that the severance involved bloodshed, and produced a hatred which rankles yet. The split should not be utter. While the two frames are separate an indestructible link should connect them, allowing to each free play for itself while making the two after all one.

Such ideas as the foregoing were not those of Thomas Hutchinson. First, he was no democrat. His great adversary, Samuel Adams, did him no injustice in declaring: "It has been his principle from a boy that mankind are to be governed by the discerning few, and it has been ever since his ambition to be the hero of the few." Matthew Arnold's doctrine of the "remnant," in fact, that in every society a select company of choice natures must exist and exercise leadership in order to a proper consummation, would have had the hearty approval of the Massachusetts worthy. Such a doctrine had the approval of John Winthrop,[1] as it has at the present day, even in democracies, the approval of numbers perhaps constantly increasing. If Hutchinson felt that in these guiding few a foremost place in his own time and land belonged to him, it can properly be said that he was not presumptuous, for his career quite justified in him a good estimate of his own wisdom. Government by the people was no principle of his. King, Lords, and Commons, the three ancient pillars of the British polity upon which should be apportioned and balanced with all care the weight of authority, were institutions good enough for him. They had satisfied Pym and Hampden before him; so, too, the framers of the Bill of Rights in the time of William and Mary; so, too, in his own time, Mansfield, and even Chatham and Burke, liberal though they were. No one dreamed then of popular sovereignty but the wild soci-

---

[1] "The best part of a community is always the least, and of that best part the wiser part is always the lesser." *Winthrop's Journal*, vol. ii., p. 428, ed. 1853.

ety of the Friends of the People, supporters of the disreputable John Wilkes; and, in the colonies, the tumultuous crowd who presumed to decide in town-meeting what had heretofore been left to the judgment of those high in place. If Hutchinson was no democrat, so, moreover, was he no favorer of a severance of the empire. At some distant day, indeed, a time might come when parting in friendship might be well. At present, however, it was not expedient to think of it. Independence would bring calamity, not benefit, to both motherland and colonies. In his view one political frame would answer well for the whole Anglo-Saxon world; and in that frame harmony required that the British Parliament should be supreme. That supremacy, once recognized, he would have kept well in the background and as far out of sight as possible, while perfect freedom was accorded to the dependency in all local affairs. What he desired, in fact, was the relation existing today between mother-land and colony, the voice of the home legislature never heard save in imperial concerns. The wisdom of division with a brotherly link to connect the distinctly separated parts, after the fashion of the lumberman's sled, was not apparent to him; but then, in the time of his activity, separation was contemplated by everybody, excepting Samuel Adams, with feelings of dread.

Hutchinson's ideas were not those which have come to prevail upon the soil which he ardently loved and from which he was ruthlessly driven; but his ideas he held with the utmost honesty and fought for with the stoutest courage. In his beliefs and in his championship he had in his day excellent company; many, possibly an increasing number, in our own day will say he was nearer right than his enemies. At any rate the struggle he waged was so manful, his general spirit through it was so humane, the good he wrought for his country was really so substantial, that his fame well deserves a *rescue* after the long obloquy. To attempt this *Rettung* has been a grateful task.

There is no lack of materials for the biography of Hutchinson. The patriots of his day have been, as they deserved to be, profusely commemorated. The deeds of James Otis, Joseph Warren, Josiah Quincy, John and Samuel Adams have found recorders; and in the case of each it has been quite impossible to tell the story without making, up to the Revolutionary outbreak, nearly as prominent as the principal figure, the form of the opposing royal chief magistrate omnipresent in all the battle. Hutchinson himself, while an exile in England in his old age, prepared an autobiographical sketch, recounting his career from childhood to the troubles of the Revolution. At that point the story is taken up in the third volume of his " History of Massachusetts Bay," which also was written during his exile, and is, of necessity, simply his personal record, as he wrestled with the men who at last bore him down. The autobiographical sketch, with large extracts from the diary and letters which he wrote during his exile, have been published in two volumes[1] under the care of his great-grandson, Peter Orlando Hutchinson. The third volume of the history, a most precious Revolutionary

[1] *Diary and Letters of Thomas Hutchinson* ; Houghton, Mifflin & Co.

document, was not printed till 1828, nearly fifty years after the death of the writer.

More interesting, however, as a source of information concerning Hutchinson is the large mass of manuscript material left behind him in his hasty flight in 1774, and now preserved in the Massachusetts archives in the office of the Secretary of State. He was the most painstaking and methodical of men, in the case of every important letter or document, and often of quite unimportant notes, making a draft to be carefully preserved in his letter books. These papers, sometimes copies of the perfected document, sometimes apparently the rough outline from which the production was afterwards finished, are contained in three thick folio volumes, marked 25, 26, and 27, and labeled "The Hutchinson Correspondence." The collection comprises some fifteen hundred letters, the greater part written by him, though a few are addressed to him. Occasionally one finds the work of an amanuensis, usually one of his own children, no doubt; but for the most part it is the laborious hand of the old Governor which fixes the line upon the page. Still a fourth volume, labeled "Hutchinson's Manuscript History," contains the first part of vol. ii. of the history, and a few other matters. When Hutchinson fled from his home on Milton Hill, June 1, 1774, he left his house in charge of his gardener, it is said.[1] The

---

[1] *Collections of Massachusetts Historical Society*, vol. x., pp. 117–133; "Report on the Hutchinson Papers," by George E. Ellis, Emory Washburn, and Joel Parker, Feb. 13, 1868. See also Justin Winsor's careful account of the vicissitudes of the Hutchinson papers; *Narrative and Critical History of America*, vol. viii., pp. 431, etc.; Appendix, "Manuscript Sources of the History of the United States," pp. 19, etc.

authorities under the new order of things did not meddle with it until after April 19, 1775. Meantime the house had been entered and much carried away. April 29, General Thomas, the Provincial officer in command on that side of Boston, was ordered to take possession of the Hutchinson papers, when the letter-books were found in the keeping of Captain Hugh McLean or his brother-in-law, Mr. John Boies. A tradition says that they had been hidden in the sacks of beds. Fifty pounds were paid for them by the State, in the expectation that evidence from them would implicate the Governor in plots against the people. When recovered, committees to examine them were appointed by the Provincial Congress, selections being afterward published in Massachusetts papers, and also in the London Liberal organ, Almon's " Remembrancer."

At the present day, these four old volumes form certainly one of the most interesting relics extant of our Revolutionary days. As the student pores over them, the doughty soul of the Tory Governor almost seems to be yet close at hand; the red pencil marks of his enemies, the committees of the Provincial Congress, noting with microscopic eye every phrase which might tend to incriminate him, have a heat and truculence which the lapse of a century and a quarter has not destroyed: there are pages to which still adhere mud and the stains of rain, got while they lay in the street into which they had been flung by the mob at the time of the Stamp Act.

While no careful life of Hutchinson has ever been written, his career has several times been sketched in brief articles. Noteworthy among these are the accounts of his contemporary, John Eliot, in his "New England Biographical Dictionary;" and, in later times, of W. H. Whitmore,[1] W. F. Poole,[2] and especially of the late lamented president of the Massachusetts Historical Society, Dr. George E. Ellis.[3] These later authorities, basing their conclusions largely upon the revelations of the "Diary and Letters," have portrayed Hutchinson with much fairness, and helped essentially toward a reconstruction of the popular verdict concerning him. His figure has, however, sufficient significance to justify a more elaborate picture.

The present writer has studied with care everything important, both in print and in manuscript, which Hutchinson has left. As authorities, the manuscripts have an especial value, and have been much depended upon.[4] By the courtesy of the state officials, the collections in the Massachusetts archives were freely thrown open. The important correspondence of Hutchinson with Colonel Israel Williams, preserved in the library of the Massachusetts Historical Society, was examined through the kind permission of Dr. S. A. Green. The character of the journal kept by Hutchinson in England during the sad and uneventful years of his exile is abundantly illustrated in the volumes of his great-grandson. Certainly nothing is contained

---

[1] N. Y. *Nation*, xxxviii, 298.

[2] Chicago *Dial*, v. 53 ; vii. 102.

[3] *Atlantic Monthly*, liii. 662 ; lviii. 561. A fair English account is given in the *Dictionary of National Biography*.

[4] Referred to in the footnotes as *Massachusetts Archives Historical*, or *M. A. Hist.*, xxv., xxvi., and xxvii.

there not in accord with the records of his vigorous time.

Besides consulting what the Governor has left, the effort has been made to gather from other sources what knowledge seemed to bear upon the topic. In particular, the writer's acquaintance with the literature relating to Samuel Adams has been of value to him. It was while writing the life [1] of that sturdiest and trustiest of the Sons of Liberty, indeed, that the worth and greatness of his opponent became plain to him. To draw one without drawing the other is as impossible as it would be to photograph a wrestler in action without catching at the same time the champion with whom he was locked. In his previous book, the present writer has already made a portrait of Hutchinson: it is, however, meagre, and the idea has constantly pressed that this man, so long neglected and misrepresented, one of the worthiest of the sons of Massachusetts, ought to have a book to himself. Though traversing to a large extent the same ground as in the "Samuel Adams," the author has made the attempt to repeat himself as little as possible. Some documents, quoted in the earlier book, it was necessary to give also in the present work. A few pages also have been quoted from the earlier text. It will be found, however, that the chapters here are not reproductions of the former considerations; in great part, it is the pen of Hutchinson himself which describes events, the present writer appending comments to elucidate or modify, as the case seems to require.

[1] *Samuel Adams* (American Statesmen Series); Houghton, Mifflin & Co., 1885.

Large quotations have been made in the text and in the Appendix from the Journals of the Massachusetts Provincial Legislature during the years immediately preceding the Revolution. To follow Hutchinson's career is a study in political embryology. In the controversy between the Governor on one side and the Council and Assembly on the other, a frame no less important than the United States was taking shape : those struggles were the pre-natal stirrings of one of the mightiest births of time. The record of them is contained in documents not printed since the year 1818,[1] seldom consulted in our generation even by students ; documents, however, of the greatest value and interest as memorials of a contest so important, and, according to eminent authorities, of extraordinary ability. They embalm, in fact, the great word-war which came before the actual clash of arms upon the battle-field. America has had no more earnest or able sons than some of the men from whom these papers proceeded. They are the most elaborate utterances of those men, and should not remain in neglect.

No satisfactory portrait of Hutchinson exists. A likeness by Edward Truman, supposed to have been painted in 1741, much defaced, it is said, by the bayonets of Revolutionary soldiers, hangs in the hall of the Massachusetts Historical Society. The Society possesses still another portrait, attributed to Copley ; but showing a face much too youthful for that of the

[1] *Massachusetts State Papers*, 1765–1775, edited by Alden Bradford ; Russell & Gardner, Boston, 1818 : described also on the title-page as "Speeches of the Massachusetts Governors from 1765 to 1775 and the Answers of the House of Representatives to the Same."

Hutchinson of Copley's time. Copley may have copied the earlier work, but can hardly have wrought from the life. He presents a young man of handsome and intellectual features, but with few marks of the force and grave dignity to be expected in the countenance. It is unfortunate that the skillful painter who has preserved so vividly for us the traits of John Hancock and Samuel Adams, should have set forth inadequately their great opponent.

In conclusion, it must be stated that this book, like the lives of Samuel Adams and Young Sir Henry Vane, and the "Short History of Anglo-Saxon Freedom," has been written for the late lamented Mrs. Mary Hemenway, — a carrying out of her Old South work. That noble woman's candor was as remarkable as her patriotic enthusiasm. While stimulating, in every way she could, interest in and love for our country and the men who brought it into being, she had a kind thought for the foe who honestly stood against them, and she desired to have justice done the victim, as well as to have praise rendered the victors.

J. K. HOSMER.

MINNEAPOLIS PUBLIC LIBRARY.
February 7, 1896.

THE LIFE OF THOMAS HUTCHINSON.

CHAPTER I.

YOUNG MANHOOD AND ENVIRONMENT.

THE first mention of Thomas Hutchinson, son of Thomas Hutchinson and Sarah Foster, his wife, is contained in an account-book kept by his mother, from which his great-grandson, Peter Orlando Hutchinson, makes many extracts.[1]

" 1711, September the 10th Martha Pue came to suckle my child Thomas Hutchinson for 6 shillings per week and 4 weeks ; after this nurse came on Monday the 8 of October. I paid her 1 : 4."

The boy had been born on the day previous, September 9th, being the fourth child in a family which came to number twelve. No mention of his boyhood is to be found except in a brief account by himself contained in an autobiographical sketch which he prepared late in life. His home was the handsome mansion in Garden Court Street, at the North End of Boston, pictures of which have come down to us.[2] It was the finest house

---

[1] *Diary and Letters of Thomas Hutchinson*, edited by P. O. Hutchinson, vol. i., p. 41.

[2] *American Magazine*, February, 1836.

in town; Thomas was the first child born into it. He
became in due time its possessor, and it continued to
be his home until its destruction by a mob in 1765.
When five and a half years old, he began to go to the
North Grammar School, proceeding thence, at the age
of twelve, to Harvard College. He speaks slightingly
of his college life, declaring that he knew little more at
his graduation in 1727 than he did when he entered.
The following scrap from the autobiography may serve
to show his lack of a sense of humor, if nothing else :
" It was part of the exercise of the scholars to read a
verse or two each out of a Latin Testament into Greek
every morning at prayer-time before prayer in the Hall ;
and it was a practice of some to take a leaf of the
Greek Testament and put it into the Latin Testament,
which was termed 'hogueing.' Young Hutchinson
was tempted once to follow so base an example ; but
guilt appeared so strong in his face that the President
ordered him to show his book, which he did in great
confusion, and received this severe reproof : "A $t\bar{e}$ $n\bar{o}n$
$expect\bar{a}v\bar{\imath}$,' and a small pecuniary punishment. The
first part made the deepest impression, and cured him
of the disease of 'hogueing' for the rest of the time
he remained at college." [1]   Three years after graduating,
he took the degree of Master of Arts, reading on Com-
mencement afternoon a thesis on the topic, " Is a College Education of Service to one who Travels ? "

He was apparently a grave and proper boy, taking
hold precociously of serious work. He carried on small
trading ventures in vessels owned by his father, keep-

---

[1] *Diary and Letters*, vol. i., p. 46.

ing strict accounts in the methodical way which marked him through life. At once, on graduating, he became a merchant-apprentice in his father's counting-room, but found some time for books. He studied Latin, working also at French with Le Mercier, the Huguenot minister, until he became well versed in the two languages. His reading was largely of history, for which he showed a fondness even thus early. He mentions as favorite books, Morton's " New England Memorial," Church's " History of the Indian War," and Mather's " Lives of the New England Governors." Baker's " Chronicle " and Fox's " Martyrs " also interested him, while the sufferings and death of Charles I. made him weep. As he grew toward manhood, he mingled in such life as Boston afforded, counting among his friends Hawke, Fitzroy, and other young officers, some of them in later years famous commanders, who then were midshipmen or lieutenants attached to ships on the North American station. Though companionable, he was serious and thrifty, having amassed at twenty-one £400 or £500 by his own schemes. In 1732, when Governor Belcher went to Casco Bay to make a treaty with the Indians, young Hutchinson was in his company, in a ship of which he was half owner, on board which he entertained a party of young fellows of his own age, among them the Governor's son.

A youth well-to-do, well born, and of good character, he did not need to wait long for a wife. In a quaint old-fashioned description, he records the story of his connection with Mary, Margaret, and Grizel Sanford, daughters of a Governor of Rhode Island, and heiresses.

Mary Sanford became the wife of Andrew Oliver, a man with whom the career of Hutchinson is closely knit. Grizel remained unmarried, an inmate through life of Hutchinson's household. Margaret became his wife, in her seventeenth year. She was tenderly loved through nineteen years; and after her death the references to her are pathetic, which here and there occur in her husband's notes. In 1735, he joined the church; in 1737, he became selectman of Boston; and a month or two later, having been elected Representative to the General Court, with Elisha Cooke, Thomas Cushing, and Timothy Prout, at the age of twenty-six he entered upon a public career strangely and sadly varied, to the study of which we must now address ourselves.

When Thomas Hutchinson stepped into leadership, he seemed simply to come to his own; for, since the foundation of Massachusetts Bay, there had been no time when some of his name and line had not been in the foreground. The first of the family to acquire prominence was that eccentric but strong-souled enthusiast, Mrs. Anne Hutchinson, heroine of the Antinomian controversy, who won to her side even men of such power as John Cotton and young Henry Vane. Her grandson, Elisha Hutchinson, became, under the old charter, the first Chief Justice of the Common Pleas, and afterwards Assistant and Commander of the Forces. Under the new charter, while retaining his judicial position, he became also Councilor, being still in office at his death in 1717, a citizen of the first eminence. His son, Thomas Hutchinson, Councilor from 1714 to 1739, had note scarcely less. He was

colonel also of the 1st Suffolk regiment, a man of independent and resolute character. " He was the man who
seized the famous Captain Kidd, when he resisted the
officers of justice sent against him."[1] He was the
father of our subject.

To sketch the institutions with which Thomas Hutchinson was concerned, and the environment into which
he was born, it must be noted that the first charter of
the Colony of Massachusetts Bay was that of a trading corporation, drawn with much indefiniteness, and
converted without color of law into an instrument of
government for a political body.[2] A Governor, Lieutenant-Governor, and eighteen Assistants, elected by the
stockholders of the company, managed affairs. The
colonists were to possess " the rights of Englishmen,"
but were without voice in the polity. Very soon, however, the interests of the company were transferred
across the sea, the plantation becoming self-governing.
For fifty years, according to an enactment of the General Court of 1631, only church members could become
freemen, a provision which put power into the hands of
a few ; but with the accession of William and Mary a
great change came to pass. In spite of the reluctance
of the New England rulers, Massachusetts, Plymouth,
and Maine, combined into one Province, were forced to
receive a new charter, radically different from that of
the preceding time. Toleration was prescribed for all
sects excepting papists, and the right of suffrage, in-

---

[1] Eliot's *New England Biographical Dictionary.*
[2] Chalmers : *Political Annals*, ch. vii.

stead of being limited to church members, was bestowed on all inhabitants possessing a freehold of the annual value of forty shillings, or personal property to the value of £40. The King appointed the Governor. Lieutenant-Governor, and Secretary. A House of Representatives or Assembly formed one branch of the General Court or Legislature, the members of which were elected every year by the towns. The second branch was formed by the Council, a body of twenty-eight members, appointed in the first instance by the King, but afterwards elected each year jointly by the old Council and the Assembly; the Governor possessed the power of negativing thirteen out of the twenty-eight. The Governor possessed, too, the power of a negative upon all acts of the General Court, which he could also summon, adjourn, and dissolve. He was commander-in-chief of the militia, whose officers he could appoint. The Assembly had, among other powers, the important power of the purse. As to the Council, in all official acts its concurrence was necessary; its members were besides the special advisers of the Governor. To the King was reserved the power of disannulling any act within three years after its passage.[1]

Of the judicial institutions established by the General Court in 1692, and continued with little change until the Revolution, the Superior Court was at the head, consisting of a Chief Justice and four associate judges. To this Court was assigned all the jurisdiction of the English Common Pleas, King's Bench, and

[1] For the text of the two charters, see Ben: Perley Poore : *Constitutions and Charters*, vol. i.

Exchequer. In the counties, Courts of Common Pleas cared for smaller civil cases ; Courts of Sessions, composed of Justices of the Peace, for smaller criminal cases; Courts of Probate, for settling the estates of persons deceased. Public prosecutions were conducted by an Attorney-General. The functionaries of this system held office under appointment of the Governor, the confirmation of the Council being necessary. From 1694 a Court of Vice-Admiralty existed, empowered to try without jury all maritime and revenue cases, an institution which from the first was strenuously opposed.[1]

In 1728, the charter of William and Mary was amended, after violent disputes between Governor Shute and the House, by the addition of a clause giving the Governor power to negative the Speaker chosen by the House ; and also a clause making it impossible for the House to adjourn by its own vote for a longer term than two days.

To these institutions of the Province of Massachusetts Bay must be added the one which, though lowest of all, is much the most celebrated and important. The question as to the origin of the Town-Meeting is by no means satisfactorily answered. The claim of E. A. Freeman, that the Town-Meeting is the ancient Anglo-Saxon folk-mote, persisting in all its essential features through nearly two thousand years, has been challenged, and is to-day more cautiously advanced than once. Since Seebohm[2] and Coote[3] have written, historians

---

[1] Washburn : *Judicial Hist. of Massachusetts*, ch. ix.

[2] *The English Village Community*, 1883.

[3] *The Romans of Britain*, 1878.

will scarcely dare to paint the self-government of our
Teuton forefathers with such definite traits as those
which mark the picture of J. R. Green. The book of
Douglas Campbell,[1] however one-sided, has nevertheless
made it clear that when no thought is given to influences from Holland, the story of early New England is
unsatisfactorily told.

The plain basis of the town system in Massachusetts is an order of the General Court passed in 1635,
which, copied substantially in 1641 by Nathaniel Ward
into his "Body of Liberties," stands as follows: "The
freemen of every township shall have power to make
such by-laws and constitutions as may concern the welfare of their town, provided they be not of a criminal,
but only of a prudential nature, and that their penalties exceed not twenty shillings for one offense, and
that they be not repugnant to the public laws and orders of the country. . . . The freemen of every town,
or township, shall have full power to choose yearly, or
for less time, out of themselves, a convenient number
of fit men to order the planting or prudential occasions
of that town, according to instructions given them in
writing, provided nothing be done by them contrary to
the public laws and orders of the country; provided
also the number of such select persons be not above
nine." The colonists followed English precedents, no
doubt to some extent unconsciously, but also to some
extent consciously. In 1647, the town of Boston, to
which all the other towns of the Province from the
beginning looked for guidance and example, voted to

---

[1] *The Puritan in Holland, England, and America,* 1892.

procure for the town's use various English law-books, among them Dalton's "Justice of the Peace," and Coke upon Lyttelton and upon Magna Charta. With the new charter of William and Mary's time came in the broader suffrage, the franchise no longer being restricted to church members, but being extended to "the free-holders and other inhabitants of each town ratable at twenty pounds estate." Practically, the voting at Town-Meeting came, before the American Revolution, to be universal. "The free-holders and other inhabitants" at Town-Meeting not only cast votes, but formed also a deliberative body, which, as the Revolution came on, far from confining itself to petty local matters, discussed topics wide as the British empire; not hesitating, too, to pass judgment upon them, and to seek in turbulent ways to give effect to their decisions.[1]

However originating, the New England Town-Meeting of Hutchinson's day was an assembly to which all flocked, high and low. The selectmen, of their own volition, or upon application of several of their townsmen, were authorized to issue the warrant. In this the business to be engaged in was specified, and only that could come up for action. The inhabitants having been warned to attend, those that were present had a right to proceed, though but a fraction of the population. Liberty of speech was shared by all, rich or poor; character and ability coming to the front, while wealth and family were treated often with scant cere-

<hr>

[1] J. H. Bugbee : *The Founders of Boston*, p. 6. *Johns Hopkins Univ. Studies*, 5th series, No. 3.

mony. Every freeman could vote as he chose, and the votes of all weighed equally. Such is the account of a writer of the time.[1] As the Town-Meeting of the Revolutionary period was an evolution, so the business with which it dealt as time went on constantly enlarged. Following the records of Boston, for instance, the town of towns, in which the Town-Meeting can be studied to best advantage, the minutes at first relate to matters of purely local interest. With the coming into office of William Cooper, however, town clerk of the Revolutionary period, the sphere greatly broadens. Boston is in its fight with George III., and questions wide as two hemispheres become the subject of speech and vote. Hutchinson, as we shall hereafter see, believed this expansion of the functions of the Town-Meeting to be unconstitutional and a thing to be repressed. Certainly it was without precedent, not only in America, but in England, except in that shadowy freedom of the forests clear knowledge of which it is so difficult to recover.

Probably the greatest service the Town-Meeting has rendered has been as an instrument of education. In managing affairs both great and small, it has often done unwisely. When it has delegated power to a superior mind, in any difficult emergency, it has too often tied the hands of its delegate so that his superiority has become impotent for good. In Town-Meeting action at the present moment, as well in New England as in the great communities of the West which have followed more or less closely New England ex-

---

[1] Gordon : *Hist. of the Independence of the United States of America*, vol. i., p. 382.

ample, meanness and folly are too often the outcome;
nor has it ever been otherwise, as those know who read
the documents, unblinded by any glamour thrown over
a past time.[1] Yet when all is said that can be said, the
plain people in Town-Meeting assembled have done the
right thing at the right time more often than not. Set
the New England way side by side with any more restricted polity, management by a few, or management
by one : it may be confidently claimed that way will
come out of the comparison with credit. The record
of sordidness and stupidity is finely balanced by acts
heroic and full of prudence; and were the page of its
failures far more impressive than it is, the debt due
the Town-Meeting, as a school for the development of
self-reliant, self-respecting manhood, will make up for
its failures many times over.

Indeed, not the Town-Meeting itself does so much
to educate, as the conditions which in any society
the Town-Meeting necessitates. The Town-Meetings
usually are infrequent, often not more than one or
two in a year. They, however, presuppose or inev-
itably bring to pass an atmosphere, so to speak, highly
salutary. As Bryce puts it : —

" The existence of public opinion, the practice of
always reading, talking, and judging of public affairs
with a view to voting, — this, rather than the possession
of political rights, gives to popular government that
educative and stimulative power which is so frequently
claimed as its highest merit. History does not sup-

[1] See C. F. Adams' study of the past of the town of Quincy, in *Three
Episodes of Mass. Hist.*

port the doctrine that the mere enjoyment of power fits large masses of men, any more than individuals and classes, for its exercise. Along with that enjoyment must be one or more of various auspicious conditions, such as a direct and fairly equal interest in the common welfare, the presence of a class or group of persons respected and competent to guide, an absence of religious or race hatreds, a high level of education, or at least of intelligence, old habits of local self-government, the practice of unlimited free discussion. In America, not simply the habit of voting, but the briskness and breeziness of the whole atmosphere of public life, and the process of obtaining information and discussing it, of hearing and judging each side, form the citizen's intelligence. The voting power must supplement this." [1]

Such were the institutions into the midst of which Hutchinson was born, — in the higher range devised and imposed by an outside power, a shackle under which the community forever fretted, until at last the shackle was burst and laid aside ; in the lower range an outgrowth as natural as the shell which develops upon the mollusk, shaped accurately to the figure of the wearer, giving free play to its members, a defense and at the same time an instrument of efficiency.

The people inhabiting the two hundred towns of Massachusetts Bay, whose Representatives sat thus yearly in the Assembly Chamber in the Old State House, with the Governor and Council close at hand across a narrow corridor, were among the sturdiest of the sturdiest race, perhaps, which the world has ever seen.

---

[1] *American Commonwealth*, vol. ii., p. 356.

Whatever may be said to-day for other stocks, the 130,000,000 of English-speaking men have been able to make themselves masters of the world to an extent which no people has thus far approached; and, with a might unexampled and often ruthless, are laying hands upon the fairest portions of all the continents. Of this masterful seed, the Puritans of the seventeenth century are undoubtedly the sifted wheat. What ruler of circumstance has sprung from this stock comparable to Oliver Cromwell! He was but the central and culminating figure in a generation similarly endowed, — the men of the English Commonwealth, brethren of whom sunk deep the pillars of a new society in the new world, while the Stuart was smitten at Naseby and the sceptre of the seas for the first time won to English grasp. Grandsons of these men were the people with whom we at present have to do, of strain quite unmixed, except as a trace of Huguenot blood had become injected into it from France, pressed out through the Revocation of the Edict of Nantes.

But let us be under no delusions as to our Revolutionary forefathers. While so forceful and in the main honest, the careful student finds that they were coarse and violent in a way in which their descendants are not, while public spirit was as rare a virtue among them as it is in our own time. They were indeed strangely unsensitive in points where their great-grandchildren have come to feel acutely. The story told of a Boston minister in the first half of the eighteenth century, that, wishing to get a negro slave cheap, he dispatched to the coast of Africa a hogshead of rum, promptly receiving in return a kidnapped black boy, is probably not exaggerated.   The distilling of rum was one of the chief industries; and the ships created so abundantly in the New England shipyards were, in the opinion of that time, quite innocently employed when used as slavers. The business of some traders counted as of good repute was of a kind to make one's hair stand on end.   The merchants of Newport, in the time of the Stamp Act, when their trade was threatened, detail in a naïve memorial to the King, with no compunction, a commerce with Africa which to-day ruffians would scarcely confess to.[1]   As regards intemperance, any faithful picture of pre-Revolutionary times will be full of unpleasant features.   In humane effort, the $a\ b\ c$ was yet to be learned: the treatment of prisoners, paupers, and insane was barbarous.   Hard, too, was the lot of children.   "It is safe to say that if, by any chance, the Braintree village school of the last century could for a single fortnight be brought back to the Quincy of 1890, parents would in horror and astonishment keep their children at home until a Town-Meeting, called at the shortest possible legal notice, could be held; and this meeting would probably culminate in a riot, in the course of which school-house, as well as school, would be summarily abated as a disgrace and a nuisance."[2]   This is hardly too energetic.   It was indeed the reign of King Rawhide, whose dominion comprehended the home scarcely less than the school.

The world of that time seems curiously incongruous.

[1] *Massachusetts Gazette*, Dec. 13, 1764.
[2] C. F. Adams : *Three Episodes of Mass. Hist.*, p. 782.

From the crowd, often so rough and besotted, representatives came forth whose state papers, as we shall see, have the highest tone.   The manifestoes of the Town-Meetings, which a drunken mob sometimes turned into a bear-garden, have frequently a manly, indeed a lofty, spirit.   If the advertisements of the day can be trusted, there was a better market in Boston for solid literature than in some modern American cities ten times as large. Men and women, humane and amiable, bore their part in the midst of this turbulent life, no better type of whom can be found than Thomas Hutchinson himself.

Vigorous the community was, of course, to the last degree.   In the interior, the farmer resolutely wrung a living from the sand and granite upon which the colony in the beginning had been dropped.   In the coast towns, the most enterprising of merchants sent to sea sailors as fearless as Leif or Eric.   The navigation laws of the statute-book were, for the most part, only recognized to be broken.   Of manufacturing, there was little.   On farm and ocean, however, the outlet for energy was abundant : and energy was the note of Massachusetts life, marking the husbandman as he reaped and delved ; the trader as he schemed ; the rover as he chased the whale, or bartered his lumber and rum, now on arctic, now on tropic coasts.   Every peaceful channel was followed with ardor ; and if opposition came, a spirit at once was aroused which in formal war could rout Dieskau and capture Louisburg, or in domestic disorders could set the streets of Boston in an uproar to the light of mob-ignited conflagrations.

CHAPTER II.

MAY 31, 1737, Thomas Hutchinson took his seat in
the House. Running down the pages of the House
Journal, we may follow after a fashion the steps of the
young statesman, as he rapidly rises. The record is
meagre; but from the frequency of mention and the
responsible character of the business in which he is
concerned, it is quite plain that, however at first wealth
and influential connections may have smoothed his path,
ability in him soon becomes manifest, and a front place
is conceded to his merits.

His first duty is, as one of a committee, to congratu-
late King George II. on his safe return through a storm
from Germany,[1] entering thus upon a course of loyal
deference destined to last through life. From the first,
too, he is set to deal with questions of finance, being
appointed as early as June 3 to wrestle with a tax-bill;
before the year ends he is settling boundary disputes.[2]
It is perhaps significant that he is once charged to see
justice done a slave, who, though freed by his dead
master's will, is still claimed as a bondsman by his master's son.[3] He early, too, reports a bill for the relief of

---

[1] House Journ., May 31, 1737.

[2] House Journ., Oct. 14, 1737.

[3] Oct. 24, 1737.

1741] FINANCIAL SERVICES.

those imprisoned for debt.[1] With business of all these several kinds, we shall find him hereafter to be much concerned, working out by his action great good, — now to individual men and women, now to communities and States. The boundary dispute in particular brought the young member into prominence. In running the line between Massachusetts Bay and New Hampshire, a large tract of land had been taken from the former, the inhabitants of which desired to return to the jurisdiction of Massachusetts. It was a great mark of confidence when, in 1740, he was appointed, being then twenty-nine, to go to England to represent the case to men in power. His mention of his English journey is brief in his autobiography; nor are there letters extant which bear upon it. He made a stormy November passage in a deep-laden ship. Without fault of his, the business came to naught through the failure of the proper parties to supply the necessary evidence. He was ill at ease in England, homesick for the Province and his family, gladly returning after thirteen months of absence.

A far more memorable service than the English agency had already been entered upon by Hutchinson, — a service resumed at once upon his return. In this he was thoroughly successful in spite of great difficulties, the sequel being most salutary at the time, and having a close relation with the coming into being of the United States. Throughout the first half of the eighteenth century New England was crippled by foolish financial management. In Massachusetts, the use

[1] Dec. 20, 1737.

of paper money dates from the year 1690, when it was introduced to defray the expenses of an unsuccessful expedition against Canada.[1] Notes to the amount of £40,000, payable in one year, were issued, the plausible idea being to anticipate by a few months only the payment into the Treasury of the annual tax. New issues of notes followed in succeeding years, which at first were punctually redeemed ; but a looser practice crept in. In 1704, the time of redemption was extended to two years ; the printing-presses teemed more than ever, the period of redemption growing longer, until at last it reached thirteen years. The confusion and depreciation became intolerable. Madame Knight, who made a journey through New England early in the eighteenth century, of which an account remains, sometimes graphic and racy, describes the trading of the time : —

"They give the title of merchant to every trader, who rates his goods according to the time and specie they pay in ; viz., ' pay,' ' money,' ' pay as money,' and ' trusting.' ' Pay ' is grain, pork, and beef, etc., the prices set by the General Court. ' Money ' is pieces of eight, ryals, Boston or Bay shillings, or good hard money, as sometimes silver coin is called ; also wampum, viz., Indian beads, which serve as change. ' Pay as money ' is provision aforesaid one third cheaper than the Assembly set it ; and ' trust,' as they agree for the time. When the buyer comes to ask for a commodity,

[1] Authorities for the financial sketch : Felt : *Hist. of the Mass. Currency.* Douglas : *Financial Hist. of Mass.* Columbia Coll. Stud. in Hist., Econ., and Public Law, 1892. Palfrey, vols. iv. and v. Hutchinson : *Hist. of Mass. Bay*, vol. ii. Douglass : *Summary of the British Settlements of North America*, Boston, 1755.

sometimes before the merchant answers that he has it, he says : ' Is your pay ready ? ' Perhaps the chap replies, ' Yes.' ' What do you pay in ? ' says the merchant. The buyer having answered, then the price is set ; as suppose he wants a sixpenny knife, in ' pay ' it is twelvepence ; in ' pay as money,' eightpence ; and hard money, its own value, sixpence. It seems a very intricate way of trade, and what Lex Mercatoria had not thought of." [1]

The condition grew from year to year more chaotic. To the classes of money described by Madame Knight, the successive issues of bills added constantly new ones. Other colonies kept pace with Massachusetts, and sometimes became even more demented ; until with " old," " middle," and " new tenor," with " pay," " trust," and " pay as money," with Rhode Island bills and Connecticut bills of several different issues, hard money at the same time becoming constantly rarer, the shrewdest Yankee brains became quite unequal to the work of trading. The depreciation of the currency wrought great suffering. Rev. Daniel Appleton, in a Fast-Day sermon in 1748, states the case of a widow who received in money £3 a year. Originally, this would buy two cords of wood, four bushels of corn, one bushel of rye, one bushel of malt, fifty pounds of pork, and sixty pounds of beef, which went far toward her maintenance. Now, says the minister, her income will purchase only one half or one quarter as much. Those having fixed incomes or money at interest especially suffered, but the distress was universal ; and worse than

---

[1] Quoted by Felt, p. 54.

the distress was the sinking of the moral tone of the
Puritan state, made inevitable by the unfortunate conditions : scarcely less, in fact, was threatened than a
destruction of the social organism. Since the immense
class of debtors were gainers through the depreciation
of the bills, their debts being diminished the longer
they remained undischarged, the temptation was strong
to keep out of their just rights the creditors, who were
obliged to accept twenty, a hundred and ten, and even
a hundred and sixty per cent. less than the real value of
their debts. Debtors disposed to fraud were greatly
encouraged by the fact that the excessive fall in value
of the currency in which the fees of the Court were
paid brought the costs of a suit often below the interest
on the debt. It became a common practice, even in the
case of indisputable obligations, to avoid payment until
the creditor brought suit, the feeling being that it paid
the debtor well to stand the small costs, which he must
do if the suit went against him, and enjoy for the
longer time the use of his creditor's money. So insensible did men become to the discredit of this "that it
was not infrequent for persons of some circumstances
and character to suffer judgments to be given against
them by default in open court for such debts, and to
appeal from one court to another merely for delay;
whereby lawsuits were scandalously multiplied, and a
litigious, trickish spirit promoted among the lower sort
of people." [1]

Says another authority of the time : —

[1] Shirley : *Report of Board of Trade*, Dec. 23, 1743 ; quoted by Palfrey,
vol. v., p. 103.

" All our paper-money-making Assemblies have been legislatures of debtors, the representatives of people, who, from incognitancy, idleness, and profuseness, have been under a necessity of mortgaging their lands ; lands are a real permanent estate, but the debt in paper currency by its multiplication depreciates more and more . . . to the disadvantage of the creditors, or industrious frugal part of the colony ; this is the wicked mystery of this iniquitous paper currency." [1]

For long there seemed to be in the Province neither force nor brains to bring help in this dreary state of things. In 1714, a " Public Bank " was talked of, through which money was to be lent by the Province for a definite period, secured by mortgage on real property of the borrower. This scheme was frustrated by one for a " Private Bank," — a measure neither safe nor honest, — which was refused incorporation. The disputes over these expedients lasted for years, the few wiser heads who desired a return to a coin basis, at last, in despair, trying to uphold the Public Bank as the smaller of the two evils. At length, royal instructions were received prohibiting, except on express permission from the King, the issue of new notes until those already outstanding had been redeemed, and fixing the year 1741 as the time of redemption. This was wholesome restriction, and was welcomed and helped forward by the Governors of the time, the Council, and many of the wiser sort. The Assembly, however, reflecting faithfully the people, only plunged deeper into

[1] Douglass : *Summary of the British Settlements of North America*, vol. i., p. 310, note. Boston, 1755.

trouble, representing so energetically the hardship suffered under the King's prohibition that it was finally
withdrawn.

It is not necessary to do more than thus outline the
folly of that generation and the misery which it brought
upon itself. The New England of that day was saved
by one of its own children, and at this point of the
distress he reveals himself. Hutchinson's election to
the Legislature in 1737 was in spite of the well-known
fact that his views on the all-absorbing question of
finance were opposed to those of the majority. The
year following he was again elected, but the party for
paper money intended to put it out of his power to hurt
them by preparing a set of instructions enjoining the
Representatives to promote the emitting of more paper
money. When the instructions were reported in Town-
Meeting, Hutchinson was at once on his feet in opposition to them, and declared he would not observe them.
" Mr. Balston, a vociferous man, called out, ' Choose
another Representative,' but this was not seconded, nor
could it be done. During the session, Hutchinson consistently threw his influence on the hard money side, in
that way so far losing popularity that in 1739 he was
dropped.[1] He had roused the wrath of the majority
by proposing in the House to borrow in England a sum
in silver equal to all the bills then extant, and therewith
to redeem them from their possessors and furnish a currency for the inhabitants; and to repay the silver at
distant periods, which would render the burden of taxes
tolerable by an equal division on a number of future

[1] Autobiography.

years, and would prevent the distress of trade by the
loss of the only instrument, the bills of credit, without
another provided in its place." [1]

The effort of the young deputy toward hard money
was summarily rejected as quite impracticable, the Province turning in preference to a revival of the " Private
Bank" or " Land Bank" of twenty-five years before.
For the details of this arrangement, Hutchinson him-
self is the best authority.	Seven or eight hundred per-
sons, some few of rank and good estate, but generally of low condition, many of them perhaps insolvent,
were to give credit to £150,000, to be issued in bills.
Each person was to mortgage real estate in proportion
to the sum he subscribed, or to give bond with two
sureties; but personal security was not to be taken for
more than £100 from any one person.	Ten directors
and a treasurer were to be chosen by the company.
Every borrower was to pay every year three per cent.
interest and five per cent. of the principal of the sum
taken out; it being understood that, besides bills, produce and manufactures of the Province might also be
rendered at such rates as the directors from time to time
should set.	The plan won great favor.	The Assem-
bly returned for 1740 in large majority favored it, and
was known therefore afterwards as the " Land Bank
House."	Men of estates and the principal merchants in
the Province abhorred the project, and refused to receive the bills, but many small traders gave them credit.
The looseness of the scheme soon became apparent.
The directors issued bills without any fund or security

---

[1] Hutchinson : *Hist. of Mass. Bay*, vol. ii., p. 351, etc.

that they would ever be redeemed. They purchased every sort of commodity, though ever so much a drug, for the sake of pushing off their bills, until they had put out £50,000 or £60,000. The Governors, Belcher and afterwards Shirley, and the Councils exerted themselves to blast the scheme. Prompt displacement took place of such civil and military officers as became directors, and even of such as received or paid out any of the bills. Shirley negatived the person chosen Speaker of the Assembly on the ground that he was a director, and also thirteen of the Councilors whose connection with the Land Bank was more or less close. It could not, however, be suppressed. The majority of the people favored it openly or secretly, and the private corporation threatened to become more powerful than the government itself.

What saved the Province in the crisis was the intervention of Parliament, which, in consistency with its preceding action, now, when appealed to for aid, put down the new scheme, as it had sought to foil the calamitous policy which had gone before. Though the Land Bank company was dissolved, yet the Act of Parliament gave the holders of the bills a right to sue every partner or director for the sums expressed, with interest. The company was in a maze. If the bills had been issued at their face value, no grounds for complaint would have existed that Parliament required their redemption at the same rate. They had not, however, been issued at their face value; in the depreciation that set in, many of the holders of the bills had acquired them for half the face value. The hardship

upon the company was very great, a fact about which
Hutchinson declares Parliament was not anxious, the loss
they sustained being only a just penalty for their unwarrantable proceeding. His contempt for the folly of
his contemporaries was unmeasured. " It would be just
as rational, when the blood in the human body is in a
putrid, corrupt state, to increase the quantity by lux-
urious living, in order to restore health. Some of the
leading men among the Representatives were debtors,
and a depreciating currency was convenient for them."
A way out was found at last.

The capture of Louisburg, though so noteworthy an
event in New England history, requires only brief mention in a biography of Hutchinson. It was an extraordinary piece of good luck, and nothing else.[1] The
expedition was undertaken in a great financial strait,
conducted quite without skill, and was embarrassed by
want of a good understanding between the land and
sea forces. Had one single thing gone wrong for the
English after the army set sail, it has been said, or
had one single thing gone right for the French, the
expedition must have failed. It succeeded triumphantly.
Hutchinson was at the front in public life at this time.
Returning from England at the end of 1741, as has
been described, he was at first rejected by the electors
in the spring of 1742; but when presently one of the
" Boston seat " was selected for the Council, Hutchinson
was chosen in his place. He was continuously chosen

---

[1] " The very, very, very rash, but very, very, very fortunate expedition
against Cape Breton or Louisburg I hope may terminate public paper
currency." Douglass : *Summary*, etc., vol. i., p. 314 (1755).

until the year 1749; in 1746, 1747, and 1748 serving as Speaker. In 1745, he became unpopular for being willing to allow a French deputation from Louisburg treating for an exchange of prisoners, a certain number of wood axes; he was accused of supplying them with tomahawks. But his position on the currency was the main cause of the public wrath. His fine place at Milton, seven miles from the city, a recent purchase, many thought should be protected by a guard; and once when his town-house caught fire, there were cries in the street, " Curse him, let it burn! "

The warlike enterprises into which Shirley had led the country had immensely increased the public debt. Bills to the amount of between two and three million dollars had been issued; but these had so depreciated that when the war closed £1100, or even £1200, were scarcely equal to £100 sterling. Fortunately for the Province, its agent in England at this time was William Bollan, a son-in-law of Shirley, a lawyer, a man of force and insight. Through his effective representations, the English government was brought to the resolve to reimburse Massachusetts for her expenditures during the Louisburg campaign. On land, it had been purely a provincial enterprise; and resulting as it did greatly to the advantage of England, it was felt to be only equitable that there should be a generous acknowledgment. The fact that at the peace of Aix-la-Chapelle, in 1748, Louisburg was returned to its old possessors, making the entire effort for its seizure utterly vain, as far as the Colonies were concerned, was enough to touch even the most obtuse sense of justice.

Bollan was able not only to secure a reimbursement, but to get hold of an amount equal to the full value of the money when issued. Money had greatly depreciated, but the advocate persuaded his audience that that should be disregarded: there was no deduction on that account. The House Journal records, under date April 21, 1749: "Voted, that his Excellency the Governor, the Secretary of the Province, and the Speaker of the House [Hutchinson], be impowered, in the name and behalf of the Province, to sign and deliver a proper deed or instrument, with the seal of the Province thereunto affixed, authorizing and impowering the Hon. Sir Peter Warren, Kt. of the Bath, William Bollan, Esq., Agent for the Province at the Court of Great Britain, and Eliakim Palmer, Esq., of London, Merchant, them or any two of them, the said William Bollan, Esq., except in case of his death always to be one, to receive the whole and every part of the sum of £183,649 2s. and 7d. halfpenny sterling, granted by Parliament to reimburse the Province their expenses in taking and securing for his Majesty the island of Cape Breton and its dependencies, and to give a full discharge for the same." What followed may best be told in Hutchinson's own words: —

"Mr. Hutchinson, who was then Speaker of the House of Representatives, imagined this to be a most favorable opportunity for abolishing bills of credit, the source of so much iniquity, and for establishing a stable currency of silver and gold for the future. About £2,200,000 would be outstanding in bills in the year 1749. £180,000 sterling, at eleven for one, which was

0269079

the lowest rate of exchange with London for a year or two before, and perhaps the difference was really twelve for one, would redeem £1,980,000, which would leave but £220,000 outstanding ; it was therefore proposed that the sum granted by Parliament should be shipped to the Province in Spanish milled dollars, and applied for the redemption of the bills as far as it would serve for that purpose, and that the remainder of the bills should be drawn in by a tax on the year 1749. This would finish the bills. For the future, silver, of sterling alloy, at six shillings and eightpence the ounce, if payment should be made in bullion ; or otherwise, milled dollars at six shillings each, should be the lawful money of the Province ; and no person should receive or pay within the Province bills of credit of any of the other governments of New England. This proposal being made to the Governor, he approved of it, as founded in justice, and tending to promote the real interest of the Province ; but he knew the attachment of the people to paper money and supposed it impracticable. The Speaker, however, laid the proposal before the House, where it was received with a smile." [1]

In fact, Hutchinson was almost alone. Though the Governors, the Councils, and the more substantial people generally had long recognized the nature of the evil from which for fifty years the Province had suffered, no one was able to see any way out of it. The project was regarded as quite Utopian ; and rather out of deference for the Speaker than from a feeling that any good could result, a committee was appointed to

[1] *Hist.*, vol. ii., p. 391.

consider it. By this committee, as skeptical as the House in general, Hutchinson was nevertheless asked to prepare a formal bill, which becoming known, the democracy began to seethe. The large class of debtors were no losers by a depreciating currency, and preferred the paper to anything more solid. Those of a different mind entertained some one scheme, some another, the more sensible holding that, even though Hutchinson's plan might have merit, the bills must be put an end to in a gradual way; "a fatal shock" would be felt by so sudden a return to a specie basis. Of this view was Douglass, an anti-paper man who had written ably, but who now in the public prints was energetic against the Speaker's idea.

For a long time the fight seemed hopeless. Many weeks were spent in debating; and when voting began the bill was decisively rejected. The chance to escape from bondage seemed irrecoverably gone. Unexpectedly, however, during the night following the vote, conviction overtook some men of influence. The clear-minded, overmatched champion of honest money must have been indeed made happy when Joseph Livermore, of Weston, and Samuel Witt, of Marlboro, told him in the narrow lobby, next morning, that there was still hope. A motion to reconsider having been carried, the bill at last, for a wonder, passed; the Council and Governor were prompt to ratify, and while the people marveled, all was done. The streets were full of angry men, whose wrath might at any time become dangerous. The infatuation was so great, the wish was often expressed that the ship bringing the treasure might

98839

sink.   Many doubted whether the treasure would really
be sent, and this uncertainty perhaps helped the passage of the bill.   Why oppose a scheme which of itself
would fall to the ground ?

But the treasure came.   Seventeen trucks were required to cart from the ship to the Treasury two hundred and seventeen chests of Spanish dollars, while ten
trucks conveyed one hundred casks of coined copper.
The details of the scheme were put into execution.
Silver bullion at six shillings and eightpence an ounce,
or Spanish dollars at six shillings, became the currency
instead of paper of the " old tenor."   The " new tenor,"
and a dozen more confusing designations, sank in value
until sometimes £120 of it were scarcely worth £1 sterling.   At once a favorable change began ; there was
no *shock* but of the pleasantest kind ; a revulsion of
popular feeling followed speedily, until Hutchinson,
from being threatened at every street corner, became
a thorough favorite.   A crowd of paper-money men
coming from Abington to Boston, in the expectation of
finding sympathy, were met with the coldest of comfort.
Massachusetts Bay was on a solid basis at last.

Twelve years after this time, Hutchinson wrote : " I
think I may be allowed to call myself the father of the
present fixed medium." [1]   There is no doubt of it.
He alone saw a way out of the difficulty, and nothing
but his tact and persistency pushed the measure to success.   Democracies perhaps never appear to so poor
advantage as in the management of finances, and no
more conspicuous instance in point can be cited than

[1] Dec. 14, 1761.   Letter Book, Mass. Archives, Historical, vol. xxvi.

that of provincial New England throughout the first half of the eighteenth century. The Assembly, the members of which were usually simply the mouthpieces of the towns, surrendering their private judgment and submissive to the "Instructions" which they received at the time of their election, was uniformly, by a large majority, in favor of an irredeemable paper currency. Before the enormous evils which early became apparent and constantly grew in magnitude, the Assembly was impotent. Widows and orphans, classes dependent on fixed incomes, were reduced to distress; creditors found themselves defrauded of their just dues till almost nothing was left; a universal gambling spirit was promoted. The people saw no way to meet the evil but by new and ever new issues of the wretched scrip, until, with utter callousness of conscience, men repudiated contracts voluntarily entered upon, and 'recklessly discounted the resources of future generations by shoving off upon them the obligations their own shoulders should have borne. The action of the Council, meantime, by which in a certain way the higher class was represented, was uniformly more wise and more honorable than that of the lower House. The Governors of provincial Massachusetts were seldom men of much mark; but all who held office during this period of distress — Shute, Bellomont, Burnett, Belcher, Shirley — had insight enough to perceive the infatuation of the people, and thwarted their short-sighted plans by such means as they could use. It is especially to be noted that King and Parliament threw their influence on the right side, and sought repeatedly to save the purblind people from themselves.

The right of the home government to interfere in colonial affairs was then never questioned. Massachusetts would dodge, if she could, the government mandates; but the theories of a later time, with which we shall hereafter be much occupied, that the Houses at Westminster had no jurisdiction beyond sea, and that the King, having granted the charter, had put it out of his power to touch the provincial policy, in these days found no expression, or only the faintest. The Revolution even now was preparing; the Colonies were chafing under restrictions imposed from beyond the ocean, — restrictions, in this case, wise, but very unwelcome. It was the beginning of the long fret which was to culminate in the Declaration of Independence.

In all this time of distress, no figure is apparent so marked with traits of greatness as that of Thomas Hutchinson. The Colonies in general were infected by the same craze as that which came so near to paralyzing Massachusetts ; but no other man in America, while appreciating rightly the disastrous state of things, at the same time saw a way out. Franklin, in Pennsylvania, level-headed though he was, elaborately advocated paper money,[1] turning a good penny in its manufacture, when at last it was resolved upon. In Massachusetts, the father of Samuel Adams was one of the directors of the iniquitous Land Bank. Of hard-money men even, not one but looked askance upon Hutchinson's suggestion as to the Louisburg indemnity, however fully the mire into which the Province was sunk may have been perceived. Shirley gave the plan his assent only

[1] *A Modest Inquiry into the Nature and Necessity of a Paper Currency.*

grudgingly. In the Council and the Assembly, it was only Hutchinson's personal weight that brought about the result. His proposition, smiled at at first, then grumbled over, then causing such resentment that its author was cursed, and the hope was rife that the ship bearing the specie would sink on the voyage, he carried in spite of all, — certainly as fine a feat of statesmanship as our colonial era can furnish. Shirley in those days was brilliant in the eyes of men, but the course of events was soon to show how little was left of him when what was due to luck was subtracted. Sir William Pepperell, too, wore his baronial honors, and dressed himself in gold lace and velvet for ceremonials and the portrait-painters, — the worthy Kittery trader, and nothing more. He deserved credit for the success of Louisburg almost as little as that other famous dignitary of the North Shore, Lord Timothy Dexter, of Newburyport, deserved credit for his fortunes made in whalebone and warming-pans. Outside of New England, one man, and only one in the Colonies, was gaining a wide fame, — Franklin, in Pennsylvania. He, however, was only on the threshold of his great career, and it may be truthfully said was stumbling badly in his start, advocate and manufacturer as he was of irredeemable paper. The great leading colony, Massachusetts Bay, — at that time, it must be remembered, comprehending Maine, and so territorially of vast extent, — the leading colony, too, in the numbers, the character, and the intelligence of its inhabitants, possessed a son who, judging even by the standards of to-day, may be called a statesman of high rank ; — a man of power, moving,

too, in no confined sphere, though it was as yet un-
cleared of forests and peopled only by pioneers.

What economic views Hutchinson had in other directions than in finance are hinted at in the conclusion to
the second volume of his History, — words penned at
a time now close at hand; words breathing a spirit of
calm wisdom and humanity. " The great Creator of the
Universe, in infinite wisdom, has so formed the earth
that different parts of it, from the soil, climate, etc.,
are adapted to different produce; and He so orders and
disposes the genius, temper, numbers, and other circumstances relative to the inhabitants as to render some
employments peculiarly proper for one country, and
others for another, and by this provision a mutual intercourse is kept up between the different parts of the
globe. It would be a folly in a Virginian to attempt a
plantation of rice for the sake of having all he con-
sumes from the produce of his own labor, when South
Carolina, by nature, is peculiarly designed for rice, and
capable of supplying one half the world. Old countries, stocked with people, are ordinarily best adapted
to manufactures. Would it be the interest of New
England, whilst thin of people, to turn their attention
from the whale, cod, mackerel, and herring fishery,
their lumber-trade and shipbuilding, which require but
few hands compared with many other sorts of business,
to such manufactures as are now imported from Great
Britain; or to take their sons from clearing the land,
and turning an uncultivated wilderness into pleasant
and profitable fields, and set them to spinning, weav-
ing, and the like employments? I do not mean to

discourage any persons, who cannot improve their time to greater advantage, from employing themselves and families in any branch of manufacture whatsoever. Idleness is the certain parent of vice. Industry, introduced, will ordinarily tend to produce a change of manners. A general philanthropy will induce us to delight in and contribute to the happiness of every part of the human race, by which we ourselves are no sufferers; the state from whence we sprang, and upon which we still depend for protection, may justly expect to be distinguished by us, and that we should delight in, and contribute to, its prosperity beyond all other parts of the globe."

CHAPTER III.

HUTCHINSON begins the third volume of his History with the remark that the people of Massachusetts Bay were never more easy and happy than in 1749, when, through the application of the Louisburg reimbursement to the extinction of the irredeemable bills, the currency was in an excellent condition. It may be claimed that he himself was the main cause of this prosperity. He failed of reëlection in the spring of 1749 by a large majority, the Assembly thus losing permanently its most eloquent and influential member.[1] His unpopularity, however, was short-lived. He appeared at once in the Council, and remained in his new sphere no less than before the guiding spirit in public affairs. He was indeed watchful for the welfare of the people in matters large and small. In 1747, Boston had been in a tumult over a press-gang let loose in the streets by the Commodore of a squadron of men-of-war then in harbor. Hutchinson, who, in a quite remarkable way, was usually on the ground in times of trouble, saved from the mob a Lieutenant of the fleet who was innocent in the transaction ; then, as Speaker, drew up resolutions. These, while favoring law and order, promised that " this House will exert themselves by all ways

---

[1] Eliot : *N. E. Biog. Dict.*, art. " Hutchinson."

and means possible in redressing such grievances as his
Majesty's subjects are and have been under," protesting thus against impressment as an outrage.   By 1750,
" he was praised as much for his ' firm,' as he had
before been abused for his ' obstinate,' perseverance."
He was made chairman of a commission to negotiate a
treaty with the Indians at Casco Bay.

As the Province increased in population, the settlement of its boundaries, which so far had been only
vaguely drawn, became a matter of increasing importance.   Ten years before, he had been concerned in
the settlement of the line on the New Hampshire side.
Now, he was set to treat as to the frontier with Connecticut commissioners ; and, apropos of some effort at
sharp practice on their part, he makes in the History
this general observation : " Communities or bodies of
men are capable jointly of such acts as, being the act
of any one member separately, would cause him to be
ashamed."   A year or two later, the Council Records
speak of him as settling the Rhode Island border.   He
must have done such work well, for at a later time,
though quite broken in the esteem of his countrymen,
only he could be trusted to settle the delicate question
of the boundary on the west toward New York.   In
fact, in important public business his name now is never
absent.   In 1752, he was appointed Judge of Probate
and Justice of the Common Pleas for the County of
Suffolk, in place of an uncle, just dead, who had filled
those positions.   In the spring of 1754, he lost his
wife.   " With her dying voice and eyes fixed on him,
she uttered these words, ' Best of husbands ! ' " [1]   He

[1] Autobiography.

loved her tenderly, twenty years later taking thought for her grave, as we shall see, in the midst of melancholy circumstances. Three sons, Thomas, Elisha, and William ("Billy"), and two daughters, Sarah and Margaret ("Peggy"), formed his family, with all of whom the student of his papers becomes well acquainted.

Hutchinson was not turned from the public service by his private griefs. The French were trying to win to their side the Six Nations, and principally for the sake of circumventing their designs a convention of the Colonies, in 1754, was held at Albany. Questions as to raising men and money were to be settled, and a union to be devised, if possible, so far as was necessary for defense. Nearly all the Colonies were represented. No assembly so deserving of respect, looking at the character of the delegates and the purpose in view, had ever before taken place in America. Massachusetts sent five deputies, at the head of whom was Hutchinson; and he and Benjamin Franklin, of Pennsylvania, were the leading minds of the body. To these two the preparation of the important papers was confided, the sketch of a plan for a colonial union, and a representation of the state of the Colonies. Hutchinson, who had the latter task, sought to show that the French designed to drive the English into the sea. How best to prevent this was Franklin's theme; he presented a scheme for union, devised probably before he left Philadelphia, which has always had great interest as a forecast of what was to come. Hutchinson and Franklin no doubt came together with thorough cordiality, though one imagines their differing views on the great

question of finance may have given grounds for dispute.
With the power for fair and clear statement which he
so constantly shows in his Letters and History, the Massachusetts statesman details the suggestion of his colleague, which he does not seem at all to disapprove,
though it found favor neither in America nor England.
In each Colony, the Assembly was to elect delegates,
to serve for a term of three years, in a general convention, over which a crown-appointed official was to
preside, possessing a negative on all acts.   Matters of
general interest, but in especial, defense against the
French, were to be considered.   Hutchinson says that
Franklin favored a more intimate union with England
through the admission to Parliament of American representatives, with repeal at the same time of all former
acts restraining trade and manufactures, so that the colonists could stand on the same footing with the men of
Great Britain.   He did not suppose the Colonies could
have enough representatives to have great weight by
their numbers, but thought enough might be admitted
"to cause the laws to be better and more impartially
considered."   The Colonies were to be, as it were, so
many counties gained to Great Britain, and all to be
included within the British empire.   Franklin's plan is a
most interesting one, and in the early agitations of the
Revolution engaged the serious thought of many leaders
on both sides of the Atlantic.   In particular, it was
entertained by James Otis, whose appearance on the
stage we are about to note.   That Hutchinson ever regarded it as feasible nowhere appears.   He describes it
merely, and notes the inconsistency of Franklin, whose

ground fifteen years later was that Britain and the
Colonies were under separate legislatures, but one sovereign, — "related to one another as were England and
Scotland before the Union." Franklin was not to blame
for the change ; for, though at first by no means impossible of fulfillment, such a plan as his became at last
quite impracticable. When the powerful influence of
Samuel Adams began to make itself felt, independence
was the only cry. In the British empire, however, the
idea has never ceased to be entertained. The federa-
tion of mother land and dependencies at the present
moment is in the thought of millions, and the lines
upon which it is to be effected, if ever, are likely to be
substantially the same as were laid down by Franklin
and James Otis one hundred and forty years ago.

Braddock's defeat made the year 1755 a dark one in
America. Shirley's son was shot through the head
there, an incident which, probably more than any other,
brought the disaster home to Boston. A certain young
Lieutenant-Colonel Gage, with young Colonel Washington, of Virginia, were active in the retreat, — men whom
Boston was to know well at a later time. In 1755, too,
came the deportation of the Acadian peasants, a measure
for which excuse may be made. The pursuits of Grand
Pré and its fellow villages were by no means purely
idyllic. In the struggle to the death in which France
and England in America were locked, it was not at all
safe to overlook the fact that in the northeast lay a
considerable population ever ready to strike hands with
the Indians in merciless raids upon the English frontier.
Of nearly seven thousand French who were driven off,

about one thousand were brought to Boston, arriving at the beginning of winter, as unexpected as undesired. Hutchinson, though never a soldier, believed in stout fighting ; and the year before at Albany had made a most useful suggestion, — that the commander near Crown Point should be Sir William Johnson, a suggestion which resulted in the defeat of Dieskau. Toward enemies in distress and powerless, however, his heart was tender ; and he took the lead in Boston toward relieving the trouble of the forlorn exiles so unceremoniously thrust upon the town. " It was the hardest case since our Saviour was on earth." [1] No one was more active than. he in their behalf. He prepared a representation for them, to be laid before the English government, which was to be signed by their principal men, praying that they might either be allowed to return or receive compensation. This he offered to put into trusty hands for them. The Acadians were thankful and took the paper to consider, but returned it unsigned. They feared they should lose the favor of France if they should receive, or even solicit, help from England. They preferred to wait, believing France would never make peace until they were restored. It was certainly due to Hutchinson's tolerant spirit also that, in the midst of the Puritan community, the captives were permitted among themselves to practice their Catholic faith.

In 1756, Shirley went to England, the Lieutenant-Governor, Spencer Phips, an old and decrepit man, acting in his place. In indirect ways, the adminis-

---

[1] Hutchinson : *Hist.*, iii. 40.

tration of the Province was largely in the hands of
Hutchinson, whose appointment to the chief place was
expected by many. As Shirley retires, Hutchinson, in
his History, speaks of him depreciatingly, but not
meanly so. Shirley had strong military ambition, and
was at first much favored by fortune. When fairly
tried, however, he failed, and withdrew disappointed.
He was never accused of want of fidelity, and embarrassed himself by his outlays in the public service.
Hutchinson's time had not yet come, and into Shirley's
shoes stepped Thomas Pownall, whose brother, John
Pownall, Secretary of the Board of Trade, became in
after years Hutchinson's frequent correspondent. With
the Governor, Hutchinson's relations were never quite
cordial. Pownall was a politician of Chatham's school,
who, after his service in America (during which, from
secretary to Osborne, Governor of New York, he became Governor of Massachusetts, and afterwards of
South Carolina), returned to England, and vigorously
seconded his great leader in the House of Commons.
The handsome portrait of Pownall in the possession of
the Massachusetts Historical Society shows a bright
face above a figure elegant and richly attired. His
tastes, however, were simple ; he was easy and informal
in his ways; and " would sometimes sit in the chair
without a sword, in a plain short frock, unruffled shirt,
with a scratch-wig and a little rattan." Such a neglect
of ceremony was not at all to Hutchinson's mind, who
believed in a certain stateliness for men of high position. Pownall's ideas, too, were not those of Hutchinson, who had now settled definitely into the " preroga-

tive " notions which he was soon to be called on to defend to the uttermost. When Danvers desired to become a town, sending representatives to the Assembly, Hutchinson, in the Council, opposed it, on grounds partly technical, but also because the number in the House was already too large. The democracy ought not to weigh down the Governor and Council. Loudoun, the British commander-in-chief, having demanded quarters for a regiment in Boston on the strength of an Act of Parliament, the General Court refused the demand, when so urged, declaring that the Act did not apply to them ; then straightway passed an Act of their own making the required provision. Loudoun was testy ; and the General Court, anxious to preserve the peace, drew up an expression " which created embarrassment in later times. The authority of all Acts of Parliament which *concern the Colonies* and *extend to them* is ever acknowledged in all the courts of law and made the rule of all judicial proceedings in the Province. There is not a member of the General Court, and we know no inhabitant within the bounds of the government, that ever questioned this authority. To prevent any ill consequences which may arise from an opinion of our holding such principles, we now utterly disavow them, as we should readily have done at any time past if there had been occasion for it." Though Hutchinson himself formulated this, he insists that in 1757 these were the habitual and well-considered sentiments of the legislators. The authority of the Parliament was unanimously admitted, the point disputed in the present case being that the Act cited by Loudoun was not intended to apply to America. Had the intention been different, Massachusetts would have submitted. From this position, Hutchinson never varied; but the hour was now not far off when the Province was to abandon it.

In 1758, Hutchinson became Lieutenant-Governor, resigning then his justiceship of the Common Pleas, which was taken by his brother Foster; and in 1760, when Pownall departed for the South, Hutchinson for a brief space was supreme magistrate. The hearts of men at this time were full of hope and vigor. The excellent financial condition produced by Hutchinson's measure ten years previous had continued, and was now made even better than before. Quebec had fallen; and the mother country, made generous by success, sent over in grateful mood such reimbursements to the Colonies for the share they had taken in causing the brilliant result that the taxes became a burden of the lightest. Aside from this prosperity, the fact that the incubus was removed which had oppressed the Colony from its first settlement — the pressure of the aggressive French on the north — imparted a confident buoyancy which became apparent at once.

Hutchinson, who could never feel cordially toward men of Pownall's ways and principles, saw in Francis Bernard, his successor, who was an English country gentleman, well educated, of refined tastes and conservative ideas, a character much more to his mind. The Province received Bernard cordially; Pownall had been much liked, and all hoped as much from the new man.

The General Court addressed him in a loyal spirit, but at the same time allowed it to appear that they were well aware of the service they had rendered and of its value to the British empire. Bernard having in his speech to the Assembly referred to the benefits derived by the Colonies from their *subjection* to Great Britain, the Council were careful in their address to substitute *relation* for *subjection*, while acknowledging it was to that relation they owed their freedom. The House, while not scrupling to acknowledge their subjection, hastened to explain it thus : " They are sensible of the blessings derived to the British Colonies from their subjection to Great Britain ; and the whole world must be sensible of the blessings derived to Great Britain from the loyalty of the Colonies in general, and from the efforts of this Colony in particular, which for more than a century past has been wading in blood and laden with the expenses of repelling the common enemy, without which efforts Great Britain at this day might have had no Colonies to defend." [1] The spirit of the Province was high, but certainly now no voice would have been raised against the declaration of a year or two before : " Our dependence upon the Parliament of Great Britain we never had a desire or thought of lessening." Says Hutchinson : " An empire distinct from Britain no man then alive expected or desired to see. From the common increase of inhabitants . . . in distant ages, an independent empire would probably be formed. This was the language of that day." The Colonies claimed territory through to the Pacific, the

[1] Hutchinson : *Hist.*, iii. 83.

filling of which with people, now that the French were broken, might at once go forward, making it inevitable that the mother country would soon be surpassed in wealth and importance. Feeling this pride and confidence in themselves, they naturally, says Hutchinson with candor, looked invidiously at advantages enjoyed by people in England over those in America.[1]

In September, 1760, Chief Justice Sewall died, and the question as to a successor became important at once. Hutchinson tells the story of the appointment both in the History and Autobiography, and as the matter proved momentous, it is proper to use detail. The morning after Sewall's death, Hutchinson was met in the street by Jeremiah Gridley, the first lawyer of the Province, who told him he must be the successor of Sewall. Other principal lawyers also pressed the matter, together with the senior surviving judge of the Superior Court and two others of the same bench. The position was attractive to Hutchinson, though he distrusted his ability to fill it, since he had had no systematic legal education. In those days the law was much less definitely a profession than it has since become. Hutchinson, quite without previous training, had filled satisfactorily the positions of judge of Probate and of the Common Pleas, his industry and quickness helping him readily to the necessary knowledge. His most capable contemporaries saw no bar to his undertaking the chief judicial functions, and easily made him feel it would be safe for him to accept the post, if offered.[2]

---

[1] Hutchinson : *Hist.*, iii. 68, 69.

[2] Gordon's account is quite different. He says Hutchinson hurried to Bernard and begged for the appointment, " by which he gratified both his

A day or two after, Hutchinson had a call from a vigorous young lawyer destined soon to great distinction, James Otis, Jr., a native of Barnstable, afterwards settled in Plymouth, and now making his way in Boston. Otis supposed that Lynde, already a member of the Superior Court, would be appointed; and came to beg the influence of the Lieutenant-Governor with Bernard that his father, James Otis, Sr., then Speaker of the Assembly, who claimed to have been encouraged by Shirley to expect at some time such a position, might be put in the place of the promoted Lynde. The younger Otis in a friendly way told Hutchinson, if he himself had any thought of the place of Chief Justice, he would not say a word as to his father. Hutchinson says he did not conceal the fact that the matter was in his mind, but declared he was undetermined as to whether or not he should accept the place if offered. So the interview ended, and in the weeks that followed the Otises, both son and father, pressed zealously for the appointment of the latter. A month passed, when Bernard informed his lieutenant he had been urged by many persons to appoint him. Hutchinson asserts that he refrained from all solicitation. On the contrary, he warned the Governor of trouble likely to come in case the Otises were disappointed. Bernard, however, ran the risk of this, declared he would in no case appoint Otis, and presently named Hutchinson, who says he had reason to feel, though not of the profession, that the lawyers in general were pleased.

ambition and covetousness, his two ruling passions." *Hist. Am. Rev.*, i. 141. This certainly is a misrepresentation.

So far, probably, we may trust Hutchinson's account. What follows in his story is more doubtful. At once, he says, the younger Otis vowed revenge, a threat which he soon after proceeded to execute by embarrassing Bernard, including the new Chief Justice also in his enmity. Though before friends to government, the Otises now became its opposers; and as the younger man presently developed power as an unequaled popular leader, he became a most dangerous foe. " From so small a spark," exclaims Hutchinson, " a great fire seems to have been kindled." [1]

To attribute thus the position which James Otis presently after assumed entirely to chagrin over a personal grievance is what no one at this day can admit. He was often violent and eccentric, guilty of conduct almost intolerable, according to the testimony of men of all parties. The morbid taint, which before the flash of lightning took his life was to reduce him to imbecility, early began its ravages. His endowments, however,

---

[1] "April 29, 1779," says Eliot (*N. E. Biog. Dict.*, art. "Hutchinson"), speaking of an old judge of the Superior Court, "I passed the afternoon at Cambridge with venerable Judge Trowbridge, who said, after a solemn pause : 'It was a most unhappy thing that Mr. H. was ever Chief Justice of our Court. What O—— said, " that he would set the Province in flames, if he perished by the fire," has come to pass. He, poor man ! suffers ; and what are we coming to ? I thought little of it at the time. I made every exertion in favor of Mr. H., and think now he was the best man to be there, if the people had been satisfied, and he had never looked beyond it. But I now think it was unhappy for us all. And I freely believe this war would have been put off many years, if Governor H. had not been made Chief Justice.' He spoke " (says Eliot) " of H. as a man of great abilities, who could fit himself in a very little time for any business ; and told likewise how their friendship was broken off, which manifested that Governor H. could be guilty of mean resentment and sordid ingratitude."

were imperial. Both in his strength and in his weakness, he bore resemblance to Chatham, with whom he has been rightly compared. In eloquence, he did not fall behind the lofty earl. His voice in those days seemed unimportant as compared with the tones that filled the historic spaces of St. Stephen's Chapel; but it was the Tyrtæan note which nerved America, as she marched out to those early conflicts, — conflicts through which she was to pass to an unparalleled supremacy. In height of soul, few statesmen have surpassed him, as all must feel who ponder the few fragmentary harangues which are all that have been transmitted from him. Strange power of partisan bitterness that could blunt the perceptions of a man like Hutchinson till he misjudged him to be only self-seeking and crazily voluble! Henceforth the two men are to have no feelings for each other but dread and hatred. Just as the Chief Justice enters upon his new duties at the end of 1760, George III. is proclaimed King. As if a bell had struck, an agitation begins in which the two men, now at odds, are at first the conspicuous figures, — an agitation destined before it closed to affect most profoundly the history of the whole future human race.

The fall of Quebec in 1759 was a crisis of great importance in the history of America, and in the career of Hutchinson as well. With the event itself, he was not unconnected. In the interval of a summer between the going out of Shirley and the coming in of Pownall, Hutchinson as Lieutenant-Governor was chief magistrate, and sent three hundred men to serve as pioneers under Wolfe. But it was not until Wolfe had done

his work, and its far-reaching consequences began to
become apparent, that its significant relations to the
story we are considering were perceived. The issue of
the Seven Years' War, triumphant for England in
India, on the continent of Europe, and in America, together with much glory brought to England a great
burden of responsibility and debt. Ministers, energetic
and sharp-eyed, though deficient in tact, casting about
for means to meet the emergency, determined upon a
vigorous enforcement of old customs enactments which,
as far as America was concerned, had been a dead letter, though long inscribed upon the statute-books.
Since the time of the English Commonwealth, the
Navigation Laws[1] had been in existence. The Rump
and Council of State of that day, with Young Sir
Henry Vane as leader, in a certain way a Massachusetts worthy, had passed these acts to restrain the
Dutch, at that time active in the Stuart interest ; and
out of them largely grew the great sea war, in which
the conspicuous figures on the two sides were Blake and
Van Tromp. The laws remained unrepealed when the
Stuarts came back ; and now in the Hanoverian days,
as venerable long-unused instruments, were conveniently
at hand for service. More important, however, than
these, the "Sugar Act" of 1733 imposed a duty of
sixpence a gallon on foreign molasses, the idea of Parliament at the time being to protect the English West
India planters, exposed to the sharp competition of their
neighbors of the French islands. In administration, all
had gone loosely. The dust-covered regulations of the

[1] Edward Channing : *Navigation Laws.*

century before had been known only to legal antiqua-
rians here and there; the Sugar Act was nearer at
hand, but had never been enforced. From a legal
point of view, the immense commercial activity of New
England was for the most part illicit. In serene igno-
rance of the statute-books, the Yankee sailors penetrated all harbors, conveying in their holds from the
ports where they belonged various sorts of interdicted
merchandise, and bringing home cargoes equally interdicted from all the ports they touched. The merchants,
who since 1749, through Hutchinson's excellent statesmanship, had been free from the embarrassment of a
bad currency, greatly throve. The shipyards teemed
with fleets; each nook of the coast was the seat of
mercantile ventures; in all the shore towns the fine
mansions of the traders, in that buff and square comeli-
ness which, under the name of " colonial," the architects of to-day take pleasure in reproducing, rose along
the main streets. Within the houses, bric-a-brac from
every clime came to abound. The merchants and their
wives and children, clothed gayly in fabrics of fantastic
names [1] from remote regions, went to and fro, sitting
sometimes for their portraits to Smibert, or Stuart, or
Copley, thus transmitting to us an idea of the purple
and flowered state which was becoming common. Glowing reports of the gayety and luxury of the Colonies
reached the mother country.[2] The efflorescence and
the substantial wealth which formed the soil from

---

[1] See the extraordinary list in Alice Morse Earle's *Customs and
Fashions in Old New England*, p. 329.
[2] Gordon : *Hist. of the American War*, vol. i., p. 157, London, 1788.

which it sprang were in great part of contraband origin. The merchants and sailors were to a man lawbreakers ; and this universal lawbreaking it was which, after the fall of Quebec, the English ministry, hard put to it for means to administer the widely extended British empire, undertook to stop. The custom-houses were to be something more than cosy nooks on the wharves where holders of sinecures might doze comfortably ; the ships of war everywhere were to be instructed to enforce the revenue laws. The new scheme was zealously pushed, and the friction at once gave rise to fire, — fire which was destined to increase until the ties' between mother land and dependency were quite consumed.

In February, 1761, Hutchinson, just warming to his work as Chief Justice, was a principal figure in the famous stir about the Writs of Assistance, during which, according to John Adams, the child Independence was born. Even in the time of slack administration, customs - officers, merely on the authority of their commissions, had sometimes forcibly entered warehouses and even dwelling-houses, upon information that smuggled goods were concealed in them. Shirley, while Governor, when appealed to for authority by customs-officers who were thus acting, had in his character as a civil magistrate sanctioned such entrances. Hutchinson at the time thought this extraordinary in a man of sense and legal education, since, by law, not the Governor, but the Courts, must give such sanction. Hutchinson himself was instrumental in bringing the illegality to light. When the customs - officers one day

were about to break into the warehouse of his brother,
upon information that smuggled Spanish iron was concealed there, he, being on the spot, challenged the
officers for their authority, and was shown in answer the
Governor's warrant. Sending for the keys, he showed
the searchers that their information was wrong, for no
iron was there; but at the same time he declared that
if they had made an entry they would have been prosecuted, as only the Courts could give the proper authority. Shirley became more cautious, referring the
officers to the Superior Court for their warrants.[1]

In the new state of affairs, the ministry pressing on
the one hand for a thorough collection of the revenue,
and the people on the other hand being full of spirit
through commercial prosperity, military success, and relief from fear of the French, the authority of even the
Superior Court to grant warrants was questioned. This
was just before the death of Chief Justice Sewall, who
was understood to have doubts of the legality of such
Writs. The matter came before Hutchinson in the
early weeks of his incumbency. James Otis, Jr., held
at this time the lucrative position of advocate-general,
and as such was applied to by the customs authorities
to defend them. He refused to do it, resigning his
office. "In such a cause," said he, "I despise all
fees." [2] Candid though Hutchinson in general is, the
heat with which he fought the protagonists of popular
ideas is still warm in the phrases in which, twenty years
later, he sets down his narrative. He attributes the
course of Otis entirely to the personal resentment he

---

[1] Hutchinson : *Hist.*, iii. 92.   [2] Tudor : *Life of Otis*, 57.

felt because his father had failed to be made Chief Justice, — a construction which the words and course of Otis make it plain is unfair. Hutchinson does better in his statement of the legal principles involved; here he is clear and judicial.[1] It was objected that the "Writs of Assistance," as the warrants were technically called, were general in their nature. Though formerly, in searching for goods which had been stolen, there had been an employment of general warrants, the practice had ceased for many years. Special warrants, issued by Justices of the Peace, had taken their place, in which the spots to be searched must be carefully set forth. In like manner, as regards search for contraband goods, general writs should be given up for special writs; to such special writs it was declared no objection would be made, if the place where the search was to be were mentioned, and information given upon oath. It was declared that the practice in England now was to use only such special writs in searching for smuggled goods; on authority, however, quite unsatisfactory, for all that could be cited was a passage in a London magazine. The judges, Hutchinson continues, were certain that such special writs would rarely, if ever, be applied for, as no informer would expose himself to the rage of the people by taking oath as to particular places of deposit for stolen goods. The position of the Chief Justice was an embarrassing one. His own proclivities were for free trade; his friends had been concerned in contraband commerce, according to the universal practice in the time of slack administra-

[1] Hutchinson : *Hist.*, iii. 93, 94.

tion. A change had come about: government had declared the laws must be enforced, and it lay upon him
to determine the laws, and see to their enforcement. A
statute of the fourteenth year of Charles II. authorized
the issuing of Writs of Assistance from the Court of
Exchequer in England. Statutes of the seventh and
eighth of William III. required of the Colonial Courts
to give to officers all such aid as was given to officers
by Courts in England. Did the Superior Court correspond to the Court of Exchequer? Was the London
magazine right in its account of the proper author-
ization for a search? One feels that the Superior
Court could do no otherwise than hesitate, and that it
would be proper to suspend judgment until the Chief
Justice could send to England and have the doubtful
points set at rest.

Before this determination was reached, James Otis
made that memorable plea, one of the epoch-making
events in the history of America. In Hutchinson's
eyes it scarcely merited notice; but fortunately there
sat at the table in the Council Chamber where the Court
was held, wigged and gowned, a young lawyer, twenty-
six years old, of compact, well-set frame surmounted by
a head and face suggestive of brains and a most com-
bative temper, who had come up from his home in
Braintree to be present at the trial, — John Adams.
His famous description, written in old age to William Tudor, cannot be omitted here. "The Council
Chamber was as respectable an apartment as the House
of Commons or the House of Lords in Great Britain,
in proportion; or that in the State House in Philadel-

phia, in which the Declaration of Independence was signed in 1776. In this chamber, round a great fire, were seated five judges, with Lieutenant-Governor Hutchinson at their head as Chief Justice, all arrayed in their new, fresh, rich robes of scarlet English broadcloth ; in their large cambric bands and immense judicial wigs. In this chamber were seated at a long table all the barristers-at-law of Boston and of the neighboring county of Middlesex, in gowns, bands, and tie wigs. They were not seated on ivory chairs, but their dress was more solemn and more pompous than that of the Roman Senate, when the Gauls broke in upon them. Two portraits, at more than full length, of King Charles the Second and of King James the Second, in splendid golden frames, were hung up on the most conspicuous sides of the apartment. If my young eyes or old memory have not deceived me, these were as fine pictures as I ever saw ; the colors of the royal ermines and long, flowing robes were the most glowing, the figures the most noble and graceful, the features the most distinct and characteristic, far superior to those of the king and queen of France in the Senate chamber of Congress, — these were worthy of the pencils of Rubens and Vandyke. There was no painter in England capable of them at that time. They had been sent over without frames in Governor Pownall's time, but he was no admirer of Charles or James. The pictures were stowed away in a garret, among rubbish, until Governor Bernard came, who had them cleaned, superbly framed, and placed in council for the admiration and imitation of all men, no doubt with the advice and concurrence of Hutchinson and all his nebula of stars and satellites. One circumstance more. Samuel Quincy and John Adams had been admitted barristers at that term. John was the youngest; he should be painted looking like a short, thick archbishop of Canterbury, seated at the table with a pen in his hand, lost in admiration."

The court-room thus described was the Council Chamber of the Old State House, still preserved in all its original features, and containing the table at which John Adams sat. The room has been the theatre of as many great events probably as any one spot in America, several of which it will be for the follower of this narrative to consider. Most important of all, perhaps, is the scene of that dull February day, the firelight dancing on the handsome pictures, the dignitaries of the Province ranged before them, and the scarlet judges, with Hutchinson at their head, — the pompous circumstances of the occasion being a novelty which he had introduced. With Otis in the case was employed Oxenbridge Thacher, an advocate of ability, who at the same time was prominent in the Assembly, — a patriot too early lost, — whose death by consumption, in 1765, opened the way into public life for Sam Adams. There is some reason for thinking that Thacher found Otis an uncomfortable associate. "When he [Thacher] happened to think differently from Mr. Otis, Jun., in the House of Assembly, the latter treated him in so overbearing and indecent a manner that he was obliged at times to call upon the Speaker to interpose and protect him." [1]

[1] Gordon : i. 205.

The case was opened by Jeremiah Gridley, a veteran of the bar, with whom Otis had studied, who, with clearness and dignity, made a plea for the customs officials. Thacher followed, cool and quiet; but Otis, according to John Adams, was a "flame of fire;" and enough remains of the impassioned sentences to make plain to us how it was that every man of the immense crowd went away prepared to take arms against Writs of Assistance. The extant portrait of Otis gives no impressive presence. A contemporary describes him as "a plump, round-faced, smooth-skinned, short-necked, eagle-eyed politician." In black gown and wig, his exterior advantages can hardly have been great. But his words still burn after more than a hundred years.

"If the king of Great Britain in person were encamped on Boston Common at the head of 20,000 men, with all his navy on our coast, he would not be able to execute these laws. They would be resisted or eluded. . . . One of the most essential branches of English liberty is the freedom of one's house. A man's house is his castle; and whilst he is quiet he is as well guarded as a prince in his castle. This writ, if it should be declared legal, would totally annihilate this privilege. Custom-house officers may enter our houses when they please; we are commanded to permit their entry. Their menial servants may enter, . . . and whether they break through malice or revenge, no man, no court, can inquire." Most important of all, the Acts of Trade, he contended, "impose taxes, — enormous, burthensome, intolerable taxes; and on this topic he gave full scope to his talent for powerful declamation and invective, against *the tyranny of taxation without representation.* From the energy with which he urged this position that taxation without representation is tyranny, it came to be a common maxim in the mouth of every one. . . . I do say, in the most solemn manner, that Mr. Otis's oration against Writs of Assistance breathed into this nation the breath of life."

John Adams, whom we are following, was greatly moved, too, by certain minor incidents of the occasion. As to Otis's treatment of his old teacher, Gridley, he says : " It was a moral spectacle more affecting to me than any I have since seen upon the stage to observe the pupil treating his master with all the deference and respect, esteem and affection, of a son to a father, and that without the least affectation ; while he baffled and confounded all his authorities, confuted all his arguments, and reduced him to silence."

That Otis's plea was a powerful one is certain. Boston at once made him its Representative in the Assembly, adopted his phrase, " no taxation without representation," as a rallying-cry, and conceded to him for many years after a leadership that was scarcely broken even when he became insane. He could not enter a Town-Meeting without being received with clapping of hands ; and at last became a great embarrassment to his party from the fact that, although his wits were gone, the people would still follow him. Hutchinson, it is plain, quite fails to do justice, not only to the good purpose, but also to the ability of Otis. He looked back upon the scene through years charged with the smoke of a tremendous conflict, during which he and

Otis had been locked in an almost continuous struggle. What to Adams seemed in the retrospect extreme eloquence seemed to Hutchinson extreme violence. Adams declares that Hutchinson had been made Chief Justice by Bernard, that the Writs of Assistance might be sustained. This can by no means have been true. Hutchinson had long felt that such Writs were issued too loosely; and his interference with the execution of one, as appears from the account which has been given, caused that the Governor ceased to issue them on his own responsibility, making it necessary that there should be an application to the Court. Sewall had been in doubt what to do about them; Hutchinson was in doubt; and it really was easy for well-meaning and sensible men in that time to see nothing improper or inexpedient in the Writs. The government certainly needed revenue, which could be got only through taxation. "No taxation without representation," though a principle as old as Magna Charta, had been long out of the minds of men; and when Otis enunciated it anew, time was required to have it sink fairly into the world's comprehension. The taxes were evaded, the whole country being given over to unlawful trade in a way most demoralizing. The warehouses were few indeed in which there were no smuggled goods. Freedom, to be sure, was outraged when a customs-officer invaded a man's house, his castle; but high tariffs cannot exist without outrages upon freedom. The measures taken for tariff enforcement in the days of Grenville and Bernard were perhaps no more objectionable than those employed in the days of McKinley. Writs of Assistance were legal and usual in England. If they are ever justifiable, said then, and still say, English authorities, they are justifiable under such circumstances as prevailed in America.[1] Once recognize it as equitable and expedient for government to put heavy fetters upon commerce, and it follows, as the night the day, that espionage and infringement of personal liberty must be called into play to make the scheme effective. Writs of Assistance should not be found fault with, but the commercial system of which Writs of Assistance, or something equivalent, are the indispensable accompaniment. Adam Smith at that very time was living and seeking to spread wiser ideas in a tariff-ridden world. His views, however, were as yet little known and less followed. To hamper trade between nations was almost universally held to be legitimate ; Writs of Assistance, or other means as arbitrary, were inevitable, in order to make the restriction effective. Hutchinson was as yet a novice in the Chief Justiceship ; but he made no mistake in postponing a decision. It was eminently proper for the Court to wait until the English practice could be known. When news came from England, a form was settled on as near to that employed in England as circumstances would permit. Writs were issued to customs-officers, for whom application should be made to the Chief Justice by the Surveyor-General of the customs. Little, however, was heard of them from this time forth.

Hutchinson appears to have been far enough from friendly to the arbitrary method, but his popularity from now begins to wane. People were taught, he

---

[1] Lecky : *Hist. of XVIIIth Cent.*, vol. iii. p. 330.

says, that innovations under pretense of law were now confirmed by judgments of court incompatible with English liberties, and that the authority of the Courts of Admiralty and powers of customs-officers, always deemed grievous because unconstitutional, were now established by judges devoted to the prerogative. The main hand in this teaching was no doubt James Otis; but he at this time, with the vacillation of disease, distributed praise and blame almost with the same breath. Peter Oliver, who succeeded Hutchinson as Chief Justice, is quoted by John Adams as saying to him that Otis would at one time declare of the Lieutenant-Governor " that he would rather have him than any man he knows in any one office ; and the next hour will represent him as the greatest tyrant and most despicable creature living." [1]

[1] *Diary*, June 5, 1762.

The reasonableness of the position of Hutchinson in the case of the Writs of Assistance has been maintained and exhibited in detail by so high an authority as Horace Gray, Jr., Esq., now justice of the Supreme Court of the United States. See Quincy, Massachusetts Reports, 1761–1772, Appendix I.

The records of the old Superior Court are preserved entire in the Court House in Boston, among the records of the Supreme Judicial Court. The original papers are now being arranged under the supervision of John Noble, Esq., Clerk of the Supreme Court for Suffolk County. These papers, when available for consultation, will fully illustrate Hutchinson's judicial career.

CHAPTER IV.

A CURRENCY dispute took place in 1762 between the
Council and House, headed respectively by Hutchinson
and Otis, in which the former, true to the policy which
had already been of such advantage, set himself once
more against a course certain to lead to a disastrous
depreciation. He tells the story himself clearly and
dispassionately : —

" The currency of Massachusetts Bay had been under
as good regulation as possible from the time that paper
had been exchanged for silver, which was made the
standard at 6s. 8d. the ounce. Gold was not a lawful
tender, but passed current at fixed rates, — a guinea at
28s., a moidore at 36s., etc., being nearly the same proportion that gold bore to silver in Europe at the time
when paper money was exchanged. Silver bullion, for
a year or two past, had advanced in price in England
from 5s. 3d. to 5s. 7d. an ounce. A greater proportion
of silver than of gold had been exported, and people
who observed the scarcity of silver were alarmed. A
bill was brought into the House of Representatives and
passed, making gold a lawful tender at the rates at
which the several coins had been current for many years
past. A conference ensued between the two Houses,
the Lieutenant-Governor being at the head of the man-

agers for the Council, and Mr. Otis of those for the House. The only argument on the part of the House was the danger of oppression upon debtors by their being obliged to procure silver at disadvantage. On the part of the Council, it was said that the proportion between silver and gold was different at different times; that one only ought to be the standard, and the other considered as merchandise; that silver being made the standard in the Province, it behoved government rather to reduce the rate at which gold coin should pass, so as to make gold and silver the same in the Province as in Europe; that in such case there would be the same profit upon exporting gold as silver; but as one metal was made the standard and the only lawful tender, it was not advisable for government to regulate the other, but to leave it to take its chance; and that there was no other way of securing the currency from depreciation.

" The House was much engaged to carry the bill through, but the Council stood firm and rejected it. In a session of the Assembly, some time after, this bill passed into an act, and gold, as well as silver, was made a lawful tender. But about the same time, the price of silver bullion in England fell to 5s. 3d., or 5s. 2d. the ounce, and there was no longer any profit by the exportation of silver rather than gold. There seems to be no reason for engaging men more on one side the question than the other in this dispute, only as one side might appear to them more just and reasonable than the other; but the Lieutenant-Governor having taken one side of the question, Mr. Otis took the other; and the court

and country parties took one side and the other with
much of the same spirit as if it had been a controversy
between privilege and prerogative." [1]

To comment for a moment on this account, let it be
observed that the status of the two metals, as compared
with that of our time, is reversed. Silver it is which
rises in value, leading to its export and consequent
scarcity. Silver rising, gold properly should fall; but
the House, using the argument which in our ears has
such a familiar sound, are afraid of hardship to debtors, and insist that through legislation the value of
gold shall be maintained, that obligations may be more
easily met. Unquestionably, the Council's view was
sound finance, as had been the case in the great struggle against paper money a dozen years before. In the
whole matter, Hutchinson is very much in the foreground, aided by a noteworthy figure whom in later
controversies we shall see in strong opposition to him,
a substantial, most intelligent merchant of Huguenot
descent, James Bowdoin. Fortunately, the fluctuation
in silver was only temporary, and serious trouble in the
currency was at this time escaped. Some heat was
evolved in the debate, which the leader of the Council betrayed by omitting mention in his letters of his
antagonist; while Otis charged his sentences with the
sarcasm which he so well knew how to employ effectively. "Instances may be found," he says, "where
a man of abilities shall monopolize a power proportionate
to all those of Lord Chief Baron of the Exchequer,
Lord Chief Justice of both benches, Lord High Treas-

---

[1] Hutchinson: *Hist.*, vol. iii., p. 98, etc.

urer, and Lord High Chancellor of Great Britain, united in one single person. There is no axiom in mathematics clearer than that no man ought to be sole legislator of his country and supreme judge of his fellow-citizens." [1] Here first, probably, the charge is recorded which afterwards was reiterated constantly through Hutchinson's life, and has been repeated by every historian who has touched his career, — that he was a rapacious seeker of office, absorbing into his own hands through mere lust of pelf and power an extraordinary variety of functions. From a superficial view one indeed may get the impression that Hutchinson was a " Pooh Bah," scarcely less absurd than the functionary of the " Mikado." At this time, he was Lieutenant-Governor, President of the Council, Chief Justice, and Judge of Probate. A fair study of the case, however, will lead one to conclude that certainly gain had nothing to do with the matter. As Chief Justice, he received an uncertain salary, probably never more than £200 a year, when it was fully paid. In fact, the House in caprice did not hesitate at times to abridge the amount or cut it off entirely. In his subordinate judicial employments, he received pittances still more trifling. As Judge of the Common Pleas, he had £100 ; as Probate Judge, no doubt less ; while to his executive and legislative positions it does not appear that any emoluments were attached until after he succeeded Bernard. The case seems to have been this : with his means, for that day so ample, he had leisure such as few men of that community possessed ; his abil-

[1] Tudor : *Life of Otis*, p. 106.

ity and high character, revealed abundantly in his great
services, brought it about that office came to him.
There is good evidence in his letters to his friends, now
and at later periods, that he would have resigned willingly his dignities. " I had no views of personal advantage, no thought of ever seeking my advancement ;
and if I had lost the small emoluments of the posts I
sustain, I have sufficient income from my own estate to
free me from anxiety." [1] " Not that I am anxious for
the continuance of my commission. I am every day
more and more reconciled to parting with it, and whenever there shall be a new appointment of a Governor I
shall chuse to resign it." [2] He probably enjoyed the
activity which his positions brought him, as an energetic man always enjoys work which he can do well.
A fair mind, however, will not doubt that he was full
of public spirit, willing to sustain great burdens and
sacrifices to serve the community. As our story proceeds, we shall see how stubbornly he kept his shoulder
to the wheel, in the way in which he thought his duty
lay, until at last he underwent ruin, saving his life only
by exile.

Otis, nevertheless, in exposing and satirizing as absurd and improper the union in one public man of
functions judicial, executive, and legislative, was speaking by the book. He was one of the few men in
America at that time familiar with Montesquieu's doctrine, afterwards so famous, and so potent in moulding
the federal instrument in 1787, of the necessity in a

[1] Oct. 15, 1764.
[2] Nov. 8, 1764. *Mass. Archives Hist.*, vol. xxvi.

free constitution of separating the three powers. At
the present day the French publicist has fewer followers
than once. The constitution of England and her dependencies has been evolved on lines not in accord with
what he approved ; and it is by no means certain that
the Fathers, in our case, did well by keeping the executive and the legislative so rigidly apart.[1] Hutchinson
was not embarrassed by any consciousness of incon-
gruity; and Otis, in his criticism, was in harmony with
an illustrious company, the men of 1787. In the winter session of 1762, a bill was introduced to exclude
the judges of the Superior Court from holding seats in
the Council or Assembly, which was lost by only seven
votes. Here, again, Otis and Hutchinson faced one the
other, the disciple of Montesquieu in this case losing.

As yet no definite line was drawn between patriots
and prerogative men. Hutchinson had not broken with
Otis, who now and always scouted the idea of independence for the Colonies as disloyal folly. Otis's most
cherished idea, that the Colonies should have representatives in Parliament, an idea which, as we have seen,
Franklin urged in 1754, and which leading statesmen
in England, Grenville for instance, were not unwilling
to grant, seems never to have been, in Hutchinson's
view, a feasible scheme. He mentions it, but without
commendation ; and soon after, with the rise of Samuel
Adams into influence, it ceased to be regarded as a
practicable thing : the distance from England was felt
to be too vast. Oppressive duties were dreaded by all.

---

[1] The valiant championship of "G. B.," in the New York *Nation*, is
certainly known to the intelligent reader.

Hutchinson disliked as much as Otis harsh revenue laws ; and Bernard himself we shall presently find in strong opposition to the Stamp Act. It was natural enough, then, that not long after the great case of the Writs of Assistance Bernard and the Otises stood on good terms. The accession of the new King made necessary many changes of officials, and the senior Otis was allowed to do pretty much what he pleased in appointments in the county of Barnstable, an opportunity which he seems to have used to the full. Shortly after, the younger Otis showed on his side equal favor to Bernard by advocating the grant to him by the Assembly of the valuable island of Mt. Desert.

Soon, however, the officials and the Otises were again at odds. The Governor and Council took it upon themselves to appropriate a small sum of £300 or £400 in bounties for sailors, to be employed in defending fishermen against the French. The Assembly, in September, hereupon maintained the ancient English doctrine, that all money bills must originate in the lower House, a doctrine upon which much dust had accumulated. Otis called the plan of the Governor and Council an annihilation of one branch of the legislature ; and in newspaper articles with which he was more or less directly concerned attacked the Council, and especially Hutchinson, its leader and president. The financial controversy in which Hutchinson, with his usual wisdom, had withstood what was sure to lead to depreciation of the currency, led to unpopularity; and Hutchinson wrote in March to Bollan, the able agent who had secured, twelve years before, the Louisburg reimbursement which Hutchinson had put to such good use : " This trial (the Writs of Assistance) and my pernicious principles about the currency, have taken away a great number of friends, and the House have not only reduced the allowance to the Superior Court in general, but have refused to make any allowance at all to me as Chief Justice. I shall make no complaint under this cloud, but please myself with hopes of its blowing over. At worst, I hope to keep a *conscia mens recti.*" [1] Bollan at this time was superseded as agent in spite of his great services, becoming a victim of the *odium theologicum.* He was a churchman, a creature which the Puritan stomach at this crisis could less than ever abide. The always present danger of the establishment of an episcopate in America, dread of which had much to do with the Revolution, seemed just now unusually imminent. Into Bollan's place as agent was put, therefore, Jasper Mauduit, of London, with whom was associated Richard Jackson, already agent for Connecticut ; moreover, private secretary of Grenville, Chancellor of the Exchequer, — a cherished friend to whom Hutchinson often wrote.

At the Peace of Paris, in 1763, which concluded the Seven Years' War, general content prevailed in Massachusetts Bay, and the dispositions of men were very loyal. At the first Town-Meeting in Boston after the event, Otis, as usual now, being the Moderator, spoke eloquently of the British empire and constitution : "The true interests of Great Britain and her plantations are mutual, and what God in his providence has united

[1] From the Autograph, *Mass. Archiv. Hist.*, vol. xxvi., p. 9.

let no man dare attempt to pull asunder." But the Revolution was even now in the air. No historic fact can be more clearly shown than that the contest, the threshold of which we have now reached, was really not one between England and America, but a dispute which went on both in England and America, in each land between two parties not far from equal in strength. In America the strife was bloody and not prolonged; in England it was bloodless, but very gradual, the closing scenes of the struggle not being unfolded until our own time.[1] Soon after the coming in of the new King, John Wilkes became famous, a champion of the people against strongly intrenched privilege. Unfortunately, he was in himself but a poor creature, though endowed with considerable powers. He became, however, the instrument of Providence through whom memorable changes came to pass in the condition of the mass of Englishmen. " Wilkes and liberty ! " was heard in these days scarcely less often in the streets of Boston than in those of London. Suddenly the names of Whig and Tory became designations of parties in America as yet only vaguely defined. On both sides of the sea the same line was being drawn ; on both sides, too, the classes ranging up, the one against the other, were the same ; in the one host the supporters of the Crown and those high in place, in the other the plain people whose voice had as yet had little weight. A powerful impulse was given to the dissatisfaction, when it became known that America was to be taxed

---

[1] Mellen Chamberlain in Winsor : *Narrative and Critical Hist. of America,* vol. vi., ch. i.

as never before. The vast glory accruing to England from the successful Seven Years' War was accompanied by expenses and responsibilities correspondingly vast, and the whole empire, America included, was to feel a burden quite new. A forerunner of what was to come was an order to the Governor to number the people. This the Assembly set itself against, partly through a superstitious fear that the Province might suffer like Israel in the day of David; partly through a well-grounded suspicion that it was preliminary to something unpleasant. What was in store soon came into view. The practical free trade which had been so long enjoyed, already interfered with, was to come to an end. The Sugar duties, in particular, for long so nearly a dead-letter, after undergoing some reduction were to be strictly enforced. The positions of the revenue officers were no longer to be sinecures. More energetic prosecution of smugglers was expected from them, and every available ship of the British fleet was to be held ready to support. The best trade of the Colonies was thus about to come to an end, unless steps were taken to save it. Jasper Mauduit, appointed agent in place of Bollan shortly before, had proved quite inadequate to his duties. A strong representation of the feelings of Massachusetts, it was felt, must be made at head-quarters, and all eyes turned on Hutchinson as the man to send. It is curious to see how, when crises arise, the carping as to his absorption of offices becomes suddenly quiet, his fellows being only too glad to put his capable hands to still new uses. In consistency with the views he has expressed in his History, Hutchinson was in full sympathy with the spirit of resistance. He believed that the vigorous trade with the West Indies was beneficial to England as well as to the Colonies, and should be encouraged. When both Houses voted strongly in his favor, he was ready to go. Bernard, however, threw difficulties in the way : he was Lieutenant-Governor, and ought not to leave the Province without permission from England. While Hutchinson was hesitating, Oxenbridge Thacher, now influential in the Assembly, took ground against the appointment of Hutchinson. He was a willing agent of the Crown. Ought he, then, to become also the agent of the people, whose grievance was with the Crown and its ministers ? He was well known to be a "prerogative man," ready to defer to the home government in important things ; or at least preferring to meet encroachments with remonstrances quite too quiet for the denunciatory mood into which the people were rising. Through Thacher the idea of Hutchinson as agent lost favor in the Assembly, and before the matter was settled, early in 1764, word came that the duties were imposed. It was too late to send an agent ; with a wrathful emphasis which was something new, the cry of Otis, " No taxation without representation," became very frequent on the lips of men.

The case was indeed a hard one. The colonists could lawfully export the chief products of their industry to no country but Great Britain, not including Ireland; nor could any foreign ship enter any colonial harbor. No ship, carriage, or pack-horse could carry wool, or anything made from it, from one Province to another. The

trade of the hatter, the iron industry, were blotted
out. There were some exceptions. Salt might be imported from any place. Wines, too, could be brought
from Madeira and the Azores; not, however, without
paying a duty in American ports to the British exchequer. Food, horses, and indentured servants might
be brought from Ireland.[1] There were some make-
weights. The whaling industry of the Colonies, for
instance, was left unrestricted, while such duties were
placed upon whaling in the British isles that it was
quite swept away. For some important articles the
people of Great Britain were restricted to American
sources of supply. The bonds, however, could scarcely
be breathed under. In most cases, Great Britain was
not only the sole market for the products of America,
but the only storehouse whence her supplies could be
drawn. Worst of all, the Sugar Act, passed in the interest of the British West Indies, drove at the vitals of
colonial prosperity. The active, buoyant-spirited community felt choked. Hutchinson was heartily with his
countrymen in feeling the policy to be unjust and foolish; and would gladly and effectively, no doubt, have
used his fine powers of presentment, at Court, in favor
of a freer course, had the opportunity been granted.

In the fall of 1764, Hutchinson, as chairman of a
joint committee of the Council and House, drafted an
address, which did not demand as a *right* that the
Province should be left free to tax itself, but asked it
as an *indulgence*. He in no way denies the right of
Parliament to tax, but sets forth the impolicy of the

[1] Bancroft: *Hist. of the U. S.*, vol. iii., p. 463, etc.

present measures. He prays that the Colonies may be
relieved from the burden of the Sugar Act ; that as to
internal taxes the Province may be allowed as heretofore to impose them by its own legislature ; or at least
that the imposition of the taxes may be delayed until
the Colonies in general may make a full representation
of their views. This address was unanimously agreed
to.[1] The position here taken by Hutchinson he ad-
hered to to the end. While the Colonies remained part
of the British empire, he believed a supremacy in Parliament must be recognized. Once recognized, however, he believed it should be kept in the background
as much as possible, the Colonies being allowed to manage themselves. As to parliamentary supremacy, Otis
in these days is much more emphatic than Hutchinson :
" The power of Parliament is uncontrollable but by
themselves, and we must obey. There would be an
end of all governments, if one or a number of subordinate provinces should take upon themselves so far to
judge of the justice of an act of Parliament as to refuse obedience to it. . . . Forcibly resisting the Parliament and the King's laws is high treason. Therefore
let the Parliament lay what burthens they please upon
us ; we must, it is our duty to, submit, and patiently to
bear them till they will be pleased to relieve us." [2] Otis
conceded to Parliament supremacy, but insisted that the
Colonies should have representatives there. Hutchinson, while nowhere expressing interest in this idea of
representation, probably feeling it impracticable, never-

[1] Gordon : *Hist. Am. War,* vol. i., p. 154.
[2] *Rights of the British Colonies.*

theless concedes supremacy, — that thought, however, to be kept well in the background while the Colonies manage for themselves.

Great Britain has really always held to this position, even to the present day. " Although the general rule is that the legislative assembly has the sole right of imposing taxes in the Colony, yet when the imperial legislature chooses to impose taxes, according to the rule of law they have a right to do it." So decided the English judge, Blackburn, in 1868, in a case in which Jamaica was involved.[1] Lecky, too, goes as far, claiming that Mansfield's position, that the Colonies were *virtually* represented in Parliament, thereby shutting off any infringement of Magna Charta, was an entirely reasonable one. Parliamentary supremacy in the British empire is, indeed, kept well in the background at the present moment. Let any great emergency arise, however, such as some peril to the parent state, if the Colony should remain apathetic, or give in any way aid and comfort to the enemy, the dependency would be as arbitrarily ridden over by the fleets and armies of the mother land as in the days of George III. So long as America remained dependent, parliamentary supremacy was necessary. It could only be got rid of by such a declaration as that of 1776: for such a declaration Hutchinson was not ready; nor was any other man in the Colonies, with one exception, ready until many years after this time.

When Bernard transmitted the petition drafted by

---

[1] Yonge : *Const. Hist. of Eng.*, p. 66. See, also, Todd : *Parl. Government in the Brit. Colonies*, 1894, for fuller discussions of this point.

Hutchinson, he wrote himself, November 18: " Massachusetts is the only one of the old Colonies that I know of, that enjoys a specie currency. This reflects great honor on the Province itself, as it is a great instance of their prudence who took hold of a singular opportunity to destroy their paper money, which other Colonies who had it equally in their power neglected. But I fear that if the great sums which are expected to be raised in America are to be transported to Great Britain, there will soon be an end of the specie currency of Massachusetts, which will be followed by a total discouragement for other Provinces to attempt the same in future; in which case perpetual paper money, the very negative power of riches, will be the portion of America." The Governor went on to show at length the impolicy of the proposed levies, arguing that England would be benefited if colonial trade could be left unrestricted.[1]

It is not becoming in our generation to accuse the English statesmen of 1764 of criminal folly. Patriotism then indeed was but a narrow sentiment. If England flourished, other countries might suffer; it was quite legitimate to build up prosperity for one's own land upon the ruined welfare of lands elsewhere. Though the Colonies were in a certain way a part of the empire, in a certain way also they were outside, — members not fully compacted and united with the main trunk, — members at whose expense the home trade might be aggrandized, the dependencies meanwhile suffering loss and embarrassment. Does the patriotism

[1] Gordon : vol. i., p. 155.

which forces home energy into unnatural channels,
destroying at the same time the industries of foreign
and dependent peoples, quite careless whether or not
benefit shall come to any country but one's own, have
in it a larger element of selfishness, or of some more
amiable principle? Such patriotism abounded then,
and is not yet out of vogue. The British statesmen of
1764 acted according to their lights. The administration of the great empire that had just fallen to them
was a hard task, with which they coped in a way not
wise, but in a way very natural. They fettered America, but they meant at the same time to grant America
great compensations. They erred, and the consequence
of their error was the dismemberment of the Anglo-
Saxon race. But as Freeman has said, it was quite
impossible for George III. and his ministers to act
otherwise; as on the other hand it was quite impossible
for America to act otherwise.

Though much had been done to make the Colonies
justly incensed, no schism probably would have come to
pass but for that Act, certainly one of the most momentous in the legislative history of the world, the Stamp
Act. The latest British historian of the eighteenth
century,[1] while not denying that the Stamp Act was a
grievance, declares that there have been gross exagger-
ations. There is not a fragment of evidence that any
English statesman, or any class of the people, desired to
raise by direct taxation anything for purposes purely
English. The colonists were not asked to contribute
for the navy that protected the coast, nor for the Eng-

[1] Lecky : vol. iii., p. 341, etc.

lish debt. The colonists had gained by the successful
war incomparably more than any other British subjects.
Until the destruction of the French power, a hand
armed with a rifle or a tomahawk seemed hard by the
threshold of every New England home. The threatening hand was paralyzed; at the same time, since the
fringe of plantations on the coast became now immeas-
urably extended westward by the addition of forest
territories, their title to which there was no one longer
to dispute, their wealth and dignity were greatly increased. They were only asked to bear their share in
the burden of the empire, by contributing to the sum
required for maintaining ten thousand men, intended
primarily for their own defense against Indians and
French. If only the Assemblies could have been induced of themselves to make the necessary grant!
The attempt was not tried; perhaps if it had been tried
it would have failed. But here came in the grievance:
the tax was demanded by a body in which there was no
representation of the people taxed, and "that taxation
and representation are inseparably connected, lay at the
root of the English conception of political liberty." [1]
The right of Parliament to regulate commerce by im-
posts had not been questioned, though the wisdom of
the measures resorted to was severely criticised, and the
Colonies were growing restive. Now, however, besides
these external taxes, an internal tax was to be levied, a
tax for revenue, of a kind heretofore only imposed by
the lower Houses. Of course it brought an outburst.
The well-meaning Grenville intended to proceed in

[1] Lecky : vol. iii., p. 353.

the kindest way. He explained to the agents of the
different Colonies the difficulties of his situation. Before the war, the American civil and military establishments had cost only £70,000 a year. In 1764, they
cost £350,000 : this additional expense was incurred
on American account, and he thought America should
contribute toward it. He claimed that the Stamp tax
was the easiest to manage ; also the most equitable that
could be devised, since it would spare the poor and fall
upon property. " I am not, however, set upon this
tax," he said. " If the Americans dislike it, and prefer
any other method, I shall be content. Write therefore
to your several Colonies, and if they choose any other
mode, I shall be satisfied, provided the money be but
raised." [1]   A timely concession of a few seats in the
upper and lower Houses of Parliament would have set
at rest the whole dispute. Franklin had suggested it
ten years before, anticipating even Otis ; Grenville was
quite ready to favor it ; Adam Smith advocated it.
Why did the scheme fail? In these days a man was
rising into provincial note, who was soon to show a
heat truly fanatical in favor of an idea quite inconsistent with this, — Samuel Adams. He from the first
seems to have felt that representation of the Colonies in
Parliament was quite impracticable, or if gained, would
result in no benefit to the Colonies ; their influence
in deliberation would always be too feeble to avail.
There was no fit state for them but independence. His
voice at first was but as a solitary cry in the midst of a
tempest, but it prevailed mightily in the end.

[1] Lecky : vol. iii., p. 347.

Nothing was said or done after the announcement of the impending Stamp tax to make Grenville think better of his plan. England was apathetic ; some of the colonial agents favored it ; even Franklin, then agent for Pennsylvania, quietly accepted it, thinking, probably, that representation might wait for a more convenient time; and in his canny way he took steps to have a friend appointed stamp-distributor in his Province. In America, to be sure, there was tumult. From the "flame of fire" that John Adams describes so well as burning to such effect in the case of the Writs of Assistance, Boston, of necessity, went up in conflagration. One royal Governor, too, no other than Bernard, was strongly opposed to it, winning warm praise from Lord Camden, the most liberal of the English peers. Hutchinson, also, though less hot than Otis, stood on the same ground with him, declaring with decision, of this and other taxes : " It cannot be good policy to tax the Americans : it will prove prejudicial to their natural interests. You will lose more than you will gain. Britain reaps the profit of all their trade and of the increase of their substance."[1]   But the Colonies were far away, and of little account. After mature consideration and consultation with representatives of all opinions, Grenville introduced his measure, honestly supposing it thoroughly reasonable. It passed late at night, in a thin House, which paid grudging attention to the protests of Barré. In April, 1765, it was known in Boston that it had become law, and the doughty little town received the news with an outburst.

[1] Gordon : *Hist. of Am. Rev.*

A man forty-two years old, but already gray, and with a physical infirmity which kept his head and his hands shaking like those of a paralytic, had just come upon the stage. He was a man of broken fortunes, — a ne'er-do-weel in his private business, a failure as tax-collector, the only public office he had thus far under-taken to discharge. He had long, however, been an effective political writer in the newspapers, and pos-sessed marked power in the management of the Town-Meeting, in which the life of the community centred. In May, 1764, as one of the committee appointed to "instruct" the representatives chosen for that year, he had produced a document no more appreciated at the time than was the character of the Stamp Act in Eng-land that same year, but destined to make an epoch. Samuel Adams submitted his instructions, in behalf of himself and his colleagues, May 24. They contained the first public denial of the right of the British Par-liament to put in operation Grenville's scheme of the Stamp Act, just announced; and the first suggestion of a union of the Colonies for a redress of grievances. The important but questionable position was also stated that the judges should be dependent for their salaries on the Assembly ; moreover, that if burdens were not removed, agreements would be entered into to import no goods from Britain, this by way of retaliation upon British manufacturers. We shall see how momentous these suggestions became. The man that made them was fast rising into great influence, though his ways were quiet, and the fact of his leadership was thus far little recognized. Before 1765 expired, the death of

Oxenbridge Thacher was to open the path for him to a seat in the Assembly. Already he was superseding the influence of Otis, though in stealthy ways, of which neither Otis nor those who made an idol of him were sensible, putting into the minds of men, in the place of the ideas for which Otis stood, radical conceptions which were to change in due time the whole future of the world.

The " Virginia Resolutions," through which Patrick Henry first acquired a continental fame, voted by the House of Burgesses in May, a month after the coming of the news that the Stamp Act had passed, denied very definitely the authority of Parliament to tax America. At first men recoiled from them. Otis was reported to have condemned them publicly in King Street, a rumor no doubt well founded ; for as we have seen, he fully admitted the supremacy of Parliament. The temper of the time, however, soon changed, and Patrick Henry's words were adopted as expressing the true sentiments of America. A congress was appointed to take place in New York the first Tuesday in October, to consider the situation, delegates to which were Timothy Ruggles, an able and influential veteran of the French wars, who in the times now beginning, through loyalty to the Crown, was about to sink out of sight a brilliant fame won through bravery and much honorable service ; Oliver Partridge, a man of mark in the western counties ; and, of course, James Otis. Now, too, the threatened non-importation arguments began to play their part. The use of mourning was given up. No lamb was to be eaten, the abstinence being designed to favor the production of wool. Whatever was likely to balk the English merchants, in whose interest it was believed the restrictions upon colonial trade and manufacture were powerfully operating, — all such measures were eagerly canvassed and prepared for adoption.

The position of Hutchinson was a most trying one. He favored neither Stamp Act nor Sugar Act. The whole course of government he disapproved; he had been ready to cross the ocean to remonstrate for the Colony against the impolitic treatment. On the other hand, the disloyal tone which daily grew more rife about him was utterly against his mind. He saw no outcome for it but independence, a most wise forecasting of the situation; in fact, there was no middle ground. Independence seemed to him and to every man then, except Sam Adams, a calamity. If that was to be avoided, there was nothing for it but to admit the supremacy of Parliament. Otis and Franklin, with their scheme for parliamentary representation of the Colonies, were proposing something quite impracticable. So Hutchinson felt; so Franklin was already coming to feel; into the same belief Sam Adams was about to swing New England in general. If only the home government would be forbearing and keep parliamentary supremacy well in the background! If only the Colonies would be patient and think they were virtually represented, even though the Town-Meetings sent no direct delegates to St. Stephens! So in these times Hutchinson sighed and prayed. But the Province to which he had been like a father was growing away from him, and before the summer ended, he was to receive a blow as ruthless and ungrateful as it was possible to administer.[1]

Before the disgraceful incident to which reference is made engages us, it is proper to mention a certain activity which the Chief Justice, busy though he was in so many places in behalf of the public, had found time to carry forward. In 1764 was published, in Boston, the first volume of his "History of Massachusetts Bay," a carefully studied work quite unparalleled in the meagre colonial literature, — a work which still is, and will always remain, of the first authority respecting the beginnings of New England. In the following year this first volume was republished in England. In 1767 came volume ii., which, like its fellow, at once appeared in an English reprint. Writing, January 18, 1765, to an English friend who had criticised his abundant use of footnotes, he says : " I am ashamed to give you the reason of this fault, but really it was to save me trouble, finding it easier to insert things which occurred to me after I had passed the time they related to in this way, than by altering the page. . . . Indeed, I wonder more fault is not found with the whole performance. I think from my beginning the work until I had completed it, which was about twelve months, I never had time to write two sheets at a sitting without avocations by public business, but was forced to steal a

---

[1] " I ever thought the taxing of America by Parliament not advisable, but as a servant of the Crown I thought myself bound to discountenance the violent opposition made to the Stamp Act, as it led to the denial of Parliament's authority in all cases whatsoever." Hutchinson wrote this in England, May 4, 1776. *Diary and Letters*, vol. ii., p. 58.

little time in the morning and evening while I was in town, and then leave it for weeks together, so that I found it difficult to keep any plan in my mind. I have an aversion to transcribing, and except the three or four first sheets, and now and then a page in which I had made some mistake, the rest of the work is rough, as I first wrote it. . . . I have no talent at painting or describing characters. I am sensible it requires great delicacy. My safest way was to avoid them and let facts speak for themselves." [1]

This letter gives us about the only information extant as to the composition of this important literary monument. Part of the manuscript is preserved in the Massachusetts Archives. The fair page is perfectly legible, written usually with few erasures or interlineations. The pen moved smoothly and rapidly, it is plain, following the promptings of a clear and alert intellect. He estimates correctly his limitation. He has " no talent at painting or describing characters," and in his earlier volumes seldom attempts it. Such interest as attaches to the work of Clarendon, that noble portrait-gallery within which hang the great men of the Cromwellian time, the Cavaliers in their lace and love-locks, with faces now frivolous or sensual, now aglow with self-sacrificing loyalty, — the Puritans in their buff and steel, now harsh and canting, now full of astuteness or virile power, — no interest of this kind attaches to the

---

[1] From the autograph, *M. A. Hist.*, vol. xxvi., p. 126. Mr. Charles Deane, in a *Hutchinson Bibliography*, privately printed (H. O. Houghton & Co., 1857), gives a careful account of the different editions and the various fortunes of this book.

work of Hutchinson. In his third volume, written twenty years later, not published till 1828,[1] more than forty years after his death, he does indeed paint the portraits of his contemporaries, the men who bore him down after the fiercest possible struggle. The heat of the fight is still in the heart beating behind the limning pen. Otis, Sam Adams, Hancock, Bowdoin, are unattractive figures in his picture ; still the trait-drawing is by no means without candor, and one wonders that the picture is no darker. In the main, he is fair-minded, and in the circumstances surprisingly calm. Nor is there in the volumes any trace of picturesque narrative, — graphic putting before one of critical events of the past, — that gift so marked in his famous townsmen of the succeeding century, Prescott, Motley, and Parkman. We must go still farther in the list of limitations : his work is in no sense philosophical. Moreover, though humor is a quality not essential in a historian, yet Hutchinson's want of humor is really remarkable. The " History of Massachusetts Bay " is unmistakably a sad-colored performance, unrelieved by any purple patch of brilliant description, by any sparkle of wit, or any deft portrayals of men. Grave defects these. Yet the writer has studied his authorities thoroughly, after gathering them industriously. His presentment is always clear and dignified; his judgments of men and events are usually just. It is the work of a thoughtful brain, whose comments on politics, finance, religion, the superstitions and aberrations of unenlightened

---

[1] Hon. James Savage brought about the publication, after urging it through more than ten years upon the Governor's descendants.

men, are full of intelligence and also full of humanity. Thomas Hutchinson's best titles to fame are certainly not gained from his writings. He achieved enough here, however, to merit gratitude.[1]

A letter of this same year illustrates his kindly nature. June 15, 1765, to Robert Wilson: "I am the patron of those people who cannot help themselves, and this obliges me to ask another favor of you for a poor widow, who supposes her husband had money due to him in England. She says the £60 mentioned in the inclosed letter was never received by her husband, whose name was William Bewley, and she supposes wages or prize-money was due to him on board the man-of-war. Perhaps by writing to John Mooney, at Portsmouth, and inquiring at the office, you may find something which can be received for the woman, who will then send proper powers."

Here, too, in a letter to Colonel Israel Williams, of Hatfield, is a dignified and candid utterance, April 26, 1765: "As for those men you talk of and wish for, they are only to be found in Plato's Commonwealth. We that fancy we are most like them, although we durst not pursue any measure which appears to us to

---

[1] "The researches of Governor Hutchinson into the early annals of Massachusetts are of the highest historical value. He had opportunities of access to original papers such as no person now possesses. He had the tastes, the capacity for close application and research, the judicial understanding, and the freedom from prejudice and partisanship which characterize the genuine historian. His style, if not always elegant, is clear and simple, and singularly free from that sensational and rhetorical method of statement which is the bane of much of the historical writing of the present day." W. F. Poole, Introduction to Hutchinson's *Witchcraft Delusions of 1692*, privately printed, 1870.

be against the publick good, yet we see things many times through a false medium, and are balanced, though insensibly, by one prejudice and another. Perhaps the case is the same with some who are opposite to us in public affairs, who vote quite different from us, and are under insensible bias the other way. This consideration should tend to keep us from discontent and disturbance in our minds when measures are pursued contrary to what appears to us to be right. Possibly we may be mistaken." [1]

After the adoption in Massachusetts of Patrick Henry's resolves, the people brooding over the injury they had received in the Stamp Act became fiercer in temper. The rough population which abounded about the wharves and shipyards grew riotous, and, with the usual want of discrimination shown by mobs, were not slow to lift their hands against even their best friends. Andrew Oliver, brother-in-law of Hutchinson and Secretary of the Province, had without his solicitation been appointed Stamp-Collector, though he did not approve the Act. He was hung in effigy, a drunken crowd carrying the effigy through the Town-House, even while the Governor and Council were in session in the chamber above. Oliver's house was attacked, until at last he made public recantation. The houses of the Customs and Admiralty officials were also attacked, the disturbances culminating in an extraordinary outrage. As to Andrew Oliver, John Adams exclaims: " Has not the

[1] These valuable papers, now in possession of the Massachusetts Historical Society, I was allowed to examine and quote, by Dr. Samuel A. Green.

blind undistinguishing rage of the rabble done that gentleman irreparable injustice ? " [1]

Why Hutchinson should have fallen into great disfavor, it is not easy to say. Gordon, a writer of Whig leanings, but a fair-minded witness of all that occurred, suggests that there were some who still entertained rancor toward him for doing away with paper money in 1748: [2] moreover, " that the mob was led on to the house by a secret influence, with a view to the destruction of certain papers known to be there, and which, it is thought, would have proved that the grant to the New Plymouth Company on Kennebec River was different from what was contended for by some claimants." [3] Hutchinson himself speaks, as having given rise to animosity against him, of certain depositions in the interest of government taken before him in his character of Chief Justice, to which his name was signed. They were purely official acts : for the depositions he had no responsibility whatever ; but the unreasoning mass confused him with others. There was nothing in his course at the time of the Writs of Assistance at which the people needed to feel aggrieved. He was with the people in opposing the external taxes; also in disapproving the Stamp Act. Now that they were imposed, he to be sure thought nothing would answer but submission ; but certainly in his declarations here he was nothing like so emphatic as James

---

[1] John Adams's Diary, Aug. 15, 1765.

[2] His position, in 1762, on the currency, was, as we have seen, not popular.

[3] *Hist. of Am. War*, vol. i., p. 180.

Otis, who still remained the popular idol. Otis had said in May : " It is the duty of all humbly and silently to acquiesce in all the decisions of the supreme legislature. Nine hundred and ninety-nine in a thousand will never entertain the thought but of submission to our Sovereign and to the authority of Parliament in all possible contingencies."

In private talk he was more vigorous than in his formal utterances. " Hallowell tells stories about Otis. . . . Otis told him, he says, that the Parliament had a right to tax the Colonies, and he was a d—d fool who denied it ; and that this people never would be quiet till we had a Council from home, till our charter was taken away, and till we had regular troops quartered upon us." [1] Hutchinson had never expressed his thoughts so definitely as that.

He was, however, made a mark for the most unmeasured outrage. Here is the story in the words of the victim taken from the autograph.

TO RICHARD JACKSON.

" BOSTON, Aug. 30, 1765.

"My dear Sir, — I came from my house at Milton, the 26 in the morning. After dinner it was whispered in town there would be a mob at night, and that Paxton, Hallowell, the custom-house, and admiralty officers' houses would be attacked ; but my friends assured me that the rabble were satisfied with the insult I had received and that I was become rather popular. In the evening, whilst I was at supper and my children

[1] John Adams's Diary, Jan. 16, 1766.

round me, somebody ran in and said the mob were coming. I directed my children to fly to a secure place, and shut up my house as I had done before, intending not to quit it; but my eldest daughter repented her leaving me, hastened back, and protested she would not quit the house unless I did. I could n't stand against this, and withdrew with her to a neighboring house, where I had been but a few minutes before the hellish crew fell upon my house with the rage of devils, and in a moment with axes split down the doors and entered. My son being in the great entry heard them cry: 'Damn him, he is upstairs, we 'll have him.' Some ran immediately as high as the top of the house, others filled the rooms below and cellars, and others remained without the house to be employed there. Messages soon came one after another to the house where I was, to inform me the mob were coming in pursuit of me, and I was obliged to retire through yards and gardens to a house more remote, where I remained until 4 o'clock, by which time one of the best finished houses in the Province had nothing remaining but the bare walls and floors. Not contented with tearing off all the wainscot and hangings, and splitting the doors to pieces, they beat down the partition walls; and although that alone cost them near two hours, they cut down the cupola or lanthorn, and they began to take the slate and boards from the roof, and were prevented only by the approaching daylight from a total demolition of the building. The garden-house was laid flat, and all my trees, etc., broke down to the ground.

"Such ruin was never seen in America. Besides my

plate and family pictures, household furniture of every kind, my own, my children's, and servants' apparel, they carried off about £900 sterling in money, and emptied the house of everything whatsoever, except a part of the kitchen furniture, not leaving a single book or paper in it, and have scattered or destroyed all the manuscripts and other papers I had been collecting for thirty years together, besides a great number of public papers in my custody. The evening being warm, I had undressed me and put on a thin camlet surtout over my waistcoat. The next morning, the weather being changed, I had not clothes enough in my possession to defend me from the cold, and was obliged to borrow from my friends. Many articles of clothing and a good part of my plate have since been picked up in different quarters of the town, but the furniture in general was cut to pieces before it was thrown out of the house, and most of the beds cut open, and the feathers thrown out of the windows. The next evening, I intended with my children to Milton, but meeting two or three small parties of the ruffians, who I suppose had concealed themselves in the country, and my coachman hearing one of them say, 'There he is!' my daughters were terrified and said they should never be safe, and I was forced to shelter them that night at the Castle.

"The encouragers of the first mob never intended matters should go this length, and the people in general expressed the utmost detestation of this unparalleled outrage, and I wish they could be convinced what infinite hazard there is of the most terrible consequences from such demons, when they are let loose in a government where there is not constant authority at hand sufficient to suppress them. I am told the government here will make me a compensation for my own and my family's loss, which I think cannot be much less than £3,000 sterling. I am not sure that they will. If they should not, it will be too heavy for me, and I must humbly apply to his majesty in whose service I am a sufferer ; but this, and a much greater sum would be an insufficient compensation for the constant distress and anxiety of mind I have felt for some time past, and must feel for months to come. You cannot conceive the wretched state we are in. Such is the resentment of the people against the Stamp-Duty, that there can be no dependence upon the General Court to take any steps to enforce, or rather advise, to the payment of it. On the other hand, such will be the effects of not submitting to it, that all trade must cease, all courts fall, and all authority be at an end. Must not the ministry be excessively embarrassed ? On the one hand, it will be said, if concessions are made, the Parliament endanger the loss of their authority over the Colony : on the other hand, if external force should be used, there seems to be danger of a total lasting alienation of affection. Is there no alternative ? May the infinitely wise God direct you." [1]

Here is another graphic contemporary picture from an authority who soon after becomes an interesting figure. Josiah Quincy, then twenty-one years old,

[1] *M. A. Hist.*, vol. xxvi., p. 146, etc. The picture of Hutchinson's house is from a cut in the *American Magazine*, February, 1836. His minute inventory of the property destroyed is given in Appendix A.

THE HUTCHINSON HOUSE GARDEN, COURT STREET, BOSTON
DESTROYED BY THE MOB IN 1765

writing in his diary, August 27, 1765, says that Hutchinson's life, " it is more than probable, was saved by his giving way to his eldest daughter and leaving the house." Quincy describes the coming into Court next day of the stripped Chief Justice, " his look big with the greatest anxiety, clothed in a manner which would have excited compassion from the hardest heart, though his dress had not been strikingly contrasted by the other judges and bar, who appeared in their robes. Such a man, in such a station, thus habited, with tears starting from his eyes, and a countenance which strongly told the inward anguish of his soul, — what must an audience have felt, whose compassion had before been moved by what they knew he had suffered, when they heard him pronounce the following words, in a manner which the agitation of his mind dictated : —

" ' GENTLEMEN, — There not being a quorum of the Court without me, I am obliged to appear. Some apology is necessary for my dress; indeed, I had no other. Destitute of everything, — no other shirt ; no other garment but what I have on ; and not one in my whole family in a better situation than myself. The distress of a whole family around me, young and tender infants hanging about me, are infinitely more insupportable than what I feel for myself, though I am obliged to borrow part of *this* clothing.

" ' Sensible that I am innocent, that all the charges against me are false, I can't help feeling : and although I am not obliged to give an answer to all the questions that may be put me by every lawless person, yet I call God to witness, — and I would not, for a thousand worlds, call my Maker to witness to falsehood, — I say

I call my Maker to witness, that I never, in New England or Old, in Great Britain or America, neither directly nor indirectly, was aiding, assisting, or supporting — in the least promoting or encouraging — what is commonly called the Stamp Act; but, on the contrary, did all in my power, and strove as much as in me lay, to prevent it. This is not declared through timidity; for I have nothing to fear. They can only take away my life, which is of but little value when deprived of all its comforts, all that was dear to me, and nothing surrounding me but the most piercing distress.

" 'I hope the eyes of the people will be opened, that they will see how easy it is for some designing, wicked man to spread false reports, to raise suspicions and jealousies in the minds of the populace, and enrage them against the innocent; but if guilty, this is not the way to proceed. The laws of our country are open to punish those who have offended. This destroying all peace and order of the community, — all will feel its effects; and I hope all will see how easily the people may be deluded, inflamed and carried away with madness against an innocent man.

" 'I pray God give us better hearts!' "

The Court then adjourned to October 15. Quincy goes on in a boyish declamation which hints vaguely at the supposed reasons for Hutchinson's sudden unpopularity, his outburst reflecting vividly the hot passion rife in the town that August day.

" Learn wisdom from the present times! O ye sons of Ambition, beware lest a thirst for power tempt you to enslave your country! O ye sons of Avarice, beware lest the thirst for gold excite you to enslave your native country ! O ye sons of Popularity, beware lest a thirst for applause move you groundlessly to inflame the minds of the people ! For the end of slavery is misery to the world, your country, fellow-citizens, and children ; the end of popular rage, destruction, desolation, and ruin.

" Who that sees the fury and instability of the populace but would seek protection under the arm of power ? Who that beholds the tyranny and oppression of arbitrary power but would lose his life in defense of his liberty ? Who that marks the riotous tumult, confusion, and uproar of a democratic, the slavery and distress of a despotic, state — the infinite miseries attendant on both — but would fly for refuge from the mad rage of the one, and oppressive power of the other, to that best asylum, that glorious medium, the British Constitution ? Happy people who enjoy this blessed constitution ! Happy, thrice happy people, if ye preserve it inviolate ! May ye never lose it through a licentious abuse of your invaluable rights and blood-purchased liberties ! May ye never forfeit it by a tame and infamous submission to the yoke of slavery and lawless despotism !

> " Remember, O my friends ! the laws, the rights,
> The generous plan of power delivered down,
> From age to age, by your renowned forefathers,
> So dearly bought, the price of so much blood !
> Oh, let it never perish in your hands,
> But piously transmit it to your children.
> Do thou, great liberty, inspire our souls,
> And make our lives in thy possession happy,
> Or our death glorious in thy just defence." [1]

Mass. Hist. Soc. Proceed., vol. iv., April, 1858.

CHAPTER V.

THE REPEAL OF THE STAMP ACT.

Boston and the Province were generally ashamed of the outrage upon Hutchinson, but the mob still dared to show its hand. Though in the first rush of feeling many of the rioters were sent to jail, they were afterwards set free; absconding for a time, they soon returned, ready for further mischief. The chief actor seems to have been a shoemaker named Mackintosh, who, though arrested, was presently discharged; Hutchinson declares this was through the interference of men of good position, who feared that a confession from him would implicate them. Hutchinson, who at first felt safe with his family nowhere else than at the Castle, in the harbor, received much sympathy. Dr. Jonathan Mayhew, a sermon by whom it was supposed had acted as an incitement to the disorder, wrote to him: " God is my witness, that from the bottom of my heart I detest these proceedings; and that I am sincerely grieved for them, and have a deep sympathy with you and your distressed family on this occasion. I indeed . . . spoke of the Stamp Act as a great grievance, likely to prove detrimental in a high degree, both to the Colonies and the mother country, and I have heard your Honor speak to the same purpose." [1]

[1] Gordon : vol. i., p. 178.

The Assembly condemned the transaction, declaring the violence to be not the act of the people, but of a knot of abandoned men. When Hutchinson claimed compensation, many of the towns appeared well disposed to grant it. The disposition was, however, frustrated for the time. The most curious memorial now extant of this old-time outrage is the manuscript of a portion of Hutchinson's History, which, after lying all night in the mud of the street into which it had been flung, was rescued in the morning and handed over to Dr. Andrew Eliot. He restored it to its owner, and it still remains among his papers in the Boston State House, its leaves yet limp and stained from their soaking, one hundred and thirty years ago.

In the difficult situation Bernard behaved in a manly way. Declaring that a law might be inexpedient, and yet it could not be denied that Parliament had authority to make the law, he did what he thought was right, announcing at much risk that he would stand in the place of Oliver as stamp-distributor. He had done what he could to prevent the Act, but now that it was passed in spite of him, as a resolute magistrate he would execute it to the letter.

The legislature met in September, but was summarily prorogued by Bernard, when he found an obstinate resistance to his idea of parliamentary supremacy. Mark, however, that at this abortive session Samuel Adams took his place, being sworn in just in time, and then and there beginning one of the most influential of political careers, which was destined to continue almost to the end of the century. In October the legislature met once more, promulgating in two documents a response to Bernard and a series of resolves soon very famous as the " Massachusetts Resolves," sentiments quite in advance of what had been hitherto formally uttered. The powers of Parliament were definitely limited, and a plain refusal given to assist in the execution of the Stamp Act. This bracing up in tone was due to the influence mainly of the new member, who, as Clerk of the House, prepared these documents, — a function which he was to fulfill through many an important year to come. Otis was absent at the Stamp Act Congress in New York, and no other man could put plausibly to the Assembly the idea of submission. From this moment, too, the idea of colonial representation in Parliament ceases to be heard of, men generally acquiescing in Samuel Adams's view that it was quite impracticable. " We think," wrote he, " the Colonies cannot be fully and equally represented, and if not equally, then in effect not at all. A representative should be, and continue to be, well acquainted with the internal circumstances of the people whom he represents." [1]   Three thousand miles of ocean prevent this.

As vagueness now disappears, Whig or Son of Liberty, and Tory or Prerogative man, standing up against one another in clear and definite opposition, no authority gives the situation in a way so fair and straightforward as does Hutchinson, both in his History and his letters. Without any improper resentment, he writes, in the months immediately following, of the outrage

[1] To Dennys Deberdt, colonial agent, December 21, 1765.

upon him, of his own views, and of those of the people.

_After the riot he wrote as follows to Governor Pownall : —

BOSTON, 31 Aug. 1765.

" Whilst the Act of Parliament was depending I never made any scruple in America or in my letters to England, of setting the privileges of the colonists with respect to internal taxes in the most favorable light I could, nor did I in any instance act a double part in the affair ; but now the Act is passed, I have always considered it as legally right, and declared that the oaths I had taken bound me in discharge of my public trust to a conformity to it. This, with the reports that there were copies of letters in town which I had wrote to England in favor of the Stamp Act, has made me the principal object of popular resentment ever since Mr. Oliver has been compelled to declare his resignation. But this violence is by no means to be charged upon the whole country : nine tenths or more of the people in it, I am sure, would detest their barbarous proceedings against me. It is, however, the consequence of an impression made upon the minds of almost the whole continent that they are deprived of English liberties which the better sort are for defending they say by all lawful means in their power, and the most abandoned say they will do it _per fas aut nefas._ We are in the most deplorable state, and all who are in authority stand in need of more than human wisdom and fortitude upon this occasion." [1]

[1] M. A. Hist., vol. xxvi., p. 149.

March 8, 1766 (marked " not sent "),[1] he writes : —

" A thought of independence I could not think it possible should enter into the heart of any man in his senses for ages to come. You have more than once hinted that I was mistaken, and I am now convinced I was so, and that the united endeavors of the friends to Britain and her Colonies in Europe and America were necessary to restore the Colonies to a true sense of their duty and interests. It would be presumption in me to suggest measures to his Majesty's ministers. If I am capable of doing any service, it must be by acquainting you with the rise and progress of this taint of principles and the degree to which it prevails. It is not more than two years since it was the general principle of the colonists that, in all matters of privilege or rights, the determination of the Parliament of Great Britain must be decisive. They could not, it is true, alter the nature of things; and the natural rights of an Englishman, to which no precise idea seems to have been affixed, would remain in him; but the exercise of that right during the continuance of such determination or act must be suspended. To oppose by armed force the execution of any Act of Parliament, grand juries without offense have been often instructed, was high treason, as well in America as in Europe; and that his Majesty, as King of Great Britain, had no subjects in any part of the world upon whom an Act of Parliament was not binding. You will give me leave to mention to you how these principles have gradually changed for others which approach very near to independence. You

---

[1] *M. A. Hist.*, vol. xxvi., p. 200, etc.

are sensible the Parliament had scarce in any instance
imposed any Act or duty upon the Colonies for the purpose of revenue. The 18th sugar duty was considered
for the regulation of trade; the Molasses Act of the 6th
of George II. was professedly designed merely as a
prohibition from the foreign islands, and the Greenwich
hospital duty was upon seamen, who generally are
rather inhabitants of the world than any Colony; and
the post-office was supposed to be established for public convenience, and until the late Act which lowered
the duty upon molasses and sugar with a professed design to raise a revenue from them, few people in the
Colonies had made it a question how far the Parliament
of right might impose taxes upon them. The Massachusetts Assembly was the first body which took this matter into consideration. . . . Several [addresses?] were
prepared which expressed in strong terms an exclusive
right in the Assembly to impose taxes. I urged the ill
policy when they had the resolution of the House of
the Commons before, of sending an address in express
words asserting the contrary, and after a fortnight
spent, at the desire of the committee[1] I drew an address
which considered the sole power of taxation as an indulgence we prayed the continuance of, and this was
unanimously agreed to. . . . It will be some amusement to you to have a more circumstantial account of
the model of government among us. I will begin with
the lowest branch, partly legislative, partly executive.
This consists of the rabble of the town of Boston,
headed by one Mackintosh, who, I imagine, you never

----

[1] Hutchinson was chairman.

heard of. He is a bold fellow, and as likely for a Ma-
saniello as you can well conceive. When there is occasion to burn or hang effigies or pull down houses, these
are employed ; but since government has been brought
to a system, they are somewhat controlled by a superior
set consisting of the master-masons, and carpenters, &c.,
of the town of Boston. . . . When anything of more
importance is to be determined, as opening the custom-
house on any matters of trade, these are under the
direction of a committee of merchants, Mr. Rowe at
their head, then Molyneux, Solomon Davis, &c. : but
all affairs of a general nature, opening all the courts of
law, &c., this is proper for a general meeting of the
inhabitants of Boston, where Otis, with his mob-high
eloquence, prevails in every motion, and the town first
determine what is necessary to be done, and then apply
either to the Governor or Council, or resolve that it is
necessary the General Court correct it ; and it would
be a very extraordinary resolve indeed that is not carried into execution. . . . About a fortnight ago the
distracted demagogue of Boston attacked my history of
the Colony, and censured me in his newspaper for charg-
ing the government with a mistake in imagining that
no act of the Colony was necessary to give force to an
Act of Parliament regulating trade. A few days after,
upon a seizure of molasses and sugar at Newbury, half-
a-dozen boats, well manned, went after the officer, took
the goods from him and the boat he was in, and left
him all night upon the beach. A proclamation, with
promise of reward on discovery, is nothing more than
the show of authority : no man will venture a discovery,

and I imagine a few more such instances will make it
settled law, that no act but those of our own legislature
can bind us."

The remark " not sent " prefixed to the foregoing
letter, and occasionally to others, may possibly have
given rise to an accusation brought at a later day
against Hutchinson, namely, that he often wrote letters, ostensibly for foreign correspondents, but without
any intention of sending them : they were prepared to
produce popular effect, — with sentiments sometimes
not really those of the writer; having served this turn
they were laid aside.[1] A most inadequate basis this for
such a suspicion, but there is no other scrap of evidence
that he ever descended to such a trick.

Hutchinson dearly loved the Province, believing to
the last that the hearts of the people were sound, if
only " incendiaries " would let them alone. Nine
tenths of the Province he felt sure now detested violence,
but over the whole continent the impression was coming
to prevail that the Colonies were deprived of English
liberties. The better sort desired to use lawful means
alone in defense of those vaguely defined liberties, —
the most abandoned only would do it *per fas aut nefas.*
Being advised to go to England with his children, when
they were in semi-concealment at Milton in reasonable
fear of further violence, he could not bear the thought
of leaving his country while he could do it service.

Events moved rapidly. The Stamp-Act Congress, at
which nine of the thirteen Colonies were represented,

---

[1] The earliest instance of the charge, probably, is in Eliot's *New Eng.
Biog. Dict.*, art: " Hutchinson."

took action little to the taste of the three Massachusetts delegates, after much stormy debate. The conclusion was quite in harmony with the contemporaneous Massachusetts Resolves. Otis returned home discomfited, his ideas of submission and parliamentary representation getting here a quietus from which they never recovered; while Timothy Ruggles, who had been president, from this time on threw in his part with the Tories, proving to the last an uncompromising fighter.[1] The Stamp Act went into operation November 1,

[1] We shall have little occasion to refer to Ruggles hereafter, though he stood stoutly to his principles in the Massachusetts Assembly, as he had stood stoutly to his work in many a field of the old French war. In the small loyal minority, he was Hutchinson's bravest and ablest helper. He was one of the best lawyers of the Province, being particularly marked by a fine vein of humor which makes his figure attractive in the midst of the fierce controversy. This element is so woefully lacking in Hutchinson, the temptation cannot be resisted to give a story or two about this henchman of his, if only by way of relief to a sombre narrative. When Ruggles was in college, he was one of a party which stole a sign, the booty being carried to his room. The proctors got wind of it and pursued the depredators. Arriving at Ruggles's door, they heard sounds indicating that a prayer-meeting was going on inside, an exercise which by college prescription could not be disturbed. The culprits, knowing they were tracked, had put the sign on the fire to burn, holding the prayer-meeting meantime until all evidence should be consumed. While the proctors waited, the unctuous voice of Ruggles was heard through the door, as he wrestled in devotion : " A wicked and adulterous generation seeketh after a sign, and there shall no sign be given them but the sign of the prophet Jonas." At a later time Ruggles was trying a case before a Court of Sessions, composed of county Justices of the Peace, whom he for some reason held in much contempt. A dog had curled himself up in a seat on the platform where the Court was placed, causing Ruggles to rise to a point of order : " He had no objection to the dog being on the bench : on the contrary, he thought the companionship was eminently fit. But the proper forms should be observed, and he accordingly moved that the dog should be sworn in as a Justice of the Peace."

1765, amid doleful bell-tolling and firing of minute-
guns. Bernard, hating the law, resolutely did what he
thought his duty in executing it. The stamps were at
the Castle, with an additional force to guard them, and
the Governor was ready to distribute them at all risks.
But the sullen Assembly devised means to do business
without stamps, and roasted the Governor for taking
money from the treasury without their consent, to
pay the additional force. Non-importation agreements
threatened to put a stop to English trade. In every
way the sky was black. Boston petitioned to have the
Courts opened in defiance of the Act, John Adams, in
conjunction with James Otis and Jeremiah Gridley, appearing before the Governor for the town, and then
and there beginning his public career. But Grenville
and his ministry passed out of power, while the Mar-
quis of Rockingham, with the liberal Conway as Secretary of State, and Edmund Burke as his chief adviser,
stood in their places.

The surprise had been great in England that the
Stamp Act had met with such opposition. Government supposed it had proceeded upon the best information and advice. Shirley, for fifteen years Governor of
Massachusetts, together with several others presumed to
be well acquainted with the temper of the Colonies, had
been consulted, and had seen no reason to hesitate at
such a course. Some of the colonial agents had favored
it. It was of course likely to be a bitter pill, thought
the ministry. When is it otherwise with a scheme of
taxation ? But we will sugar-coat it abundantly ; so,
to appease the South, the trade in rice was favored,

while the North received a sop in various encourage-
ments. Most unexpectedly, however, both old and new
world were in a blaze of excitement, — the latter vocif-
erating that they were taxed while unrepresented; the
former stirred up into terror by the traders with America, who saw ruin for themselves in the discontent of
their trans-Atlantic customers.

Early in 1766 came that debate, one of the most
memorable which ever took place at St. Stephens,
whether we consider the ability and character of the
participants, or the gravity of the issues involved. Pitt,
Burke, Camden, and Barré were for the repeal of the
Stamp Act. The great Chief Justice of England,
Mansfield, led the opposing host; while Franklin, close
at hand, called to the bar of the Commons, gave to a
committee of the House his weighty testimony that the
colonists held allegiance to be due to the King alone, and
that instead of Parliament only the General Court in
each Province should have power to tax. We in America, holding, as has been our fashion, that all the wisdom was on one side in that combat, and that only folly
and ruthlessness characterized the party of the King,
need to restudy the matter.[1] Pitt's position, that the
Colonies should tax themselves, but in every other point
be under the dominion of Parliament, has been regarded in England from that day to this as untenable.[2]
Between legislation for taxing and legislation for other
purposes no distinction can be drawn. The Colonies,

[1] See the able presentment of an unusual view by Professor Moses
Coit Tyler : *American Historical Review*, vol. i., No. 1, " The Party of the
Loyalists in the American Revolution."

[2] Massey : *Hist. of Reign of George III.*, vol. i., p. 262.

too, at this very moment, practically pronounced Pitt's position untenable. Not simply the power to tax, but the power to pass laws of any kind, was denied : this soon became the general doctrine, — doctrine, let it be noted, which, had disease allowed Pitt capacity to act, would have been fought by him as vigorously as by any Tory of his day.

Nor, on the other hand, is that doctrine of *virtual representation*, presented by Mansfield, so scored by Pitt and James Otis, and scouted ever since in America as quite absurd, at all deserving to be set aside so summarily. " The notion now taken up," said Mansfield, " that every subject must be represented by deputy, is purely ideal.

" A member of Parliament chosen by any borough, represents not only the constituents and inhabitants of that particular place, but he represents the inhabitants of every other borough in Great Britain. He represents the city of London and all other the Commons of this land, and the inhabitants of all the Colonies and dominions of Great Britain, and is in duty and conscience bound to take care of their interests." [1]

The most recent and most authoritative English historian of the eighteenth century declares these closing sentences of Mansfield to be grandly true, and calls attention to the fact that Burke not long after insisted upon the same ideas to the electors of Bristol. What trouble has come, and still comes to the United States, from the general failure to recognize the expediency and the justice of this position of Mansfield and

[1] Hansard's *Parliamentary History*, vol. xvi.

Burke! In high places and low, the delegate stands only for the knot that sent him. In the municipal council each deputy has only his ward in thought, not the city at large. In the Senate at Washington, his particular State, not the whole land, too often limits the sympathy of the Senator. From lowest to highest, our legislatures here are honeycombed with an evil which has done us incalculable harm, and is as yet not at all stayed. "I will vote for your scheme, which I really think wrong or know nothing of, if you will vote for mine. You are for your section; I have no responsibility except to look out for my particular constituents. Why need I care for the land in general?" So it is that legislation becomes a constant log-rolling, and the statesmen can be counted upon the fingers whose view and whose hearts comprehend the country *in toto*. In the debate on the Stamp Act, the ablest men in Parliament defended America, — men who sat in Parliament through elections far enough from being free and just; but after all, elections of such a nature that they could follow quite unhampered the course prescribed by their sense of justice, or their idea of the welfare of the empire. If each one of the Thirteen Colonies had had its two or more deputies at`that time at Westminster, can it be believed that the case of America would have been any more effectively presented? In Westminster Abbey, the statue of Mansfield sitting in his robes, the grave judicial face seen from afar through the arches, is one of the most impressive of the marble presences. Not otherwise does he appear in the landscape of his time, — one of the

ablest and sturdiest characters of his day; nor did he
fall below his usual mark in the debate on the repeal
of the Stamp Act.

Let us not go too far, however. Lecky, while com-
mending Mansfield, and claiming that it is no abuse of
terms to say that the Colonies were virtually represented, acknowledges that the claim cannot be made
without some straining, and that the Stamp Act did
really infringe on a great principle, lying at the very
root of the English conception of political liberty,
namely, that taxation and representation are inseparably connected.[1] That any reputable citizen should
be without his vote is something which no American
will admit; which few English-speaking men anywhere
will admit. Inconveniences may be connected with a
broad suffrage; nothing human is without inconveniences; and among such drawbacks may be the holding of the representative by his constituency in too
tight a grasp, until he has eyes to see and hands to
work only for the narrow local interest, leaving uncared
for the interest of the great whole. But the draw-
back is a thousandfold compensated. If there were
nothing else but this, that there is no other such educative power as that of the ballot, that and the conditions under which it must be thrown, it would be
much more than a make-weight for the evil. There is
an ideal state for an Anglo-Saxon community, perhaps
not unattainable, in which a broad suffrage shall select
with a fair degree of accuracy the worthy man, and
then leave him free to do what good he is capable of

[1] Lecky: vol. iii., p. 353, etc.

doing for the greatest number. The instinct of America in the Stamp Act times was right, a genuine prompting of the Anglo-Saxon spirit, transmitted from remote times and pervading the breasts of men even though the original seats had long been exchanged for new homes, — the instinct demanding that only those should act for the people in whose selection every good citizen of the land had had a voice. Mansfield and his group showed, in belittling the principle, that their finer perceptions had become benumbed. How natural it was, however, that such a state should have come about in their circumstances! If one goes from under a clear sky into a room where people sit in bad air, though instantly impressed himself by the foulness in contrast with the purity he has just left, he may find the people in the room comfortable, quite unconscious, perhaps, that the atmosphere is vitiated. The statesmen of George III.'s day lived when parliamentary corruption was at its worst: in their political conditions they knew nothing else, and appreciated but feebly the enormity of the departure of their generation from a proper standard. The man of our time (in spite of all that may be said against it, the best time the world has ever seen), making real to himself in his imagination that past state, is appalled at the abuses, and impatient of the men that lived in the midst of them and suffered them to exist. Those men of the past should, however, be treated with thorough candor. When so treated they stand out well meaning and able, deserving honor for all the good they saw and practiced, even if at the same time they must have reproach, because their eyes in some ways were blinded. Side by side with the agitation in America went forward an agitation in England, the cause in the two cases being substantially one and the same, — a conviction in the mass of the people that the "liberties of Englishmen" were withheld. The belief expressed by Grenville in the great debate to which reference has just been made — that the trouble in America would never have become threatening but for encouragement from England — was well founded: Hutchinson saw it also, and repeatedly expressed the thought.

Hutchinson, thoroughly disapproving of the Stamp Act as a most impolitic measure, and as thoroughly disapproving of the position of the people that Parliament had no right to pass it or any other measure for them, tried in his public work to steer the middle course to which his feelings forced him. In business of the Superior and Probate Courts, he refused to undertake any matter requiring stamps. The popular feeling was scarcely less outraged by such a course than if he had gone to the full Tory extreme, and he had thoughts of England again as an asylum which he might be obliged to seek. "I often think," he writes, "how quiet and contented I was before I quitted my mercantile life for a political one, and it adds to my misfortune that from my present station I cannot return to my former condition with honor." Early in the spring, however, rumors of a probable repeal of the Stamp Act became current; and in May, before the Assembly met, the news of repeal arrived. That the revocation was accompanied by the Declaratory Act, maintaining the su-

premacy of Parliament in all cases whatsoever, not only
as to taxation, but as to legislation in general, excited
at the time little remark. The rejoicing was universal. The bells pealed, flags were waved, liberty-tree
was dressed with streamers and lanterns, joyful crowds
thronged the streets. Bernard held with his Council a
congratulatory meeting, then mingled affably with the
multitude. Governor and citizen were for the moment
heartily happy and sympathetic, — an instant of peace,
with discord before and discord far worse in the immediate future.

In a few days, the election took place for members
of the Assembly. In the " Boston seat," which of late
had been growing greatly in influence, the power of the
Otises having sufficed to thrust into the background
the jealousy which the country entertained toward the
capital, there sat beside Samuel Adams the new member of the preceding fall, — John Hancock, — a young
merchant who lately, through the death of an uncle, had
come into possession of the largest property in the Province. Another new member, abler and worthier than
Hancock, was Joseph Hawley, of Northampton, a man
of such force and gifts that one is always wondering
why he did not do more. His prestige in the western
counties was very great, and he made a strong impression in his new sphere. He appears to have had a
morbid taint in his nature something like that of Otis;
which indeed never made him an object of disgust and
dread, but rendered him fitful and uncertain, and was
probably the reason why, as the Revolution advanced,
he fell back into obscurity. The chief characters in

the drama with which we have to do are now upon the scene. To Otis have been joined the Adamses, Hancock, Bowdoin, and Hawley; confronting whom stand Bernard, Hutchinson, and the Olivers, now definitely marked as prerogative men or Tories.

Not many data for Hutchinson's home life are given in his letters and journals, full though they are. As appears from the documents of the time when his house was torn down, his sister-in-law, Grizel Sanford, was an inmate who we may suppose had much to do with bringing up her motherless nephews and nieces. Thomas and Elisha, the sons, were now men, Harvard graduates of 1758 and 1762, and will soon appear as merchants. Sarah was soon to be the wife of Dr. Peter Oliver.[1] "Peggy," a beauty, no doubt, on evidence about to be adduced, was now often her father's amanuensis; a child much loved, whose death, when it came, was one of the last and heaviest strokes her father received. "Billy," the youngest boy, was to have an English career, setting out from home in April of this year. The Chief Justice lays it down to him as "a good general rule, to say and do everything you can with a good conscience to obtain every man's favor, and to avoid as far as possible giving offense," — advice, it must be acknowledged, which might well have come from Polonius or Mr. Worldlywiseman. "We were all employed in watching you from Milton all the day you sailed, and did not wholly lose sight of you until late in the afternoon."

---

[1] Son of Peter Oliver, soon to be Chief Justice.

At Milton the family lived now, for the most part. The place was a superb one, greatly loved by the Governor, who thus described it to King George in 1774 : —

" My house is seven or eight miles from town, a pleasant situation, and many gentlemen from abroad say it has the finest prospect from it they ever saw, except where great improvements have been made by art, to help the natural view." [1]   Certainly the view is very lovely ; and " improvements made by art" would enable the Governor, if he could describe the spot to-day, to praise it without qualification.   Southward, at the distance of three or four miles, lie the Blue Hills, from whose Indian title of Massachusetts the land derives its name.   Seen from Hutchinson's home, the noble range presents itself in its most picturesque outline, the granite shoulders thrust boldly under the heaven in the horizon, as wild and forest-grown to the eye to-day as they were a century ago.   Toward the north, beyond a league or two of meadow, where the haymakers are at work in July, and through which the dark Neponset winds to the sea, the entire expanse of Boston harbor lies outspread, from the wharves to the outer light, dotted with its islands and forts and thronged with ships.   The golden dome of the State House crowns the great city, far to the left; and close at hand as well as in the distance, along the blue sea, lies a landscape whose beauty is everywhere heightened by the power of wealth, refinement, and industry.

---

[1] Account of conversation with George III., *Diary and Letters of Hutchinson*, vol. i., p. 164.

CHAPTER VI.

THE END OF BERNARD.

WHILE the people in general were disposed to be quiet, the leaders were under no illusion as to the Declaratory Act. With that on the statute-book, no peace was possible between the Province and the powers at home, and there was encouragement from home to think that an active policy might gain all. At once, after the election, trouble began. Otis, having been chosen Speaker, was negatived by Bernard, Thomas Cushing being put in his place, an inoffensive, honorable man, whose name for ten years to come was very prominent, since he was regularly made Speaker. He had, however, little significance in himself. Hutchinson, Andrew Oliver, Secretary of the Province, Lynde, of the Superior Court, and Trowbridge, the Attorney-General, men whom Bernard much desired for the Council, were rejected by the legislature, the hand of Otis appearing plainly in the transaction. The reason alleged was that it was dangerous to unite the legislative with judicial or executive powers. This Hutchinson made light of as quite new doctrine, urging that there was abundant precedent for judges to act as Councilors, and claiming for himself a right to a seat in the upper House by virtue of the Lieutenant-Governorship.[1] The Lieutenant-Governor, Hutchinson says, had sat in the Council from 1692 to 1732, not voting except when elected ; but Hutchinson had been elected to the Council constantly since 1749. The House, however, stood firm, and the home government declined to interfere ; so into Hutchinson's place as leader of the Council came James Bowdoin, the able merchant of Huguenot strain, who in preceding years had stood with Hutchinson in his financial schemes. Now, however, he was with the Whigs, and under his influence the Council sometimes went farther in opposition than the Assembly itself. While the Council spoke of a " due submission " to Parliament as proper, and the House used the phrase " constitutional subordination," Hawley at last startled his fellows by denying in set terms *all* right in Parliament to legislate for the Colonies. A noteworthy incident of the summer session was the demand by Otis that a gallery should be provided in the House for the use of the public, to whom the debates should hereafter be thrown open. Now for the first time in the history of the world, says Tudor, such provision took place, a thing which has been followed in all countries where constitutional government prevails, and which has modified profoundly the character and proceedings of deliberative bodies.[2]

In the fall a special session of the legislature was called by Bernard, to consider the matter of restitution to Hutchinson for his loss through the mob of the pre-

[1] When the State of Massachusetts afterwards adopted a constitution, the Lieutenant-Governor became *ex-officio* President of the Council.

[2] *Life of Otis.*

vious year. At this time nothing was done, the members
of the House pleading that they could not act without
instructions from their constituents, and Hawley showing an unfriendliness which cut Hutchinson, who was
inclined to like him, to the quick. As regards the matter of instructions, a letter of Hutchinson of this time [1]
contains a few sentences which show that he held with
Burke,[2] that a legislator should be his own man and
not a mere mouthpiece.

"November 7, 1766. In the recess of the Court
most of the members applied to their towns for in-
tructions, and now suppose themselves at all events
held to conform to them. This I always thought unconstitutional and absurd, and contrary to the idea of
a Parliament ; but upon instructions prevailing so much
as they have done of late years in England upon any
important point, we must mimic you, and by means
of it continue the public embarrassment, as well as my
private distress ; for I am assured that more than one
half the negatives, if they had not feared their towns,
would have been on the other side of the question, and
that from attachment to me, for I never stood better
with the Assembly in general."

What Hutchinson writes as to Hawley's course is
manly and pathetic. "March 27, 1767. I have never
met with any misfortune more sudden and unexpected
than Major Hawley's violent prejudice and opposition.
. . . When a general charge is made against me by a
gentleman of so fine a character as Major Hawley has
always sustained, that I am of unconstitutional princi-

[1] *M. A. Hist.*, vol. xxvi., p. 250.   [2] To the Electors of Bristol.

ples, am ambitious and lustful of power, and when he has repeatedly declared that he is loth to enter into particulars, I should not wonder if the most extravagant things should be said of me in one part of the country or another. We are not always upon our guard, and resentment upon the first notice of fresh injuries may lead me to drop some expressions which I wish to avoid. I only desire my friends to suspend forming any judgment upon such ill reports until they have better evidence than merely the reports themselves. . . . Some of my friends, as they have told me, were really afraid something criminal would be produced. I am informed that all the particulars of the general charge was my taking the place of Chief Justice when I was Lieutenant-Governor. It was not a place of my seeking ; and if he should prevail upon the people to think I ought not to continue in it, I will resign it, for I do not desire any public position any longer than I can give satisfaction. Indeed, if all the gentlemen of the bar should think it allowable to persecute one of the justices of the Court as often as he differed from him in sentiment, a man had better be employed in any menial office." [1]

Hutchinson thought that the temper of the Province this year was, on the whole, good. With his lights the following letter to Jasper Mauduit cannot be regarded as otherwise than reasonable.

" December 31, 1766. I wish the Colonies may have a just sense of the great tenderness of their mother country. There will be some restless spirits in all gov-

[1] *M. A. Hist.*, vol. xxvi., p. 271.

ernments. In general there is at present in this Province a disposition to promote government and good
order. I cannot say that we have the same apprehension of our relation to Great Britain which we had two
years ago. It is not to be wondered at. You are divided
in your sentiments about it in England. Most of the
political performances reach us, and those which favor
liberty and a state the least dependent are most approved. Besides, it is an age of liberty. If we have
right notions of the constitution of Great Britain, it has
been growing more and more popular since the Revolution, and some of the other nations of Europe are wishing and making their feeble attempts to recover a greater
degree of freedom. However, I am not apprehensive
that any man in the Colonies who has a cool head thinks
it possible they could long subsist if Britain should leave
them to themselves; much less, that they could maintain their independence contrary to the mind of the
nation: but our misfortune is the different apprehension of the nature and degree of our dependence. I
wish to see it settled, known, and admitted; for while
the rules of law are vague and uncertain, especially in
such fundamental points, our condition is deplorable in
general. But no particular part of the community have
so difficult a task, and are so exposed to censure, malice,
and personal resentment, as those persons who are the
judges of the law. Some think we may continue in this
state until the Colonies arrive to manhood, when the pa-
rental right of control will determine [end]. It is not
possible. Our internal disquiet will make the body of
the people wish to have the point determined, although

it should not be done exactly to their own sentiment. I have in some degree relieved myself from my anxiety the last year, by applying my leisure time to completing a second volume of the history of the Province to the year 1750, which is now ready for the press." [1]

To this letter the statement of Hutchinson in the History respecting the position that the Province had come generally to occupy by 1767 forms an excellent supplement. The authority of Parliament to pass any acts whatever affecting the interior polity of the Colonies is, he says, challenged, as destroying the effect of the charters, to which great sacredness is attached. People have been induced to settle in the plantations on the strength of the charters, relying on the continuance of the privileges. King, Lords, and Commons form the legislature of Great Britain: the Governor, who is the King's representative, the Council, and the Assembly form the legislature of the Colony. But as Colonies cannot make laws to extend further than their respective limits, Parliament must step in in all cases to which the legislative power of the Colonies does not extend. Parliament ought to go no farther than this: all beyond is infringing upon the domain of the colonial legislatures. From Virginia to Massachusetts this has now come to be the accepted doctrine.[2]

Hutchinson's demand of the legislature for compensation for the destruction of his house, made formally October 29, 1766, was at last effectual.[3] He is

---

[1] M. A. Hist., vol. xxvi., p. 257.

[2] Hist. of Mass. Bay, vol. iii., p. 172.

[3] "In Massachusetts, Rhode Island, and New York, the Assemblies slowly and unwillingly complied with the injunction of the Secretary of

said to have received £3,194 17s. 6d., a fair indemnity. After some discussion of the plan of a lottery to raise the means, an expedient which in those days no one thought questionable, an Act was passed to make the grant directly, which, however, had for a " rider " pardon to all who had taken part in the disturbances connected with the Stamp Act. This rider was the work of Hawley; he was greatly interested to clear certain rioters in Hampshire County, who had employed him as their counsel. Though Hawley did not appear to wish to excuse them from all blame, he yet urged that the basis of the trouble was the unjust law which, in unthinking minds, must necessarily work exasperation sure to go great lengths. Bernard hesitated to sign the Act, but was finally induced to do so by his earnest wish to have Hutchinson receive justice. When the Act was sent to England, the King disallowed it; such lawlessness could not be condoned even that a faithful official might receive his rights. But the money had been paid before the news of the King's displeasure arrived.

Rockingham's ministry, marked by the repeal of the Stamp Act and the passage of the Declaratory Act, after a few months was succeeded by a government which contained indeed Pitt, now the Earl of Chatham, but the leader in which was Charles Townshend, Chatham being incapacitated through infirmity. Town-

---

State to award compensation to the sufferers by the recent riots." Lord Mahon : *Hist. of Eng.*, vol. v., p. 145. The Massachusetts Archives contain a minute inventory of the contents of the destroyed house, drawn up by Hutchinson himself, in many ways a curious and interesting list. Vol. marked *Colonial*, vol. vi., 1724–1776 ; this is given in Appendix A.

shend had no patience with colonial restiveness; nor
was he at all under the sway of the great chief at his
side, now fast sinking toward his grave. He made light
of the distinction sought to be drawn between external
and internal taxes, as a distinction without a difference ;
but in levying a tax, destined to have momentous consequences, he declared he would humor the Americans :
to external taxes they had professed a readiness to submit; his tax should be external, upon paper, glass,
red and white lead, painters' colors, and lastly upon tea.
Here, said Townshend, the colonists shall have things
to their advantage. The export duty on tea, payable
in England, of 12d. a pound, was taken off entirely ;
an import duty of 3d., to be collected in the Colonies
themselves, being imposed in its place. Tea regularly
obtained, therefore, was to be had more cheaply than
before. But a principle was infringed. The ideas of
the colonists were shifting; they had come to feel, as
well as Townshend, that the distinction between external
and internal taxes could not be made, even though
it was doctrine taught by Pitt and Franklin.

The new measure brought all the old feeling into
life once more, the consideration of advantage counting for little, no doubt, from the fact that thus far it
had been possible to get at a cheap rate much smuggled tea, through the Dutch. Hutchinson approved of
Townshend's tax no more than he did of the Stamp
Act, his ground consistently being that though it was
right for the Supreme Legislature to impose it, it was
impolitic : having been imposed, however, he thought
it should be enforced.[1] It was sought through Town-

---

[1] *Hist.* vol. iii., p. 178.

shend's taxes to obtain means to defray the salaries of a civil list. Officers in the civil and judicial services were to be paid from the proceeds, in that way being freed from dependence upon the legislatures, though still supported by the Colonies. Townshend further provided for the establishment of a Board of Commissioners of Customs, with large powers, to superintend all the laws relating to trade, members of which were Paxton, Robinson, and Temple, characters who will hereafter appear in our story. Still another blow that Townshend struck was a suspension of the legislature of New York for contumacy in the treatment of royal troops that had been ordered to that Province. These Acts were accomplished on the 13th of May. Soon after, the rash and brilliant young statesman, for whom a career of prominence, though hardly of usefulness, might have been hoped, died.

The following letter written at this juncture by Thomas Pownall is interesting, as the expression of a sensible man and a well-wisher to America, who favored its representation in Parliament. After acknowledging the second volume of Hutchinson's History he writes, London, September 9, 1767 : —

" Without your knowledge or application I took the liberty upon the establishment of the Board of Revenue in America, to apply to have you named as one, and as I wrote you in my last, I thought it was decided that you were to be named, and to be first. I did not, indeed, totally rely on it, as you will have seen by my last ; and the Duke of Grafton's letter decides that point. However, I may venture to explain to you the first part of his letter. It is meant that you shall have a handsome salary fixed as Chief Justice, as soon as the American revenue shall create a fund. I think on that occasion it would be right to solicit a patent from the Crown for that place. If all on this last ground succeeds as meant, I think 't will be much better for you, and what you will like better.

" If the people of the Province would be advised, one might serve them and the Colonies in general. The point of being exempt from being taxed by Parliament they will never carry, but will every time lose something by the struggle. The point of having representatives, if pursued prudently, and in the right line, I am sure they might and ought to carry. And whatever they may think of keeping the power of taxing themselves by their own legislatures in general matters, exclusive of Parliament, they will be disappointed, and by aiming at the shadow lose the substance. Now, from principle of opinion, thinking it best both for Great Britain and the Colonies, on the plan of a general union of the parts, I shall always support the doctrine of the Colonies sending representatives to Parliament. I have done, and shall do it as long as I am in Parliament, both in Parliament and out of the House. From principle of affection and gratitude, I shall ever support and defend the people of the Massachusetts Bay as I did last sessions, when some people were for extending the censure laid on New York to the Massachusetts." [1]

Resistance was manifest as soon as the news of the new duties was received. As the Town-Meetings gath-

---

[1] *Mass. Hist. Society Coll.*, 3d series, vol. i., pp. 148, 149.

cred, men became familiarized with the advanced positions toward which the leading minds were so swiftly
making their way. Otis and Samuel Adams swayed
the crowds in Faneuil Hall, the one by his eloquence
and straightforward personal force, the other by ways
more subtle and indirect, but no less effective. Hawley
held a similar place at Northampton ; so, too, James
Warren, brother-in-law of Otis, at Plymouth ; and John
Adams, at Braintree. When the towns came together
at the Boston State House in their delegates, Otis,
Adams, and Hawley were there again in the front as
they had been at home. Committees of Correspondence
in the various colonial legislatures were taking form,
and already knitting the bond which was to grow into
the Union. As the year went on, the air was full of
" non-importation." Rather than pay the taxes imposed
by a body in which they were not represented, the
people would renounce. The use of superfluities, enumerated in long lists, was reduced. All was done
that could be done to stimulate colonial manufactures.
Active minds were at work in the newspapers, the most
radical spirit in these preliminary days being the youth
of twenty-three, Josiah Quincy, a touch of whose fer-
vor we have already felt the force of. He went so far
as to advocate even at this time an armed resistance, —
over-hot counsel, which no one was ready to follow.

In spite of all, however, a good degree of quiet prevailed. The non-consumption arrangements were not
to go into operation until the end of the year. The
Tories took great encouragement from the course pursued in the fall by James Otis, who made a speech then

thought to be quite reactionary, but which is really consistent enough with all he had ever claimed. In Town-Meeting, November 20, he asserted in a long harangue the right of the King to appoint officers of customs in what number and by what name he pleased, and declared it inexpedient to oppose the new duties. What the Colonies should demand was representation in the taxing body. Pownall would have said the same thing. Two years before, probably few persons in the Province would have taken other ground. The duties were plainly external; to cavil at such duties was a very recent matter. To enforce them, of course, there must be officials. Hutchinson's position was that, though justified by precedent, the laying of such duties by Parliament was inexpedient; when laid, however, it was inexpedient in the Colonies to resist. The point where Otis and Hutchinson differed was as to representation in the taxing body, which Otis so fiercely fought for. Hutchinson would have been glad to have the representation, had it been practicable; since it seemed impracticable, he was quite ready to take up with Mansfield's doctrine of " virtual representation."

How hollow the opposition to Hutchinson was, on the score that he filled so many functions, appears from the fact, which one has frequently to note in studying his career, that in a remarkable way, whenever an occasion comes up demanding prudent management upon which large interests depend, no one but Hutchinson can be trusted to transact the business. We have seen heretofore [1] that, had he been properly seconded, he

[1] See p. 17.

would have made a satisfactory settlement of the Massachusetts boundary on the side of New Hampshire. Afterwards he had settled it on the side of Connecticut; then Rhode Island. A still more difficult negotiation remained with New York; and in this year the Province was willing to commit this delicate task to no one but him. Associated in a commission with Brattle and Sheaffe, respectable but inconspicuous citizens, who were expected to be little more than lay figures in the transaction, Hutchinson met in October the New York commissioners at New Haven. He demanded that the western line of Massachusetts should be twelve miles east from the Hudson River; New York demanded a line thirty miles east of the river. It was not possible at this time to hit upon any compromise.[1] The final settlement six years later by Hutchinson was, as we shall see, the last important service he was to render to his country.

Hutchinson was not long in recognizing Samuel Adams as the "Chief Incendiary" among the more ardent spirits of the Whigs; and in the winter session of the legislature, 1767–68, there came from the hand of Adams, writing for the Assembly, two documents which made it certain that submission to Townshend's policy, now adopted by Lord North, who after Townshend's death came into his place, would not be thought of. The first of these missives was a letter to Dennys Deberdt, the London agent of the Assembly. The lower House, which increased all the time in influence

[1] See Hutchinson's autograph report, *Mass. Archiv.* (*Colonial*, 1721–1768), vol. iv., p. 217.

and size (the new towns, as the Province grew, sending members, while the Council remained at twenty-eight, the number ordained by the charter), had lately set up an agent of its own, although until now one agent had sufficed for the whole legislature. The letter was intended to be published : it was, in fact, a manifesto to the King, government, and people of England. There is no hint in the paper at a disruption from the mother country, toward which an " English affection " is professed. The injustice of taxation without representation is dwelt upon, and the impossibility of colonial representation in Parliament made plain. A voluntary subsidy is suggested as the only proper way in which a revenue can be gained from the Colonies. In an energetic passage, speaking of the appointment of an American bishop, which had so long been threatened, the Assembly " hopes in God such an establishment will never take place in America. . . . The revenue raised in America, for aught we can tell, may be as constitutionally applied towards the support of prelacy as of soldiers and pensioners ; " that would, indeed, cap the climax ! In still other passages, after citing as a grievance the establishment of the Board of Customs Commissions, the impropriety of giving to Governors and judges stipends from other sources than distinct legislative appropriations is asserted ; and here the writer must have had Hutchinson particularly in his mind, for it had been proposed to pay him as Chief Justice a salary of £200 from the proceeds of Townshend's taxes, — this to take the place of the £150 to which he was entitled from legislative appropriation, a sum from which £30 was often deducted, and which was liable to be withheld entirely. The adroit hand by which the epistle was penned caused it to be provided with qualities which now and henceforth mark the state papers of the Massachusetts Assembly, — a superficial gloss of courtesy spread over an uncompromising statement of advanced political ideas, — each sentence cool, polished, and even, but driving at the mark with utter plainness, with wide knowledge of appropriate examples from past history, with inflexible purpose to win.

The Circular Letter with which the one to Deberdt was associated in time was sent to each House of Representatives in the Thirteen Colonies. A large majority of the Assembly had shrunk from the idea of such a measure when it was first proposed, well knowing the jealousy with which any approach to a banding together of the Colonies was sure to be received at home. A change, however, was soon wrought, and in little more than a fortnight from the inception of the idea the letter was ready for sending. The Colonies were urged to concert a uniform plan for remonstrances against the government policy. What Massachusetts had done was detailed, and information asked as to what had been done elsewhere. With all possible tact the idea of assuming leadership was disclaimed, and local sensitiveness soothed into repose. It was at once dispatched, and at once met with a good response, while prerogative men in all the Provinces were correspondingly exasperated. Representations went to England that stringent measures were imperative. Bernard in particular was outraged, enlarging in his communication upon the older grievance, the determination to exclude all Crown officers from the Council. These sentiments he expressed without reserve, and from this time until the day of his departure, his relations with his charge were bad as bad could be. The voice through which the popular animosity in particular found expression at this time was that of Joseph Warren, a young physician, twenty-seven years old, for some time a writer for the papers, but who now first created a sensation by the following vehement arraignment in the " Boston Gazette " of February 29, 1768.

" We have for a long time known your enmity to this Province. We have had full proof of your cruelty to a loyal people. No age has, perhaps, furnished a more glaring instance of obstinate perseverance in the path of malice. . . . Could you have reaped any advantage from injuring this people, there would have been some excuse for the manifold abuses with which you have loaded them. But when a diabolical thirst for mischief is the alone motive of your conduct, you must not wonder if you are treated with open dislike ; for it is impossible, how much soever we endeavor it, to feel any esteem for a man like you. . . . Nothing has ever been more intolerable than your insolence upon a late occasion, when you had, by your jesuitical insinuations, induced a worthy minister of state to form a most unfavorable opinion of the Province in general, and some of the most respectable inhabitants in particular. You had the effrontery to produce a letter from his lordship as a proof of your success in calumniating us. . . . We never can treat good and patriotic rulers with too great reverence. But it is certain that men totally abandoned to wickedness can never merit our regard, be their stations ever so high.

> 'If such men are by God appointed,
> The Devil may be the Lord's anointed.'

A TRUE PATRIOT." [1]

If ever a man's friends had cause to fly to his rescue, those of the Governor had such cause, in the appearance of an attack so utterly intemperate. A man of refinement and good purposes, who had done well in his place in many ways, and who at first had received from the people committed to him many evidences of friendliness, was struck at in this unqualified diatribe. Hutchinson would have been neither true man nor proper judge had he failed to do what he straightway did, try to induce the grand jury to indict Warren for libel. The jury, however, returned "ignoramus." The incensed Governor was forced to stomach the affront, which was only the first blast of a storm of abuse directed against him during the rest of his American sojourn. It was sought to enforce the taxes, for the effective collection of which the Writs of Assistance were fully legalized and put into operation. The air was full of rebellion ; and Hutchinson notes in the History with an approach to a chuckle, that even the Harvard students, under their Liberty-tree, decreed that the rule of the faculty was unconstitutional. This was fire in their own camp : here the provincials could see

---

[1] Frothingham : *Life of Warren*, pp. 40, 41.

how it was themselves. Quite inconsistently, however, as the friends of the government no doubt thought, the people sustained the overseers in putting down the recalcitrant young men, while they themselves kicked sky-high at King George and all his mandates. As the grand jury was indifferent to Warren's letter, so the legislature could not be induced to notice it. Bernard prorogued it in indignation; not, however, until resolutions had been passed favoring non-importation and non-consumption agreements. The only break in unanimity was the vote of bright Timothy Ruggles, now and always a Tory of the bravest.

The letters form a continuous commentary upon the events as they succeed each other. We are rarely at a loss to understand just the nature of Hutchinson's connection with them, or his judgment of men and measures. February 3, he writes to the Duke of Grafton, who had proposed to him a seat on the Board of Customs. The pay attracts him, being more than three times greater than his uncertain pittance as Chief Justice. In the latter place, however, he can do more to head off the incendiaries. " I will do as your Grace thinks proper." [1] With a premonition of great trouble in store for him in a future year, he declares, February 17: " When we write with freedom it is of importance that it should not be known." [2] March 23, his word to Jackson, to whom many of his best letters go, runs as follows: " The claim of right to independence of Parliament is now become almost universal. . . . Either my brain is turned, or the brains of most of the people about me

---

[1] *M. A. Hist.*, vol. xxvi., p. 287.   [2] *Ibid.*

are so ; " and on the 27th, he reasons logically to the
Duke of Grafton : " It is by force of an Act of Parliament that all the Princes since the Revolution [of
1688] have been sovereign, . . . and I cannot see why
the advocates for sedition may not with equal reason
make one step more, and deny the regal as well as parliamentary authority, although I do not think a man of
them at present has it in his thoughts."

March was marked by riots, which proved once more
that side by side with the community of intelligent and
law-abiding men dwelt a mob as brutal as that of London.   When the drunken, blasphemous horde poured
up from the waterside into the better streets, the officials
had good reason to feel they held their lives in their
hands.   Though banned as a Tory, Hutchinson's popularity was not yet entirely wrecked.   It cost the patriots a hard fight to defeat him for the Council this year,
in the election for which he fell short only three votes.
June 17, he writes about it to the Duke of Grafton :
" Our great incendiary [Otis] was enraged and ran
about the House in a fury, with votes for my competitor,
crying, ' Pensioner, or no Pensioner.' " He was charged
with receiving a salary from the Crown, or being about
to do so, and this was what defeated him.   Some months
before, in the perturbed condition of the Colonies, the
Earl of Hillsborough had been made a special secretary
for colonial affairs, and at present his name fills a large
space on the English side.   He transmits to Bernard
the royal instructions for the treatment of the Circular
Letter, which was regarded as distinctly seditious.   Virginia, New Jersey, Connecticut, and Georgia early re-

plied to the Letter in cordial terms, and there was no
doubt that other Colonies would soon do the same.
Bernard, following his instructions, required that the Circular Letter should be at once rescinded. When it came
to a vote, the Assembly refused to rescind by ninety-
two to seventeen. Some of those who had disapproved
of the Circular Letter were now in the majority against
rescinding, the position taken being that royal dictation
should not be submitted to. Bernard's instructions were
to prorogue as long as contumacy existed. This he did,
becoming odious to the last degree. He was believed
to have brought the mandate upon the Assembly by
his "misrepresentations," though the journals of the
House told the whole story with sufficient plainness.
Hutchinson says the Governor really tried to make
things easy for the people to such an extent that his
friends thought he would be censured in England. He
was, however, clamored against in Massachusetts as the
sole cause. Moreover, he was censured for receiving
the Customs Commissioners into the Castle ; and when
the fleet in the harbor moored so as to command that
fortress with their guns, he was censured for doubting
the fidelity of the Provincial troops who formed the
garrison. The legislature adjourned, and Bernard naturally began to feel that another position might be
more agreeable, if less lucrative. His departure would
bring Hutchinson once more to the front, as had been
the case before, at the departure of Pownall. For
some months more, however, Hutchinson was to remain
in the second place.

One of his contemporaneous comments on events is

as follows. July 14, to Jackson : "Whatever measures you may take to maintain the authority of Parliament, give me leave to pray they may be accompanied with a declaration that it is not the intention of Parliament to deprive the Colonies of their subordinate power of legislation, nor to exercise the supreme legislative power, except in such cases and upon such occasions as an equitable regard to the interests of the whole empire shall make necessary. . . . My hopes of tranquillity have been confined to one plan, — that we should be convinced the Parliament will not give up their authority ; and then find by experience that it is exercised in the same gentle, tender manner that a parent exercises his authority over his children." [1]

There is perhaps no better statement by Hutchinson of his view than the foregoing, and the reader is asked to consider it well. 'England to-day is commended for her attitude to her dependencies; and the idea has often been expressed that, had she stood in the same attitude toward the Thirteen Colonies, the Anglo-Saxon schism need never have taken place. What is Hutchinson's notion but that England should stand toward America as she does toward her dependencies to-day, — the Colonies to legislate for themselves without interference except when the interests of the whole empire are concerned ? the authority of Parliament, if ever exercised, to be exercised with the gentle tenderness of a parent, until the day came when it might entirely disappear?

The legislature refused to rescind the Circular Letter, and stood prorogued, the Governor's instructions mak-

[1] M. A. Hist., vol. xxvi., p. 313.

ing it necessary for him to prorogue while contumacy existed. General Gage, Commander-in-Chief of the forces in America, stationed at New York, had orders from home to bring troops to bear. Ships of war were also sent to Boston, the first arrival taking place in May. It was the fifty-gun ship Romney which signalized its approach through New England waters by attempting impressments, a procedure sure to aggravate the popular fever. When John Hancock's sloop, the Liberty, soon after fell into difficulties for violating the revenue laws, the trouble at once became acute. The Commissioners of Customs went to the Castle, and Bernard to his house in Roxbury; while Demos in Faneuil Hall or the Old South growled and grumbled ominously in its bitter discontent. Restrictive laws had wrought their usual effect. Trade had become to a large extent lawbreaking, and from that flowed copious demoralization. "We have been so long habituated," says Hutchinson in November, "to illicit trade, that people in general see no evil in it. Justices and grand juries, whose business it is to suppress riots and tumultuous assemblies, have suffered mobs against informers and to rescue seized goods, to pass unnoticed. Breach of law in one instance leads to others, and a breach of oaths at the custom-house is one cause of so frequent perjuries in judicial proceedings. That temper which for many years has been too prevalent, of dislike to all government, is very much encouraged, as well as a disregard to the rules of morality in general." [1]

The Boston world was becoming more and more out

1 *M. A. Hist.*, vol. xxvi., p. 325.

of joint, and in the trouble none were in so poor a plight
as the Governor and Lieutenant-Governor, held, as they
were, responsible for measures of repression which they
did not approve,[1] which they felt must aggravate the
difficulty, and which they sought to carry out only
because their official oaths made them of necessity the
instruments of the ministry behind them. Why could
they not resign? Bernard already had resignation in
his thoughts. Wanting sympathy with the government
he represented, wanting sympathy with the people in
his charge, who had no appreciation of his effort in
their behalf to mitigate the severity, he was soon to
withdraw. His companion, thinking it his duty to stay,
was destined to continue the struggle five years longer,
hoping against hope all the time, on the one hand, that
the government would become more moderate, and on
the other hand, that the people would become less punctilious as regarded the letter of their rights.

Since the legislature must of necessity be prorogued
until the Circular Letter was rescinded, in the summer
Massachusetts Bay had no legislature practically, and
Boston Town-Meeting, with characteristic boldness and
enterprise, set on foot an expedient to meet the situation. This was to call a convention of the towns of
the Province for September, the understanding being
that Boston should be the place of assembly, and the
delegates the Representatives legally elected for the
General Court. It was, in fact, convening the General
Court at the instance of a town, the agency in the
matter of the Governor, who by the charter alone had

---

[1] Hutchinson : *Hist.*, vol. iii., p. 197, etc.

the power to summon, being entirely dispensed with. There was a precedent for such action in the revolutionary year 1688, an ominous date. Four hundred muskets lay on the floor of Faneuil Hall at the meeting, over which, as usual, Otis presided. Two royal ships suddenly left the harbor, on the other hand, the understanding being that they were dispatched to Halifax for troops. September 22, the convention assembled, nearly a hundred towns responding to the call. Otis here was faltering and uncertain, embarrassing action much by failing to appear in the first days. His strange spell was unbroken as yet, although his freaks and vacillations were beyond reason. To this in part, and besides to a natural fear before the unknown threatening danger from the impending military occupation, it was due that the country members held back, and Samuel Adams, with his knot of radicals, was forced to be satisfied with what seemed to them a maimed result. The manifesto of the convention was moderate ; and after a session of a week, while the ships bringing the troops were sailing up the harbor, an adjournment came.   " I assure you," writes Hutchinson to Bollan in November, " that when the troops arrived we were upon the brink of ruin, and their arrival prevented some most extravagant measures. The party now say they were not in earnest." [1]

Part of the thousand men in the Halifax regiments, the 14th and 29th, were encamped on the Common, part quartered in the town-house and in Faneuil Hall. Of course no hospitality was shown ; the supplies

[1] *M. A. Hist.* vol. xxvi., p. 328.

demanded could not be obtained, and Dalrymple, the Lieutenant-Colonel in command, provided for his men at the expense of the Crown. The government was feeble and fluctuating. The Assembly was practically out of existence ; the Council, whose only constitutional function was to advise and assist the Governor, assumed now to act independently, addressing of itself the Commander-in-Chief, who came from New York to the seat of trouble, and also writing to Bollan in England, whom they named as their agent. As the year drew to a close, a considerable score had been run up by the Province, which the King and his friends could by no means overlook. The riotous opposition to the laws of trade and the new Board of Commissioners had been frequent and flagrant. The Assembly had vindicated instead of rescinding its former action as to the Circular Letter and the practical confederation of the Colonies. The illegal convention had taken place, which the home government could only look at as distinctly seditious. The Councilors had transcended their proper limits ; from satellites of the Governor, they had presumed to roll away into space. Not strangely Boston, whose Town-Meeting was in the lead in all this, was declared to be in a state of confusion, and Lords and Commons determined to maintain inviolate the supreme authority of Parliament.

As always, the vigor of the government was held in check by a back fire, which required to be faced and fought no less than the conflagration before. The dispute in England between the popular and prerogative parties was scarcely less well defined and bitter

than in the Colonies. The Boston patriots, being assured from beyond sea that nothing serious would ever
be done, and that Townshend's Act was likely to be repealed like the Stamp Act before it, kept a bold front.
The Town-Meeting demanded to know from Bernard
what representations had been made at home, that they
might defend themselves. It was intended Barre should
present a remonstrance against the "misrepresentations" and the sending of the troops. The threat to
deport the Boston leaders to England and try them for
treason according to a long disused statute of Henry
VIII. was presently mocked at, as were also the unfortunate regiments, as soon as the people became familiar
with their presence. Few, if any, of the Loyalists, says
Hutchinson, had any share in counseling harsh measures. They might even think them not founded in
good policy.[1] The hampered government seemed unen-
ergetic, and its action was construed as timidity.

Hutchinson would fain in these days have pursued a
middle course. April 19, 1768 : "An ingenious writer
who would keep the mean between a slavish subjection
on the one hand and absolute independence on the
other, would do great service. Where the fundamentals of a constitution are unsettled and vague, the people must be miserable indeed."[2]   He loses his temper
over the calumnies of unscrupulous newspaper-writers.
December, 1768 : "I think sometimes we have a dozen
of the most wicked fellows among us of any on the
globe. They stick at nothing."[3]   He is not a demo-

---

[1] *Hist.*, vol. iii., p. 221.   [2] *M. A. Hist.*, vol. xxvi., p. 303.
[3] *Ibid.*, p. 332.

crat, yet by no means unfriendly to freedom. " A thirst
for liberty seems to be the ruling passion, not only of
America, but of the present age. In governments
under arbitrary rule it may have a salutary effect, but
in governments where as much freedom is enjoyed as
can consist with the ends of government, as was the case
in this Province, it must work anarchy and confusion
unless there be some external power to restrain it." [1]
Now it was that he wrote a letter to Richard Jackson,
which in time to come was to give him much trouble.
January 20 : " I never think of the measures necessary
for the peace and good order of the Colonies without
pain. There must be an abridgment of what is called
English liberty. I relieve myself by considering that in
a remove from a state of nature to the most perfect
state of government there must be a great restraint of
natural liberty. I doubt whether it is possible to project a system of government in which a colony 3,000
miles distant from the parent state shall enjoy all the
liberties of the parent state. I am certain I have never
yet seen the projection. I wish to see the good of the
Colony when I wish to see some restraint of liberty
rather than the convulsion . . . I am sure such a
breach must prove." The Town-Meetings he thought
should deal with local interests, and were in these days
quite overstepping their proper functions.[2]   Yet he declares now, as he came in later years to asseverate with
all possible solemnity : " I have never proposed an alteration of the constitution. I rather wished for something to show them the danger of it and to effect a

[1] *M. A. Hist.*, vol. xxvi., Jan. 28, 1769.   [2] *Ibid.*, Aug. 18, 1769.

reforniation.[1] . . . If we could be prudent, I think I may say, only silent, we might save the country and retain the Rights we contend for ; or, which is the same thing, might rest assured that the Parliament would not exercise the right of Taxing which they claim and we may be assured will not give up ; but if we go on denying the right and asserting our independence, the Nation will by force compel us to acknowledge it. I wish this force may be kept off as long as you and I live." [2]

Whatever awe the troops inspired at their first coming soon wore off, and their situation before long became most uncomfortable. From the government point of view, they were in the crisis quite indispensable. The people in vast majority were passionately against the laws which Bernard and the officers of customs were bound by their oaths to administer. They were quite isolated, and had every reason to be afraid for their lives from mob violence. It was only proper prudence which made Bernard again and again go to his Roxbury home, and the customs-officers seek refuge in the Castle, although they were jeered at in the papers as absconding from their duty. To the popular cry that the prerogative men were bringing calamity upon the country by their misrepresentations of the state of things in America, Bernard replied, they need not fear misrepresentations. Nothing could be worse than their own declarations. The Assembly was convened in May, a body sullen to the last degree. The manifestoes of the Governor, on the one hand, and the Council and Assembly, on the other, were full of warmth. When

<hr/>

[1] *M. A. Hist.*, vol. xxvi., Feb. 26, 1769.   [2] *Ibid.*, May 6, 1769.

Council and Assembly refused to go to business because they were under duress from the close-at-hand troops, Bernard adjourned them to Cambridge, a move for which there was a precedent, and which before long was to be memorably repeated, giving rise to a controversy with which soon we shall have much to do. Bernard still tried to be conciliatory, making public letters he had just received, with the tenor of which he no doubt was fully in sympathy. The administration in England, it was asserted, was disposed to relieve all real grievances as to revenue acts: no further taxes were proposed, and those still in force, the Townshend taxes, namely, on paper, paint, glass, and tea, were quite certain to be greatly mitigated. The legislative authority of Parliament once admitted, all might go well.

The cause of the Colonies was forcefully upheld across the water, not only in the streets of London, but also in Parliament, where the most effective voice on that side had come to be that of Edmund Burke. Even Grenville declared the order requiring the rescinding of the Circular Letter an illegal one. Lord North, however, and the Earl of Hillsborough, the Secretary for the Colonies, were for breaking the spirits that murmured ; while the Duke of Bedford was active in favor of carrying to England the ringleaders for trial among strangers. Little probably would have resulted but for pressure from the traders. These, finding their American business ruined by the non-importation agreements, urged that Townshend's taxes should go the way of the Stamp Act, and this at last to a great extent came about. Paper, paints, and glass were freed; but to make it clear that the principle was not given up, the tax remained on tea, a scarcely appreciable impost in itself, but most heavily influential among the factors that brought about the Anglo-Saxon schism.

But Bernard's American days were over. His term in Massachusetts Bay had lasted eleven years, during the first part of which, as Hutchinson declared, he won much favor. Had his administration ended after five years, he would have been accounted one of the best of the Massachusetts Governors. But as determination grew among the people to govern themselves, he could by no means keep pace with the idea. He was a country gentleman and an Oxford scholar, and like all of his class in that day, an aristocrat. He was, however, a kindly man, with helpful instincts. He was a capital story-teller; [1] while his refined habits and accomplishments must have made him a distinguished figure in those days in any society not blinded by prejudice. The fact that he appreciated Shakespeare so keenly that he is said to have learned him by heart, indicates a literary taste quite unusual in that time. He was an excellent architect. He was an earnest friend of Harvard College, for which he designed Harvard Hall, showing in that and in other constructions that he was a master and leader in that colonial style whose decorous and comely grace our modern architects are pleased enough to catch. Had he been the blackest of traitors and villains, he could not have received worse

---

[1] "The best stocked with anecdotes of any man I ever knew, and fond of communicating them, which he could do with a good grace," says Hutchinson.

treatment than was poured out after him, when on the
last day of July he sailed down the harbor in the
Ripon, bound for home. He was accused of having
by his misrepresentations brought the troops to Boston
and put the Colony in danger of a change of charter.
Bollan, the son-in-law of Shirley, who had in a former
time done much toward getting for the Province the
Louisburg indemnity, was still on the stage, as agent
for the Massachusetts Council; for the Council now
as well as the House, it will be remembered, had its
English agent. Through him it was that six letters of
Bernard, written to affect parliamentary action at the
end of 1768, were obtained and sent back to America.
They were so important, it was felt, that they were considered on a Sunday by the Council, a procedure quite
extraordinary. The letters made it impossible for him
to live in the country. Yet it was entirely proper for
the chief magistrate to give his views as to what needed
to be done ; and not an idea was expressed as to a
policy expedient in the circumstances, different from
what he had expressed in the most open manner in his
papers to the legislature, and in his talk to those who
came in contact with him : there was, moreover, no
allegation respecting the conduct of the Province which
was not completely borne out by facts. He thought
the provincial governments should be brought to a uniform type ; the Assemblies he would have remain composed of popular representatives, but he thought the
Councils should consist of a kind of life-peers appointed
directly by the King. He believed also that government officers should be removed from dependence upon

legislative grants for their salaries. If governors, judges, and civil officers generally depended thus upon the people, how could any unpopular law ever be enforced; and how could any criminal who might succeed in ingratiating himself with the crowd ever be brought to justice? Certainly, for a prerogative man, these views were not unreasonable. Who will say now that such direct dependence upon the popular breath is expedient for governors and judges? Bernard never made pretense of holding other views; yet because they were advocated in these letters, which accompanied the plain story of what was said and done every day in the Province, he was denounced. He no doubt felt himself well compensated by the government favor he received. He was made a baronet; though absent from his post, he remained titular Governor, receiving half the salary, an equitable arrangement, since he was expected to contribute his time and knowledge to the Provincial service, though at Westminster instead of in Boston. The other half of the salary was to be paid to Hutchinson, who for two years was destined to remain Lieutenant-Governor, before becoming Governor in full. Could a son of the Province, born of its best stock, bred in the midst of its best influences, adorned with all sorts of honors won by long-continued and successful public service in places large and small, — could such a man do better with the administration than the man from beyond sea?

CHAPTER VII.

HUTCHINSON assumed his new prominence without alacrity, — with reluctance rather. On September 8, he urgently wishes that he may be allowed to retain the Chief Justiceship, and not be made Governor. In the former place he is sure he can do more good, and there he would prefer to work, even although the stipend is small and precarious.[1] The administration, however, would not have it otherwise, and he now stepped into the first place. He was fifty-eight years old, indeed a veteran. For ten years he had been Representative, during three years of which period he had been Speaker of the House. From 1749 to 1766, he had been every year of the Council. Besides these legislative positions, in the judicial field he had been Judge of Probate, of the Common Pleas, and Chief Justice; in the executive field, he had long been Lieutenant-Governor. Some years before, upon becoming Lieutenant-Governor, he had resigned his Justiceship of the Common Pleas in favor of his brother Foster. He now resigned as Judge of Probate, we may believe regretfully, from the following memorandum : —

" It gives me so much pleasure to relieve the widow and fatherless, and direct them what steps to take in

[1] *M. A. Hist.*, vol. xxvi., p. 374.

managing their estates, and also in reconciling contending parties, that I would rather resign my other offices, and discharge this alone without fee or reward."[1] While still nominally Chief Justice, he ceased to discharge the functions of the office. The assertion of the editor of the "Diary" is no doubt quite correct, that as Judge of Probate, Chief Justice, and Lieutenant-Governor combined, he had not received enough from the united stipends for the decent support of his family.

Precisely at the moment when Hutchinson's functions became thus simplified and exalted, a single figure stands out over against him in the front of the opposition with a definiteness which he has not before possessed, — Samuel Adams. Until now James Otis has, though with much fitfulness, been well forward in the leadership. From the departure of Bernard, however, he falls into the background, and henceforth needs to be reckoned with only seldom. How disease was making inroads on his fine powers, we best know from John Adams, who on September 3 writes: "Otis talks all; he grows the most talkative man alive; no other gentleman in company can find a space to put in a word. . . . He grows narrative like an old man."[2] On September 5, while at the British Coffee House in King Street, an altercation having arisen in which Otis, thus infirm, no doubt bore himself offensively, he was badly beaten by Robinson, one of the Commissioners of Customs, receiving injuries which apparently aggravated his insanity. From this time on he was to the Whig leaders

---

[1] Hutchinson's *Diary and Letters*, vol. i, p. 120.

[2] John Adams's Diary.

a subject of great perplexity. His judgment was quite
gone; he veered from opinion to opinion as his moods
swayed him ; his talk and conduct were often those of a
man demented; yet his eloquence to some extent remained, and the spell with which he influenced the
people was long in breaking. " Otis is in confusion
yet; he loses himself ; he rambles and wanders like a
ship without a helm ; attempted to tell a story which
took up almost all the evening. . . . In one word, Otis
will spoil the club. He talks so much, and takes up so
much of our time, and fills it with trash, obsceneness,
profaneness, nonsense, and distraction, that we have
none left for rational amusements or inquiries. . . . I
fear, I tremble, I mourn, for the man and for his
country ; many others mourn over him with tears in
their eyes." [1] One more extract may be quoted from
John Adams bearing upon Otis, which shows, among
other things, that others besides Hutchinson were open
to the charge of rapacious office-seeking. After detail-
ing certain detractions of which he had been the victim,
the diarist breaks out testily : " This is the rant of Mr.
Otis concerning me. . . . But be it known to Mr. Otis
I have been in the public cause as long as he, though I
was never in the General Court but one year. I have
sacrificed as much to it as he. I have never got my
father chosen Speaker and Counselor by it ; my brother-
in-law chosen into the House and chosen Speaker by it ;
nor a brother-in-law's brother-in-law into the House and
Council by it ; nor did I ever turn about in the House,
and rant it on the side of prerogative for a whole year,

[1] John Adams's Diary, Jan. 16, 1770.

to get a father into a Probate office and a first Justice
of a Court of Common Pleas, and a brother into a
clerk's office.   There is a complication of malice, envy,
and jealousy in this man, in the present disordered state
of his mind, that is quite shocking." [1]   In this incapa-
city of Otis, who was at last carried, bound hand and
foot, to confinement, Samuel Adams comes to the front
of the opposition, his adroitness being perhaps no more
conspicuous anywhere than in the manner in which he
humored and exploited the colleague, whom, though
sick, the people would not suffer to be withdrawn.

Hutchinson remarks [2] that the position of the chief
magistrate in 1769 was particularly discouraging.   He
was bound by his oath and the nature of his office to
submit to an authority which the majority had come
to reject.   As soon as the supremacy of Parliament
was called in question, a certain authority being still
conceded to it, but with no criterion to set the limits,
the chief magistrate's authority at once became ener-
vated.   At first this supremacy seemed to be admitted
in everything except taxes ; but exception had gradually
extended from one case to another until all functions
had become included.   A profession of subordination
remained, but it was a word without meaning.   The chief
magistrate, says Hutchinson, had now no aid from the
executive powers under him.   Not only did the Assembly refuse to join him in measures for repressing opposition, but the Council had gradually been brought to
the same sentiments.   Hutchinson could not even apply
to the troops for help.   They could not legally be

[1] John Adams's Diary, Oct. 27, 1772.   [2] *Hist.*, vol. iii., p. 256.

used except upon the requisition of a civil magistrate. Though chief executive, he thought it beyond his powers to make such a requisition, and he could find no civil magistrate, in the strong set of the popular current, who would come to his aid.

The Townshend duties were to be repealed, excepting upon the article tea. While the law stood on the statute-book, Hutchinson, though disapproving, thought it must be executed. As the year proceeded the opposition became constantly more bitter, the especial instrument of resistance being non-importation agreements, which all engaged in trade were now forced to sign. Boston, as ever, was the principal seat of agitation, and "merchants' meetings" were the means by which the popular party, convening with little discrimination the orderly elements with the rough crowd, forced the agreements upon the reluctant. October 28, a case of tarring and feathering occurred in the midst of much tumult, the victim being an informer against illicit traders; and at the same time the case of John Mein came up, a humble but most reputable sufferer, upon whom we can afford to spend a few minutes' attention. Mein, a Scotch printer, published the "Independent Chronicle," whose files, as they are preserved, do great credit to his skill in his craft: it is a handsome sheet, even judged by modern standards, but of Tory proclivities, and at this time had contained some ridicule of members of the caucus. Mein was also a bookseller: his advertisements give in long detail his importations, and speak favorably for his intelligence and enterprise. As the founder of circulating libraries in

Boston, his name should not be forgotten.[1] Mein, attacked by the mob, was goaded into firing a pistol, and was forced to take refuge at the main guard. In the Hutchinson papers is preserved the following appeal, copied here from Mein's autograph, written as he lay in durance : —

"Hon. Sir, — I now write to you as the principal civil officer in this province, to claim that protection to which every man in my situation has a legal right; I was last afternoon in open daylight attacked by a number of persons in a most vitious manner, and it was owing to the providence of Almighty God that I escaped with my life. Soon after I acquainted you with my situation and received no assistance ; and such is the disposition of my enemies in this town, that unless I am properly protected I cannot say what will be the consequence. I have just wrote to Mr. Foster Hutchinson desiring he would accompany a friend to the house where I now am to take some depositions against the persons who assaulted me ; and he refused to attend. I have desired two friends to sign this letter, that whatever may happen the blame may be fixed on the proper persons.   I am informed that the very persons who attacked me, and who struck me without even my returning it, only presenting a pistol to keep them off, have taken out a warrant against me. I am ready to surrender myself, provided I have a proper force to prevent any injury to my person from a licentious mob, and I make no doubt

[1] *The Massachusetts Gazette*, October 31, 1765, has a quaint and curious announcement of the establishment of Mein's Library.

I shall clear myself to the satisfaction of the impartial
world.　Also in the conversation with your Honour, I
asked if on the 5th of Nov. being a riotous day in
Boston, you could inform me of the name of any Justice of Peace that would engage to be at any particular
place if necessity required him to be called; to this
you answered you did not know any that would refuse
to do his duty.[1]　I then asked if your Honour would be
in town that night; you said you could not tell, and
told me, often, no previous steps could be taken, and
advised me against the memorial to you in Council.
The matter has now arisen to such a pitch that a proper
Guard of Military appears to me and my friends, to be
necessary, to attend to and from the Justices.

JOHN MEIN."[2]

Hutchinson describes this as the first mob since the
coming of the troops.　It was prepared for outrage;
like the mobs before and after, putting the town in terror; but it was not interfered with.　Hutchinson summoned the Council to him, who declared it inexpedient
to call out the troops.　He also convened the justices of
the peace, whom he instructed solemnly in their duties as
to the preservation of order, but could make no impression, one declaring that a man must be in danger of
being torn in pieces " for opposing the whole continent
in the only measure which could save them from ruin."
In all their disorder the people were greatly encouraged from England, from which quarter they had been

---

[1] A little later Hutchinson would not have said this.
[2] *M. A. Hist.*, vol. xxv., p. 455.

abundantly taught by great men, both in the Lords and
Commons, that there should be no taxation without
representation. The body of the people, it was said
probably with truth, strongly upheld the colonists; in
fact was embarked in the same cause with them. Nothing is plainer than that this struggle, becoming now
so acute, was not between England and America, but
between two parties, both of which existed as well in
England as in America. At this time pamphlets came
to the American Whigs from their fellow-fighters in
England, maintaining what till recently had been such
advanced doctrine, that the King, by his Governor,
Council, and House, made up the rightful legislature of
the Colony, and that Parliament must be excluded.
Hawley was thus emboldened to declare, " he knew not
how Parliament could have acquired a right to legislate
over the Colonies;" and Samuel Adams said in Town-
meeting: "Independent we are, and independent we
will be!"[1] As yet this was called bold language.
A certain supremacy in Parliament was still generally
admitted, but so attenuated and undefined as to be
scarcely palpable. An indispensable part of a Govern-
or's duties was to make a report of public matters to
the King's ministers. The simplest recitals of events,
claims Hutchinson, were pronounced misrepresentations
made with a view to bring on vindictive measures.

With the beginning of 1770, it became plain that a
fierce explosion was not far off, though the fire was still
for a time suppressed. Thomas and Elisha, the Lieutenant-Governor's sons, now men grown, and starting in

[1] *Hist.*, vol. iii., p. 264.

their native town as traders, suddenly became prominent figures with their father in the anti-popular party.
Under force the young men had signed the non-importation agreements; but resenting what they felt to be
restrictions quite uncalled for and unauthorized, they
had caused a padlock placed upon the door of their warehouse to be broken, and in other ways proceeded too
spiritedly against the popular will.   The mob came at
once to Hutchinson's house, and its inmates must have
had very vividly in mind what they had gone through
five years before.   Others who had taken the same stand
as Thomas and Elisha were in similar danger.   Hutchinson convened the Council, urging them to join with
him in requiring the justices to order out the troops.
They, as before, declined acting though declaring their
disapproval of mobs.   He then summoned the justices
and exhorted them on his own responsibility to discharge
their duty.   Their straightforward answer was "that
the assemblies might be unwarrantable, but there
were times when irregularities could not be restrained.
The people were now much disturbed by danger to
their just rights and liberties.   It was therefore not
incumbent on them to act."   The assemblies meantime
declared they unanimously believed that their coming
together was lawful, and that they should act conscien-
tiously.   With February came the first actual bloodshed in connection with the tumults, an inferior custom-
house officer, whose windows were being broken by the
mob, killing with a pistol-shot, fired at random, a
German boy of twelve, who was forthwith buried with
immense demonstration.   Though there is no reason

to think that Hutchinson's nerve failed at all through these difficult scenes, he was tortured by indecision as to what was the wise and legal course for him to pursue. And how could it be otherwise? Whether or not it lay within his power to call out the troops was something he could not decide. No civil magistrate could be found to do it. If it was done, he must do it. He afterwards regretted he did not assume the responsibility. He yielded to advice to remain inactive " without sufficiently considering the consequences," and felt more distress of mind from this error than when his house was destroyed.[1] He was triumphed over and reproached for the concession by the men who under color of friendship advised it.[2] But the collision which he was so anxious to postpone must of necessity come. Dalrymple, the Lieutenant-Colonel in command, was a prudent officer, and it must be said kept his men under remarkable control in the midst of the provocations that were showered upon them. The grievance of the people was real; their resistance manful and quite justified; though the insults and assaults in which they vented their discontent were coarse and terrible. Nothing is better known

[1] *Hist.*, vol. iii., p. 266.

[2] When Hutchinson went to England at a later time, he talked this matter over with Wedderburn, afterward Lord Loughborough, the famous English lawyer. Wedderburn told him the King's law servants, especially the Lord Chancellor, thought the chief magistrate could call on troops to fire in a riot ; that he himself, however, was in doubt. Hutchinson's uncertainty seems to have been not without grounds. *Diary and Letters*, vol. i., p. 183.

What care was thought necessary in calling out the troops in case of riots appeared singularly at the time of the Gordon riots in London, in 1780.   Lord Mahon : *Hist. of Eng.*, vol. vii.

among the events of our history than the Boston
Massacre. Hutchinson gives it with full detail in the
History. Here is what he wrote at the time to Hillsboro, his heart palpitating with the agitation of the
moment.

"BOSTON, March, 1770.

" MY LORD, — There has for a long time subsisted
great animosity between the inhabitants of this town
and the troops. . . . The 5th, in the evening near ten
o'clock, one of the bells of the town near where I dwell
was rung, and I supposed it to be for fire, but in a few
moments several of the inhabitants came running into
my house intreating me immediately to come out or the
town would be all in blood, the soldiers having killed a
great number of the inhabitants, and the people in general being about to arm themselves. I went out without delay in order to go to the Council Chamber, as the
people were killed in King Street near to it, but was
soon surrounded by a great body of men, many of them
armed with clubs, some with cutlasses, and all calling
for their firearms. I discovered myself to them and
endeavored to prevail on them to hear me, but was
soon obliged for my own safety to go into a house and
by a private-way into King Street, the people having
returned there expecting me. After assuring them that
a due inquiry should be made and justice done as far as
it was in my power, and prevailing with the commanding officers of the troops in the street to retire with
them to their barracks, the people dispersed. Expresses had gone out to the neighboring towns, and the
inhabitants were called out of their beds, many of whom

armed themselves, but were stopped from coming into town by advice that there was no further danger that night. A barrel of tar which was carrying to the Beacon to set on fire was also sent back. Upon examination before two Justices of the Peace, Capt. Preston of the 29th, who had the command of the Guard, was committed to prison for being charged with ordering the troops to fire, and seven or eight privates charged with firing. Four persons were killed, two more are said to be mortally wounded, divers others wounded, but not in such danger. Among them is a gentleman of the town, who, standing at his door, was shot in the arm and the bones splintered. How far the affronts and abuses offered by the inhabitants may avail to excuse this action is uncertain, but it is certain that nothing more unfortunate could have happened, for a very great part of the people were in a perfect frenzy by means of it.

"I summoned all the members of the Council who were near enough to meet the next morning. When I came to them I found the selectmen of the town and a great part of the Justices of the county waiting for me at the Council Chamber, to represent to me their opinion of the absolute necessity of the troops being at a distance that there may be no intercourse between the inhabitants, to prevent a further effusion of blood. The selectmen acquainted me they had been applied to, to call a town-meeting, and that the inhabitants would be under no restraint whilst the troops were in the town. I let them know that I had no power to remove the troops. I then sent to desire

Col. Dalrymple and Col. Carr to be present in Council. Soon after a message came by a large committee from the town to me being in Council. I told the Council also that the removal of the troops was not with me, and I desired them to consider what answer I could give to this application of the town whilst Col. Dalrymple, who had the command, was present. The principal quarrels had been with the 29th Regiment, and upon hearing from the Council what they had to urge, Col. Dalrymple let me know that he was willing the 29th should go into the barracks at the Castle, and engaged that the 14th should be so disposed in Boston as to prevent occasions of dispute between the inhabitants and the regiment. I thereupon signified to the Committee of the town what Col. Dalrymple had agreed to, repeating to them also what I said to the selectmen, that the ordering of the troops did not lie with me. Upon report made to the town, they, by a general vote, declared that they could not be satisfied unless both regiments were at the Castle.

"I met the Council again in the afternoon, when the commanding officers of both regiments, and also Capt. Caldwell, of his Majesty's Ship Rose, were present. I would have desired some other Crown officers to have been there, but I knew the Council would not consent to it. The town soon sent a second committee to me, and with their vote, which I required the Council to give me their advice upon. They advised me to desire Col. Dalrymple to remove the 14th regiment also to the barracks at the Castle, and with one voice most earnestly urged it upon me." [1]

[1] *M. A. Hist.*, vol. xxvi., p. 452.

Samuel Adams's famous " Both regiments or none!" carried the day. In almost the only exultant passage of his writings, he described afterwards how before him Hutchinson's eye quailed and his knees trembled. It was not, however, through cowardice. The embarrassments of the situation for the chief magistrate were really appalling. Respectable men at that time and at other times disavowed the outrages ; Lord Mahon's remark cannot, however, be regarded as hitting wide of the facts : " No doubt in a large majority of cases these disavowals were perfectly well-founded : still, however, the suspicion remains that the rabble on these occasions was set in movement and directed by some persons of higher rank and larger views of mischief than themselves." [1] None of the mobs, of that time of mobs, was more brutal and truculent than that which provoked the firing of the little group of baited men, standing their ground with steady discipline, among the clubs and missiles resorted to now to enforce the usual foul and blasphemous abuse. Hutchinson fulfilled at this time with complete adequacy the functions of chief magistrate. He was at once, in the street, in imminent danger of having his brains dashed out,[2] expostulating, entreating that order might be observed. It was a fine exhibition of power and courage, that, standing in the

---

[1] *Hist. of England,* vol. v., p. 265.

[2] " Witness at trial of soldiers said : ' He stood close behind me, . . . and that one of the mob lifted up a large club over my head, and was going to strike, but that he seized him by the arm and prevented it.' I remember some people hurried me into the Town-House and told me I was not safe there [in the streets], but I did not then know the occasion of it." Letter, May 22, 1770, *M. A. Hist.,* vol. xxvi., p. 491.

east balcony of the State House, with the snow reddened beneath by the blood of the massacred, with the
regiments kneeling in rank ready for street firing, and
several thousands of enraged men on the other side on
the point of rushing into fight, he was able to hold
both parties in check. His prompt arrest of Preston
and the squad which had done the killing was his full
duty; and it is to the credit of the troops that the
officer and his men, in the midst of the exasperation,
gave themselves quietly into the hands of the law.

In the famous scenes which followed, the next day,
— the pressure of the town for the removal of the
troops, brought to bear with such consummate force
and address by Samuel Adams, the resolute, manful,
self-assertion of the matchless Town-Meeting leader is
admirable; but, on the other hand, neither the Lieutenant-Governor nor the troops, if their position is rightly
estimated, were wanting in good conduct. Two weak
regiments, together amounting to not more than six hundred effective men, isolated in a populous Province
which hated them, were in great peril of life. It does
not appear that they showed the white feather at all,
but rather that they wished to be law-abiding. Hutchinson refused to order the removal of the troops at the
demand of the town, on the ground that it transcended
his powers to do so, — a position quite correct. The
troops had come not through him, but through the
ministry; and his assertion that Gage alone, the commander at New York, could order them here or there,
was true. The position of Dalrymple was trying in
the extreme; but if scanned closely it will appear that

he was solicitous to be prudent and forbearing, rather than that he wanted courage. Sir Samuel Hood, afterwards one of the best naval captains of the great period of Rodney and Nelson, at this time commander on the Boston station, testifies in strong terms to Dalrymple's excellence as an officer.[1] Although from that day to this it has been held that the British uniform was driven with ignominy out of the streets of Boston, the "Sam. Adams Regiments" deserve no discredit for their conduct. Dalrymple was not censured by his superiors at the time, though the popular outcry, on the one hand exultant, on the other full of mortification, was very loud. As to the troops, probably few organizations of the British army have a record more honorable. The 14th was with William III. in Flanders; it formed, too, one of the squares at Waterloo, breasting for hours the charges of the French cuirassiers until it had nearly melted away. The 29th was with Marlboro at Ramillies; with Wellington in the Peninsula it bore a heavy part, as may be read in Napier, in wresting Spain from the grasp of Napoleon. A mistaken policy had put the regiments into a position where they deserved pity; to fight it out with the mob would no doubt have been far easier and pleasanter than to yield. For brave soldiers, to forbear is harder than to charge; and one may be sure that, in the long history of those regiments, few experiences more trying came to pass than those of the Boston streets.

Again, the town of Boston was quite right in its contention. The basal principles of Anglo-Saxon free-

[1] Frothingham's *Warren*, p. 116.

dom were being violated by the people in power; the
stubborn resistance of the town, however unlovely and
coarse its incidents may have been, was thoroughly right
and manly, and of incalculable advantage to all future
generations of English-speaking men. Very fine, too,
was the determination of the town soon afterward,
that Preston and his men should have a fair trial; and
the standing forth in their defense of the two conspicuous patriots, John Adams and Josiah Quincy, who
left no stone unturned to secure full justice for their
clients. Instead of a bloody battle, there was sub-
stituted a well-ordered civil process, due delay being
observed that the passions of both sides might subside,
and the evidence, pro and con, be calmly weighed. A
mild and thoroughly just verdict was the outcome, to
which all submitted.

Men they were, all of the same stock, for the time
being fallen into antagonism. All saw but a little
way, — had but a feeble comprehension of how the
trouble had come to pass, and no foreknowledge of
the momentous sequel that lay before. All, however,
bore themselves like good Anglo-Saxon men, showing
strongly the quality which has made the race a mighty
one.

Hutchinson so far in his life had had nothing so trying to meet as the circumstances which had prevailed
in Massachusetts from the departure of Bernard at
the end of July to the Boston Massacre at the beginning of March. Naturally, we shall find in his letters
a more unreserved expression of his mind than in his
formal History. To Lord Hillsboro he was in duty

bound to make reports of news and suggestions as to remedies for the trouble. To Bernard, an old friend, who still nominally was his superior, he would, of course, write, and more unreservedly than in his official notes to the Secretary for the Colonies. To Richard Jackson, also, he unbosomed himself quite fully, as to a man he cordially liked. To Bernard he says, October 4, 1769, " I must entreat you not to suffer the contents of my letters to come to the knowledge of any New England man, for everything they hear to have been wrote from hence comes back in their letters," — a reasonable caution enough, and one which he often hereafter expresses, in view of the case of Bernard's letters, such use of which had been made to thrust the Governor into disfavor. From Hutchinson's point of view the " merchants' meetings," urging the rigorous nonimportation schemes by way of resistance to the Townshend Tax Act, were distinctly seditious. These, therefore, are consistent expressions to Jackson, October 4 :[1] " I wish I could write you agreeable news of the temper of the people here. The confederacy of the merchants is certainly a very high offense, and the Sons of Liberty are the greatest tyrants which were ever known, for they will suffer no man to use his property but just in such a way as they approve of, and I can find no one to join with me in an attempt to discourage them. . . . People in general here suppose that they have a strong party in England which think all that has been done here is constitutional, and an expedient measure to bring Parliament to reason."[2] " A thousand acts of

[1] M. A. Hist., vol. xxvi., p. 383.   [2] M. A. Hist., vol. xxvi., p. 385.

Parliament will never have the least force, if combinations to prevent the operation of them and to sacrifice all who will conform to them are tolerated, or if towns are allowed to meet and vote that measures for defeating such acts are legal. A vigorous spirit in Parliament will yet set us right. Without, the government of this Province will be split into innumerable divisions, every town, every parish, and every particular club or connexion will meet and vote, and carry their votes into execution just as they please. . . . As to the non-importation agreement, if Parliament pass it over, I shall have nothing left but to sit down and pray silently, Lord, open the eyes of these men that they may see." [1]

The clearest expression of his displeasure with the Town-Meeting, and how he would have it restrained, I find in the following : " The powers given to towns were never intended by law to extend farther than for the management of the immediate concerns of each town, such as choosing their officers, raising money for their necessary charges and the like, and if the law had its course, I think every meeting for any other purpose would be an unlawful assembly, and it would be an aggravation of the offense that law is made a pretense for it. These meetings introduced the mob meetings to support the non-importation scheme which have weakened govt. beyond every thing else, having convinced the people that whenever they thought fit to assemble there is no interior power to disperse them or to punish them for anything they do when assembled. There is at present no chance for suppressing such illegal meet-

[1] Letter to Bernard, October 6, 1769.

ings by any power within the province. My hopes have been from an Act of Parliament subjecting all persons concerned in any such confederacies to incapacities for civil privileges and such penalties of the statute of Præmunire as may be judged proper." [1]

"January 9. There has prevailed in all the Colonies an opinion that by a resolute opposition we should bring Parliament to submit. We have some mad, desperate people amongst us who would be for resisting to the last drop of blood rather than we should submit ourselves; but I flatter myself this is the sense of but a very few; and the best, when they see Parliament determined to maintain at all costs its authority over the Colonies will think it madness to resist; and when they find this authority exercised with the utmost tenderness, and feel the revival of internal government and good order, they will cheerfully submit." [2]   In the foregoing passage we have again the doctrine from which Hutchinson never departs. The Colonies must acknowledge a supreme authority in Parliament in all imperial questions; that once admitted, the ruling hand must wear the glove of velvet, the power obtruded only in the rarest instances. So he wrote in the hope that it would be heeded in England.

In 1754, at Albany, Hutchinson had been not at all unfavorable to Franklin's scheme for a Colonial union. Such a thing still might be an advantage. "One of the Council of New York writes by the last post that nothing can restore America but a Lord Lieutenant and

[1] To Hillsboro, October 9, 1770, *M. A. Hist.*, vol. xxv., p. 443.
[2] *M. A. Hist.*, vol. xxvi., p. 430.

an American Parliament, and however jealous they may
be of it in England, yet they will find the spirit of
democracy so persevering that they will be obliged at
last to come into it." Hutchinson thinks one government of this kind quite impracticable: there must be
three, the Colonies occupying a territory 1500 miles in
extent. 1, Nova Scotia and New England. 2d, New
York and Virginia. 3rd, the Southern Colonies.
With such a division he thinks a scheme for broader
unions feasible, — possibly desirable. " February 18. In
settling the several parts of the plan occasion may be
taken to reform the constitution of the several governments of which the general governments shall consist,
and to ascertain the general authority of Parliament
over the whole. There is one visible advantage from
such a plan. If the general government shall be
persons of rank and of the nobility who have the best
talents for government, and they continue only two or
at most three years, by their knowledge after their
return of the state of America Parliament would be
better able to make such provision from time to time
as shall be necessary. Be this as it may, it is certainly
best to make some stir. To be still only gives time for
the principles of independence to spread and to be confirmed. Every year they gain strength, and in a short
time will be universally avowed. What a noise it made
when Hawley said in the House that he doubted the
authority of Parliament to legislate for America! But
now we see every newspaper asserting we are not subject to acts of Parliament farther than we consent to
receive them. Nay, I am frequently told in Council

that unconstitutional acts are not obligations."[1] " Erving said to me in Council that it would be time enough for them to advise against such meetings when they had intelligence that the Supporters of the Bill of Rights were suppressed in England."[2]

Turning from these high and serious matters, it will be a relief to take a look at the chief magistrate in quite a different phase. Here is his order for clothes, sent to London after his elevation. We may suppose them to have arrived by the time of the Massacre, and can narrowly know how the handsome man of fifty-nine must have looked as he schemed and argued against his contumacious people. " October 5, 1769. To Mr. Peter Leitch : I desire to have you send me a blue cloth waistcoat trimmed with the same color, lined, the skirts and facings, with effigeen, and the body linnen to match the last blue cloath I had from you : — two under waistcoats or camisols of warm swansdown, without sleeves, faced with some cheap silk or shagg. A suit of cloaths full-trimmed, the cloath something like the enclosed, only more of a gray mixture, gold button and hole, but little wadding lined with effigeen. I like a wrought, or flowered, or embroidered hole, something though not exactly like the hole upon the cloaths of which the pattern is enclosed ; or if frogs are worn, I think they look well on the coat ; but if it be quite irregular, I would have neither one nor the other, but such a hole and button as are worn. I know a laced coat is more the mode, but this is too gay for me. A pair of worsted breeches to match the color, and a pair of black velvet breeches,

[1] February 18, 1770.   [2] *M. A. Hist.*, vol. xxvi., p. 443.

the breeches with leather linings. Let them come by
the first ship. P. S. If there be no opportunity before
February, omit the camisols, and send a green waistcoat,
the forebodies a strong corded silk, — not the *cor du
soie*, but looks something like it, — the sleeves and
bodies sagathee or other thin stuff, body lined with
linen, skirts silk. My last cloaths were rather small in
the arm-holes, but the alterations must be very little,
next to nothing." [1] The Lieutenant-Governor grows a
little stout with years, but holds his shape well.

[1] *M. A. Hist.*, vol. xxvi., p. 386.

CHAPTER VIII.

ACCESSION TO THE GOVERNORSHIP.

" MAY 18th. Hitherto we have gone no farther than to disown the authority of Parliament; but now even the King is allowed little or no share in the government except the appointing of a Governor, who is not to be directed by his Majesty, nor subject to his instructions. This publication is not indeed the act of the Province, but it is the act of a town whose influence extends to every other town in the Province." [1]

These words to Hillsboro will serve to introduce the controversy with the legislature which had succeeded to the earlier disagreements, and which was destined to be long and important, — as to how far the chief magistrate could be bound by royal instructions.

As yet, since the departure of Bernard, there had been no session of the General Court. In March, one took place, which at the very beginning was signalized by a new dispute between the Lieutenant-Governor and the legislature. Says Hutchinson : " The Assembly was prorogued to meet at Boston the 14th of March, 1770, but before that time arrived there came a further signification of the King's pleasure that it should be held in Cambridge, unless the Lieutenant-Governor had more weighty reasons for holding it at

[1] To Hillsboro, *M. A. Hist.*, vol. xxvi., p. 485.

Boston than those which were mentioned by the Secretary of State against it.   He was not able to offer such reasons as he had any ground to suppose would justify him with the King, and therefore he considered the instructions tantamount to a peremptory order." [1]

On the 15th of March, therefore, the legislature met in the "Philosophy Room," in Harvard College, in Cambridge.   After the customary opening speech of the chief magistrate, the following remonstrance was at once presented against the removal of the legislature from Boston, the Council joining with the House : " By an act passed in the tenth year of his late Majesty, King William, of glorious memory, which received his royal approbation, and is now in force, the form of a writ for calling the General Assembly is established ; wherein it is ordered that the General Assembly be convened, held, and kept in the Town House in Boston.   Hence it appears that the Town House in Boston is by law established as the only place for holding the Assembly ; and we take the liberty to express our sentiments that no instruction ought to be deemed of sufficient force to invalidate the law.   With regard to the instruction, which seems to lie with so much weight on your Honor's mind, we would observe that when a bill was brought into the British Parliament to give the royal instructions in the Colonies the force of laws, the Commons then asserted the rights of the people, and rejected it with disdain." [2]

[1] *Hist.*, vol. iii., p. 280.   See, also, letter to Daniel Leonard, Sept. 2, 1775, *Diary and Letters*, vol. i., p. 526.

[2] Bradford : *State Papers*, p. 200.

To this Hutchinson saw fit to reply "that with as much reason they might except to the authority of the King to give instructions in many, if not all, other cases, as in the removal of the Assembly. The Crown, neither by charter, nor in any other way, had ever divested itself of its authority to instruct its Governor." [1] That the King, by his prerogative, could interfere to remove the legislature from the "Town House in Boston," did not in his mind admit of a doubt, and therefore he disregarded the remonstrance.

During this session of the legislature Samuel Adams wrote most of the state papers, and was the working member of the important committees. Hawley stood at his right hand, exercising an influence over the country members (who were not always without jealousy of the "Boston seat") even greater than that of Adams, though he was less constantly active. In the Council, James Bowdoin occupied a position corresponding to that of Adams in the House. Hutchinson declares that the legislature, much more the people at large, ought not to be judged from the votes and messages. "They were the compositions of a very few, probably most of them of one person in each house." [2] He thought he could manage the legislature and the Province but for the one town and its representatives. "All the House can do will be a perfect trifle compared with the trouble the town of Boston gives me. If the town could be separated from the rest of the Province ! Something must be done to humble the leaders of the town. The body of the people are all of one mind,

---

[1] *Hist.*, vol. iii., p. 304.   [2] *Hist.*, vol. iii., p. 306.

and there is no stemming the torrent. It is the common language of Adams and the rest that they are not to be intimidated by acts of Parliament, for they will not be executed here." [1]

The House took pains, while proceeding to business, to make it clear that they did not renounce their claim to a legal right to sit in the town-house in Boston; and after a session of a few weeks were dissolved, near the end of April. When the elections for the new Assembly took place, as usual at the beginning of May, the popular leaders were enthusiastically sustained, Samuel Adams receiving all but three out of five hundred and thirteen votes cast in Town-Meeting, and John Hancock all but two. Otis was replaced by James Bowdoin; and since he went at once into the Council, John Adams was chosen in his stead, appearing now in the legislature for the first time, and assuming at once a position of importance. On the 15th of May instructions of unusual eloquence were addressed to the new representatives, prepared by the young Josiah Quincy. In more distinct terms than ever before revolt was anticipated. Resistance was recommended even to the uttermost; the deputies were urged to use means to rouse a military spirit in the people, to cultivate union with the other Colonies, and hints were dropped about " dogs of war, let loose and hot for blood, rushing on to waste and havoc."

Hancock, who, through his wealth and popular gifts, was a most important man, required to be managed

---

[1] Letter of March, 1770, cited in Wells : *Life of Samuel Adams*, vol. i., p. 335.

with almost as much care and tact as the crazy Otis. His sensitiveness was easily touched, and a little wise manipulation from the "Master of the Puppets," Samuel Adams, was often required to keep him well at work in the company of the Whigs. Generally, throughout the lives of the two men, Hancock's admiration and friendship for Samuel Adams were sincere and hearty, broken, however, by intervals of estrangement, which, later on, were sometimes long continued.

During the session, which began at the end of May, Cushing as usual being Speaker and Samuel Adams, clerk, the controversy with the Lieutenant-Governor proceeded, as to the confining of the General Court to Cambridge. Efforts were also made to obtain the accounts transmitted to England by the royal officials of the conduct of Boston at the time of the Massacre, — accounts upon which the action of the government would be based, and yet which were carefully withheld from the Colonists, so that it should be out of their power, the Whigs declared, to answer misrepresentations. In the correspondence, the pen of Samuel Adams was as usual employed. Hutchinson, dissatisfied, prorogued them in June, to meet again in July, at which time Samuel Adams for the House replied to the address of Hutchinson in terms which indicate how rapidly the growth of indignant and independent feeling had proceeded : —

"After the most attentive and repeated examination of your speech, we find nothing to induce us to alter our opinion and very little that is new and material in the controversy. . . ."

" You are pleased to say, ' you meet us at Cambridge, because you have no reason to think there has been any alterations in his Majesty's pleasure, which you doubt not was determined by wise motives, and with a gracious purpose to promote the good of the Province.' . . .

" This House have great reason to doubt whether it is, or ever was, his Majesty's pleasure that your Honor should meet the Assembly at Cambridge, or that he has ever taken the matter under his royal consideration; because the common and the best evidence in such cases is not communicated to us.

" It is needless for us to add anything to what has been heretofore said upon the illegality of holding the Court anywhere except in the town of Boston. . . .

" The opinion of the Attorney and Solicitor-General has very little weight with this House in any case, any further than the reasons which they expressly give are convincing. This Province has suffered so much by unjust, groundless, and illegal opinions of those officers of the crown, that our veneration or reverence for their opinions is much abated. We utterly deny that the Attorney and Solicitor-General have any authority or jurisdiction over us, any right to decide questions in controversy between the several branches of the Legislature here. Nor do we concede, that even his Majesty in Council has any constitutional authority to decide such questions, or any controversy whatever, that arises in this Province, excepting only such matters as are reserved in the charter. . . .

" The House are still ready to answer for the ill con-

sequences which can be justly attributed to them ; nor
are they sensible of any danger from exerting the power
which the charter has given them, of doing their part
of the business in their own time. That the Province
has enemies, who are continually defaming it and their
charter, is certain ; that there are persons who are en-
deavoring to intimidate the Province from asserting and
vindicating their just rights and liberties, by insinuations of danger to the Constitution, is also indisputable.
But no instance happened, even in the execrable reign
of the worst of the Stuart race, of a forfeiture of a
charter, because any one branch of a legislative, or even
because the whole government under that charter, refused to do business at a particular time under grievous
circumstances of ignominy, disgrace, and insult ; and
when their charter had explicitly given to that government the sole power of judging of the proper season
and occasion of doing business. We are obliged, at
this time, to struggle with all the powers with which the
Constitution has furnished us, in defence of our rights,
to prevent the most valuable of our liberties from being
wrested from us by the subtle machinations and daring
encroachments of wicked ministers. We have seen of
late innumerable encroachments on our charter : Courts
of Admiralty extended from the high seas, where by
the compact in the charter they are confined, to num-
berless important causes upon land ; multitudes of civil
officers, the appointment of all which is by charter confined to the Governor and Council, sent here from
abroad by the Ministry ; a revenue not granted by us,
but torn from us ; armies stationed here without our

consent ; and the streets of our metropolis *crimsoned* with the blood of our fellow-subjects. These and other grievances and cruelties, too many to be here enumerated, and too melancholy to be much longer borne by this injured people, we have seen brought upon us by the devices of ministers of state. We have seen and heard, of late, instructions to governors which threaten to destroy all the remaining privileges of our charter. In June, 1768, the House by an instruction were ordered to rescind an excellent resolution of a former House on pain of dissolution : they refused to comply with so impudent a mandate, and were dissolved : and the Governor, though repeatedly requested, and although the exigencies of the Province demanded a General Assembly, refused to call a new one until the following May. In the last year, the General Court was forced to give way to regular troops, illegally quartered in the town of Boston, in consequence of instructions to crown officers, and whose main guard was most daringly and insultingly placed at the door of the State-House ; and afterwards they were constrained to hold their session at Cambridge. The present year the Assembly is summoned to meet, and is still continued there in a kind of duress, without any reason that can be given, any motive whatever that is not as great an insult to them and breach of their privilege as any of the foregoing. Are these things consistent with the freedom of the House ? or could the General Court's tamely submitting to such usage be thought to promote his Majesty's service ? Should these struggles of the House prove unfortunate and ineffectual, this Province will submit, with pious resignation, to the will of Providence ; but it will be a kind of suicide, of which we have the utmost horror, thus to be the instruments of our own servitude." [1]

Hutchinson, in answering, referred particularly to their having called the instructions an " *impudent mandate*." " It may not," he says, " be presumed you would have done this, had you known it to be an order from his Majesty. I wish however that you had spared this coarse and indecent epithet . . . The freedom you have used with the characters of the Attorneys and Solicitors General will, I fear, likewise bring dishonor upon you." [2]

He argued ably the right of convening the General Court elsewhere than in Boston, and again prorogued the Assembly, this time to September. He thought he had in some measure weakened the opposition, and hoped for still greater advances. To a friend in London he wrote the next day : —

" The House having persisted in their refusal to do business, I have prorogued them to a further time, having gained over, in this short session, enough of the Council to prevent Bowdoin from obtaining a vote for an address which he had prepared conformable to the sentiments of the faction of the House ; and I hope to keep a party there strong enough to defeat his future attempts. Neither Worthington, Murray, Ruggles, nor any member capable of opposing Adams, &c., came to the session. Many, if not a majority of the members, wish to go to business, but are afraid. I will have a full House another session, and have yet encouragement

[1] Bradford's *State Papers*, p. 240, etc.   [2] *Ibid.*, p. 249.

that I shall carry the point then, notwithstanding the
unanimity now.

"I did not design to enter into any argument with
them, but I found it necessary to undeceive the people,
and, since my speech, I perceive a great alteration among
them, and it will certainly have a good effect. The
answer, drawn by Adams, breathes the seditious spirit
which has appeared in Edes and Gills's paper. The
rudeness to the King, to the House of Commons, to the
Ministers of State, the declarations of independence,
the menaces of an appeal to Heaven, and the people's
no longer bearing with their injuries without seeking
redress, — plainly hinting a downright revolt, — are so
criminal and at the same time so daring, that some
notice will be taken of it, if the nation is to be aroused
by anything." [1]

And two days later : " Worthington, Ruggles, Murray, nor any other persons not afraid of Adams and the
Bostoneers, would attend. If I could persuade a few to
exert themselves, the point would be carried in the
House another session." [2]

A glance at the Journal of the Assembly during this
session shows at once the prominence to which the
" Boston seat " had attained, and that of the four members the Adamses were the moving spirits. Governor
Shirley, now old and living in retirement at his house
in Roxbury, used to follow the controversies in the
newspapers. " Who are the Boston seat ? " he one day
asked, during the discussion of this session. He was

[1] Hutchinson to Bernard, August 3, 1770.
[2] Hutchinson to Bernard, August 5, 1770.

answered, " Mr. Cushing, Mr. Hancock, Mr. Samuel
Adams, and Mr. John Adams." " Mr. Cushing I knew,
and Mr. Hancock I knew," replied the old Governor,
" but where the Devil this brace of Adamses came from,
I know not." " This," says John Adams, " was archly
circulated by the ministerialists, to impress the people
with the obscurity of the original of the *par nobile fra-
trum*, as the friends of the country used to call us by
way of retaliation." [1]

As the summer proceeded, the non-importation
agreement weighed heavily upon many among the merchants ; it was broken extensively in New York, and
the example was followed elsewhere. The government,
too, took an important step which must be related.
By an order coming from the King in Council, Boston
harbor was made the rendezvous of ships stationed on
the North American coast, while the Castle, it was in-
dicated, must be garrisoned by regular troops. The
charter of the Province distinctly required that the
Castle and forts should be under command of the Governor ; so when General Gage sent instructions to
Hutchinson to deliver Castle William to Colonel Dalrymple, a violation of the charter seemed to the Whigs
inevitable, if the order were complied with. Hutchinson
at once obeyed, withdrawing the Provincial troops who
had made up the garrison, and turning the fortress with
its stores over to the regulars. In so doing he felt he
by no means violated the charter. " I told the Council," he writes, " I should give up no right which they
had by charter. The Governor was to commit the cus-

[1] *Works*, vol. ii., p. 233.

tody and government of forts to such persons as to
himself should seem meet. It now seemed meet to me
to commit the Castle to Colonel Dalrymple, to be garrisoned by the regulars. What induced me to this, I
was not liable to be questioned or called to account
for." [1] Hutchinson declares that this affair was one
of the most difficult to manage which came up during
his administration. "There happened," he says, "to
be a very grand meeting of merchants and tradesmen
upon the subject of importation, when Adams made an
attempt to inflame them, declaring I had given up the
Castle and would give up the charter; but some of
the merchants declared that was not the business of the
meeting, and repeatedly stopped him from going on."

Before the excitement had in any degree subsided,
the legislature, prorogued to September, met, and at
once took the Lieutenant-Governor to task for his conduct. He replied substantially in the terms already
quoted, always wary and plausible, and taking positions
which in one friendly to Parliament and prerogative
were quite reasonable. The Assembly on their side,
through Samuel Adams, pressed him hard, and the
leader spoke out in the public press still more strongly;
for there he could lay aside the conventional formalities
and terms of assumed respect, proper in a legislative
document.

The non-importation agreement had now thoroughly
fallen through everywhere. Samuel Adams expressed
regret at its failure, but said it had lasted longer than
he had expected. He began to hint significantly at

[1] Wells : *Life of Samuel Adams*, vol. i., p. 356.

other means of resistance, and held himself ready to revive also this scheme, if opportunity should occur. Gradually, too, there had appeared in the legislature a disposition to yield the point for which they had lately been struggling with the Lieutenant-Governor. The House had at one time been nearly unanimous against proceeding to business while constrained to meet in Cambridge. In the fall of 1770, the House was small, many country members being discouraged from attending by the prorogations, which made their journeys from home of no avail. The spirit of opposition, too, was much weakened, and symptoms of schism appeared in the ranks of the Whigs, which were ominous of trouble to them in time to come. A Committee of Correspondence, too, set on foot at the instance of Samuel Adams, to communicate with the agent in England and the Speakers of the different Colonial Assemblies, had only a languishing activity. Such a committee had long been a favorite scheme of Samuel Adams. We have seen the first hint of it in the instructions of 1764. The " Circular Letter " of 1768 had been a step in the same direction : the time for its full realization had not arrived ; a vivid remembrance existed of the resentment produced by the previous attempts of the Colonies to reach an understanding with one another, which few as yet cared to arouse again. The present committee was, however, the precedent for one which was at length to come, and which was to produce extraordinary results.

On the third anniversary of the Boston Massacre, John Adams wrote in his diary: " The part I took in defence of Capt. Preston and the soldiers procured me anxiety and obloquy enough. It was, however, one of the most gallant, generous, manly, and disinterested acts of my whole life, and one of the best pieces of service I ever rendered my country. Judgment of death against those soldiers would have been as foul a stain upon this country as the executions of the Quakers or witches anciently. As the evidence was, the verdict of the jury was exactly right. This, however, is no reason why the town should not call the action of that night a massacre; nor is it any argument in favor of the Governor or minister who caused them to be sent here. But it is the strongest of proofs of the danger of standing armies." [1]

John Adams is entirely just in the estimate he puts upon his conduct in these frank terms. His defense of the soldiers was one of the manliest things that thoroughly manly man ever did, and his summing up of the matter at the end is quite right. The soldiers having been summoned, the conflict was inevitable. Through bad trade laws, fear of ecclesiastical encroachment, and taxation without representation, the town was justly afire, and the Province behind it. The people in general would have been law-abiding in their remonstrance, however energetic; but the rough element was no less existent then than in every modern American municipality. Hence, with such abundant heat developed, a roaring flame was sure to catch. If John Adams showed himself here a man of sense and a hero, as much cannot be said for his cousin Samuel.

---

[1] John Adams's Diary, Mar. 5, 1773. The trial of the soldiers was postponed until the fall.

The driving out of the regiments, in which Samuel Adams led his townsmen, was indeed good service, accomplished with all possible ability and energy; but in the vindictive persecution which followed, the attempt to arouse in England and America indignation against the soldiers by documents based on evidence hastily collected in advance of trial, from witnesses utterly unworthy, and in the attempt to precipitate the trial while passion was still hot, the misbehavior of the people was grave. In all this no leader was more eager than Samuel Adams; and in no time of his career, probably, does he more plainly lay himself open to the charge of being a great demagogue, a mere mob-leader, than at this moment.

Hutchinson's position was a most forlorn one, and if all its embarrassments are considered, it is hard to see how he could have done better. He was scarcely more in agreement, it must always be said, with the government policy, really, than the Whigs themselves. The trade-laws he was no friend to; the establishing of a bishop he had no desire for, though his tolerant spirit made him more indifferent here than were the zealous Puritans. The Stamp Act and the Townshend taxes he would never have counseled, though taxation without representation had never come home to him as such a crying outrage upon English freedom as Otis and his company had felt it to be. He did not like the laws; but since they were laws, they ought to be enforced, and he, through no seeking of his own, was in a position where he must be the enforcer. There is little evidence that up to this time he had favored the coming of the soldiers; but being at hand he would have used them, if a civil magistrate could have been found to help him out, to preserve order; and he desired to have them held in respect as the arm of the government to which in his heart, and as bound by his oath, he was loyal. He was no democrat. Samuel Adams did him no injustice in saying: "It has been his principle from a boy that mankind are to be governed by the discerning few; and it has ever since been his ambition to be the hero of the few." [1]   Matthew Arnold's doctrine of the "remnant" he accepted, — that what must save the world is a small leaven of excellent men, hidden and active within the mass. If he felt that he himself was a hero of that few, how could he form any other conclusion as he reviewed his near forty years of public life, crowded as they were with acts on his part, which he without any unreasonable self-pride could see had been of great public benefit!

In the spring, the Townshend taxes had been all repealed except as regards the one article, tea; the preamble to this Act, asserting the right in Parliament to legislate for the Colonies in all cases whatsoever, was maintained, and the tax on tea was to secure its acknowledgment.   Hutchinson would gladly have had the Act repealed without exception.   "I know not what reason," he wrote October 15, 1770, "may make it necessary to continue the duty on tea; but I think the repeal of it, or making the same duty payable in England, is necessary to prevent disorders in the Colonies." [2]   The

[1] Letter to Stephen Sayre, Nov. 23, 1770, quoted in Frothingham's *Life of Warren*, p. 159.

[2] Quoted by Frothingham : *Life of Warren*, pp. 157, 158.

Massacre affair turned out at last just as he would have had it, except that he could not extinguish a popular resentment which was destined to crop out each year, on the anniversary, in a fierce commemorative address at the Old South. The likelihood of his succession to the governorship grew greater as the year passed ; and he had reason to entertain confidence that, should the appointment come, he might conciliate those estranged. If there could only be an acknowledgment of Parliamentary supremacy, all would be well. Let the Colonies allow that, — then let the Home government forbear the obtrusion of it except on the rarest occasions and in the gentlest way, and only in cases where the welfare of the whole empire was concerned, — then would follow what seemed to him the ideal relation, — the ideal relation, at least, until that remote future should come of which he sometimes spoke, when America, constituting in itself a mighty empire, might with advantage cut loose.

At the prospect of promotion, however, his attitude is always that of reluctance rather than eagerness. Soon after the Massacre, he begs Hillsboro to be allowed to resign. "I must humbly pray that a person of superior powers of body and mind may be appointed to the administration of the government of this Province. I shall faithfully endeavor to support such person according to the best of my abilities, and I think it not improbable that I may be capable of doing his Majesty greater service in the Province, even in a private station, than at present." [1] To Jackson also he

[1] *M. A. Hist.*, vol. xxvi., Mar. 27, to Hillsboro.

writes : " I have received your most obliging letter of
the 18th of November, and thank you for your kind
offer in case I had been appointed to succeed Sir
Francis Bernard. I find my constitution is not strong
enough to bear so great a burden, and I hope the next
vessel will bring us news of a person of weight and
importance appointed to the government." [1] The Town-
Meeting seems to him more and more unlovely. To
John Pownal, now confidential secretary of Lord Hillsboro, he writes : " There is a Town-Meeting, no sort
of regard being had to any qualification of voters, but
all the inferior people meet together ; and at a late
meeting the inhabitants of other towns who happened
to be in town, mixed with them, and made, they say
themselves, near 3000, — their newspaper says 4000,
when it is not likely there are 1500 legal voters in the
town. It is in other words being under the government of the mob. This has given the lower part of the
people such a sense of their importance that a gentleman
does not meet with what used to be common civility,
and we are sinking into perfect barbarism. . . . If this
town could be separated from the rest of the Province,
the infection has not taken such strong hold of the
parts remote from it. The spirit of anarchy which prevails in Boston is more than I am able to cope with." [2]

The grand cause of all the trouble is, in his mind,
the example of discord set in England ; for in studying
Hutchinson's story we are never left in the dark that a
strife scarcely less bitter than in America raged in England, and that America constantly drew encouragement

[1] Mar., 1770.   [2] Mar. 26, 1770.

in her sedition from the seditious spirits over sea, who, in his view, threatened dire ill, as they fought for the rights of the people.

May 11, 1770, to Robert Wilson : " You [English-men] are carrying your indecent, illiberal, even savage harangues to such lengths as is inconsistent with that respect and reverence, which, be the form of govern-ment what it may, is due to the supreme authority, and which, if not preserved, the authority itself must soon fall. You do not consider the extensive consequences of such irregularities. They are not confined to the island of Britain ; they reach to the Colonies. We ape you in everything, especially in everything which is a reproach to you ; and for fear of falling short, we go beyond you, and are more licentious than even the people of England. This is in part to be attributed to a cause which does not exist in England. The supreme authority with you nobody disputes where it lies. With us there are such divisions about it that we begin to think it best there should be none, and that every man should do what is right in his own eyes. Nobody now dares say that Parliament has a right to tax us. Lord Chatham, Lord Camden, and others support us [our Whigs] in that. We have not penetration enough to conceive of their subtle distinctions, and some of us suppose that if you once set bounds to the supreme authority, the subjects will never agree among them-selves where the line shall be drawn ; and our people now say, that if we ought not to be taxed by a power without us, we ought not to be bound by any laws whatsoever made by such power ; for it is idle to say

we are not subject to a Tax Act which takes a small
sum out of our pockets, and yet are subject to an Act
restraining our trade which prevents a very large sum
from coming into our pockets. You have brought all
this trouble upon yourselves and upon us by your own
imprudence. You never ought to have made any concessions from your own power over the Colonies, and
you ought not to have attempted an exertion of power
which caused such a general dissatisfaction through the
Colonies. God only knows when the effects of this
mistake will cease. I fear not until you can unite
among yourselves; for till then you will have a party
who will encourage disorder and confusion in the Colonies for the sake of distressing administration. When
your political frenzy is over I hope ours will abate, and
that the confusions will be less than they are at present;
but government will never recover its vigour until the
relation the Colony bears to the parent state is better
ascertained." [1]

To Stephen Sayre, afterwards Sheriff of London, by
the efforts of the Supporters of the Bill of Rights,
Samuel Adams wrote, November 23, the following passage copied here from the autograph: [2] —

" Good God ! " [This is crossed out in the draft, but
can be read under the lines.] " Could it be possibly
imagined that a man that is bone of our Bone and flesh
of our flesh, who. boasts that his Ancestors were of the
first Rank and figure in the Country, who has had all
the Honors lavished upon him which his Fellow-Citizens

---

[1] *M. A. Hist.*, vol. xxvi., p. 479, etc.
[2] Now in the Lenox Library, New York.

had it in their power to bestow, who with all the Arts
of personal address professes the strongest attachment
to his native Country, and the most tender feeling for
its Rights, could it be imagined that such a man should
be so lost to all sense of Gratitude and publick Love,
as to aid the Designs of despotick power for the sake of
rising a single step higher?

" Who would not weep if such a man there be ?
Who would not weep if H——n were he ? "

While Samuel Adams pays his compliments in these
terms to Hutchinson, the latter is not behindhand in
his tributes.   He took great hope from the failure of
the non-importation agreements, the subsidence of opposition to his policy in the legislature, the acquittal of
Preston and most of the culprits of the Massacre, and a
general quiet which at the beginning of 1771 prevailed
in the Province.

" We have not been so quiet these five years.   The
people about the country have certainly altered their
conduct, and in this town, if it were not for two or
three Adamses, we should do well enough.   I don't
know how to account for the obstinacy of one [John
Adams], who seemed to me, when he began life, to
promise well.   The other [Samuel Adams] never appeared different from what he does at present, and, I
fear, never will.   The name of ' Vindex,' which he has
assumed, is characteristic; but, as it is the custom now
for people to give their children two or three names, I
could wish he would add ' Malignus ' and ' Invidus,' to
make his names a little more significative."

Had skies been calmer, the governorship would not

have been distasteful to Hutchinson. "In common times a life of business would be agreeable to me, and I am not so devoid of ambition as not to be pleased with the honor conferred upon me by my Sovereign; but when the state of the times is such as that a Governor must be deprived of that tranquillity of mind without which life itself is scarcely endurable, you will not wonder that I am not fond of the place." The unwisdom of the ministry was scarcely less a trial to him than the sedition of the people. "I wrote the 18th of Feb. that in my opinion it was better to leave all the duties in force than to take off three and leave the other."[1] As to the tumults: "I have many months ago wrote to the ministry my sentiments upon it, but nothing is done. If it has not already been too long neglected, I think if this session of Parliament should rise without something more than Declaratory Acts, without some new provision for carrying the acts into execution, this Province will never submit to their authority unless compelled to it by superior external force."[2] "I cannot help flattering myself that the late doings of the town and Province have before this time caused such measures as shall restore both to their former subordination."[3] He throws out all the incitements he can to a vigorous interference by the government. "May 22. I shall have trouble enough with such an Assembly, but I would willingly undergo it a whole year rather than undergo the trouble I meet with from

[1] *M. A. Hist.*, vol. xxvi., to Commodore Hood, May 21, 1770.
[2] *Ibid.*, to the same, Apr. 9, 1770.
[3] *Ibid.*, Apr. 19, 1770.

the dissolute state of the town of Boston for one month." [1] The merchants' meetings he speaks of as "made up of Tom, Dick, and Harry." "Will the nation never have any sense of these indignities offered them?" He writes to Hillsboro that he keeps Gage and Hood informed so they can be ready on occasion, with troops and ships. "Opposition never will expire until the Colonists are brought to know that their ancestors remained subjects of England when they removed to America, as fully as if they had only removed from one part of the island of Britain to another part of the same island." If only Boston could be disciplined! "The town at present is led by several persons of profligate habits, both for religion and morality, and about an equal number of the most precisely devout. It is difficult to say which are capable of the most illegal and violent acts for promoting the cause they are engaged in. By this union they have this great advantage, that the body of the people who are divided in proportions not very different are more easily brought to enlist, some under the one sort, and some the other." Still more plainly: "At present, it [the Democratic tyranny in the town] is kept up by two or three of the most abandoned atheist fellows in the world, united with as many precise enthusiast deacons, who head the rabble in all their meetings." [2] "He is sure," if the members from Boston were out of the House, he should have a majority in favor of government. "In this Province the faction is headed by the lowest. dirtiest, and most abject part of the whole community, and so

[1] *M. A. Hist.*, vol. xxvi., p. 491.   [2] June 26, 1770.

absurdly do the Council and House of Representatives reason that they justify this anarchy, the worst of tyranny, as necessary to remove a single instance of what they call oppression. . . . They have persecuted my sons with peculiar pleasure." [1]

August 26, 1770, to William Parker, of Portsmouth: "You certainly think right when you think Boston people are run mad. The frenzy was not higher when they banished my pious great-grandmother, when they hanged the Quakers, when they afterwards hanged the poor innocent witches, when they were carried away with a Land Bank, nor when they all turned ' New Lights,' than the political frenzy has been for a twelvemonth past. If we were not mad, I have no doubt we might enjoy all that liberty which can consist with a state of government, and that the affair of taxation has given them so much trouble in England as to prevent any future attempts, unless our breaking a challenge and suffering indignities, insults, and defiances, shall provoke them to it. I believe the delay in the act you refer to is occasioned merely by the pressure of the affairs of the kingdom." [2]

August 28, 1770, to Bernard: " The distresses of the town of Boston have not yet opened its eyes. They do not consider that it is only a few merchants in England who are losers by their non-importation, and that the tradesmen and manufacturers do not feel it. The infamous Molineux and Young, with Cooper, Adams,

---

[1] To Mr. Silliman, July 28, 1770, *M. A. Hist.*, vol. xxvi.

[2] In the hand of an amanuensis, as is now frequently the case. *M. A. Hist.*, vol. xxvi., p. 540.

and two or three more, still influence the mob who threaten all who import; but it seems impossible it should hold much longer; many who at first were zealous among the merchants, against importation, are now as zealous for it. . . . An Act of Parliament for the severe punishment of all who shall in like manner offend for the future, will be necessary; for these fellows having had power so long in their hands, will reassume it upon the lightest pretence."[1] What follows is interesting as showing that the Lieutenant-Governor had to supply backbone to the judges at the trial of Preston and the soldiers. "I have persuaded Judge Lynde, who came twice to see me with his resignation in his pocket, to hold his place a little longer. Timid as he is, I think Goffe is more so: the only difference is, little matters as well as great frighten Lynde. Goffe appears valiant until the danger, or apprehensions of it, rise to considerable height; after that he is more terrified than the other. Judge Oliver[2] appears to be very firm, though threatened in yesterday's paper; and I hope Cushing will be so likewise. The prospect is certainly much better than with any new judges I could have appointed who would have accepted. You advise me not to be concerned about my salary. I am not. It never shall have the least influence, and I will never remove the Court to Boston a minute sooner upon that account; nor will I give the ministry any trouble about it as long as I can find money from my own estate to support me."

[1] *M. A. Hist.*, vol. xxvi., p. 540.
[2] Peter Oliver, who succeeds Hutchinson as Chief Justice.

He is convinced that independence is more and more
the aim of the Whigs, and so short-sighted as to think
it would be certain ruin to the country. July 26: "I
have not the least doubt that if Parliament shall fail
the next session as it has done the last, this will be the
case in every Colony. It is not now time to grudge at
a small expense to save the whole Colony, for we are
strengthening ourselves every year against the authority
of Parliament, and the reduction will grow every year
more difficult." [1] As often, he would be glad to have
the tea duty repealed. October 3, 1770: "I wish that
[tea] had been joined with the other articles in the last
repealing act; or that it may be still done, and the
same duty remain in England. . . . Levelling principles have had such spread, that the principal men of
the Province for understanding and estate have been
excluded both from the Council and House, and a few
artful persons have governed all the rest." [2]

October 3, 1770, to Whately: "I think it must
puzzle the wisest heads in the kingdom to restore America to a state of government and order. . . . In general
I can say that the wound may be skinned over, but can
never be healed until it be laid open to the bone. Parliament must give up its claim to a supreme authority
over the Colonies, or the Colonies must cease from asserting a supreme legislative among themselves. Until
these points are settled, we shall be always liable upon
every slight occasion to fresh disorders."

No reader of these extracts will fail to see that
Hutchinson, in his constant letters to men in power

[1] *M. A. Hist.*, vol. xxvi., p. 524. [2] *Ibid.*, vol. xxvii., p

and to those in confidential and close relations with
them, was communicating always intelligence and advice. That there was any misrepresentation cannot be
said. He reported what his eyes saw and ears heard;
though another mind than his would have seen and
heard in the spectacles and speeches things quite different. It was his business to report and advise. But
he was laying up trouble for himself, the beginnings of
which were already apparent. In view of what was
before long to come, there is something pathetic in his
frequent and earnest petitions in these days to keep
secret what he writes. September 20, 1770, to Bernard:
"It will hurt my interest with the Council, which was
every day increasing. Indeed, a Governor must cease
from transmitting what passes here, unless some way can
be found to keep it from coming back again; for it not
only makes him obnoxious to the particular persons to
whom what he transmits more immediately relates, but
he is exposed to the rage of the people and destitute of
every protection and defence." [1]

September 28, 1770, to Bernard: "Either they [cer-
tain letters] came from copies that were laid before the
House of Commons, or they have corrupted some of
the clerks in the office. I cannot conceive of a third
way of coming at them. I heard a gentleman say he
went into Dr. Cooper's room, and saw a large table
spread with them. Pray endeavor that more care may
be taken to prevent copies of letters coming among us.
I have said something to Lord Hillsboro of the temper
people were in and their opposition to government,

[1] *M. A. Hist.*, vol. xxvii., p. 5.

which though strictly true and incumbent on me to
mention, yet if they must be laid before the House
of Commons, and from thence or by any other means
come over here, I have no security against the rage of
the people." [1]

September 28, 1770, to Hillsboro: "I have wrote
nothing which I cannot justify; but in these times it is
not safe to speak what in ordinary times would meet
with no exception." [2]

In time now not far off, Hutchinson was to be accused of wishing to have the constitution changed.
How far this was from the truth appears from passages
in a letter to Hillsboro, published in the "Proceedings
of the Massachusetts Historical Society," vol. xix., p.
129, etc.: "Measures for reforming the constitution of
any people under such circumstances will probably be
ineffectual, and tend to increase their disorders. . . .

"I was not insensible of the peculiar defects in the
constitution of this Province, and I have complained of
the Council as being under undue influence, and casting their weight into that scale which had much too
great proportion before; but I was doubtful myself,
and I found some judicious persons in whom I could
confide to be doubtful, also, whether, while the body of
the people continued in the state they were then in,
such councillors as should be appointed by the Crown
would dare to undertake the trust; or if they should
do it, whether the people in general would not refuse
to submit to their authority; and I feared the conse-

[1] *M. A. Hist.*, vol. xxvii., p. 6, etc.; not in Hutchinson's hand.
[2] Quoted in Almon's *Remembrancer*, 1776, p. 158.

quences of either would more than countervail the advantages which would arise merely from an alteration in the constitution if accomplished."

To glance for a moment at Hutchinson's private life. His two sons, Thomas and Elisha, as we have seen, were playing a part in the eye of the public as merchants to whom the non-importation agreements were obnoxious. The latter was soon to marry Miss Mary Watson, of Plymouth. " Billy," the youngest boy, had gone to England, his father, with affectionate eyes, from Milton Hill, watching the disappearance of the ship that bore him, as the breeze carried it to sea past Nantasket. He was apparently a heedless and selfish youth, for his father often chided him for indifference to the friends he had left behind, shown in the fact that he almost never wrote.[1] The two girls were growing into attractive womanhood. " Sallie," the elder, now the wife of Dr. Peter Oliver, lived at Middleboro, at the handsome estate of her husband's father, Chief Justice Peter Oliver. " Peggy," the younger, seems especially to have been her father's darling, a delicate figure, destined like her mother to an early death by consumption. The student of the Letter Books comes into a close relation with her, for she was often her father's amanuensis, and the fine, childlike hand becomes very familiar. She must have been a beauty, for she made an easy capture of the son of a nobleman, a young naval officer

---

[1] Dec. 22, 1772: " I could not have thought it possible that in seven months I should have received only two short letters from you, and none of the rest of your friends so much as one."

attached to the Boston, one of the ships of the fleet at anchor in the harbor. The following correspondence is interesting. The courtliness and prudence of Hutchinson's note are quite in character : —

"SIR, — The various methods there are of writing on the following subject, make me rather at a loss which to take, as I am a stranger to you, — but as the nature of it requires plain dealing, I shall take the liberty to consider you as a friend, and write to you as such : you will perhaps, Sir, think it rather strange, and be much surprised at the receipt of this letter, particularly as I am going to ask a great favor; no less, Sir, than the honor of an alliance to your family. I have had the honor of seeing Miss Hutchinson, but never in my life spoke to her. I need not tell you I admire her when I say I wish to call her mine ; on seeing her the first time, I determined to endeavour to cultivate her acquaintance, but have not been so happy as to succeed ; therefore I should wish as the most *honourable* method of proceeding, to get acquainted with her through the means of her father ; and I should be happy in obtaining *your* permission, Sir, to visit her. I would say more on the occasion, but yet not near so much as what I could say to you in person ; therefore, Sir, if you 'll favor me with a line, directed to me at Mr. Perkins', near the old Brick meeting House, I will do myself the honour of waiting on you, any time you 'll apoint.

" You will find me act, from beginning to end, as a man of honour, and I am very certain that you, on

your part, will do the same. I have the honour to remain with the utmost esteem and respect,

> "Sir,
>> Your very obedient and
>>> most humble servant,
>>>> WM. FITZWILLIAM.

"April ye 6th, 1771."

[Written on the same sheet with the above.]

> "BOSTON, 6 Ap., 1771.

SIR, — I am not insensible that such an alliance as
you have proposed would be doing the greatest honour
to me and my family. I am at the same time very sensible that it cannot be approved of by the Noble Family to which you belong. In my station, from respect
to My Lord Fitzwilliam, I should think it my duty to
do all in my power to discourage one of his sons from
so unequal a match with any person in the Province,
and I should most certainly be highly criminal if I
should countenance and encourage a match with my
own daughter.

" I hope, sir, you will think this a sufficient reason
for my not acceding to your proposal. I sincerely wish
you happy in a person more suitable to your birth and
rank, and who may be approved by your R. Honourable
Parents." [1]

Here is a letter to a tenant who leased a farm in
Rhode Island, in which the Governor appears to good
advantage. " February 15. You judge wrong if you

[1] *M. A. Hist.*, vol. xxv., p. 474.

think the arrival of my commission will lessen my friendship or make me expect any sort of ceremony ; and if
you should use any, you could not disoblige me more.
Pride is always odious, but in an old man whose dust,
be his station what it may, in a very little while will not
be distinguishable from that of the beggar, is unpar-
donable. I do not despair, as I go sometimes to see
my daughter and grand-daughter at Middleborough, of
being able to run away in an afternoon and drink a
dish of tea with you, before summer is out." [1]

In March, Hutchinson received his Commission as
Governor, his wife's brother-in-law, Andrew Oliver, being
at the same time commissioned Lieutenant-Governor, and
Thomas Flucker, Secretary. At his inauguration, while
the Assembly and the Congregational ministers were
silent, there were many felicitations. Harvard College,
among the rest, addressed him with congratulations,
the students singing in Holden Chapel the anthem,
" Thus saith the Lord : From henceforth, behold ! all
nations shall call thee blessed ; for thy rulers shall be of
thy own kindred, your nobles shall be of yourselves,
and thy governor shall proceed from the midst of thee."
In the better prospect for the Tory cause, which had
come to exist, Hutchinson was cheerful and hopeful.
His letters now are seldom in his own hand, his amanuensis being often his daughter.

March 9, 1771, to Hillsboro : " My friends may flatter me, but they assure me that a very great majority

---

[1] Feb. 15, 1771, to Chesebrough. His Rhode Island estate was one of
the finest in that Province. *M. A. Hist.*, vol. xxvii., p. 118.

of the people in the country towns rejoice at the appointment. In Boston they say nothing to my charge but my bad principles in government. The late newspaper performances which undoubtedly came from one or more of the representatives of the town, boldly assert an independence of all parliamentary authority, and declare the King, by his representative, the Council, and the Assembly in each Colony, to be a distinct legislature, subject to no other power upon earth. A great part of the people easily embrace the principle without perceiving that it destroys their connexion with Great Britain, and leaves them no better claim to protection than the King's subjects have in the electorate of Hanover. It would be to no more purpose to reason with them than with an enthusiast who holds an absurd tenet in religion ; and whilst principles are avowed and published in England with impunity which are equally criminal, and equally tend to sedition, the judges here seem to be of opinion that it can do no good to bring information against the publisher of such libels, as the juries would probably acquit them, as they have lately done in several instances in Westminster Hall. These acquittals, the infamous libels of Junius, and some speeches said to be made in Parliament, all which are immediately republished and greedily swallowed down, have in some degree revived the spirits of the faction among us, but I hope not so far as to cause any fresh disorders ; for the people in the country seem generally convinced of the folly of those which are past." [1]

March 17, 1771, to Josias Lyndon, Esq., of Rhode

[1] *M. A. Hist.*, vol. xxvii., p. 128.

Island : " I am much obliged to you for your kind congratulations on my advancement to the chief seat of
government. A sense of the difficulty attending so important a trust prevailed for some time over the desire
of honor and fame which we all have more or less of,
and I desired to be excused from the post. I really
expected that a new appointment would be made unless
the commissions were issued before my letters arrived ;
but my Lord Hillsboro refused to make any alteration
until he should receive answers to letters which he had
just before wrote advising me in form of the appointment. My friends who agreed with me before in the
expediency of declining then urged me to accept, especially as I was told it was uncertain how long I should
be obliged to hold the place of Lieutenant-Governor
and Commander-in-Chief, which subjected me to all the
burdens, but did not entitle me to all the advantages of
the Chief-Governor's place." [1]

April 1, 1771, to Colonel Williams, Hatfield : " It's
certain all the valuable part of the town have shown
me as much respect personally, as well as in my public
character, as I could desire. Two Adamses, Phillips,
Hancock, and two or three others, who, with the least
reason, have been the most injurious, are all of any
sort of consideration who stand out. I cannot expect
any great mark of regard from the House whilst the
Boston members are aided by a gentleman of your
county who has so much influence." [2]

The first anniversary of the Massacre having been

[1] *M. A. Hist.*, vol. xxvii., p. 131.
[2] *Ibid.*, p. 149. Hawley is referred to.

commemorated by an oration, in which the power of
Parliament to legislate for the Colonies was denied,
Hutchinson writes, April 3, 1771, to Secretary Pownal:
"It must show to Parliament the necessity of such an
alteration in the constitution of the town,[1] as some time
ago you gave me a hint of, and will be sufficient to
render an act for that purpose unexceptionable. . . . It
has been some inconvenience to me to be without my
salary for more than twenty months, the only grant I
have received from the Province just enabling me to
pay the fees of my commission."

April 19, 1771, to Hillsboro : " In these votes and
in most of the public proceedings of the town of
Boston, persons of the best character and estate have
little or no concern. They decline attending Town-
Meetings where they are sure to be outvoted by men of
the lowest order, all being admitted, and it being very
rare that any scrutiny is made into the qualification of
voters." [2]

May 24, 1771, to Bernard : " The town of Boston is
the source from whence all the other parts of the Province derive more or less troubled water. When you
consider what is called its constitution, your good sense
will determine immediately that it never can be otherwise for a long time together, whilst the majority which
conducts all affairs, if met together upon another occasion, would be properly called a mob, and are persons

---

[1] He is thinking here of no change in the charter, but only of bringing back the Town-Meetings to the limited functions originally laid down
for them, and from which he believes they have illegally departed.

[2] *M. A. Hist.*, vol. xxvii., p. 151.

of such rank and circumstance as in all communities constitute a mob, there being no sort of regulation of voters in practice ; and as these will always be most in number, men of weight and value, although they wish to suppress them, cannot be induced to attempt to do it for fear not only of being outvoted, but affronted and insulted. Call such an assembly what you will, it is really no sort of government, not even a democracy, at best a corruption of it. There is no hopes of a cure by any legislative but among ourselves to compel the town to be a corporation. The people will not seek it, because every one is sensible his importance will be lessened. If ever a remedy is found, it must be by compelling them to swallow it, and that by an exterior power, — the Parliament." [1]

[1] *M. A. Hist.*, vol. xxvii., p. 173.

CHAPTER IX.

In April the legislature assembled, received from Hutchinson the formal announcement of his promotion, and at once requested him to remove them to their usual seat, the town-house in Boston. Hutchinson declined, stating that one of the obstructions to the desired removal was the denial by the House of the right reserved by the Crown to convene the Court in such place as was thought proper.[1] Samuel Adams replied in a dignified strain to the Governor's address, speaking of the Assembly as "His Majesty's Commons;" a style which his adversary did not fail to note as something new and to be disapproved, rightly surmising that the intention was to assert for the House supreme and independent legislative power. The tedious controversy, however, over the removal of the legislature, was about giving way to a new topic of dispute.

Early in the session bills were passed granting the usual sums for the salary of the Governor and defraying public expenses. When three weeks had gone, upon inquiry of the Secretary of the Province, it did not appear that the bills had been approved by the

---

[1] Hutchinson declares he would never have permitted a royal instruction to justify a departure from law ; he allowed to it force only in cases where there was no law. *Hist.*, vol. iii., p. 342.

Governor. Among the Samuel Adams manuscripts is contained the following draft: —

"In the House of Representatives, April 25, 1771. Ordered, that Mr. Samuel Adams, Brig. Ruggles, Mr. Hersy, Coll. Bowers, and Mr. Godfrey be a committee to wait on his Excellency with the following message. May it please your Excellency, the House of Representatives, after enquiry of the Secretary cannot be made certain whether you have yet given your Assent to two Bills which were laid before your Excellency early in this Session ; The one for granting the sum of five hundred and six pounds for your services when Lieutenant-Governor and Commander-in-Cheife ; and the other for granting the usual Sum of Thirteen hundred Pounds to enable your Excellency as Governor to carry on the affairs of this Province. And as your Excellency was not pleased to give your Assent to another Bill passed in the last Session of this Assembly for granting the sum of three hundred and twenty-five pounds for your services when in the Chair as Lieutenant-Governor, the House is apprehensive that you are under some Restraint; and they cannot account for it upon any other Principle but your having Provision for your Support in some new and unprecedented manner. If the apprehensions of the House are not groundless, they are sollicitous to be made certain of it before an End is put to the present Session and think it their Duty to pray your Excellency to inform them whether any provision is made for your support as Governor of this Province independent of his Majesty's Commons in it." [1]

[1] From the autograph.

The Whigs felt that their cause would be much hurt if the Governor and judges were permitted to derive their support from other sources than the people. So one form of disagreement succeeded another : whatever form came up, it was promptly met ; and always, at the front of the patriotic picket, it was the voice of Samuel Adams that challenged the danger. Hutchinson, on the other hand, believed that by charter the Governor was intended to be independent, a condition not at all possible if his support were a popular grant.[1]

The hopes of the Tories were high in the spring of 1771. Among the Whigs, men like Andrew Eliot thought "it might be as well not to dispute in such strong terms the legal right of Parliament. This is a point which cannot be easily settled and had therefore best be touched very gently." Otis, who at this time had a return of reason, and who was promptly chosen, together with Hancock, Cushing, and Samuel Adams, to the Assembly, on the 7th of May, reduced to a mere wreck, and in his weakness the prey of a contemptible jealousy towards Samuel Adams, pursued a strongly reactionary course. Hancock, too, gave such signs of disgust at his former associates and opinions, that the Governor had strong hopes of bringing him over to the Tory side. Cushing, courtly and complaisant, regularly elected Speaker, no doubt, in good part, because Hutchinson, fearing him less than any other in the "faction," did not veto him as he would have done a stronger man, was little more than a figure-head. John Adams, out of conceit with public

[1] *Hist.*, vol. iii., p. 359.

life, where abuse, he alleged, was more often the reward of service than fame or profit, had withdrawn
himself to his law practice.   Hawley was absent far in
the interior except during the sessions ; and even then,
able and respected though he was, his unevenness of
temper made him an unstable prop.   Samuel Adams,
almost alone, his resolution not a whit abated by his
isolation, took up the burden.   Courteous, calm, per-
sistent, when the deputies were scattered he spread his
thoughts in the newspapers ; he was busy, too, in a
score of unrecorded ways, consummate manager that
he was, talking, sending letters and messages, winning
a wavering friend by a smile and a hand-shake, running
under some Tory mine by a cunning counter-mine, —
forever trying to stem the reaction that had set in.
" Our sons of sedition," writes Hutchinson to Bernard,
" are afraid of a change of members in many towns,
and make a strong effort in the newspapers to prevent
it.   In this week's paper you see the black art of
Adams."   But for Samuel Adams, the patriot cause
at this time must have gone by the board.

When, on May 29, the legislature met, Adams as
usual being chosen Clerk of the House, the change of
tone became instantly manifest.   Otis, even in his decay, had an overmastering charm.   At his instance,
while the remonstrance was passed, as had become
usual, against the removal of the legislature from Boston, the clause was struck out which denied to the
Crown the right to remove.   The principle so long contended for was thus sacrificed, the right of prerogative
to infringe upon the charter at this point was acknow-

ledged, and it would be easy to proceed to the ground
that the Crown might take what liberties it pleased with
the charter. Otis's change was indeed startling. Wrote
John Adams: "John Chandler, Esq., of Petersham,
gave me an account of Otis's conversion to Toryism.
Adams was going on in the old road, and Otis started
up and said they had gone far enough in that way; the
Governor had an undoubted right to carry the court
where he pleased, and moved for a committee to represent the inconveniences of sitting there, and for an
address to the Governor. He was a good man; the
ministers said so, and it must be so; and moved to go
on with business; and the House voted everything he
moved for. Boston people say he is distracted."[1]

Hutchinson had high hopes of future advantages
from the position the repentant Otis was inclined to
take. "The House," he wrote, "having acknowledged
my right to convene the Court where I think proper,
have strengthened government, and given me more
weight in the Province than they intended. The people being made sensible that I claimed no more than
the just prerogatives in this instance, think more favorably of me and of the principles I avow in other points
in difference. The return of the Court to Boston, in
consequence of this concession, will give me further
weight, and it may be, enable me to obtain other points
equally reasonable for them to concede."[2]

Bad as was the defection of James Otis, that of Hancock was not less harmful. His wealth, popular man-

[1] John Adams's *Works*, vol. ii., p. 266.
[2] Wells : *Life of Samuel Adams*, vol. i., p. 396.

ners, and some really strong qualities, made his influence great, in spite of his many foibles. Samuel Adams had exploited Hancock, with all his consummate art, ever since his appearance in public life, making him a powerful pillar of the popular cause. Contemptuous allusions to Hancock as little better than an ape whom Samuel Adams led about according to his will have come down from these times. Vain and shallow though Hancock may have been, he deserved no such disparagement; there were times when Hancock was manly and rendered great service. The scoff, however, partially indicates the relation between the two men. It may well have been the case that, through some Tory source, some such uncomplimentary description of the relation of Hancock to Adams reached the ears of the former. Such things were flying in the air, and Hancock was feeble enough to be moved by them if they came to his ears. Whatever may have been the reason, Hancock forsook his old guide, voted with the party of Otis for the acknowledgment of Hutchinson's right to convene the legislature when he chose, and so far coquetted with the Tories that his introduction into the Council through their agency began to seem probable. His recreancy, however, was only short.

Samuel Adams probably never experienced a greater mortification than when, as a member of a committee, by command of the House he waited upon Hutchinson, to present an address acknowledging the right of the Governor to remove the General Court " to Housatonic, in the western extreme of the Province," if he would; nor, on the other hand, did the Governor ever enjoy

a greater triumph. Hutchinson must have felt that
he was even with his adversary for the humiliation
of the preceding year, the driving out of the regiments.
The great Whig saw his influence apparently far on the
wane. He suffered keenly, but gave no sign of it, and
was as unremitting as ever to retrieve the lost ground.
So hopeless did his fall seem that the Tories thought
they could afford to pity him. Speaking of a conversation with a noted Tory, John Adams writes: " Spar-
hawk mentioned the intrepidity of Samuel Adams, a
man, he says, of great sensibility, of tender nerves, and
harassed, dependent, in their power. Yet he had borne
up against all ; it must have penetrated him very
deeply." [1] While the Assembly followed other guides,
the faithful " Boston Gazette " gave Samuel Adams
opportunity to reply to the writers whom Hutchinson
kept at work in the Tory sheets. As " Candidus," he
writes June 10 : " A firm and manly opposition to the
attempts that have been made and *are still* making to
enslave and ruin this continent has always been branded
by writers of this stamp by the name of a FACTION.
Governor Bernard used to tell his Lordship that it was
an ' *expiring* faction ; ' with as little reason it is now
said to have *given up the ghost :* Gladly would some,
even of the clergy, persuade this people to be *at ease ;*
and for the sake of peace under the administration of
' a son of the Province,' to acquiesce in unconstitutional
revenue acts, arbitrary ministerial mandates, and absolute, despotic, independent governors, etc., etc. But the
time is not yet come ; and I am satisfied that, notwith-

1 *Works*, vol. ii., p. 285.

standing the address of *a few* who *took the opportunity*
to carry it through, while *only* the small number of
twenty-four were present, there is in that venerable
order a great majority who will not go up to the house
of Rimmon or bow the knee to Baal."

The revulsion was not long in coming. Before
Hutchinson had had time to restore the repentant legislature to the town-house in Boston, their hearts again
became hardened against him. A protest came forth
bearing all of Samuel Adams's well-known marks, in
which the old ground, the illegality of the removal, was
reasserted; the payment of a salary, too, to the Governor, independent of the legislative provision, was dwelt
upon after the old fashion. The strong opposition had
been beaten down by the sudden rally. The protest had
a saucier ring than ever, and was regarded in England,
when at length the news reached there, as a greater insult than had at any time been offered. The most was
made of their victory by the Whigs. By the end of
June, the resolution of the previous year, establishing
the Committee of Correspondence, was again carried,
with Cushing, Adams, Otis, Hancock, and Heath as
members. The first-fruits of the Committee, a letter to
Franklin, who had now become agent, show that there
was no quailing before external danger or internal
defection.[1]

In a letter of this time, undated and undirected,
Hutchinson thus characterizes his chief adversary: —

"I doubt whether there is a greater incendiary in the
King's dominion or a man of greater malignity of heart,

[1] For the letter, see Wells: *Samuel Adams*, vol. i., pp. 408, 409.

who less scruples any measure ever so criminal to accomplish his purposes; and I think I do him no injustice when I suppose he wishes the destruction of every friend to government in America. This is the man who is of the committee and the *instar omnium* with which the agent corresponds and from which he takes his directions in the recess of the Court. The doctrine advanced in these letters of independence upon Parliament and even upon the King to whom they deny the right of supporting or even instructing his Governor, must rouse the people of England and they will sooner or later express their indignation. I see the principle spreading every day, and the silence in England is construed to be a tacit acknowledgment or acquiescence. It cannot, as they threaten, be expressly acknowledged, but it may, and as soon as we [our Whigs] think ourselves strong enough, will be openly asserted and all attempts to secure our dependence openly resisted." [1]

At midsummer, Hutchinson informed the House that in obedience to instructions from the King, he could not give his consent to bills levying a tax upon the incomes of Crown officers, an instruction unexpected and apparently not approved by him. In his History, he states the position of the Assembly as regards royal instructions, while recording his dissent.[2] " The safety of the people requiring that every power should have a check, therefore it was ordained by the charter, that the full power of convening, adjourning, proroguing, and dissolving, should be in a Governor residing in the Province, and supported by the free grants of the people;

[1] *M. A. Hist.*, vol. xxv., p. 437.   [2] Vol. iii., pp. 342, 344.

and the King, they say, covenanted that the Governor shall exercise this power, ' as he shall think fit,' and not another : therefore an endeavor, meaning the instruction from the King, to restrain the Governor in the exercise of this power, is clearly an attempt to infringe and violate the charter." Samuel Adams, writing for the committee of which he was a member, denounced the position of Hutchinson, in refusing, in obedience to the King's instructions, to sanction the taxation of the Crown officers.[1]

" The reason you are pleased to assign for withholding your assent to the tax bill is surprising and alarming. We know of no Commissioners of his Majesty's Customs nor of any revenue his Majesty has a right to establish in North America ; we know and feel a tribute levied and extorted from those who, if they have property, have a right to the absolute disposal of it.

" By the royal charter it is expressly granted that the General Assembly shall have full power and authority to impose and levy proportionable and reasonable assessments, rates, and taxes upon the estates and persons of all and every the proprietors and inhabitants of this Province. Hence it plainly appears that the power of raising and levying taxes is vested in the General Assembly ; and that power which has the sole right of raising and levying taxes has an uncontrollable right to order and direct in what way and manner, and upon whom, such taxes shall be raised and levied. Therefore for your Excellency to withhold your assent to this bill, merely by force of instruction, is effectually vacat-

[1] Bradford : *State Papers*, p. 307.

ing the charter, and giving instructions the force of laws within this Province. And we are constrained to say, that your Excellency's present determination is to be governed by them, though this should be the consequence. We must further observe, that such a doctrine, if established, would render the representatives of a free people mere machines; and they would be reduced to this fatal alternative, either to have no taxes levied and raised at all, or to have them raised and levied in such way and manner and upon those only whom his Majesty pleases.

" As to the operation of law, mentioned in your Excellency's message, the law of this Province, at least in this respect, has rightly operated as it ever ought to. And we know no reason nor any semblance of reason why the Commissioners, their superior or subordinate officers, who are equally protected with the other inhabitants, should be exempted from paying their full proportion of taxes for the support of government within this Province."

The session came to a close, and the legislature, again and again prorogued, did not meet again until the spring of 1772. In spite of the rallying of the Whigs, after the reactionary proceedings at the beginning of the session just ended, there was a widespread disposition to make some compromise with government and have rest from controversy.

A scheme which Hillsboro had entertained for changing the Massachusetts charter, according to suggestions of Bernard, so that the members of the Council should be appointed by the King, was postponed on account of a threatened war with Spain. In August, a fleet of twelve men-of-war, under Montagu, Rear-Admiral of the Blue, and brother of the Earl of Sandwich, a noted opponent of the Colonial claims, cast anchor in Boston harl or. The probable war with Spain was the pretext f)r the presence of the unusual force, but no one doubted that an effect upon the Province was also designed.

Samuel Adams began to form in his mind, in the fall of 1771, a project which before long was to become very famous. In the light of events which are to follow, a letter written to Arthur Lee is very memorable.

"BOSTON, Sept. 27, 1771.

"The Grievances of Britain and the Colonies, as you observe, spring from the same root of Bitterness and are of the same pernicious Growth. The Union of Britain and the Colonys is therefore by all means to be cultivated. If in every Colony Societies should be formed out of the most respectable inhabitants similar to that of the Bill of Rights, who should once in the year meet by their Deputies and correspond with such a society in London, would it not effectually promote such an Union? And if conducted with a proper spirit, would it not afford reason for the Enemies of our common liberty, however great, to tremble? This is a sudden Thought and drops undigested from my pen. It would be an arduous Task for any man to attempt to awaken a sufficient Number in the Colonies to so grand an undertaking. Nothing, however, should be despaired of." [1]

[1] Copied from the autograph; now in the Lenox Library, New York.

The strife over the receiving by the government officers of stipends independent of the people has begun, and is soon to become more violent. As yet the complete denial of the authority of Parliament over the Colonies has not been made with any formality. In the days of the Stamp Act, only the right of Parliament to *tax* America was denied. We have seen Hawley soon after in the Assembly advance a further claim, but in an incidental way. Franklin, too, as we know, had taken advanced ground. The question of Parliamentary authority, however, was about to receive most elaborate discussion, and for a forerunner to the controversy, Samuel Adams printed in the " Boston Gazette " for October 28, 1771, a carefully studied paper, which exhibits well his wide reading of all the best authorities, his logical power, and his ability in calm statement. Hutchinson sent the paper to England with these remarks : —

" You may depend upon it, that the leaders of the people are in earnest, and flatter themselves they shall maintain their ground and make further advances until they have rejected every Act of Parliament which controls the Colonies. The paper which I enclose to you speaks their real sentiments, and is the language of the Chief Incendiary of the House. If they meet with nothing to deter them, it is not improbable that the next session may obtain a vote for a message or declaration in the very terms of the exceptionable declaration in the paper."

It was natural that he should write at this time, Octo-

---

[1] See Wells : *Samuel Adams*, vol. i., p. 427, etc.

ber 9 : " I have still a great way to go before I reach the mark and attain to a state of order and tranquillity. I am afraid sometimes that such a state is not attainable. The principles of the continental colonists will not admit of a supreme legislative Parliament, and consequently the King and his ministers will never concede to a colony an independent legislature. Whilst the point remains in dispute, the measures of administration in a colony will continually be affected by it. For some time past the correspondence between the several Colonies has been interrupted, but it is easily revived. It would be happy for the kingdom and the colonies if every province was a distinct island. Sooner or later the strength of the whole will be employed to effect what they call an emancipation." [1] When a Town-Meeting at the end of October begged that the Assembly might meet December 2, Hutchinson's reply was that the law had not made it the business of Town-Meetings to determine when the Assembly should meet. Their right he holds to rest upon a Province law, which authorizes them " when there shall be occasion for them for any business of public concernment *to the town* there to be done." [2] This he interprets as confining them within narrow limits.

In a lighter vein he writes from Milton, October 31, 1771, to Gambier : [3] " You would have made some humorous remark upon the company if you had been present among us to-day. About one half had been yesterday at a turtle-feast at the Peacock, which they

---

[1] *M. A. Hist.*, vol. xxvii.   [2] *Hist.*, vol. iii., p. 363.
[3] Afterwards a well-known Admiral.

did not quit until between three and four this morning, in a high storm of wind and rain. Lady William [Campbell] [1] has changed in one evening a tolerably healthy Nova Scotia countenance for the pale, sickly complexion of South Carolina; Mrs. Robinson [2] her natural cheerfulness and fluency for an unusual gravity and taciturnity. Poor Paxton's [3] usual refreshing nap after dinner was turned into a waking coma, more insensible with his eyes open than he used to be when they were shut. In fact, there was no need of any discernment to ascertain who had and who had not been of the party. The physicians, Parsons and Tetlow, may well contribute to the support of the Peacock. I only wish, instead of my good friends, the company might consist of Otis, Adams, Cooper, Hancock, Molineux, and half a hundred more of the same sort."

At the end of the year the Tories were rubbing their hands over the dissensions of their opponents. December 1, 1771, to Gage : " The pretended patriotism of this Province has always followed the example of those who make the like pretenses in England. They are now quarrelling among themselves. Hancock has declared he will never again connect himself with Adams. They both have their partisans, and like Wilkes and Oliver, they both declare they will never give up any part of the cause of liberty. I hope, however, it is like the faction in England; when divided, it will be weakened. It will be easier to manage them when the bundle

---

[1] Wife of the royal governor of South Carolina, then his guest.

[2] Wife of the Commissioner of Customs, the assailant of James Otis.

[3] Commissioner of Customs.

is broke than when tied together. Otis is a maniack, and under a guardian regularly appointed." [1]

The winter of 1771–72 was indeed a dark time in Massachusetts as regards the prospects of the Whigs. A powerful fleet was anchored in the harbor; the legislature was scattered; the patriotic strength had no opportunity for combined action. Samuel Adams struggled almost alone in the " Boston Gazette," against a number of Tory writers, some of them able, and all paid and inspired by the energetic Governor. " Chronus," " Probus," " Benevolus," and " Philanthrop," the latter believed then to be Jonathan Sewall, attorney-general of the Province, were vigorous opponents whom it was no child's play to encounter. "Except in this town," wrote Hutchinson to Hillsboro, " there is now a general appearance of contentment throughout the Province, and even the persons who have made the most disturbance have become of less importance. A gentleman who had assisted them much by his money and by the reputation which his fortune gives him among the people, seems weary of them, and I have reason to think is determined to leave them. The plain dispassionate pieces in our newspapers which are now published with freedom and dispersed through the Province, have done great service."

Hancock's defection, at this time, from the patriot cause seemed imminent to both Tories and Whigs. When Hutchinson fled to England three years later, and his papers fell into the hands of the patriots, it was found necessary to suppress certain documents per-

[1] *M. A. Hist.*, vol. xxvii., p. 258.

haps belonging to this time, as compromising Hancock, who in 1774 was once more firmly on the side of the Colonies. To quote Hutchinson again : —

"Hancock and Adams are at great variance. Some of my friends blow the coals, and I hope to see a good effect. They follow the opposition in England in everything they are able to do. I compare this to the quarrel between Oliver and Wilkes. Otis was carried off to-day in a post-chaise, bound hand and foot. He has been as good as his word, — set the Province in a flame, and perished in the attempt. I have taken much pains to procure writers to answer the pieces in the newspapers which do so much mischief among the people, and have two or three engaged with Draper, besides a new press, and a young printer who says he will not be frightened, and I hope for some good effect." [1]

Hutchinson claims that Massachusetts was never freer from real evils than in the beginning of 1772. From the surpluses of former funds and debts due government for lands, there was money enough for public needs for some time to come without taxes. Commerce had never been more flourishing. While the Colonies in general languished under the curse of paper money, Massachusetts had, through Hutchinson's beneficent work, a hard currency. Parliamentary duties had been reduced, until molasses and tea were the only articles which it was worth while to smuggle. As it was, tea cost twice as much in England as in America, twelvepence export duty having been taken off in England, while only threepence import duty in America had been

---

[1] To Bernard, Dec. 3, 1771.

imposed. Prosperity tended to mitigate discontent, and injure the plans of the Whigs.[1]

In March, 1772, the second anniversary of the Massacre was celebrated, Samuel Adams serving on the town's committee to procure an orator. John Adams was at first selected; but since he declined, adhering to his determination to hold aloof from public life, Joseph Warren was chosen, who received great applause, raising much his own prestige and cheering the hearts of the patriots.

The unusual interval of nine months had passed before the legislature was called together again on the 8th of April. Hancock, Speaker in the temporary absence of Cushing, who was ill, was still in opposition to Samuel Adams, and exerted his influence to have the right of the Governor recognized to remove the General Court to any place in obedience to instructions from the ministry. This measure Samuel Adams barely managed to de. at. Bowdoin in the Council also contrived to procure a similar vote. Temperately but firmly, Samuel Adams addressed the Governor for the Assembly: —

"We are still firmly of the opinion that such instruction is repugnant to the royal charter. . . . Nothing in the charter appears to us to afford the least grounds to conclude that a right is reserved to his Majesty of controlling the Governor in thus exercising his full power. Nor, indeed, does it seem reasonable that there should; for it being impossible that any one, at the distance of three thousand miles, should be able to foresee the most

[1] *Hist.*, vol. iii., p. 349, etc.

convenient time or place of holding the Assembly, it is
necessary that such discretionary power should be lodged
with the Governor, who is by charter constantly to reside within the Province." [1]

Nothing of importance was done during the session.
The enmity of Hancock toward Samuel Adams continued, as did the general apathy among the Whigs.
Hutchinson looked forward most hopefully; while his
rival, in spite of discouragement, was active as ever,
though apparently with small result. In the election of
the 6th of May, the Tories made a strong effort to defeat Samuel Adams. Of the 700 votes cast, Cushing
received 699, and Hancock 690, which showed that
their disposition to temporize (for Cushing was at this
time also weak-kneed) had conciliated the Loyalists
without alienating the Whigs. Phillips, the third can-
didate, received 688 votes, and Samuel Adams 505.
The majority, largely due to the influence of the
North End Caucus, was indeed sufficient. The patriots
were, however, alarmed, and took such measures that
the Tories soon saw they had only brought harm upon
themselves by their course. "It caused," said Hutchinson, "a more vigorous exertion, and no endeavors
were spared to heal all breaches in the opposition and
to guard against a renewal of them."

When the Court met, May 27, the number in attendance was unusually small, and twenty-three towns
were fined for neglecting to send Representatives. Hancock and Cushing waited upon the Governor before the
session began, "to inquire upon what terms I would

[1] Bradford : *State Papers*, p. 315.

consent to their returning to Boston. I let them know
that if there was anything in their address or message
which tended to a denial of the King's authority to
give instructions to the Governor, I would not consent
to it. , . . They encouraged me they would comply
with my proposal if Mr. Adams did not prevent it,
against whose art and insidiousness I cautioned them."
Mr. Adams, however, did prevent it. The House maintained the position from which it had been driven only
for a moment, under the influence of James Otis, the
preceding year, and Hutchinson felt the struggle was
useless. Adams and Hancock became reconciled, the
former magnanimously striving to palliate the inconsistency of his colleague; and as a first sign of the
restored friendship of the two men, Hancock refused
the position of Councilor for which the Governor had
approved him, preferring to remain in the House.

Since the House flatly refused to proceed to business
in any other place than the town-house in Boston,
Hutchinson at last yielded. For four years the struggle had been maintained, much of the time almost
solely by Samuel Adams. The insistence upon the point
produced a profound effect upon public opinion, though
in history its importance has not been appreciated.

CHAPTER X.

THE COMMITTEE OF CORRESPONDENCE.

AGAIN in the town-house in Boston, the legislature turned almost at once to the matter of the Governor's salary, which Hutchinson now plainly announced he should receive from the King. The House protested in its usual temper, the set of the opposition being so powerful that several of the Loyalists withdrew disheartened. A sullen refusal to repair the neglected Province House, which was falling into dilapidation, followed, and Hutchinson, after a vigorous reply to the Assembly's manifesto, prorogued the Court to September. During the summer Hillsboro gave place to the Earl of Dartmouth, in the Secretaryship for the Colonies, declaring to the Lords of Trade, as he laid down his office, that provision had been made by the King for the support of the Massachusetts Crown officials. When it became known that the decision had been taken, and that warrants for the payments had been drawn on the Commissioners of Customs, the wrath of the people became heavy, the voice of Samuel Adams, as usual, leading the discontent, as he muttered in the columns of the "Boston Gazette." What Hutchinson's frame of mind during this year was, we shall learn from the "Letter Book."

Writing, February 14, to John Hales Hutchinson,

perhaps a distant relative, who lived at Palmerston, near Dublin, in Ireland, he says : " Lord Hillsboro acquainted me with his Majesty's determination to allow his Governor £1500 sterling, to be paid annually out of the revenue, instead of the £1000 for which he used to be dependent on the people. . . . Is not an unwarrantable desire of independence at the bottom of all the discontent both in Ireland and in the Colonies ? In a government which has anything popular in its form or constitution, the remote parts will grow more dissatisfied with any unfavorable distinctions in proportion as those parts increase and become considerable. A doubt or scruple in the supreme authority of its absolute, uncontrollable power, and a relaxation in consequence, will increase the dissatisfaction and endanger a disunion or total separation. The words of Mr. Pitt, when he said, 'I am glad America has resisted,' gave a deeper wound to the peace of America than all the tumultuous resolves and rebellious acts which preceded them. For thirty years before that I had been concerned in government, and never knew the authority of an Act of Parliament called in question. All which had any respect to us were printed immediately and made a part of our code. Since that time the members of the Assembly grumble and mutter, and ask by what authority Acts of Parliament are mixed with our Provincial laws ; and the House of Representatives have repeatedly resolved that it is unconstitutional for the people to be governed by laws made by any power in which they are not represented. . . . It is not likely that the American Colonies will remain part of the dominion of Great Britain another century; but while they do remain, I cannot conceive of any line to be drawn. The supreme absolute power must remain entire, to be exercised over the Colonies so far as is necessary for the maintenance of its own authority and the general weal of the whole empire, and no farther. In the 27th and 29th books of Livy we find an instance of refractoriness in the Roman colonies not altogether unlike to that of the British colonies, and of the spirited and successful doings of the Roman senate upon that occasion. I have often wondered that in all the publications in the late controversy, no notice has been taken of so pertinent a piece of history. . . . So far the family has done worthily. I hope, therefore, and I think I shall demonstrate that the information you had of our relation to the regicide was not well founded. It is certain neither of us are descended from him." [1]

In the spring he received, in the midst of the fault-finding of the Sons of Liberty, a mark of confidence from the General Court at which he was greatly pleased, as he had a right to be. The boundary of Massachusetts on the side of New York, not settled in 1767 and still in dispute, it became very necessary to adjust, and no one but Hutchinson could be trusted to do it. April 27, 1772, he writes to Hillsboro : —

" After all the illiberal treatment I have received for so many years together, this is a greater mark of real confidence than I have known any Assembly to place in a Governor. I have made no concessions to occasion

---

[1] *M. A. Hist.*, vol. xxvii., p. 296. Quoted in Almon's *Remembrancer*, 1777, pp. 110, 111.

it. . . . They could not be prevailed upon to make any addition to the salaries of the judges of the Superior Court, and I think there is no room to hope that any Assembly will give what is adequate to their service." The settlement of the boundary was adjourned till the year following.

The Boston Town-Meeting is thus set forth. March 29, 1772, he incloses to Hillsboro certain proceedings, accompanying instructions to Representatives, "which however criminal are looked upon as matter of course, the meetings of that town being constituted of the lowest class of the people under the influence of a few of a higher class, but of intemperate and furious dispositions and of desperate fortunes. Men of property and of the best character have deserted these meetings, where they are sure of being affronted. By the constitution £40 sterling, which they say may be in cloaths, household furniture or any sort of property, is a qualification ; and even with that there is scarce ever any inquiry, and anything with the appearance of a man is admitted without scrutiny."

June 22, 1772, to Governor Pownal : "If you was now in America you would be sick of it in a week and leave it. Ten years ago they had some notion of government. They have none now. Can anything be more absurd than for the representatives of a people to admit the prerogative of the Crown, and yet to declare that all power is to be exercised for the good of the people, and they are to judge when it is so exercised, and to submit accordingly ! What they hold in theory they have not yet been able to carry into practice, and

I hope never will. . . . Indeed, I never had an instruction but what appeared to me consonant with the charter. I rather think we do not differ much as to the affair of the Castle, and that you have been misinformed as to facts. The Castle remains under the Governor, and did. The stores are as absolutely under my direction as ever, and all the apartments and buildings. The garrison would immediately remove if I should give orders for it." [1]

As to the case of the Gaspee, the British man-of-war which excited the rage of the people about Narragansett Bay by its effective interference with smuggling, and which was at length burned while aground by a party from Providence, such an expression is to be expected as the following : —

June 30, 1772, to Gambier: "I hope if there should be another like attempt, some concerned in it may be taken prisoners and carried direct to England. A few punished at Execution Dock would be the only effectual preventive of any further attempts. In every Colony they are sure of escaping with impunity. . . . I have brought the Assembly to such a state that though there are a small majority sour enough, yet when they seek matter for protests, remonstrances, etc., they are puzzled where to charge the grievances which they look for, in the first place ; and then consider whether [what] they complain of are grievances or not. Under such circumstances, and the advantage of having them in the town of Boston, where I can see a company of them every day, which by the way, you would think

[1] *M. A. Hist.*, vol. xxvii., p. 346.

to be dearly earning your salary, I hope to pass through a session without much trouble. Some foolish thing or other from such people is always of course." [1]

He advises strenuous measures.

August 23, 1772: " A declaratory Act of Parliament signifies nothing. What objection can there be to a penalty upon the denial of the authority of Parliament, and when done by any Assemblies or bodies of politicians in any part of the King's British dominions, why should not all subsequent proceedings of such Assemblies or bodies political be declared to be mere nullities? Or if this be inexpedient, can no other way be found to punish this offence?"

August 25, 1772: "If copies of private letters can be obtained we are never safe." [2]

A good head and heart speaks out of the following words: —

August 27, 1772, probably to Mauduit: "When I was young, at college or soon after, I read with attention what Mr. Locke had wrote upon toleration. I was astonished that ever anybody who thought at all, should have thought differently upon the subject; and yet all the world until then easily received the absurdities of the contrary doctrine. My poor ancestors, of my country I mean, and not of my family, I look back upon with pity, — in their intolerant spirit, which was the more inexcusable because they were at the same time vehemently inveighing against the same spirit in others.

---

[1] *M. A. Hist.*, vol. xxvii., p. 354. Quoted in Almon's *Remembrancer*, 1776, Pt. II., p. 57.

[2] *M. A. Hist.*, vol. xxvii., p. 373, etc.

I am not sure that if we were unrestrained, we have not a majority of the same spirit at this day. It's certain we have but little catholicism among the laity ; and the clergy in general, of every denomination, are bigots. My education has been among the Congregationalists, and I generally attend the publick worship with them. . . . As I have no scruples I frequently attend at the King's Chapel. Considering the commission I sustain, I think there is a decency and propriety in my so doing; and although I cannot approve of the good bishop's reason for not allowing toleration in England, yet I have no objection to a bishop upon the proposed plan in America. I think the inhabitants of the Episcopal persuasion have a right to it. It's a degree of intolerance to oppose it." [1]

November 7, 1772, to Governor Wentworth, of New Hampshire: "It's happy for the King's servants in the Colonies that Lord Hillsboro is succeeded by a nobleman of so amiable a character as that of Lord Dartmouth.[2] If God should raise up a Moses, or inspire any person now living with the same spirit, and give evidence of the same authority, I think it would have no effect on our Sons of Liberty, nor upon the rest of the sons of Levi . . . who are as much disposed to rebellion as Korah and his company of old." [3]

---

[1] *M. A. Hist.*, vol. xxvii., p. 377.

[2] Richardson, the novelist, said that Dartmouth might have been the original of Sir Charles Grandison, except that he was a Methodist. Cowper, too, celebrated his piety. Dartmouth was indeed a man of much good sense, and of far higher character than most of the society in which he moved.

[3] *M. A. Hist.*, vol. xxvii., p. 404.

At the close of the year come references to a matter of great importance in the development of the struggle, which even the Governor, with all his astuteness, at first entirely misappreciated.

November 13, 1772, to Secretary Pownal : "The restless faction in this town have pleased themselves with hopes of fresh disturbances from the salaries proposed for the judges of the Superior Court. The usual first step has been taken, a Town-Meeting. Hitherto they have fallen much short of their expectation, and even in this town have not been able to revive the old plan of mobbing ; and the only dependence left is to keep up a correspondence through the Province by committees of the several towns, which is such a foolish scheme that they must necessarily make themselves ridiculous." [1]

December 8, he writes again : " I send you the votes and proceedings of the town. The first part is Otis, the second Adams, and the third Dr. Young. Their plan is to bring as many towns as they can to adopt their resolves, and to keep up a correspondence by committees. They are vexed at the contempt I treat them with." [2]

Thus the Governor refers to what turned out to be the beginning of the end, — the formation of the Boston Committee of Correspondence, the significance of which neither he nor any one, except its institutor, Samuel Adams, at first penetrated, but the direct outcome of which was the United States.

---

[1] *M. A. Hist.*, vol. xxvii., p. 412.   Quoted in *Proceedings of Mass. Hist. Soc.*, vol. xix., pp. 139, 140, dated, however, Nov. 10.

[2] *M. A. Hist.*, vol. xxvii., p. 426.

How Samuel Adams brought into being the Boston Committee of Correspondence, probably the most important achievement of his career, the present writer has narrated elsewhere.[1]   He had not only to thwart the Tories, but to arouse and control the Whigs, whose leaders, with scarcely an exception, saw no promise in the scheme.   Hutchinson having been petitioned by Boston not to prorogue the General Court, appointed to meet December 2, took exception to the procedure as interfering with a matter " which the law had not made the business of Town-Meetings."   The town, protesting their right to petition, indignantly voted the Governor's reply " not satisfactory ; " whereupon the great manager, riding the wave as he always knew how to do, moved the establishment of the famous committee to state the rights of the Colonists, and to communicate the ideas of the town " to the several towns and to the world," and solicit replies.   Samuel Adams himself, Warren, and Church forthwith prepared and spread abroad the statement, which in a few days brought replies from important towns, evidently heralds of an almost unanimous expression.

To quote from what the present writer has elsewhere said : —

" In the last days of 1772, the document, having been printed, was transmitted to those for whom it had been intended, producing at once an immense effect.   The towns almost unanimously appointed similar committees ; from every quarter came replies in which the sentiments of Samuel Adams were echoed.   In the library

[1] *Life of Samuel Adams*, ch. xiii.

of Bancroft is a volume of manuscripts,[1] worn and
stained by time, which have an interest scarcely inferior
to that possessed by the "Declaration of Independence"
itself, as the fading page hangs against its pillar in the
library of the State Department at Washington. They
are the original replies sent by the Massachusetts towns
to Samuel Adams's Committee sitting in Faneuil Hall,
during those first months of 1773. One may well read
them with bated breath, for it is the touch of the elbow
as the stout little democracies dress up into line, just
before they plunge in at Concord and Bunker Hill.
There is sometimes a noble scorn of the restraints of
orthography, as of the despotism of Great Britain, in
the work of the old town clerks, for they generally were
secretaries of the committees; and once in a while a
touch of Dogberry's quaintness, as the punctilious
officials, though not always "putting God first," yet
take pains that there shall be no mistake as to their
piety, by making every letter in the name of the Deity
a rounded capital; yet the documents ought to inspire
the deepest reverence. It is the highest mark the
Town-Meeting has ever touched. Never before and
never since have Anglo-Saxon men, in lawful Folkmote
assembled, given utterance to thoughts and feelings so
fine in themselves and so pregnant with great events.
To each letter stand affixed the names of the committee
in autograph. This awkward scrawl was made by the
rough fist of a Cape Ann fisherman, on shore for the
day to do at Town-Meeting the duty his fellows had laid
upon him; the hand that wrote this was cramped from

[1] They are now in the Lenox Library, New York.

the scythe-handle, as its possessor mowed an intervale on the Connecticut; this blotted signature where smutted fingers have left a black stain was written by a blacksmith of Middlesex, turning aside a moment from forging a barrel that was to do duty at Lexington. They were men of the plainest; but as the documents, containing statements of the most generous principles and the most courageous determination, were read in the town-houses, the committees who produced them and the constituents for whom the committees stood were lifted above the ordinary level. Their horizon expanded to the broadest; they had in view not simply themselves, but the welfare of the continent; not solely their own generation, but remote posterity. It was Samuel Adams's own plan, the consequences of which no one foresaw, neither friend nor foe. Even Hutchinson, who was scarcely less keen than Samuel Adams himself, was completely at fault. "Such a foolish scheme," he wrote, "that the faction must necessarily make themselves ridiculous." But in January the eyes of men were opening. One of the ablest of the Tories wrote:[1] "This is the foulest, subtlest, and most venomous serpent ever issued from the egg of sedition. I saw the small seed when it was implanted; it was a grain of mustard. I have watched the plant until it has become a great tree." It was the transformation into a strong cord of what had been a rope of sand.

As an illustration of the invigoration of patriotic sentiment which at once appeared in all the Massachu-

[1] Daniel Leonard.

setts towns, the following "instructions" are given, drawn up by Concord for its Representative, Captain James Barrett, the veteran of the old French War who afterward commanded the Minute-men on the 19th of April, 1775.[1] The document is taken here from the handwriting of the town clerk, except the signatures, which stand at the end in the original as autographs of the committee.

" CONCORD : INSTRUCTION FOR THE REPRESENTATIVE.

"CAPN JAMES BARRETT :

"SIR, — We his Majesty's most Dutifull and Loyal Subjects the Inhabitants of the Town of Concord, in Town-Meeting assembled this Eleventh Day of January 1773 after Expressing our most firm attatchment to and ardent Love for our most Gracious Soverand King George, in the support of whose Person and Dignity we are always ready not only to Spend our fortunes but Lives (while we are in the Enjoyment of our invaluable Priviliges Granted us by Royal Charter) But Cannot in this time of General Concern throughout the Province Do otherwise than Express our Sentiments that Some of our invaluable Priviliges are Infringed upon by those heavy Burdens unconstitutionally as we think already Laid upon us that by some Late Laws and Innovations other if our Liberties and Priviliges Equally Dear are in Danger of being effected and Curtailed — for as a Report has of Late Prevailed that the Justices of the Superiour Court of this Province have

---

[1] His great-great-grandson feels a pious satisfaction in setting upon his page the name of this ancient worthy.

Salaries appointed them from the Crown, thereby Rendering them more Dependent on the Crown than we think any Judge ought to be on Crown or People, Whereby a foundation is laid for our Courts of Justice which always Should be Uninfluenced by any force but that of Law, being too Immediately under the influence of the Crown — and whereas an act was Passed During the Last Sessions of the British Parliament, Entitled an act for the better Preserving his Majesty's Dockyards, Magazines, Ships, ammunitions and stores by which act we in this Country are Exposed to the Rage of Some Malicious Person who out of Complasance to Some Court Sycophant may accuse any Person and thereby Cause him to be Hurried out of his native country, where he ought to be Judged and Carried to Some Distant Place thereby Deprived of all his friends and acquaintances and advantage of his Common Character, to be Judged by Strangers and Perhaps by Foreigners, and whether Innocent or Guilty is in Danger of being Ruined in Person and Estate, which we Look upon as a great Infringement on our Rights and Privileges and Contrary to the true Sense of Magna Charta and Spirit of Law.

" We think it therefore Proper at Such a time as this, to Instruct you, our Representative in General Assembly of this Province, that you in a Constitutional manner Endeavor to Prevent those Innovations we too sencebly feel and those we fear, by using your influence in the General Assembly in their Present Session for an humble Remonstrance to his Majesty, that all those Violations and Privileges which we are justly entitled to by the British Constitution and made over to us and our successors by the Royal Charter, might be Redressed, and also we further advise you, to use your best Endeavours that an Honorable and adequate Support be Granted to the Justices of the Superior Court as a recompence for their Important Services in their Exalted Station — Relying on your Loyalty & Respect for his Sacred Majesty, your Love and affection for your Country, we trust that you will in all matters that may come before you, Conduct with that Wisdom and Prudence, that Integrity and Coolness, that Circumspection and Firmness which So well Become the Senator and Patriot.

"JOSEPH LEE,
CHARLES PRESCOTT,
JOHN CUMING,
DANIEL BLISS,
THOS BARRETT,
STEPHEN HOSMER,
JOHN FLINT,
EPHRAIM WOOD JR
} *Committee.*

"The above Report Being Read in Town-Meeting Several Times, then the Vote was Called for to Know whether Town would accept of the Same and it Passed in the affirmative unanimously in a full Town-Meeting.

"A true Coppy att'   EPHRAIM WOOD JR.
                                    Town Clerk.

"CONCORD Jany yᵉ 18ᵗʰ 1773."

To Lord Dartmouth, the new Secretary, Hutchinson writes somewhat at length as to the situation.

December 13, 1772 : " I have repeatedly suggested

that nothing short of the power of Parliament would provide a cure for the distempers of the Colonies, and that I had no doubt of the sufficiency of that power, and until the proposal for taxing the Colonies by the Stamp Act nobody had ever questioned the supreme authority of Parliament in all cases. When the Virginia Resolves first appeared, it was so bold a stroke that even the Sons of Liberty with us pronounced them treasonable. However, we raised our notes immediately, but we waited until we heard how little notice was taken of them in England before we ran to their pitch. When it was advanced in both Houses of Parliament that we could not be taxed whilst we had no representative in Parliament, we embraced the doctrine with rapture, and the joy was rather increased than lessened by a new declaratory act to the contrary without any provision for enforcing it. You expected in England that time would cause truth to prevail, but error has been strengthening itself every day. A passion for independence which must be our ruin will not suffer us to discover the absurdity of two supreme powers in one state; for we are not willing to go so far as to admit of such a separation between the kingdom and colonies as will make them distinct and different states. Now if we can be brought to renounce these absurdities, we shall return to the state we were in before the Stamp Act, and Parliament can and will sooner or later compel us to it. When this is done it will appear to be the mutual interest of Kingdom and Colonies that this supreme authority should be exercised as seldom as it used to be before the Stamp

Act, and upon commercial views only, which until of
late we have thought reasonable to submit to; but if
we are let alone a little longer, we shall think any
restraint in our trade to be as grievous as raising a
revenue by internal tax.[1] I have not been forward in
proposing measures for restoring us to a state of order.
I have repeatedly suggested that no power less than
Parliament could effect it, but the way and manner in
which Parliament was to proceed, it did not become me
to suggest. I can say nothing concerning the principles or the temper of the Americans which will be
new to you. A right to independence upon the British
Parliament is more and more asserted every day, and
the longer such an opinion is tolerated, the deeper root
it takes in men's minds and becomes more difficult to
eradicate, but it must be done or we shall never return
to good government and order."

The eyes of the Governor gradually open. He
writes to Dartmouth : " As yet but small response to
the Committee of Correspondence from the towns, but
the proceeding is to be regarded as very dangerous."

Early in January, 1773, letters to Dartmouth and
Pownal narrate the progress of the Committee of Correspondence, the scheme for which, he has learned, is
intended to include the Colonies as well as the towns.
The statute of Henry VIII. relating to the carrying of
accused persons to England for trial, the Governor
wishes had been newly enacted, as there were no Col-

---

[1] This draft, apparently the rough outline from which the letter to
Dartmouth was afterwards written, is crossed out up to this point, as if
Hutchinson felt he had gone into particulars to an unnecessary, perhaps
a disrespectful, degree. *M. A. Hist.*, vol. xxvii., p. 430.

onies when it was passed, and to extend it to their affairs might seem a strain. He thinks it, therefore, inexpedient to put it in practice if any other way can be found, as it would certainly cause great alarm. He is anxious to have Parliament interfere, and purposes himself to lay an elaborate paper before the General Court, a plan which he at once proceeds to carry out, and which produces a memorable crisis. But before we turn to this, let us see how the "Man of the Town-Meeting" justifies against the Tory the institution with which he is identified.[1]

"But were there no such Laws of the Province, or should our Enemies pervert these and other Laws made for the same Purpose from their plain and obvious Intent and Meaning, still there is the great and perpetual Law of Self-preservation, to which every natural Person or corporate Body hath an inherent Right to recur. This being the Law of the Creator, no human Law can be of force against it: And, indeed, it is an Absurdity to suppose that any such Law could be made by Common Consent, which alone gives Validity to human Laws. If, then, the 'Matter or Thing,' viz. the fixing Salaries to the Offices of the Judges of the Superior Court, as aforesaid, was such as threatened the Lives, Liberties, and Properties of the People, which we have the Authority of the greatest Assembly of the Province to affirm, the Inhabitants of this or any other Town had certainly an uncontrovertible Right to meet together,

---

[1] *Boston Gazette*, March 29, 1773. The town clerk's account of the proceedings commences with the statement that Samuel Adams was the author of the report.

either in the Manner the Law has prescribed, or in any
other orderly Manner, jointly to consult the necessary
Means of their own Preservation and Safety. The Peti-
tioners wisely chose the Rule of the Province Law, by
applying to the Selectmen for a Meeting, and they, as it
was their Duty to do, followed the same Rule, and called
a Meeting accordingly. We are therefore not a little
surprised that his Excellency, speaking of this and
other principal Towns, should descend to such an artful
Use of Words, — that ' a *Number* of Inhabitants have
assembled together, and having *assumed* the Name
of *legal* Town-Meetings,' &c., — thereby appearing to
have a design to lead an inattentive Reader to believe
that no regard was had to the Laws of the Province in
calling these Meetings, and consequently to consider
them as illegal and disorderly.

" The Inhabitants being met, and for the Purpose
aforesaid, the Points determined, his Excellency says,
' were such as the Law gives the Inhabitants of Towns,
in their corporate Capacity, no Power to act upon ! '
It would be a sufficient Justification of the Town to say,
that no Law *forbids* the Inhabitants of Towns, in their
corporate Capacity, to determine such Points as were
then determined. And if there was no positive legal
Restraint upon their Conduct, it was doing them an
essential Injury to represent it to the World as *illegal*.
Where the Law makes no special Provision for the common Safety, the People have a Right to consult their
own Preservation, and the necessary Means to withstand a most dangerous Attack of arbitrary Power.
At such a Time, it is but a pitiful Objection to their

thus doing, that the Law has not expressly given them
power to act upon such Points. This is the very Language of Tyranny : And when' such Objections are
offered to prevent the People's meeting together in a
time of Public Danger, it affords of itself just Grounds
of Jealousy that a Plan was laid for their Slavery."

This much by way of comment on the conflicting
views of Samuel Adams and Hutchinson upon the
Town-Meeting. Hutchinson, aristocratic in his political conceptions, believing that the few wise should
guide, while the many of limited wisdom should follow,
retaining in their hands but a modicum of power, turned
away from the Town-Meeting, in which the majority was
omnipotent, with disgust. That a good outcome could
proceed from the deliberations of the " plain people,"
the multitude in the Anglo-Saxon state, whom Abraham
Lincoln so loved, and whom he was so willing to trust,
the Tory Governor conceived as rarely probable. Much
less had he any conception of the mighty educative influence of such an institution upon the population in
the midst of which it exists, an influence which impressed so profoundly the spirit of John Stuart Mill.[1]
In the society which had shaped itself in New England,
the worse part, in his view, was imposing its will upon
the better part ; and he saw his duty in thwarting and
blocking by whatever means he could employ the tumultuous crowd in Faneuil Hall and the Old South that
overrode with such scant ceremony the more refined
world of the Province, and vociferated so disrespectfully
against time-honored privilege and prerogative across

[1] See *Considerations on Representative Government.*

the sea. If his view was narrow and not justified, he
had at any rate, in holding to it, much good company
in his own day ; nor is the number small at the present
hour of those who will declare Hutchinson's conception
to be entirely correct, — who, appalled by the rough
incidents and tumultuous course of democratic rule,
would, if they could, commit themselves, as men did in
the past, to the sway of the few or the sway of one.

Samuel Adams, on the other hand, thoroughly a man
of the people, was ready to apply Town-Meeting rule
through thick and thin. He was ready to admit to the
deliberations, and to the voting even, the ignorant, perhaps the vicious; and was little troubled though the
voices of the well-placed and educated were silenced.
There was no sphere, in his view, into which the Town-
Meeting might not venture. In a later time he was
ready to apply its methods to the management of the
general affairs of the United States, shrinking from any
delegation of power, even when the popular way was
cumbrous to the last degree. The student of those
times will see in the North End Caucus, in much of its
action, a prototype of the "Machine," of such ill odor
to-day in the nostrils of municipal reformers. Mackintosh, leader of the rioters who tore down Hutchinson's
house in 1765, was apparently as thorough a ruffian as
ever met justice at the hands of a vigilance committee.
Yet, after a short retirement, we find him again, unpun-
ished, in the streets of Boston ; and in the time of the
Massacre, and later, as we shall see, at the Tea-Party,
he and his "chickens" are discreditably in evidence
among the better men, suffered, indeed connived at, by

reputable Whigs in a way hard for us now to understand. Samuel Adams was himself a man of the strict-
est piety and most austere morals. His vindications of
the right of the people to rule themselves, and smite
back the interference of distant and high-placed would-
be masters and tax-gatherers, are full of dignity and the
manliest courage ; as were also his actions in further-
ance of the ideas he professed. But the query constantly suggests itself to him who ponders his career,
how could a man high-minded and wise, to such an
extent the master in the sphere in which he moved,
have admitted this and that objectionable agent, or
allowed this and that piece of policy, or stooped himself
to such questionable practices ?

Hutchinson and Samuel Adams, men alike in patriotic purpose, though so far apart in their ideas of the
methods by which their country's good might be secured, thoroughly honest and well disposed, were yet
very human instruments. Each saw the truth but partially ; each, in scheming to push the plans he believed
to be of public advantage, did things which one can
only wonder at. But when has it been otherwise, as
the world has gone forward ?

CHAPTER XI.

THE following letter, written out of the hot water in which he becomes immersed early in 1773, will well introduce an important event of Hutchinson's career : —

February 14, 1773, to Gambier : " I am involved in spite of my teeth in a fresh controversy with my two Houses. I have always avoided the point of the supremacy of Parliament, — I have taken it for granted that it was not to be disputed. The grand incendiary having tried every measure besides to bring the Province into an open declaration of independency, at length projected a plan, 1st, to bring the town of Boston into it, and then into a vote to send their resolves to every other town and district in the Province, with a desire to adopt them, and to appoint committees to correspond with a committee of the town of Boston, and to concert measures for maintaining their principles. The several towns having made these resolves, there would be but little difficulty in bringing their representatives to agree to them in the House ; and this being done, the other Assemblies throughout the continent were to be desired by a circular letter to join with the House of Massachusetts Bay. Upon the invitation of Boston the towns of Plimouth, Charlestown, Cambridge, Marblehead, Roxbury, and I suppose an hundred more of the towns, met and passed the same resolves. I could no longer dispense with passing the most open testimony against such extravagance, and at the next meeting of the Assembly, I endeavored to show them what their constitution was, and called them to join with me in supporting it or to show me where I was erroneous. I send you my speech, their reply, and my answer, which may be some little amusement to you, though I need to apologize for laboring to prove points so evident; the prejudices people were under made it necessary. Can you believe that all those cloudy, inconclusive expressions in the Council's answer came from B.?[1] They certainly did, and the contempt with which I have treated them enrages him, but he has compelled me to it. By employing them in this way, they have been kept hitherto from perfecting their plan, and about one half the towns in the Province have hitherto refrained from complying with Boston; but everything is uncertain, and nothing more is in my power than to stand my ground against a constant opposition, and now and then to throw something before them to catch at and direct them from their main object, tearing the constitution to pieces."[2]

The Governor had indeed good legal grounds for holding the establishment of the Committee of Correspondence to be "glaringly unconstitutional." One branch of the legislature seemed to assume the powers of the whole; the powers of the Representatives were continued practically after the term for which they were elected had expired.[3] The Town-Meetings, whose

---

[1] Bowdoin.
[2] *M. A. Hist.*, vol. xxvii., p. 448.
[3] *Hist.*, vol. iii., p. 396.

jurisdiction was by prescription purely local, presumed to meddle with the management of the British empire. January 6, he convened the legislature, and whereas he had before avoided discussing the supremacy of Parliament, he now proceeded to take the step. His letters now indicate a certain despondency, due no doubt to the vigor with which he is answered in the controversy which he has precipitated ; and also to the fact that his own friends often disapprove his course. He expresses a feeling of inadequacy for his position, hopes he shall not be neglected and forgotten, and begs for a passage to England on a government ship.

June 12, 1773, to Dartmouth : " It gives me pain that any step which I have taken with the most sincere intention to promote his Majesty's service, should be judged to have a contrary effect." [1] Plainly he has heard some disapproval from the Secretary of the course he has followed. " The principles so solemnly established by the Crown and Parliament were unhinged and degraded by the presumptuous, argumentative patronage of a provincial Governor." [2] There seems to have been some such feeling in England ; and in America the Whigs, at any rate, thought the Governor had made a great mistake, and were much elated. Says a letter of Thomas Cushing to Arthur Lee, September, 1773 : " I observe the Governor, by reviving the late dispute, has lost credit on your side the water, as well as on ours. The Ministry, I understand, are greatly chagrined at his officiousness, their intention having been to let

---

[1] *M. A. Hist.*, vol. xxvii., p. 494.
[2] Graham : *Hist. of U. S.*, vol. iv., p. 340.

all controversy subside, and by degrees suffer matters to return to their old channel." [1]

Says John Adams's Diary, March 4, 1773: "The Governor and General Court have been engaged, for two months, upon the greatest question ever yet agitated. I stand amazed at the Governor for forcing on this controversy. He will not be thanked for this. His ruin and destruction must spring out of it either from the Ministry and Parliament on one hand, or from his countrymen on the other. He has reduced himself to a most ridiculous state of distress. He is closeting and soliciting Mr. Bowdoin, Mr. Denny, Dr. Church, &c., &c., and seems in the utmost agony."

Hutchinson, however, was by no means unsupported. Lord Thurlow found his course admirable, and Lord Mansfield, with whom Hutchinson talked the matter over in England the following year, passed the highest encomiums upon the papers.[2]

The two documents are the most elaborate state papers of Hutchinson. The cause of the Tories in America probably never received a setting-forth more detailed and able. They well deserve, therefore, to be cited without abridgment, after long oblivion.[3] Equally important, on the other side, were the replies of the Council and House. The elder Charles Francis Adams, while giving the evidence for John Adams's connection with the controversy, calls the House document "the most elaborate state-paper of the revolution-

---

[1] *Mass. Hist. Soc. Coll.,* 4th ser., vol. iv., p. 360.

[2] *Diary and Letters,* vol. i., p. 202.

[3] See Appendix B. They were given in full the last time in Bradford's *State Papers,* 1818.

ary controversy in Massachusetts," [1] and Webster, in
the oration on Adams and Jefferson, commends "the
singular ability of the discussion."

John Adams wrote to William Tudor, March 8,
1817 : —

"Governor Hutchinson, in the plenitude of his
vanity and self-sufficiency, thought he could convince
all America and all Europe that the Parliament of
Great Britain had an authority supreme, sovereign, absolute, and uncontrollable over the Colonies, in all cases
whatsoever. In full confidence of his own influence,
at the opening of a session of the legislature, he made
a speech to both Houses, in which he demonstrated, as
he thought, those mighty truths beyond all contradiction, doubt, or question. The public stood astonished!
The two Houses appointed committees to take into consideration the Governor's speech. If any honest historian should ever appear, he will search those records.
The proceedings of the Council I shall leave to the
historian.

"The House appointed a committee to take into consideration the Governor's speech. Major Hawley, who,
far from assuming the character of commander-in-chief
of the House, pretended to nothing, still, however, insisted with the committee in private that they should
invite John Adams to meet with them, and to take his
opinion and advice upon every question. So critical
was the state of affairs, that Samuel Adams, John Hancock, Thomas Cushing, and all their friends and associates, could carry no question upon legal and constitu-

[1] John Adams's *Works*, vol. ii., p. 310.

tional subjects in the House, without the countenance, concurrence, and support of Major Hawley. John Adams, therefore, was very civilly invited, requested, and urged to meet the committee ; which he did every evening till their report was finished.

" When I first met the gentlemen, they had an answer to his Excellency's speech already prepared, neatly and elegantly composed, which I then believed had been written by Samuel Adams, but which I have since had some reasons to suspect was drawn at his desire, and with his coöperation by my friend, Dr. Joseph Warren. It was full of those elementary principles of liberty, equality, and fraternity, which have since made such a figure in the world, — principles which are founded in nature, and eternal, unchangeable truth, but which must be well understood and cautiously applied. . . . There was no answer, nor attempt to answer the Governor's legal and constitutional arguments, such as they were.

" I found myself in a delicate situation, as you may well suppose. In the first place, the self-love of the composer, who I believed to be Samuel Adams, having then no suspicion of Warren, would be hurt by garbling his infant. In the second place, to strike out principles which I loved as well as any of the people, would be odious and unpopular.

" Can I describe to you, my dear Tudor, the state of my mind at that time ? I had a wife — and what a wife ! I had children — and what children ! . . . But I had taken a part. . . . I determined to set friends and enemies at defiance and follow my own best judgment. . . . We read the answer paragraph by paragraph. I suggested my doubts, scruples, and difficulties. The committee seemed to see and feel the force of them. The gentlemen condescended to ask my opinion, what answer would be proper for them to report. I modestly suggested to them the expediency of leaving out many of those popular and eloquent periods, and of discussing the question with the Governor upon principles more especially legal and constitutional. The gentlemen very civilly requested me to undertake the task, and I agreed to attempt it.

"The committee met from evening to evening, and I soon made my report. I drew a line over the most eloquent parts of the oration they had before them, and introduced those legal and historical authorities which appear on the record. . . . The effect of them upon public opinion was beyond expectation. The Governor's reasoning, instead of convincing the people that Parliament had sovereign authority over them in all cases whatsoever, seemed to convince all the world that Parliament had no authority over them in any case whatsoever. Mr. Hutchinson really made a meagre figure in that dispute. He had waded beyond his depth. He had wholly misunderstood the legal doctrine of allegiance. In all great affairs there is always something ridiculous; *et, malheureusement, j'ai toujours trop incliné à saisir les ridicules.* I had quoted largely from a law authority which no man in Massachusetts, at that time, had ever read. Hutchinson and all his law counsels were in fault; they could catch no secret. They dared not deny it lest the book should be produced to their confusion. It was humorous enough to see how Hutchinson wriggled to evade it. He found nothing better to say than that it was 'the artificial reasoning of Lord Coke.' The book was Moore's reports. The owner of it—for, alas! master, it was borrowed—was a buyer, but not a reader, of books. It had been Mr. Gridley's."

The reply of the Council to Hutchinson's message, the work of James Bowdoin, was in every way an acute, well-studied, and happily formulated presentation. The reply of the House deserves the commendations which have been quoted, and owes unquestionably its power in great part to John Adams. That Samuel Adams, too, did an important work in shaping the telling paragraphs, all familiar with the products of that skilled and tireless hand will detect at once. Possibly the Whigs went to a distance for help. Governor Hutchinson, in England, met a Maryland refugee, who assured him that the lights of that remote Colony were appealed to.[1] The controversy is without doubt the most important which preceded the Revolution, and deserves an attention which later times have not bestowed upon it. Since the reader has the text at hand,[2] the labor of summarizing may be here spared. Especially interesting is the logical play, as regards the dilemma proposed by the Governor, that if Parliament is not supreme the Colonies are independent. The alternative is accepted, and the claim made that since the vassalage of the Colonies could not have been intended, independent the Colonies are. There cannot be two

[1] Diary, Sept. 7, 1776.   [2] Appendix B.

independent legislatures in one and the same state, Hutchinson has urged. Are not the Colonies then by their charters made different states by the mother country? queries the reply. Although, declares Hutchinson, there may be but one head, — the King, — yet the two legislative bodies will make two governments, as distinct as the kingdoms of England and Scotland before the union. Very true, may it please your Excellency, is the answer; and if they interfere not with each other, what hinders their living happily in such a connection, mutually supporting and protecting each other, united in one common sovereign? As to the dangers of independence, the answer states that they stand in far more fear of despotism than of any perils which can come to them if they are cut loose.

To Council and House the Governor at once rejoined, and to the rejoinder Council and House returned answers,[1] as they had done to the original speech, taking care to have the last word. The same acuteness and decision appear as in the earlier papers, the thin veneering of deferential courtesy covering very imperfectly the hatred that lurks in each period.

It is to be remarked, as regards this important controversy, that the opponents were worthy of each other. Acute and vigorous intellects, the best courage, the most unselfish public spirit, were engaged on each side; nor were the Whigs superior to the Tories in any one of these respects. Both sides were hampered beyond remedy in their effort to find a firm " constitutional " basis for their respective claims, by the fact that nothing

[1] See Appendix B.

has been more fluctuating and uncertain throughout its history than the English constitution. What more in contrast than the Plantagenet and the Lancastrian conceptions of that Constitution! To Tudor and Stuart again it was one thing; to Commonwealthsman, a thing how different! To the oligarchy that followed the Revolution of 1688, a thing how different still! Hutchinson was certainly correct in his contention, that for the most part throughout the colonial and provincial history the right of Parliament to regulate the affairs of the whole empire had been admitted; the patriot champions, in maintaining that the claim to be independent of Parliament was anything more than the claim of a few individuals, living in the unsettled days when the royal succession was interrupted, had no good ground to stand on. Hutchinson was quite right, also, in declaring that the position of his opponents involved an assertion of complete independence of control from home, — an independence from which, in those days, every man in the Colonies but Samuel Adams recoiled, as something sure to bring calamity. From denying the authority of Parliament to tax them, the Colonies had proceeded to a denial of the authority of Parliament to legislate for them in any way. From dealing with the Parliament, the spokesmen had latterly gone on to take in hand the King. For a time the contention had been that the relations of America and England had been those of Scotland and England before the union. Scotland had retained its own legislature for its own affairs, while the authority of the King had never been impaired. The Stuarts had all the power in the Northern Kingdom which they had in the Southern, — indeed had been followed with more loyalty by the Scots than the Southrons ; for, however it may have been the case that the Covenanters in the Civil War for a time withstood Charles I., no denial of his sovereignty was ever made, and the Scots fought unanimously by the side of the Cavaliers when the Independents tried to set up the Commonwealth. In America, however, the King had of late been practically set aside. He could not interfere in American affairs, it was said, because, eighty years before, William III. had given the Colony a charter which subsequent monarchs had no power to revoke, according to which the Governor must stand supreme, — he to judge of what was fit to be done in any emergency, because he, being on the ground, could weigh, as the sovereign from his distance of three thousand miles could not weigh, all the circumstances that bore on the case. The prerogative men said well, that from denying the right of the King to *instruct* the Governor, it was but a small step to denying the right of the King to *appoint* the Governor, and that right was the last tie that remained. Indeed, the position of his adversaries had become no less inconsistent and absurd than Hutchinson claimed. While professing loyalty, they were casting off Parliament and King. Two supreme authorities in one state are out of the question. Samuel Adams appreciated this well, though as yet the wary " Chief Incendiary " felt it to be impolitic quite to drop his mask. First, a three years' " campaign of education ; " then July 4, 1776.

It is no discredit to Hutchinson that in these years

he saw nothing but calamity in a dismemberment of the British empire. That was the general feeling, though the Colonies in this blind way were bringing about the very severance which all dreaded. Franklin, who in this view was quite in accord with Hutchinson, compared in his homely effective way the British empire to a handsome china bowl, which it was a great pity to break. In that generation dismemberment seemed certain to bring to pass ruin. Anglo-Saxondom, so thought the highest minded, would lose all chance to be preëminent, and the leadership of the world must fall into the hands of some race less masterful, with ideas less promotive of human welfare. Hutchinson could not foresee, no one foresaw, that the shock of separation would rather invigorate England, and that in a few years, even without the Thirteen Colonies, her empire and influence would be more far-reaching than ever before ; nor was it at all within human ken that, in the cleaving, the United States could come to pass, a nation so mighty, on pillars so enduring, of such good hope to mankind. To the Governor and all his world, misfortune only seemed to lie in schism, and honor rather than shame should be accorded him for his steady and uncompromising fight against it. As the reader has abundantly seen from the letters that have been quoted, what Hutchinson thought of as the happy solution of the problems of British empire was in all essential respects what has been hit upon as the English policy of the nineteenth century. Each Colonial member within its own limits administers itself, quite unvexed by interference from the mother land :

none the less, each Colonial member concedes to the
power at home — that Parliament which our Revolutionary fathers so execrated and hated, now a body
whose authority is largely increased — a precedence ;
indeed, a supremacy. In all ordinary times and affairs
the Parliament, so far as the Colonies are concerned, is
silent and unfelt. Let, however, a crisis arise involving
the interests of the whole, none of the Colonial members would to-day question the right and duty of the
English Parliament to step into the leadership, with
authority, if need were, to dictate east and west, as far
as the drum-beat extends, what measures should be
taken and what sums should be contributed to maintain the general welfare. This state of things Hutchinson would have had, if he could, a century and a
quarter ago. His world had no patience with such a
thought. From home came always exasperating inter-
meddling with local affairs ; in the Colonies there was
no disposition quietly to endure until ministers should
grow wiser. Standing directly between the contestants
advancing upon one another already with weapons bare
for use, turning now to one now to the other with
pleas, arguments, and entreaties, to which both one
and the other turned deaf ears, who will say that in
the attitude of the Governor there is not something
both pathetic and heroic !

   This much can be said for the hated Tory, while at
the same time full justice is done to those with whom
he struggled. But while Anglo-Saxon freedom en-
dures, honor will be rendered to Bowdoin, to Otis, to
the Adamses, and their sympathizers throughout the

Thirteen Colonies, who insisted, at the risk of their necks, that the principles of Magna Charta, becoming obscure, should be fully maintained. There will be honor to them for that; and honor to them also for their impetuous declaration that to the plain people belongs authority; that the plain people, in Town-Meeting assembled, or in any way seriously and solemnly convened, have a right to pass judgment on all acts that affect them, — to approve, to condemn, if need be, to denounce, even though it may be the King; and if words fail of effect, that the sword may be lawfully snatched and all ties sundered. It was inexpedient to try to justify this rule of the people from what was held to be the English constitution of that day, or from any conception of that constitution which had existed during the existence of the Colonies, except, indeed, the memorable interpretation given by the men of the Commonwealth, 1649–1653, which died out in the very uttering of it, because a sordid world was not worthy of it.[1] Far wiser was the course of the patriot champions, when at length they threw precedents away and boldly based their claims upon the law of nature, — upon inherent right, upon which human institutions should not be permitted to infringe, however hoar with age. Not until this ground was assumed (which Gadsden, of South Carolina, had counseled as far back as the Stamp-Act Congress) did the argument of the fathers become thoroughly irrefragable. In the long fence with the Governor he had them at a disadvantage, so long as it was sought to rest their justification

---

[1] See the author's *Life of Young Sir Henry Vane.*

upon what then existed, or had been in existence in preceding ages.[1]

It was a memorable controversy, during which the fiercest hate sprang up between·the contestants. Candid men to-day can thoroughly respect the champions of both sides. Certainly the claims of the fathers of the Republic need no further setting forth. In Hutchinson's case, grant that his apprehension of some precious principles was quite too weak, — that in trying to put restraints upon the people he was foolishly blind, yet in his own day he stood in company of the best; and in our day authoritative voices urge that any society, to be saved, must not be given over to itself, but be guided and ordered by a select " remnant," a doctrine to which Hutchinson would have fully subscribed. " By an unfortunate mistake," wrote the Governor to General Gage, " soon after the charter, a law passed which made every town in the Province a corporation perfectly democratic, every matter being determined by the major vote of the inhabitants; and although the intent of the law was to confine their proceedings to the immediate proceedings of the town, yet for many years past the town of Boston has been used to interest itself in every affair of moment which concerned the Province in general." [2] It was in the Governor's view

---

[1] " Adams now gives out they are on better ground ; all men have a *natural* right to change a bad constitution for a better whenever they have it in their power." Hutchinson to Col. J. Williams, April 7, 1773.

For an account of this change of base in the American Whigs from historical to natural rights, see D. J. Ritchie, *Natural Rights*, pp. 10, 11, London, 1895.

[2] Quoted in Wells : *Life of Samuel Adams*, vol. ii., p. 56.

" by an unfortunate mistake," and not by direction of
the Divine power that shapes the course of nations for
their good.   He was brave and honest, however, and
had and continues to have the best countenance.

Interspersed within this great controversy, a frequent
interchange of messages had gone on between Governor
and legislature over the question of salaries for the
judges of the Superior Court.   Government wished to
make the judges independent of the Province.   Is it
not well that judges should be independent of the community in which they are to judge?   The people, however, resisted long and fiercely, seeing a better condition
in the state of things which had prevailed since the
beginning, — a judiciary, namely, receiving at best a
very meagre stipend, — a stipend, moreover, liable to be
considerably reduced, or indeed completely withdrawn,
if decisions were given contrary to the popular will.
Were the people really wiser here than they had been
in the time of the bad currency?   This important session of the legislature came to an end on the 6th of
March.

On the 5th of March, Benjamin Church (a man now
nearly forgotten, but an honored and prominent figure until he turned traitor in 1775), in delivering the
oration on the third anniversary of the Massacre,
exclaimed: "Some future Congress will be the glorious
source of the salvation of America.   The Amphictyons
of Greece who formed the diet or great Council of the
states exhibit an excellent model for the rising Americans."   Contemporaneously with this utterance, the
House of Burgesses in Virginia debated the subject of

an intercolonial Committee of Correspondence. Before the middle of the month a measure favoring it had passed, action to some extent brought about, no doubt, through incitements from Samuel Adams's committee in Massachusetts. The natal hour being close at hand, the unborn nation was plainly stirring.

Even while the legislature were contending so hotly with Hutchinson, he made preparations for settling the boundary on the side of New York, for which he had been appointed the year before. That a state should be well secured and at peace, nothing is more important than that its boundaries should be clearly and advantageously settled. That Massachusetts has fared here fortunately is due to Hutchinson. We have already seen him as the principal figure in drawing the lines on the sides of New Hampshire, Rhode Island, and Connecticut. In 1767, an unsuccessful effort, in which he was the prime actor, had been made to fix the limit on the side of New York.[1] Some settlement had now become imperative; and although his principles were popularly denounced, and the scheme was already in progress which was to fling him out of the land, only he could be trusted to undertake the delicate negotiation upon which the welfare of the Province depended. The journal of the proceedings is still extant in the hand of the Governor. With William Brattle, Joseph Hawley, and John Hancock, Hutchinson journeyed to Hartford, where in the middle of May they discussed the matter with Governor Tryon, John Watts, William

[1] The details are given in the *Mass. Archives*, marked " Colonial," vol. iv., 1721–1768, pp. 335–344.

Smith, R. R. Livingston, and William Nicoll, commissioners of New York. On election day the dignitaries of Connecticut invited the visitors to a formal banquet, after which, until May 18, the business was debated. The New York men, although more compliant than the negotiators of seven years before, were still disposed to exact hard concessions, to which all the commissioners but Hutchinson were about prepared to agree. New York in that time was rapacious, and already deeply involved with the Green Mountain Boys in disputes as to the rightful ownership of the New Hampshire Grants, which in days following were to become the State of Vermont. Hutchinson, however, while diplomatic, was unyielding, insisting upon what had been substantially the demand of 1767. At last it was conceded, establishing for all time as part of the Bay State the beautiful county of Berkshire. He alone, too, it is said, prevented the giving up by Massachusetts of her claim to western lands; these were retained, and afterwards sold for a large sum.[1] It was really a considerable victory. The Massachusetts commissioners had been left free to do what seemed to them best; the Governor's colleagues cordially acknowledged that the success belonged to him. On the return to Boston the legislature was in the May session, and the Assembly authorized him to transmit the settlement to Dartmouth, Secretary of State, at once, without formally laying it before them. They trusted him entirely. Hutchinson with some pride declares that "no previous

[1] *N. E. Hist. and Gen. Register*, vol. i., p. 310.

instance of a like confidence of an Assembly in a Governor" can be found in Massachusetts story.[1] This transient favor and trust aggravated for him the force of the blow he was about to receive.

[1] *Hist.*, vol. iii., pp. 390, 391.

CHAPTER XII.

How bitter the home-coming of Hutchinson was, the following extracts will show : —

June 29, 1773, to Bernard: "After every other attempt to distress me they have at last engaged in a conspiracy which has been managed with infinite art, and succeeded beyond their own expectations. They have buzzed about for three or four months a story of something that would amaze everybody, and as soon as the elections were over, it was said in the House something would appear in eight and forty hours, which if improved aright, the Province might be as happy as it was fourteen or fifteen years ago. These things were spread through all the towns in the Province, and everybody's expectations were raised. At length upon motion the gallery was ordered to be cleared and the doors shut, and it was rumored that the members were sworn to secrecy. This was not true. After most of a day spent, it came out that Mr. Adams informed the House seventeen original letters had been put into his hands, wrote to a gentleman in England by several persons from New England, with an intention to subvert the constitution. They were delivered to him on condition that they should be returned not printed, and no copies taken. If the House would receive them on these terms, he would read them. They agreed to it.

"It looks as if the design at first was to form the resolves and never suffer the letters to appear to be compared with them. The name of the person to whom the letters were wrote was erased from all of them, but they appear to be all Mr. Whately's, — six from me, four from the Lieutenant-Governor,[1] one from Rogers, and one from Auchmuty to me which I had enclosed, — besides three or four more from Rhode Island or Connecticut. [So far the amanuensis, what follows being in Hutchinson's hand.]

"They broke through the pretended agreement, printed the resolves and then the letters, which effrontery was never known before. The letters are mere narratives which you well know to be true as respects remarks upon the constitution of the Colonies, and such proposals as naturally follow from the principles which I have openly avowed; but by every malversation which the talents of the party in each House could produce, they have raised the prejudice of the people against me, and it is generally supposed all the writers were concerned in one plan, though I suppose no one of them ever saw or knew the contents of the letters of any of the others unless by accident. After three weeks spent the House resolved to address the King to remove the Governor and Lieutenant-Governor. The Council, through their resolves, as you well know (for most of the facts about the Council I had from you), are more injurious than those of the House, yet conclude that the Governor and Lieutenant-Governor have rendered themselves so unpopular, that it cannot be

[1] Andrew Oliver.

for his Majesty's service they should continue, &c. There were five only out of twenty in the Council had firmness enough to withstand the cry, and twenty-eight in one hundred and eleven in the House. . . . Mr. Adams said in the House that what he had in view was to take off such people as were attached to the Governor, for the King would never confirm a Governor against the general voice of the people, and they had got rid of Sir F. Bernard in that way." [1]

The affair of the "Hutchinson Letters," which created great excitement both in America and England, an affair in which the best men of Massachusetts Bay were concerned (including Franklin, then the agent of the Assembly of his native Province, though a citizen of Pennsylvania), has been variously characterized. American writers in general have portrayed it as an instance of spirited treatment by patriots thoroughly upright and long-suffering, of an underhand and most criminal attack upon their liberties. The important assertion of Dr. George E. Ellis, in opposition to this view, however, is, that "the whole affair is a marvelously strong illustration of the most vehement possible cry, with the slightest possible amount of wool." [2] Hutchinson himself believed that he was pursued with the most treacherous and unprincipled malignity. An innocent man nearly lost his life in a duel in consequence of the transactions; a shade has rested therefrom upon the character of Franklin which cannot yet be said to have been explained away; the conduct of

[1] M. A. Hist., vol. xxvii., p. 502, etc.

[2] Atlantic Monthly, vol. liii., p. 662.

the people, so far from being admirable, seems to some, even at the present day, to have been a blind following of crafty leaders into the commission of grave injustice. Certainly, the biographer of Hutchinson is called upon to consider the matter with care.

Hutchinson throughout his public life had correspondents in England. As his manhood went forward, his prominence meantime always increasing, his letters abroad became constantly more numerous, addressed to people of all ranks, from men in humble station up to the Secretaries of State. The character of these foreign letters of Hutchinson has been abundantly illustrated in these pages. He expressed his views with entire frankness, but certainly with no more frankness than he employed in his daily private conversations, and in his open, formal declarations as a high official. Not the slightest evidence exists that he was ever doublefaced : his condemnations, his counsel, his criticisms, as communicated to Jackson, to Hillsboro, to Dartmouth, to Bernard, are of like tenor with his communications as Chief Justice, as chief magistrate, as conservative Boston townsman. Both in letters and in daily talk and manifestoes he had condemned the high flights of the Town-Meeting ; while not recommending the introduction of troops, he had yet declared that Parliamentary Acts must be backed up with some exertion of force ; he had mentioned by name the men he regarded as dangerous to the public peace, and approved of the policy of bringing such men to trial somewhere out of New England, since there they were sure to be shielded. With all this he had never favored any change in the charter; but consistently from first to last pressed his deeply-set conviction that if only Parliament would leave the Colonies to themselves in all but strictly imperial concerns, and if only the Colonies would admit Parliamentary supremacy, that, however, to be kept far in the background, — all would go as well as possible, no change at all being necessary in the existing instrument.[1]   Such were the views expressed in his letters and also to those in his Massachusetts environment.   Hutchinson, however, had, as the reader has had frequent opportunity to see, become very nervous about having the contents of his letters reported from England back to his countrymen.   Why was he nervous?   It was because he had before him the experience of Bernard. Bernard's views, though plainly expressed in Massachusetts, somehow seemed in the popular view much worse when reported back from across the water; and coming back in that way had been a main factor in bringing about his overthrow.   Hutchinson feared now a similar fate for himself.   He had never gone so far as Bernard, for Bernard wished to change the charter.   His views, however, were unpopular.   He held his chief opponents — Samuel Adams, Bowdoin, Otis, Hawley — to be full of craft and intensely hostile to him : they could sway the people as they chose.   If his letters should come back, they could give an interpretation to their phrases which would make them seem to go much farther, and to be of character quite different, from the sentiments uttered by the Governor to the world of Massachusetts.

[1] Such hints at " reform " as occur on page 169 do not imply change, but only restoration to the original intention.

Hutchinson's English friends were in the main discreet, but what he had feared at length came to pass. A package containing, with others, six letters from him was transmitted to America. The letters are mild as compared with some quoted in the foregoing pages. How they were obtained, how used, and what the consequences were, it is important to set forth.

The view of George Bancroft, subscribed to by Robert C. Winthrop,[1] is that the letters having been written to a member of ·Parliament, Thomas Whately, not a friend to government but in opposition, were shown by him to his friend George Grenville, the promoter of the Stamp Act, by whom they were retained. Grenville dying in 1770, and Whately in 1772, the letters fell into the hands in some way of Sir John Temple, the highly connected son-in-law of Bowdoin, lately a Commissioner of Customs in Boston, and after the war the first British Consul-General in the United States. Temple's sympathies were quite liberal, a disposition no doubt helped forward by his relations with the energetic leader of the Massachusetts Council ; and he it was who committed them to the hands of Franklin. Franklin, having received the originals, under strict injunctions of secrecy, was allowed at last to send them to Boston, with the understanding that the letters were to be shown only to a few leading people of the government, without being printed or copied, and that they were to be carefully returned. " They were not," he

---

[1] *Mass. Hist. Soc. Coll.*, vol. xvi., Feb. 14, 1878. W. H. Whitmore, in the *Nation*, vol. xxxviii., p. 298, gives a slightly different account of the transmission.

says, " of the nature of private letters between friends. They were written by public officers, to persons in public station, on public affairs, and intended to procure public measures. They were therefore handed to other public persons who might be influenced by them to produce those measures." Franklin did not contemplate the publication of the letters, nor did the Boston leaders to whom they had been sent. Hutchinson, too, believes they meant to keep back the documents, while persuading the people that they contained enormities not to be endured ; [1] but as Cushing told Hutchinson, " the people compelled their publication, or would not be satisfied without it." For thus making public private letters, the Whigs were roundly denounced. Wedderburn, afterwards Lord Loughborough, who was scarcely inferior to " Junius " in his power of bitter speech, lashed Franklin before a Committee of Parliament without mercy, who thenceforth had no position in the English social world. Mr. Winthrop palliates Franklin's conduct by saying that the best men in Massachusetts were in it, Chauncy, Cooper, Dr. Winthrop, and Bowdoin, the latter of whom calls it " that meritorious act." It was a time of great commotion : Franklin's own letters were thus opened. Mr. Winthrop believes it may be classed among what Burke calls " irregular things done in the confusion of mighty troubles, not to be made precedents of or justified on principle." If Franklin had done no more than to send the letters, his conduct perhaps need give little trouble to his eulogists ; but there are grounds for thinking he accom-

[1] *Hist.*, vol. iii., p. 393. See, also, the letter to Bernard, p. 269.

panied them by a letter of his own, which contained a
crafty suggestion. It is claimed that July 7, 1773,
Franklin wrote as follows to Dr. Samuel Cooper : —

"The letters might be shown to some of the Governor's and Lieutenant-Governor's partisans, and spoken
of to everybody, for there was no restraint proposed to
talking of them, but only to copying. And possibly,
as distant objects, seen only through a mist, appear
larger, the same may happen from the mystery in this
case. However this may be, the terms given with them
could only be those with which they were received."
This letter to Cooper, so far as it bears on this matter,
in Franklin's correspondence edited by Sparks, and later
by Bigelow, reads as follows.

July 7, 1773, to Samuel Cooper, London : "You
mention the surprise of gentlemen, to whom those letters have been communicated, at the restrictions with
which they were accompanied, and which they suppose
render them incapable of answering any important end.
One great reason of forbidding their publication was
an apprehension that it might put all the possessors of
such correspondence here upon their guard, and so prevent the obtaining more of it. And it was imagined
that showing the originals to so many as were named,
and to a few such others as they might think fit, would
be sufficient to establish their authenticity, and to spread
through the Province so just an estimation of the
writers as to strip them of all their deluded friends, and
demolish effectually their interest and influence. The
letters might be shown even to some of the Governor's
and Lieutenant-Governor's partisans, and spoken of to

everybody; for there was no restraint proposed to talking of them, but only to copying. However, the terms given with them could only be those with which they were received." [1]

The sentence, "And possibly, as distant objects, seen only through a mist, appear larger, the same may happen from the mystery in this case," is omitted. The claim of Tory writers is that the letter has been garbled. Governor Hutchinson himself has copied the letter " on a fly-leaf at the end of the sixth volume of his Diary." [2] The omitted sentence also appears in the letter as printed in the Tory Curwen's Journal.[3] Though such testimony of course will not go very far, Dr. Ellis can be cited as expressing a belief that it may possibly be true.[4] The free and easy way of the old-fashioned editors was to omit and emend wherever a judicious touch of that kind might veil a blotch in the hero they had in care. Franklin was the most consummate of managers, and there was perhaps nothing in his character to hold him back even from a trick like this, when such a foe as Hutchinson was to be put down. The intention was, as Franklin lets us plainly see, after showing the originals to a few selected men, "to spread through the Province so just an estimation of the writers as to strip them of all their deluded friends, and demolish effectually their interest and influence."

Following out this plan soon after the return of the

[1] Sparks : *Life and Writings of Franklin*, vol. viii., p. 72 ; Bigelow : *Works of Benjamin Franklin*, vol. v., p. 189.

[2] *Diary and Letters*, P. O. Hutchinson, vol. ii., pp. 337, 338.

[3] Appendix, art. " Hutchinson."

[4] *Atlantic Monthly*, May, 1884, p. 672.

commissioners from Hartford, Hancock informed the Assembly that within two days something most important was to transpire. This announcement went abroad, greatly exciting public curiosity. Immediately after, the public having been excluded, Samuel Adams informed the House of the reception of the letters, and of the restriction which lay upon their publication. The House, he said, could, however, be possessed of their contents, and the reading of the letters then followed. A committee then reported, taking the letters together, that they tended to annul the charter and overthrow all liberty. An almost unanimous acceptance of the report followed, and the transactions being made known in the streets, the people grew wild to know upon what the action of the House was based.

Hutchinson was at once on the alert. He demanded copies of the letters, declaring vehemently that no such documents as were described had ever proceeded from him. The House sent him the dates of the letters. He refused a request of the House to transmit them copies of the letters he had written on those dates, as there would be an impropriety in laying before them his private correspondence, and he was restrained by the King from showing that of a public nature. He declared, however, that neither private nor public letters of his "tended, or were designed to subvert, but rather to preserve entire, the constitution of the government." [1] The popular clamor to know what the letters contained became now irresistible. It may be believed that the leaders felt themselves to be most awkwardly placed.

[1] *Hist.*, vol. iii., p. 401.

They were bound by the conditions imposed by Franklin neither to print nor to copy; and besides, as far as Hutchinson was concerned, the chief *bête noire* to whom they wished to put an end, they were, of course, perfectly well aware, shrewd, cool heads as they were, that the letters signed by him were mild as mother's milk. To yield, however, became a necessity. Hancock told the House that copies of the letters had been put into his hands in the streets; they were really out then, and the House gave way. The letters were ordered printed; but beforehand the House spread far and wide a series of resolves, most carefully and elaborately worded, interpreting the letters in the most unfavorable way, as containing proofs of a conspiracy against the country, in which Hutchinson was the prime mover. The people were prepared for revelations very terrible; so hoodwinked were they that when the letters came, as Hutchinson said, " had they been Chevy Chase, the leaders would have made them *believe* it was full of evil and treason."

To justify this presentation, the full text of letters and resolves must be given.[1]

As to the letters by which those from the Governor were accompanied, also printed in the pamphlet, there is one from Robert Auchmuty, September 14, 1768, warning Hutchinson against great danger to his life from " the infernal purposes of the sons of liberty as they falsely stile themselves" — " terrible threats and menaces by those Catilines against you."

Of the four from Andrew Oliver, one of the 7th of

---

[1] See Appendix C.

May, 1767, describes the effort of the Assembly to minimize the power of Crown officials, and the bad treatment of Hutchinson, "a gentleman to whom they are more indebted than to any man in the government." The Governor ought to have more salary in these expensive days than £1000, which has been the customary pay for thirty-five years. The Lieutenant-Governor has "no appointments [salary] as such." As Captain of Castle William, he has perhaps £120. The Secretary has about £200, with some fees, but "perquisites and salary altogether are not the half of his annual expense." In the following terms, he recommends that Crown officers be provided for by the King : "The Crown did by charter reserve to itself the appointment of a Governor, Lieutenant-Governor, and Secretary : the design of this was without doubt to maintain some kind of balance between the powers of the Crown and of the people. But if officers are not in some measure independent of the people (for it is difficult to serve two masters), they will sometimes have a hard struggle between duty to the Crown and a regard to self, which must be a very disagreeable situation to them, as well as a weakening to the authority of government. The officers of the Crown are very few, and are therefore the more easily provided for without burdening the people; *and such provision I look upon as necessary to the restoration and support of the King's authority.*" [1]

Oliver's second and fourth letters are quite unimportant; in the third, however, he distinctly advises a

---

[1] The italics are those of the pamphlet of the General Court.

change of the constitution, saying that some alteration is necessary in the election of councilors; that there must be less of popular influence in order to make the resemblance as near as may be to the British Parliament. A change in the charter he thinks may be salutary.

Charles Paxton, head of the Board of Customs Commissioners, writes from the "Romney," June 20, 1768: " Unless we have immediately two or three regiments, 't is the opinion of all the friends to government that Boston will be *in open rebellion*." ·

Nathaniel Rogers writes a letter personal and unimportant about succeeding Andrew Oliver as Secretary, an appointment he did not receive. What letters remain have even less significance.

The reader must feel that these letters of Hutchinson are mild. A number have been quoted in these pages, which, while certainly not recommending any change in the constitution, go much more strongly against popular ideas than any cited in the pamphlet. Andrew Oliver does, indeed, recommend a change in the Council, and Paxton asks for troops; but there was no reason for supposing the Governor knew of their letters; no reason for supposing he sympathized with their ideas. It was indeed, as Dr. Ellis urges, a very marked case of great cry and little wool. Is it credible that those wary, able men — Franklin, Samuel Adams, Bowdoin, John Adams, Samuel Cooper — really thought these very quiet statements justified on their part such an uprising against the Governor? There is really much to make the following explanation of their course

the most satisfactory one : they had persuaded themselves Hutchinson was so dangerous that if conduct
thoroughly above board would not answer, he must be
cast out by questionable means.

In the only one of the six letters in which Hutchinson trenches closely upon controverted points, his
expressions are as follows : " I never think of the
measures necessary for the peace and good order of
the Colonies without pain : there must be an abridgment of what are called English liberties. I relieve
myself by considering that in a remove from the state
of nature to the most perfect state of government,
there must be a great restraint of natural liberty. I
doubt whether it is possible to project a system of
government in which a Colony, three thousand miles
distant from the parent state, shall enjoy all the liberty
of the parent state. I am certain I have never yet
seen the projection." In Hutchinson's own defense, he
says of these words, in his History : " To a candid
mind, the substance of the whole paragraph was really
no more than this : ' I am sorry the people cannot be
gratified with the enjoyment of all they call English
liberties, but in their sense of them, it is not possible
for a Colony at three thousand miles distance from the
parent state to enjoy them, as they might do if they
had not removed.' " [1]

In no way does the Governor say more here than he
had repeatedly said in public. He makes no recommendation that the charter should be changed or troops

[1] *Hist.*, vol. iii., p. 409. That is, to have representation in Parliament
is impracticable. See page 293.

be sent. Such liberties as the establishment of Committees of Correspondence, the discussion of great affairs of state by the Town-Meetings, the resistance to the ministerial policy in the matter of the payment of the judges and the Crown officials, Hutchinson felt, and in the most open manner had said, ought to be abridged. These, in his idea, were excesses, but could be remedied without touching the charter. He was in some points wrong, of course, but there was nothing underhanded in his fight. He declares, further, that he wishes well to the Colony, and, *therefore*, desires an abridgment of its liberty; and that he hopes no more severity will be shown than is necessary to secure its dependence.

The following letter, written a little later in the year, November 13, is clear and manly : "I differ in my principles from the present leaders of the people. . . . I think that by the constitution of the Colonies the Parliament has a supreme authority over them. I have, nevertheless, always been an advocate for as large a power of legislation within each Colony as can consist with a supreme control. I have declared against a forcible opposition to the execution of Acts of Parliament which have laid taxes on the people of America : I have notwithstanding ever wished that such Acts might not be made as the Stamp Act in particular. I have done everything in my power that they might be repealed. I do not see how the people in the Colonies can enjoy every liberty which the people in England enjoy, because in England every man may be represented in Parliament, the supreme authority over the whole ; but in the Colonies, the people, I conceive, cannot have representatives in Parliament to any advantage. It gives me pain when I think it must be so. I wish also that we may enjoy every privilege of an Englishman which our remote situation will admit of. These are sentiments which I have without reserve declared among my private friends, in my speeches and messages to the General Court, in my correspondence with the ministers of state, and I have published them to the world in my History; and yet I have been declared an enemy and a traitor to my country, because in my private letters I have discovered the same sentiments; for everything else asserted to be contained in those letters, I mean of mine, unfriendly to the country, I must deny as altogether groundless and false." [1]

On a fly-leaf of his diary two years later, after quoting a sentence from Erasmus as to the injustice of garbled quotations from a man's words, he continues : " How applicable is this to the case of my letters to Whately, and the expression, ' there must be an abridgment of what are called English liberties ! ' Everything which preceded and followed which would have given the real sentiment and taken away all the odium was left out."

Had the leaders lost in the excitement of the controversies the power of weighing words properly, and did they honestly think Hutchinson's expressions deserved such an interpretation ? Did they honestly believe it was right to hold him responsible for what Oliver and Paxton had said ?

[1] *M. A. Hist.*, vol. xxvii., p. 568.

Hutchinson claims it was deliberate artifice. " When some of the Governor's friends urged to the persons principally concerned . . . the unwarrantableness of asserting or insinuating what they knew to be false and injurious, they justified themselves from the necessity of the thing; the publick interest, the safety of the people, making it absolutely necessary that his weight and influence among them should by any means whatever be destroyed." [1]

The remark of a great historian seems here appropriate : " Tho maxim that it is as justifiable to defeat a public enemy by craft as by valor finds easy access to the breasts of even high-minded statesmen." [2]

Hutchinson's letters in this time of trial deserve still farther citation.

" I know," he writes July 11, " that the great Governor of the world always does right, and I desire to acknowledge it when I am in adversity, as well as in prosperity. . . . It cannot be many years before I shall be beyond the reach of the most envious and malicious enemy. I desire your prayers that while I remain I may be faithful to the people and to the King, — that I may preserve the *decens et rectum*. You may be assured that I have but little if any concern from any danger of my being superseded, more than a war-horse feels when his heavy accoutrements are to be taken off, and he sees a quiet stable or pasture just by him." [3]

July 20, 1773, to Colonel Israel Williams, of Hat-

---

[1] *Hist.*, vol. iii., p. 405, note.

[2] S. R. Gardiner : *Commonwealth and Protectorate*, vol. i., p. 105, London, 1895.

[3] *M. A. Hist.*, vol. xxvii., p. 515.

field: "Bowdoin in the Council and Adams in the House have certainly shown themselves very adroit, but it will be a reproach to the body of the people to the latest posterity, that they have suffered themselves to be made such dupes, especially after a public declaration in the House that all that was intended was to raise a general clamor against the Governor and Lieutenant-Governor, and then they should be sure of their removal. The deception cannot last longer than it did in the time of the witchcraft. Truth at worst will finally prevail. As for the Resolves,[1] they are every one false; most of them are villainous. I would have declared them to be so in the most open manner, if it had been in character, and would in the same manner have vindicated every part of the letters. In so plain a case, if but a few persons only remain undeceived, a free open testimony against the delusion will soon undeceive the rest. I pitied the poor members, more than one half of them being forced to vote *in verba magistri*, either directly against their judgment, or without understanding what they voted. I have no great doubt that sooner or later this proceeding will reflect more infamy on all concerned, than any public transaction since the country was settled; for it was founded on such baseness as no civilized people have ever countenanced, and has been conducted through every part of its progress with falsehood and deception, which, although for a short time they have their intended effect, yet as soon as they are discovered, prove ignominious to the authors of them." [2]

---

[1] See Appendix C.

[2] From the Williams MSS. in possession of the Mass. Hist. Society.

Though Hutchinson saw, as he thought, signs that the people would awake to the injustice done him, the Whig leaders drove astutely and energetically toward making the most of the mood toward the Governor into which the towns had been brought. " Master of the Puppets " is Hutchinson's term for Samuel Adams in these days ; and he notes the significant changes of language which show the growth of the spirit of independence. The Boston " town-house " or " court-house " becomes what it has remained to the present day, — the old " state-house," and its debates and decisions " Parliamentary " debates and acts ; the Province laws become " the laws of the land ; " the charter, originally a grant from royal grace, becomes " a compact : " as the House becomes " his Majesty's Commons," so the Council is assimilated to the Lords, and the right of impeachment, a function quite new, arrogated for it. The Revolution was indeed well along, and the disposition became more and more marked to claim that the American people were " in a state of nature," — that no thought need be given to past charters, enactments, or precedents ; but that standing on their inalienable rights to life, liberty, and the pursuit of happiness, they must strike out for a political arrangement new from the foundation. Besides the affair of the Letters, the principal topic of interest during the summer of 1773 was the matter of the salaries of the judges of the Superior Court, which the Whigs were determined should not be received from the government, but as heretofore from

The letter corresponds minutely with the draft in the Letter Book at the State House. *M. A. Hist.*, vol. xxvii., p. 516.

the vote of the Assembly. When finally the House was prorogued, the Committee of Correspondence maintained a most active life, scheming, of course under Samuel Adams's lead, for a congress of the Colonies, a project which momentarily now took on shape more and more definite.

The reflection of the passing show is vividly given in Hutchinson's letters of this time, — a true picture except as the imperfections of his mirror, due to his limited range of view and the passion aroused in him by the baiting he was undergoing, distorted the image. In what guise he moved in this stormful year, and in the next year when he stood before George III. to give an account of his stewardship (to descend for a moment to smaller matters), such a letter as the following informs us narrowly.

August 2, 1773, to Mr. James Fisher: "I desire you to send me by the first opportunity a suit of scarlet broad-cloth, full trimmed but with few folds, and shalloon lining in the body of the coat and facing, the body of the waistcoat linen, and the breeches lining leather, plain mohair button-hole; also, a cloth frock with waistcoat and breeches, not a pure white but next to it, upon the yellow rather than blue, — I mean a color which has been much worn of late, button-holes and lining the same, the coat to have a small rolling cape or collar. — Also, a surtout of light shag or beaver, such color as is most in fashion: a velvet cape gives a little life to it. The waistcoats last sent are cut rather too large in the neck, which makes them full before, but not much. Write me whether any sort of garment of the fashion of velvet coats, to wear over all, which were common some years ago, are now worn, and whether of cloth, and what color and trimmings. I should not chuse velvet." [1]

Not strangely, note was made at this time of the extent to which 'public places were held by a knot of closely connected men. Hutchinson's brother Foster was Justice of the Common Pleas; Andrew Oliver, Lieutenant-Governor, had married the Governor's wife's sister; Peter Oliver, Chief Justice, was father of the Governor's daughter's husband ; the Governor's own son Thomas had lately become Judge of Probate. This state of things, of course, does not look well ; but the reader of this narrative will hardly suppose the holders of these posts to have become plethoric through their emoluments, or puffed up with adulations rendered them. Most certain is it that the accusation that Hutchinson put his own family and friends into good positions had as slight foundation as many other charges against him. The positions involved great care and labor, with small pay and little credit; such as they were, they were not given to their incumbents by Hutchinson, with one exception. Writing to Dartmouth, August 20, 1773, he says he has seen in an English newspaper a long list of places bestowed by him upon his family, which is in every article false, the only appointment he has made being since that time, of his eldest son to a judge of an inferior Court, a post of £50 a year.[2] This he had offered to several gentlemen, who declined accepting it as not worth the trouble. Hutchinson asks

<hr>

[1] *M. A. Hist.*, vol. xxvii., p. 521.   [2] Court of Probate.

for a position for his son " Billy," then in England, a quite proper request for him to make of the Earl. He himself has been, he declares, in public service for small pay since he was very young, and has had no chance to provide for his family.[1]

As the fall went forward, a congress of the Colonies " after the plan first proposed by Virginia " was called for with increasing emphasis, and at last, October 11, in the "Boston Gazette," an " American Commonwealth " was boldly discussed. Hutchinson's letter at this time to Dartmouth, as to the situation and the prime mover in bringing it to pass, can by no means be omitted.

October 9, 1773 (marked in the Letter Book " private ") : " The conductors of the people are divided in sentiment, some of them professing that they only aim to remove the innovations since the date of the Stamp Act, or, as they sometimes say, since the expiration of the war ; for they are not always the same : and though they don't think Parliament has a just authority, yet they are willing to acquiesce, seeing it had been so long submitted to. Others declare they will be altogether independent ; they would maintain an alliance with Great Britain. Each stands in need of the other, and their mutual interest is sufficient to keep them together. Of the first sort, the Speaker of the House[2] often declares himself : so does a clergyman of Boston, who has great influence in our political measures ;[3] and so do some of the Council who have most influence there.

---

[1] M. A. Hist., vol. xxvii., p. 529.

[2] Cushing.

[3] Andrew Eliot, no doubt.

"Those of the latter opinion have for their head one of the members of Boston, who was the first person that openly and in any public assembly declared for absolute independence. From a natural obstinacy of temper, and from many years' practice in politics, he is perhaps as well qualified to excite the people to any extravagance in theory or practice as any person in America. From large defalcations, as collector of taxes for the town of Boston, and other defalcations in pecuniary matters, his influence was small until within these seven years; but since that, it has been gradually increasing, until he has obtained such an ascendency as to direct the town of Boston and House of Representatives, and consequently the Council, just as he pleases. A principle has been avowed by some who are attached to him, the most inimical that can be devised, that in political matters the public good is above all other considerations; and every rule of morality, when in competition with that, may very well be dispensed with. Upon this principle, the whole proceedings, with respect to the letters of the Governor and Lieutenant-Governor, of which he was the chief conductor, has been vindicated. In ordinary affairs, the council of the whole opposition unite. Whenever there appears a disposition to any conciliatory measures, this person, by his art and skill, prevents any effect; sometimes by exercising his talents in the newspapers, an instance of which is supposed to have been given in the paper enclosed to your Lordship in my letter, number twenty-seven; at other times by an open opposition, and this sometimes in the House, where he has defeated every attempt as often as any has been made. But his chief dependence is upon a Boston Town-Meeting, where he originates his measures, which are followed by the rest of the towns, and of course are adopted or justified by the Assembly. . . .

" I could mention to your Lordship many instances of the like kind. To his influence it has been chiefly owing, that when there has been a repeal of Acts of Parliament complained of as grievous, and when any concessions have been made to the Assembly, as the removal of it to Boston and the like (notwithstanding the professions made beforehand by the moderate part of the opposition, that such measures would quiet the minds of the people), he has had art enough to improve them to raise the people higher by assuring them, if they will but persevere, they may bring the nation to their own terms ; and the people are more easily induced to a compliance from the declaration made, that they are assured by one or more gentlemen in England, on whose judgment they can depend, that nothing more than a firm adhesion to their demands is necessary to obtain a compliance with every one of them. Could he have been made dependent, I am not sure that he might not have been taken off by an appointment to some public civil office. But, as the constitution of the Province is framed, such an appointment would increase his abilities, if not his disposition to do mischief, for he well knows that I have not a Council which in any case would consent to his removal, and nobody can do more than he to prevent my ever having such a Council.

"I have presumed thus in a private letter to give your Lordship a true state of the Province. . . . Where any unnecessary change or innovation has been made which has not a real tendency to strengthen government, or where there is any room to doubt whether a measure has been in consistency with the charter or other rights, or where the thing desired is immaterial in itself, but imagined to be of importance, I wish to see the people gratified. . . . On the other hand, where any concession is made on a demand not founded upon right, and which will cast more weight into the popular scale, your Lordship will judge whether in the present state of the Province there is no danger of its being improved to force compliance with every other demand, even to independence itself." [1]

As the autumn deepened, Hutchinson interpreted favorably toward himself the symptoms he perceived of the mood of the people, — enjoying a brief Indian summer of favor before the outbreak, now not distant, of a storm more cold and pitiless than ever. October 16, he writes : "I now see so great a change in the people wherever I travel about the country, that I have reason to think I shall rather gain than lose by the late detestable proceedings, and my friends express stronger attachment to me than ever. . . . One would be apt to think that men of common sense would never pass a set of resolves founded upon letters which had no tendency to support them ; but I have lately had reason to believe they did not intend the letters should ever appear, and that after they had spread very false reports of the tenor and purport of the letters many of the inhabitants of Boston called upon their representatives

[1] *M. A. Hist.*, vol. xxvii., pp. 549, etc.

for the publication of them, and they were obliged to submit to it." October 18, he writes : " The Council say in one of their resolves, that I have declared there must be an abridgment of English liberties. They might have just as well charged David with saying, ' There is no God.' When I wrote those letters, some of my correspondents proposed a representation of the Colonies in Parliament, and said that without, they could not enjoy the liberties of Englishmen. This caused me to write as I did. It gave me pain to think the Colonies could not enjoy every liberty which the kingdom could, but I did not see how it could be helped ; a representation was not practicable, and I had never seen any other scheme that satisfied me. No candid man will contend any other meaning. I write all such things *currente calamo*. If I had supposed they would be printed, I should have expressed myself more carefully. I explain this expression because I see they harp so much on it in the English papers. I don't see any other which can be even tortured to serve their purpose." [1]

[1] *M. A. Hist.*, vol. xxvii., p. 556.

CHAPTER XIII.

HUTCHINSON'S LAST DAYS IN AMERICA.

"THE town of Boston," Hutchinson writes to Dartmouth, "is the source of all the disorders of the government; and many persons of the best judgment in the Province often remark that if that town could be separated from the rest, which they don't suppose it can be, my administration would be as easy to me as I could wish. . . . There has hardly been an instance of any other town meddling with any affairs but what immediately concern them, except when called upon by this town, with a view by multiplying instances of irregularity, to give countenance to their own practice."

A crisis was at hand more threatening than any that had preceded. November 24, the Governor writes from Milton to Andrew Oliver :[1] —

"It is very necessary I should have a consultation with you upon the state of the Province ; I must desire you therefore to come out before dinner to-day; and if you think best to take the Secretary[2] with you, I have no objection, and could wish to have as much advice as possible. When I saw the inhabitants of the town

---

[1] Andrew Oliver's handsome home was in Dorchester, half way between Boston and Milton Hill.

[2] Thomas Flucker.

assembled under color of law, and heard of the open
declaration, that we were now in a state of nature, and
that each one has a right to take up arms; and when
in the meeting, as I am informed, the inhabitants were
accordingly called 'To arms, to arms,' and they all replied with clapping and general applause; — when a
tumultuous assembly of people can from time to time
attack the persons and properties of the King's subjects, and threaten death and destruction to them; and
when assemblies are tolerated from night to night in
the public town-hall to consult and determine upon
further unlawful measures, and very dark propositions
and resolutions are made and agreed to there; — when
the infection is industriously spreading, and the neighbor towns not only join their committees with the committee of Boston, but are assembled in Town-Meeting
to approve of the doings of the town of Boston; — and
above all, when upon repeated summoning of the Council, they put off any advice to me from time to time, and
I am obliged to consent to it because all the voices
there, as far as they declare their minds, I have reason
to fear would rather confirm than discourage the people
in their wrong proceedings, — under all these circumstances I think it time to deliberate whether his Majesty's service does not call me to retire to the Castle,
where I may with safety to my person more freely give
my sense of the criminality of these proceedings than
whilst I am in the hands of the people, some of whom
and those most active, not only in print but in cabals,
don't scruple to declare their designs against me. This
is a measure which I wish to avoid as long as I can

consistent with my duty, and the more because of the consequences of it to the Province, than from any inconvenience to me though I know it will be very great, especially as after a retreat I see but little prospect of a return until I can receive advice from England. But the point to be considered is, what am I in duty bound to do. When this is settled the event may be left to the great disposer of all events."[1]

The fume now in the wind, touching the Governor's quick sense and causing him to utter himself in such long-drawn indignation and alarm, was from the premonitory simmering of the Boston Tea Party. Townshend's Act of 1767, it will be remembered, laid a tax upon paper, glass, painters' colors, and tea. No revenue, probably, had ever been expected from it. The principle that Parliament might tax, it was felt, must be maintained; the cost of collection was greater than the proceeds, and soon the tax was entirely withdrawn except upon the one article, tea. The ministry of Lord North, now in the front, cleverly thought to entrap the Colonists into a sufferance of the tax by a neat arrangement: an export duty, paid in England, of twelvepence in the pound, was withdrawn; an import duty of threepence, paid in America, being retained. By the withdrawal of the export duty, the tea could be sold even cheaper than that smuggled in from the Dutch. It was a bait well designed to deceive the unwary. A second advantage sought was relief to the East India Company. Circumstances, among which the colonial non-importation agreements were important, had

[1] *M. A. Hist.*, vol. xxvii., p. 575.

brought it about that the great company was badly
overstocked with tea, — 17,000,000 pounds, it was said,
having accumulated, which, with a slow market, could
not be disposed of. The cheapening of tea, however,
neither relieved the East India ,Company nor brought
the Colonies, now well-schooled, to acquiesce in taxation
without representation.

The project had been decided upon in May, and
soon became known in the Colonies, where opposition
became manifest at once. The legislative Committees
of Correspondence were busy through the summer, until
from the remote South to New Hampshire a uniform
plan of resistance was decided upon. It was in the
"ringleading Colony" of Massachusetts Bay that the
crisis was to come. The consignees here, to whom it
was appointed in England that the tea should be sent,
were noteworthy persons. Two of them were Thomas
and Elisha Hutchinson, sons of the Governor; a third
was the Governor's nephew, Richard Clarke, father-in-
law of Copley, the painter, and grandfather of Lord
Lyndhurst, Lord Chancellor of England. Benjamin
Faneuil, a fourth, was of the family of the public-spir-
ited Huguenot whose name has become almost the most
familiar of Boston names; a fifth was Joshua Winslow,
also of a memorable family. These held stubbornly
to the task that had been set them, putting their property and their lives in jeopardy, until finally they were
driven to seek refuge in the Castle.

Of the figures opposed to them, Samuel Adams was
the chief; while close at hand Hancock, Bowdoin, Dr.
Thomas Young, Dr. Joseph Warren, Dr. Benjamin

Church, Josiah Quincy, John Scollay, chairman of the Boston selectmen, Samuel and William Cooper, Molineux, and others of station no less, lent their hands to action and their heads to counsel. Historic truth compels the statement that an energetic personage also of this time was " Captain Mackintosh," leader of the South End toughs in street fights with the North Enders, the same who had been conspicuous in the riot of August, 1765, in the destruction of Hutchinson's house. For his part in that he had never received punishment, and now seems to have been rather a popular pet. He was styled the " First Captain-General of Liberty-Tree," and managed the illuminations, hanging of effigies, etc. Long afterward, in speaking of the Tea Party, he said, " It was my chickens that did the job." [1]

An attempt was made to cause the consignees to resign their commissions under Liberty - Tree, after the fashion of Andrew Oliver in the Stamp Act days. This, however, they refused to do, undergoing presently in consequence a smashing-in of their windows and doors, and the reception of a tempest of missiles which put life and limb in great danger. The consignees, called upon to lay down their function by a Town-Meeting, declared respectfully that their friends in England had entered into engagements on their behalf, which made it impossible for them to withdraw ; they insisted, however, that the engagements were of a purely " commercial nature," evidently wishing to correct a prevalent notion that they were in some way government officers.

[1] Francis S. Drake : *Tea Leaves*, Introd., p. cxxvii.

Through November debate went forward with no result. The consignees, backed by the Governor and the
influential Tories, stood their ground against the plead-
ings of the selectmen and the murmurs of the Sons of
Liberty until, on November 28, the Dartmouth, owned
by the young Quaker, Francis Rotch, twenty-three years
old, sailed into port with one hundred and fourteen
chests of tea on board. What followed has been told
a thousand times, with all possible elaboration, by those
who sympathize fully with the tea-destroyers. Hutchinson set himself against them, " his course not showing
one sign of vacillation from first to last, but throughout
bearing the marks of clear, cold, passionless inflexi-
bility." [1] To candid men, the letters he wrote in those
days of struggle ought to have interest, as well as the
declarations of those who have portrayed him as the
disgraced minion of a tyrant.

December 1, 1773, to Governor Tryon, of New York:
" Notifications were posted in all parts of the town and
printed in the newspapers, requiring all persons in town
and country to assemble at the ringing of the bells;
and the appearance was too numerous for the hall,
which caused them to adjourn to one of the meeting-
houses. Nothing can be more inflammatory than the
speeches and resolutions made on this occasion. . . .
Whilst the rabble was together in one place, I was
in another not far distant, with his Majesty's Council,
urging them to join with me in some measure to break
up this unlawful assembly; but to no purpose. They
draw up a declaration of grievances which cause this

[1] Richard Frothingham.

disordered state of the people, declare against doing anything for the protection of the tea because the duty on it is unconstitutional, and conclude with desiring me to direct the justices, etc., to keep the peace. An indiscreet countenancing and encouraging the disorders! The people being assembled again the next day, I sent the sheriff with a proclamation, which he carried into the meeting, requiring them immediately to disperse, which they treated in contempt, and unanimously voted they would not disperse. Thus the affair stands at present. . . . If they go the lengths they threaten, I shall be obliged to retire to the Castle, as I cannot otherwise make any exertion in support of the King's authority." [1]

December 2, 1773, to Dartmouth : " Although this meeting or assembly consisted principally of the lower ranks of the people, and even journeymen tradesmen were brought to increase the number, and the rabble were not excluded, yet there were divers gentlemen of good fortune among them, and I can scarcely think they will prosecute these mad resolves ; yet it is possible, and if it becomes probable I shall be under the necessity of withdrawing to the Castle also, in order to defeat them as far as shall be in my power." [2]

December 3, 1773: "The whole business of the letters was turning fast to the shame of all who had been concerned in the plot, and a gentleman who is very observant had congratulated me upon the fair prospect of being a popular governor ; when a new subject — the news of the intended importation of tea by the East

[1] *M. A. Hist.*, vol. xxvii., p. 576.   [2] *Ibid.*, p. 578.

India Company — afforded occasion for renewing our disorders. The first thing suggested was that it was a plan of mine, to recommend myself to administration. . . . I must observe there is nothing in this last affair which can charge the Province in general, all being done by the people of Boston, and a few from half a dozen towns round about, drawn in by the artifices of Boston, expecting them to share in the criminality and lessen their own share. I could be content to part with what estate I have in this town, which is not inconsiderable, if the inhabitants would be content, and it could be effected to be separated from the rest of the Province. I think my government would be very easy to me." [1]

December 14, 1773, to Dartmouth : " It would be a good measure if the General Court could be brought to the enacting a law for disfranchising such towns as assemble for other purposes than the immediate concerns of the town. They really have no further power, as the Province law now stands. It looks as if the principal actors in some late Town-Meetings were afraid of being, at one time or other, called to account by some other authority than any within the Province ; for when anything very extravagant is to be done, a meeting of the people at large is called by printed notification, without signing ; but selectmen, town clerk, etc., attend. In the last assembly in the largest meeting-house in town, a gent who spoke in behalf of the consignees called upon the selectmen. Mr. Adams, the representative, corrected him, and remarked that they

[1] *M. A. Hist.*, vol. xxvii., p. 581.

knew no selectmen at those meetings. Surely, my Lord, it is time this anarchy was restrained and corrected by some authority or other." [1]

At last came the evening of December 16, with its never-to-be-forgotten event. Next day, while the broken chests covered the water far and near, and the tea, caught by the tide, washed under the wharves, then on the ebb was drawn out into the harbor in a long windrow, — while the town was all excitement over what it had done, the Whigs braced to meet the consequences, the Tories muttering of the direst punishment sure to come, Hutchinson sat down to write a calm report to Dartmouth.

December 17, 1773: "My Lord, the owner of the ship Dartmouth, which arrived with the first teas, having been repeatedly called upon by what are called the Committee of Correspondence to send the ship to sea, and refusing, a meeting of the people was called and the owner required to demand a clearance from the custom-house, which was refused, — and then a permit from the naval officer to pass the Castle, which was also refused; — after which he was required to apply to me for the permit; and yesterday, towards evening, came to me at Milton, and I soon satisfied him that no such permit would be granted until the vessel was regularly cleared. He returned to town after dark in the evening, and reported to the meeting the answer I had given him. Immediately thereupon numbers of the people cried out, ' A Mob! a Mob!' left the house, repaired to the wharf, where three of the vessels lay

<hr>

[1] *M. A. Hist.*, vol. xxvii., p. 588.

aground, having on board three hundred and forty
chests of tea, and in two hours' time it was wholly destroyed. The other vessel, Captain Loring, was cast
ashore on the back of Cape Cod in a storm, and I am
informed the tea is landed upon the beach, and there is
reason to fear what has been the fate of it. I sent
expresses this morning before sunrise to summon a
Council to meet me at Boston, but by reason of the
indisposition of three of them I could not make a
quorum. I have ordered new summons this afternoon,
for the Council to meet me at Milton to-morrow morning. What influence this violence and outrage may
have I cannot determine. Probably it may issue in a
proclamation promising a reward for discovering the
persons concerned, which has been the usual proceeding in other instances of high-handed riots. A sufficient
number of people for doing the work were disguised,
and these were surrounded by a vast body of people,
who generally, as was commonly reported, went from
this meeting, which it is said was more numerous than
any before, and consisted of the inhabitants of divers
other towns, as well as Boston ; but in what proportion
I have not been able to ascertain. The wind coming
fair, I do not expect by this vessel to be able to give
your lordship a more particular account of this unhappy
affair." [1]

He writes as follows to Israel Williams, of Hatfield : —

Boston, December 23, 1773 : " There never was
greater tyranny in Constantinople than has been lately
in Boston. Because a number of gentlemen who with-

---

[1] *M. A. Hist.*, vol. xxvii., p. 587.

out their knowledge, the East India Company made the consignees of 400 chests of Tea would not send it back again, which was absolutely out of their power, they have forced them to fly to the Castle for refuge and then have destroyed the property committed to their care. Such barbarity none of the Aborigines were ever guilty of. The Admiral asked some of them next morning who was to pay the fiddler. . . . The value of what is lost is 12 or 14,000 £ sterling. Fifty-eight chests were cast ashoar at Cape Cod." [1]

To Mauduit, he says : "Nobody suspected they would suffer the tea to be destroyed, there being so many men of property active at these meetings, as Hancock, Phillips, Rowe, Dennie, and others, besides the selectmen, and town clerk, who was clerk of all the meetings. Adams never was in greater glory." [2]

Writing to Robertson, the Scotch historian, with whom as a fellow historian he had come into contact, an interesting passage is the following : " December 28, 1773. The prevalence of a spirit of opposition to government in the plantation is the natural consequence of the great growth of Colonies so remote from the parent State, and not the effect of oppression in the King or his servants, as the promoters of this spirit would have the world to believe." [3]

" I have taken a solemn oath," he writes to Samuel Swift, on the 4th of January, 1774, " as Governor. to do everything in my power that the Acts of Trade may

---

[1] Williams Papers, in rooms of Mass. Hist. Society.

[2] Samuel. of course.

[3] M. A. Hist., vol. xxvii., p. 601.

Boston 4 Jan 1774

Sir

I am obliged to you for the favorable
opinion you express in your letter of the 30 Dec of
my general disposition, and I think you will be
satisfied of the propriety of my conduct in the
particular instance you refer to, when I put you
in mind that I have taken a solemn oath, as
governor, to do every thing in my power that the
acts of trade may be carried into execution. Now
to have granted a Pass to a Vessel which I knew had
not cleared at the Custom house would have been
such a direct countenancing & encouraging the
violation of the Acts of Trade, that I believe you
would have altered your opinion of me and seen
me ever after in an unfavorable light. I am sure
if I could have preserved the property that is
destroyed or could have complied with the general
desire of the people consistent with the duty which
my station requires I would most readily have done
it. I am
                        Sir Your most humb Ser.

                              Tho Hutchinson

FROM GOVERNOR HUTCHINSON TO SAMUEL SWIFT

be carried into execution. Now to have granted a pass
to a vessel which I knew had not cleared at the Custom-
House, would have been such a direct countenancing
and encouraging the violation of the Acts of Trade,
that I believe you would have altered your opinion of
me, and seen me ever after in an unfavorable light. I
am sure if I could have preserved the property that is
destroyed, or could have complied with the general desire of the people, consistent with the duty which my
station requires, I would most readily have done it." [1]

In all the events in this story, after the usual human
fashion, good and ill are mixed together in the conduct
of both sides. As to the Whigs, their principle that
there should be no taxation without representation was, as
always in these pre-Revolutionary contests, most clearly
apprehended, and maintained with an unflinching con-
stancy and courage that merit not only admiration, but
gratitude from all English-speaking men. " Boston is
suffering in the common cause " came in a few months
to be the cry throughout the Thirteen Colonies, as the
penalties promptly following the destruction of the tea
seemed likely to wipe the town out of existence. Boston suffered then for a far wider world than the
Thirteen Colonies; it suffered for England as well as
America, — for men now living and for generations
yet unborn, — the clear sight that her citizens had of
Anglo-Saxon rights and their boldness in upholding
them having brought it to pass that Anglo-Saxon freedom, for all the English-speaking world and for all

[1] *M. A. Hist.*, vol. xxvii., p. 611. Lord Mahon thinks Hutchinson was
"perhaps unwise " in refusing the pass. *Hist. of Eng.*, vol. vi., p. 2.

time, is recognized and established as it would not otherwise have been. Much self-denial the act required. Tea seems to have been a comfort more esteemed in those days than in ours : it was their wives and daughters who suffered through the deprivation of it more than the Fathers themselves. One pities, and smiles, too, as he reads the manifestoes of the dames and the young maids as well, pledging themselves to abstain, and contenting themselves with steeped catnip and raspberry leaves. Lord North and his ministry baited the hook cunningly. It was a master-move to withdraw the export duty and bring the tea in price below what was paid for tea smuggled from Holland. The penny-wisdom of the Yankee nature was most shrewdly appealed to in that stroke. In this case it failed to answer ; as did also all the apparatus for terrorizing, present and to come. The doughty little town showed capital nerve. Men and women, rich and poor, standing together, they threw into the sea from $70,000 to $100,000 worth of something they all prized.[1] " Oh, what a waste ! " must have exclaimed the thousands of thrifty souls, as the fragrant Bohea, flung upon the mud-flats, piled up above the bulwarks of the ships until it had again and again to be shoveled away. A mile or two down the bay — they could have floated up in a few minutes, as soon as the tide began to flow — lay Montague's great ships of war, scores of heavy cannon under control of a commander well known in the town as thoroughly ready and rough. How could they tell but that the broadsides would be at once brought to bear, and the

---

[1] Lord Mahon estimates the value at £18,000. *Hist.*, vol. vi., p. 2.

town blown into splinters before the night had passed! Immediate retribution did not come, but every soul in Boston knew that the penalty must fall, as certain as night follows day, and that it was likely to gain in weight through being deferred.

But while, in the main, the posterity of those men and women must admire, the incidents of the transaction are not by any means always pleasant. There was a mob in revolutionary Boston scarcely less foul-mouthed, pitiless, unscrupulous, than that which roared for the blood of the Bourbons in revolutionary Paris, or was on the verge of destroying London in the Gordon riots. Mackintosh and his crew were unmistakably in evidence; certainly not effectually restrained, perhaps connived at, by the better men, so that those, just as conscientious and patriotic, who tried in lawful ways to oppose, found destruction for their property imminent, and could feel that their lives were secure only when they had fled down the harbor to the Castle.

Hutchinson's limitations are plain here, as always. While it was no plan of his to tax the Colonies, while he thought and urged year in and year out the inexpediency of taxing, and the good policy of removing from America all such burdens, he felt only in a feeble way that a great principle was infringed in taxation without representation. The doctrine that the Colonies were virtually represented he would have subscribed to, quite blind to the danger that indifference at that moment might have carried the English-speaking race back into a régime as harsh as that of the Stuarts. He was, moreover, no democrat: the Town-Meeting could adequately care for certain very restricted interests, perhaps, — the fences, the commons, the school, the poor-house, within the square mile or two within which it was placed ; but to judge of politics on a large scale and call in question the administration of an empire was intolerable presumption. The few must lead, and no state could be well ordered which the mass directed. Hutchinson was un-American, but he was no less well-meaning and patriotic than those whom he opposed. The maintenance of this tax on tea was, in his view, utterly inexpedient. Why, one asks, did he remain in his place, enforcing laws in which he had no sympathy, the instrument of a policy he disliked, wrecking utterly in the minds of his countrymen the honorable name which for forty years he had been establishing ? It was certainly not for the emoluments. It was not for fame : instead of credit he had long received only abuse. No explanation can be offered except that he wished to be of public service. He kept hoping against hope, that the home government would become wiser ; that statesmen would come more and more to abound of the same mind as Dartmouth, who believed, as he did, that a supremacy in Parliament having once been recognized, that supremacy should be allowed to sink out of sight, the Colonies being allowed to control themselves. He kept hoping against hope, that in his own land the punctilio as to taxation would be less hotly pressed. Might not the Town-Meetings, too, be brought to admit that in large affairs authority should be conceded to the few ! These things being gained, the glorious empire of England might remain undivided, — mother and daughter remain-

ing in peace together, an affectionate headship dwelling
in the one, a filial and loving concession of precedence
in the other.   To attain such a consummation seemed
to the Governor a thing worth suffering and striving for.
To bring this about, as is shown by all his acts and all
his words, he contended year after year, sacrificing to
his aim his reputation, his fortune, at last, hardest of
all, his citizenship, dying in exile of a broken heart.
That end was as yet some years off. Meantime, Hutchinson fought his fight with courage and purpose to the
full as good as belonged to those who withstood him.

The 12th of January arriving, the time to which the
General Court had been prorogued, Hutchinson made
still further prorogation, to January 26.   In his message at the opening, he made no reference to the Tea-
Party, feeling certain it would call out a disagreeable
reply.   Committees of Correspondence, however, were
animadverted upon as having occasioned the King's
displeasure ; to which the House replied, that while
their rights were attacked, there must be some method
of correspondence, in order to obtain redress of grievances : since the Governor and Lieutenant-Governor
corresponded with men in power, bringing in that way
measures to pass grievous to the people, the Colonies
on the other side should be allowed to correspond, in
order that relief might be obtained.

The dispute, which for some time had been approaching an acute stage, became in this session an absorbing
one, — whether or not the judges of the Superior Court
should receive salaries from the King.[1]   Judge Trow-

· [1] Hutchinson : *Hist.*, vol. iii., p. 440, etc.

bridge, whose feeble health, perhaps, accounts for his ready compliance with the legislative demand that the salary should continue to be received from the Assembly's appropriation, was the first to yield, being soon followed, however, by three associates; this left Peter Oliver, now Chief Justice, alone. He was a man of more resolution : at once receiving the royal grant, he put it out of his power to retract. He alleged he had been a justice of the Superior Court seventeen years, during all of which time his salary of £150, often delayed, or paid only in part, had been quite insufficient for his support. He had, he declares, sunk besides £2000 of his own money in the service.[1] He had never been able to obtain any redress : he had been growing poor, and had often been on the point of resigning, but had always been encouraged to hope for something better. He had now come to the conclusion that he ought to receive the Crown grant, as much as the judges in other Colonies, and so obtain a support more ample and certain. Severe resolves against Oliver were at once passed, accompanied by a petition for his removal. An attempt was made to prevent the sitting of the Superior Court. Hutchinson, of course, was obdurate, and the effort was at once set on foot to impeach the Chief Justice, the Council for that purpose to assume powers of jurisdiction like those of the House of Lords. But one similar attempt had been made in the history of the Province, and that had not been sanctioned. Hutchinson refused to convene the Council for any such

---

[1] See Peter Oliver's account, cited in *Diary and Letters of Hutchinson*, vol. i., p. 142, etc.

unconstitutional purpose; whereupon Samuel Adams and Bowdoin, always leaders of House and Council, manœuvred to lay aside the Governor. In truth, the Whigs were getting far beyond the Constitution. The *natural right* of a great people to do as it pleased was fast becoming the popular ground; the couriers of the Committees of Correspondence were galloping from Colony to Colony; in the matter of the tea, not only at Boston, but at Philadelphia, at New York, in North Carolina, at Charleston in the far South, the temper of the people, though less impressively manifested, was no less revolutionary. They had now stepped in so far, all felt, that there could be no going back; they must hang together. What woes were to be visited upon Boston for what Admiral Montague called its "Indian caper" were, during the winter and spring, all unknown. Something direful was certain, and all America was prepared to countenance and help the ringleading town under the infliction, whatever it might be.

At the end of the winter, Hutchinson, finding the dispute over the judges' salaries more hopeless than ever, put an end to the session, this being the last act in his long and stormful partnership with them. The Court locked the door upon his messenger until they had done what business it pleased them to do, signalizing the last moments of the sitting with a more emphatic outburst than ever of anger and dislike. "If when we complain," said they, "we cannot even be heard, our case is indeed deplorable. Yet we have the pleasure of contemplating that posterity for whom we are struggling, will do us justice by abhorring the memory of those men who owe their greatness to their country's ruin." Hutchinson announced that he had obtained " discretionary leave from the King to go to England," and that he should now make preparations for his voyage.

Early in March, the news of the Tea-Party having reached England, Parliament began its discussion.[1]   A bill having been brought in for the punishment of Boston, " the principal object of attention," the first reading passed without discussion ; the second, also, with little debate.   At the third reading, however, debate became very spirited.   The Lord Mayor of London presented petitions against it from several " natives of America," and a many-voiced discussion followed, in which the champions of America, her " virtual representatives," were by no means silent.   The utterance best worth remembering was that of Barré : " Keep your hands out of the pockets of the Americans, and they will be obedient subjects."   Remonstrances, however, were looked upon by the great majority with impatience.   In the Lords the temper toward the Colonies was rather better than in the Commons, Dartmouth showing his usual good sense and excellent spirit by a speech full of conciliation.   Mansfield, however, opposed : the result was the same as in the lower House ; in both Houses proceedings were so construed that a technical " unanimity " came out, and at the end of March the result was the Boston Port Bill.

Hutchinson's intention to go at once to England, announced early in the year to the legislature, was for a

[1] Hansard's *Parliamentary History*, vol. xvii.

time frustrated by the death of the Lieutenant-Governor, Andrew Oliver, which occurred on the 3d of March. As Hutchinson's brother-in-law, associated with him, too, in business and public relations, the link between the chief magistrate and the deputy was of the closest kind. By the testimony of foes as well as friends, he was a most useful and estimable man, — modest, inde-fatigable, well-cultured, soundly sensible. He had been the most beloved member of a family greatly beloved, and no charge could be brought against him except that in his political principles he sided with the Gov-ernor. He had incurred great unpopularity at the time of the Stamp Act, which he disapproved, writing to England to that effect. But without his knowledge he received the appointment of distributor, a position which he publicly resigned under Liberty-Tree at the demand of the Sons of Liberty. From that time, as the shadow of Hutchinson, a less marked but closely connected and thoroughly sympathetic personality, he had marched step by step in the troublous times in which their lot was cast. With Andrew Oliver to take his place, the Governor could feel that in his absence the duties of the position would be faithfully attended to. With Oliver dead, however, his honest feeling was that no influence remained to hold back the country from the destruction upon which it was rushing. At the funeral, the disorder of the time was sadly apparent. The House of Representatives withdrew from the pro-cession because a certain punctilio was neglected; the mob of Boston ran hooting after the train, and in an unseemly way hilarious, gave three cheers when the mourners came out of the graveyard; his brother, the Chief Justice, intrepid as he was, did not dare to be present because his life was threatened. Hutchinson laid his friend in the grave, and took up again the burden of his office. His respite, however, was not long delayed. On May 13, General Gage arrived, appointed to supersede for a time the civilian; though it was the understanding of Hutchinson that when the sword had been brandished close at hand for a period, an operation which the ministry hoped would have a healthful effect, he was to return to power, having meantime helped the King with counsel in face to face communications. Three days before the arrival of Gage, news had come of the penalties which the Tea-Party had brought upon the town. Four bills had been triumphantly carried in Parliament, had then received the signature of the King, and now were to be executed by Gage, who was to have at his command four regiments and a powerful fleet. By the first bill the port of Boston was to be closed. The second bill was "for the better regulating the government of the Province of Massachusetts Bay:" it changed the charter in the matter of the election of the Council, abolished Town-Meetings except for the choice of town officers, or on the special permission of the Governor, and gave the Governor also power to appoint and remove sheriffs, who were to be intrusted with the returning of juries. The third bill was "for the impartial administration of justice," and transferred the place of trial of magistrates, revenue officers, and soldiers indicted for murder or other capital offense, to Nova Scotia or Great Britain.

A fourth bill legalized the quartering of troops in Boston. The leading Whigs were to be brought to punishment at once, especial emphasis being laid upon the importance of seizing Samuel Adams.

Hutchinson's work in America was done. While Gage was taking possession, the displaced chief magistrate, we may well believe with no heaviness of heart, made his final preparations, and June 1 embarked for England. Milton Hill is never lovelier than in early June; its noble trees show then their densest and deepest green ; the greater hills behind, the Massachusetts, through the atmosphere charged with fragrant mist rising from intervening blossoming fields, have all their ruggedness softened into beauty. In front, across the green waving marshes, penetrated by the black current of the Neponset, the broad bosom of the harbor bears up its islands to where in the remote distance the white lighthouse marks the edge of the ocean.

From the higher land of his noble estate Hutchinson could easily see, fifty miles to the west, the round summit of Wachusett, marking the centre of the Province. A few miles to the west of Wachusett a fair township was about to be called after him, Hutchinson ; and it may easily have been in his thoughts, as his farewell glance took in the landscape near and far, that his name would go down to future times attached to the soil to which his heart was bound.

The present writer heard at Milton Hill, from an old man who had received the story in his youth from his grandfather, the Governor's friend, that Hutchinson was in cheerful mood on the day when he left his home forever. The well-placed world of the Province for the most part approved of him, and had already bestowed upon him, or were soon to bestow, strong marks of favor. One hundred and twenty merchants and gentlemen of Boston, the members of the Bar, the Episcopal clergy, the magistrates of Middlesex, a number of citizens of Salem and Marblehead, sent him respectful addresses. He had no thought of a lasting absence. Though martial law for a time was to be tried, he was still Governor, having " received assurance that General Gage's continuance would probably not be of long duration, and that it was the intention of the King that he should be reinstated." [1] Meantime, his salary was continued. He was to give an account of his stewardship to his royal master. Boston was in an uproar through what he felt to be the folly of both ruled and rulers. The rulers he might hope, if he could but talk to them, to make wiser. As to the ruled, if Gage could not persuade, he could coerce. Hutchinson might confidently anticipate coming back to a vindicated authority. He turned away from the far-stretching farm, his possession since 1743; the ample mansion enlarged and beautified after the plans of Sir Francis Bernard; the long avenue of thrifty buttonwoods planted by himself, a few survivors of which still stand, decrepit and broken, the sole extant relics there of the man who put them in place. He walked down the hill to the Lower Mills, nodding and smiling to his neighbors on this side and that, whether Whig or Tory, for

[1] *Hist.*, vol. iii., p. 458.

he was good friends with all. His carriage, next year
to be confiscated and appropriated to the use of Washington, awaited him on the level road beneath and carried him to the foot of Dorchester Heights, a name not
yet famous. The Minerva, which was to convey him
to England, lay in the harbor; but before embarking
he was rowed to the island of the Castle, the last bit
of Massachusetts earth to feel his footfall.

Castle William, now Fort Independence, lies to-day,
as always, close to the deep water of the channel, not
to be avoided by ships, whether inward or outward
bound, frowning over the busy harbor with cannon-
crested ramparts. These have superseded the defenses
of the Revolutionary time, and now in their turn are
held to be useless, though they still impotently threaten.
The benevolent modern city has made it possible to cross
from the nearest shore the intervening water on a broad
pier, and to circle the walls in a walk full of inspirations.
On a summer day, one can get the sea-breeze there
almost as well as at Nahant or Nantasket. Interesting
indeed the excursion will become, if he who makes it,
while taking in the beauty and freshness, has in mind
the associations of the spot. From the days of Winthrop the fortress has kept guard at the gate. When
Young Harry Vane sailed for England, to do deeds
worthy to be sung by Milton, while lifting side by side
with Cromwell the pillars of the English Commonwealth
into a short but glorious day, these ramparts shook
under the salvos that marked his departure. Sir Edmund Andros, crossed in his tyrannical schemes by the
accession of William and Mary; Sir William Phips, com-

ing home to power with treasure in his hold recovered from wrecked galleons; Pepperell, setting sail for Louisburg with the flower of New England manhood; French ships of the line in stately grace, to be crushed before long under the broadsides of Rodney; the far-off boom of heavy guns from the Chesapeake and Shannon fighting in the offing, — these are among the events which have touched the old fortress in their happening. Probably no man has known it longer or more closely than Hutchinson. During the extended period of his lieutenant-governorship, he was its titular commander. Again and again, his friends, his children, he himself, had been forced to seek asylum here. How constantly during the troubled years, while Faneuil Hall and the Old South were roaring and the smoke of conflagrations lighted by the mob filled the air, must his eyes have sought, down the channel, the grass-grown mound with the cross of St. George floating above it, — the one secure spot in the Province, if all else should fail!

There must have been gloom in the Governor's soul as his eyes turned for what was destined to be his last glance, toward the spot of his birth and his lifelong striving. In the foreground lay the stubborn town that had so thwarted and contemned him, and yet which he so much loved, — Copp's Hill to the right where lay the dust of his fathers and his much-cherished wife; the Beacon on the height in the centre ready to flame its invitation to sedition inland; the third of the three summits still nearer, at the foot of which the tea had been thrown out. Across the stretch of water the westerly breeze for which the Minerva lay waiting must have

brought distinctly the sound of the tolling bells marking that the Port Bill that day went into operation, as
he no doubt felt, to the town's probable ruin. In the
background rose the high lands of the beautiful Province which the old man had lived for from the days of
his youth. He had written its history, tracing every
detail. That its boundaries swept wide and were well
ascertained was due to his watchfulness. No less was
it due to him that its laws everywhere were well admin-
istered, chief among its judges as he had been through
many years. That in all public ways the people were
honestly and diligently served, his care had brought
about; to him, too, the credit belonged that, as each
man bought and sold, the coin rang upon the counter
solid and undebased. Through him it was, in fact, that
the Province was in every way well-to-do, buoyant,
enterprising before its sister Provinces. With such a
foundation, leadership came of necessity. A sad thing
was it in the eyes of the father-statesman that the strong
child he had nourished gave its energy and initiative in
willful ways, heading its thirteen sisters in courses of
disloyal folly. On the ebb, the ship dropped down
past the headland of Hull, past the lighthouse rising
above the curl of the surf upon the Little Brewster, —

> " Even in the distance he can see the tides
> Upheaving break unheard along its base, —
> A speechless wrath that rises and subsides
> In the white lip and tremor of the face."

Was the exile's fancy sufficiently awake, as he gloom-
ily mused, to believe that even the physical New England, in that parting glimpse, wore an unfriendly look?

Probably not : in his sober mind there was little play
of imagination.   In his thought, at any rate, must
have risen vividly the memory of wrath that had not
been speechless, and that had not subsided.   Of what
that wrath was capable he was soon to know.   It was
to bar him out forever, and to cast forth into companionship with him a sorrowful multitude.

"History at this late date can certainly afford a com-
passionate word for the Tories, who, besides being forced
to atone in life for the mistake of taking the wrong side
by undergoing exile and confiscation, have received
while in their graves little but detestation.   At the
evacuation of Boston, says Mr. Sabine, in the ' American Loyalists,' eleven hundred Loyalists retired to Nova
Scotia with the army of Gage, of whom one hundred
and two were men in official station, eighteen were cler-
gymen, two hundred and thirteen were merchants and
traders of Boston, three hundred and eighty-two were
farmers and mechanics, in great part from the country.
The mere mention of calling and station in the case of
the forlorn expatriated company conveys a suggestion
of respectability.   There were, in fact, no better men
or women in Massachusetts, as regards intelligence,
substantial good purpose, and piety.   They had made
the one great mistake of conceding a supremacy over
themselves to distant arbitrary masters, which a population nurtured under the influence of the Town-
Meeting ought by no means to have made ; but with
this exception, the exiles were not at all inferior in
worth of every kind to those who drove them forth.
The Tories were generally people of substance, their

stake in the country was greater, even, than that of their opponents; their patriotism, no doubt, was to the full as fervent. There is much that is melancholy, of which the world knows but little, connected with their expulsion from the land they sincerely loved. The estates of the Tories were among the fairest; their stately mansions stood on the sightliest hill-brows; the richest and best tilled meadows were their farms; the long avenue, the broad lawn, the trim hedge about the garden; servants, plate, pictures, — the varied circumstances, external and internal, of dignified and generous housekeeping, — for the most part these things were at the homes of Tories. They loved beauty, dignity, and refinement. It seemed to belong to such forms of life to be generously loyal to King and Parliament without questioning too narrowly as to rights and taxes. The rude contacts of the Town-Meeting were full of things to offend the taste of a gentleman. The Crown officials were courteous, well-born, congenial, having behind them the far-away nobles and the sovereign, who rose in the imagination, unknown and at a distance as they were, surrounded by a brilliant glamour. Was there not a certain meanness in haggling as to the tax which these polite placemen and their superiors might choose to exact; or inquiring narrowly as to their credentials when they chose to exercise authority? The graceful, the chivalrous, the poetic, the spirits over whom these feelings had power, were sure to be Tories. Democracy was something rude and coarse; independence, — what was it but a severance of those connections of which a colonist ought to be proudest? It was

an easy thing to be led into taking sides against notions
like these. Hence, when the country rose, many a high-
bred, honorable gentleman turned the key in his door,
drove down his line of trees with his refined dame and
carefully guarded children at his side, turned his back
on his handsome estate, and put himself under the shelter of the proud banner of St. George. It was a mere
temporary refuge, he thought; and as he pronounced
upon ' Sam Adams ' and the rabble a gentlemanly
execration, he promised himself a speedy return, when
discipline and loyalty should have put down the ship-
yard men and the misled rustics.

" But the return was never to be. The day went
against them ; they crowded into ships with the gates
of their country barred forever behind them. They
found themselves penniless upon shores often bleak and
barren, always showing scant hospitality to outcasts who
came empty-handed, and there they were forced to begin
life anew. . . . Gray, Clarke, Erving, and Faneuil,
Royall and Vassall, Fayerweather and Leonard and
Sewall, families of honorable note, bound in with all
that was best in the life of the Province, who now can
think of their destiny unpitying ? " [1]

At the same time, the victors should not be judged
too harshly. Probably no unnecessary cruelty was shown
in the treatment of the Loyalists. The struggle was
a desperate one, the parties in America almost equally

[1] A page or two here has been quoted from the writer's *Life of Samuel Adams*, American Statesmen Series. The sympathetic reader will
find very interesting the article by Professor M. C. Tyler, " The Party
of the Loyalists in the American Revolution," *Am. Hist. Review*, vol.
i., No. 1.

balanced in numbers and strength, the Whigs setting
forth upon a plan quite untried, with no prospect at
first of allies; while the Tories had with them all the
power of England. The conditions were not unlike
those of the English Commonwealth in the previous
century, when two sevenths of the nation faced five
sevenths in great part actively hostile. In such times
severities become inevitable. Necessity drove Cromwell
and the Independents to be bloody and quick in
Ireland, to break Scotland in pieces at Dunbar and
Worcester, to despoil and drive out Catholics and Cavaliers, till the story of England gained many a reddened
page. Only so could their cause, could their own lives,
be secured. Not less critical was the task of the Fathers
of the Revolution. Again and again before the war
was over submission seemed inevitable, and might
easily have come to pass, had not the best strength of
the Tories been driven out. After the war was over, in
the chaotic times of the mutiny of the Pennsylvania line,
Shays's rebellion, and the Whiskey Insurrection, how
easily might a few strong men, if any such had been suffered to remain, have swung America back again into
subservience, that independence being utterly thrown
over for which, through seven years, there had been such
battles and sacrifices! The instinct was correct which
caused the Fathers to move against the Tories harshly,
to cast them out at the outset, and, during all the critical early years, to keep them from returning. Their
confiscated estates went to supply the public needs; the
land they left belonged to the new order of things; and
good men and women though they were in a thousand

private relations, there was nothing for them, and necessarily nothing for them, but to bear their expatriation and poverty with such fortitude as they could muster. It should not be overlooked that in their despoilment and expatriation the lot of the Tories was not without compensations. Vast grants were made to them by the English government of lands in Nova Scotia, New Brunswick, and western Canada.

As Hutchinson was by far the ablest and most eminent of his party, so his suffering was especially sharp. His name was held to be a stigma. Hutchinson Street in Boston became Pearl Street. The town, Hutchinson, at the heart of the Commonwealth, cast off its title as that " of one who had acted the part of a traitor and parricide," substituting for it that of Barré, the liberal champion in Parliament. The honorable note he had reached through forty years of self-denying, wisely directed public service was blotted out; for generations he was a mark for obloquy. His possessions, even to the tomb where lay his wife and his ancestors, were snatched from him and his children.[1] He became in England a royal pensioner. But for this charity, the man who for some years had been the most illustrious personage in America might have died in want in the streets of London.

[1] Under an Act of 1779 "to confiscate the estates of certain notorious Conspirators against the Government and liberties of the late Province," Hutchinson's Boston and Milton property was sold for £98,121 4s. 2¼d., his mansion-house alone, on the corner of Fleet and Hanover streets, bringing £33,500. These values are in the depreciated currency of the time. J. T. Hassam : "Confiscated Estates of Boston Loyalists," in *Proceedings of Mass. Hist. Soc.*, May, 1895, p. 163. For the estate in detail, see Appendix D.

CHAPTER XIV.

THE YEARS OF EXILE.

ARRIVING in London, Friday, July 1st, after a pleasant summer passage, Hutchinson at once sought out Lord Dartmouth, who, after near an hour's conversation, took him to the King. " I was not dressed as expecting to go to Court, but his Lordship observing that the King would not be at St. James's again until Wednesday, I thought it best to go." Contrary to custom he was admitted to the King's closet, where took place a conversation of nearly two hours. Immediately after the interview the Governor wrote down in full the incidents, a record of great interest.[1] One wishes he had possessed something of the graphic power of Peter Oliver, his companion in exile. One craves, as he reads, some picturing of the King's appearance and environment. The story, however, is told without embellishment of this kind, though as regards the utterances both of the King and the Governor, we probably receive them nearly word for word.

"*King*. How do you do, Mr. H., after your voyage ?

"*Hutchinson*. Much reduced, Sir, by sea-sickness ; and unfit upon that account, as well as my New England dress, to appear before your Majesty.

---

[1] *Diary and Letters*, vol. i., p. 157, etc.

" Lord D. observed, ' Mr. H. apologized to me for his dress, but I thought it very well, as he is just come ashoar,' to which the King assented.

" *K.* How did you leave your government, and how did the people receive the news of the late measures in Parliament ?

" *H.* When I left Boston we had no news of any Act of Parliament, except the one for shutting up the port, which was extremely alarming to people." [1]

Hutchinson stated his conviction that no Colony would comply with the request to close its ports. When Dartmouth took out of his pocket the addresses to Hutchinson from the merchants, lawyers, and Episcopal clergy, the King said he did not see how it could be otherwise, and expressed the belief that in England there had been universal approval of Hutchinson's course. For himself, he declared he was entirely satisfied with it : he knew what the Governor had faced, and sympathized with him in his sufferings, particularly with his trouble in the matter of the letters. They then discussed the probabilities as to how the letters had been obtained and forwarded. The King expressing some curiosity as to Boston men whose names he had heard, the Governor gives some account of them. He takes pride, evidently, in declaring it is only in his public character that he has been the mark of malevolence.

---

[1] Immediately after the interview, the King wrote Lord North : " I have seen Mr. Hutchinson, late Governor of Massachusetts, and am now well convinced they will soon submit. He owns the Boston Port Bill has been the only wise and effectual method." Lord Mahon's *Hist.*, vol. vi., appendix, 3d ed. The King's memory was treacherous. Hutchinson neither expresses nor implies approval of the Port Bill.

" It has been my good fortune, Sir, to escape any charges against me in my private character. The attacks have been upon my publick conduct, and for such things as my duty to your Majesty required me to do, and which you have been pleased to approve of. I don't know that any of my enemies have complained of a personal injury.

" *K.* I see they threatened to pitch and feather you.

" *H.* Tarr and feather, may it please your Majesty ; but I don't remember that ever I was threatened with it."

He goes on to say that he never had a guard, and always, so far as he could, put a bold face on, in the idea that a betrayal of fear would encourage violence. To an inquiry as to his home, one can imagine the warmth with which the exile replies, " It has a pleasant situation, and most gentlemen from abroad say it has the finest prospect from it they ever saw, except where great improvements have been made by art, to help the natural view." In a magnanimous way, when Hancock comes up in the conversation, Hutchinson corrects an impression the King has formed as to financial irregularities. The King having referred to Cushing as a leader, " A Mr. Adams," replies Hutchinson, " is rather considered as the opposer of government, and a sort of Wilkes in New England.

" *K.* What gave him his importance ?

" *H.* A great pretended zeal for liberty, and a most inflexible natural temper. He was the first that publickly asserted the independency of the Colonies upon the Kingdom, or the Supreme authority of it.

" *K.* I have heard, Mr. H., that your ministers preach

that for the sake of promoting liberty or the publick good, any immorality or less evil may be tolerated.

" *H.* I don't know, Sir, that such doctrine has ever been preached from the pulpit; but I have no doubt that it has been publickly asserted by some of the heads of the party who call themselves sober men, that the good of the publick is above all other considerations; and that truth may be dispensed with, and immorality is excusable, when this good can be obtained by such means.

" *K.* That's strange doctrine, indeed."

Hutchinson having explained to the King the ecclesiastical situation in New England, and that he himself was a dissenter, the King said : —

" I say, Mr. H., why do your ministers generally join with the people in opposition to the government ?

" *H.* They are, Sir, dependent upon the people. They are elected by the people, and when they are dissatisfied with them, they seldom leave till they get rid of them.

" *K.* That must be very dangerous. If the people oblige them to concur with them in their erroneous principles on government, they may do it in religion also, and this must have a most fatal tendency."

To the King's inquiry as to the increase of population, Hutchinson replies that in Massachusetts it doubles every twenty-five years, and that immigration seeks the milder climate of the South rather than New England. As to crops and the natural history of America, also, the King is set right. A conversation ensued as to the peculiarities of Colonial constitutions, and the comparative disloyalty of the populations. The succession in the government was then touched upon, Hutchinson's family, the present condition and prospects of the Indians, — the talk becoming desultory. Both characters appear to advantage in the record, — two sensible, well-meaning men discussing in the best temper important topics. George III. probably has never been portrayed with more agreeable traits.

Soon after reaching London, Hutchinson wrote as follows to an old neighbor at Milton, James Murray :[1] —

"LONDON, 23rd July, 1774.

"I am much obliged to you for so early a letter. You will find, before you have travelled through Cardinal de Retz, an observation of the Prince de Condé, when he was informed of the abusive charges and suspicions against him, — that the authors had no other ground, except that, if they had been in his place, they knew that they would have done themselves what they suspected him of doing. I am not only free from any share in the three Acts of Parliament, but I am also willing to own that they are so severe, that, if I had been upon the spot, I would have done what I could at least to have moderated them ; and, as to the first of them, I have all the encouragement possible to hope and believe, that my being here will be the means by which the town of Boston will be relieved from the distress the act brings upon it, more speedily and effectually than it otherwise would have been. Lord Dartmouth has more than once assured me that he is

1 *Proceedings of Mass. Hist. Soc.*, vol. v., p. 361, January, 1862.

of the same opinion, and that he should have been glad
to have seen me here, if he had no other reason for it
than that alone. I wish for the good opinion of my
countrymen, if I could acquire it without disturbing
the peace of my own mind. Those persons here whom
they have always supposed their best friends, express
themselves as favorably of my conduct as those who are
called their greatest enemies ; and Lord Rockingham
treats me with as much politeness, and makes as high
professions of esteem, as Lord North. Although the
town is said to be empty, my whole time has been taken
up in receiving visits, and complying with invitations,
from persons of the first rank, and I have but little
other opportunity for business ; but, after next week, I
hope to come to it."

The exile was keenly sensitive to opprobrium, and
defends himself in his letters and sometimes in more
formal ways. Speaking of his Letter Books, he says : —

"When I was threatened by the tea-mobs, I carried
them to Milton, and when I was obliged to retire to the
Castle upon Gen. Gage's arrival, it did not come into
my mind where I had put them. I am sure there is
nothing in them but what will evidence an upright aim,
and an endeavour to keep off the miseries which, in spite
of my endeavours, a few men have brought upon the
country ; and if they will take the whole of them, they
will find an uniform plan for preserving the authority
of Parliament, and at the same time indulging the
Colonies in every point in which the people imagined
they were aggrieved." [1]

[1] July 28, 1775, *Diary and Letters*, vol. i., p. 505.

To attacks which were made upon him by the Whigs in Parliament, he replied by a formal " Vindication," in which he speaks of himself in the third person. The paper was not printed then, and appears now for the first time in the Diary. It is a document full of clearness and dignity, and has much interest to the student of our Revolutionary history. A passage from this follows : —

" By acts of fraud and violence the late Governor Hutchinson's most private papers have, at different times, come into the possession of persons disposed to do him hurt, who for that purpose have published detached parcells of them, with Comments and remarks, torturing his words to an unnatural sense and meaning, totally different from what they were intended to convey. It is nevertheless now asserted that no one fact has ever appeared to have been materially misrepresented by him, nor any one proposal made unfriendly to the rights and liberties of mankind in general, or tending to take from the Province, of which he was governor, the privileges enjoyed by its charter, or any powers or privileges from the inhabitants of the Colonies which can be made to consist with their relation to Parliament as the supreme authority of the British dominions ; nor has it been shown that in his public character he has interested himself in controversies or disputes with the people of his Province farther than the posts which he sustained, required and made his indispensable duty. . . .

" To a person long acquainted with the temper and disposition of the people, it was easy to foresee the effects of the Stamp Act; and although Mr. Hutchinson never doubted the authority of Parliament, yet he doubted the expediency of exercising its authority in that instance, and did everything within his sphere to prevent it, by representations for that purpose to persons of character in England. . . .

" A gentleman in England had procured and sent to Boston several private letters from Mr. Hutchinson, all but one before he came to the Chair; and from Mr. Oliver, when he was Secretary of the Province, to the late Mr. Whately. Every fallacious art had been used to raise the expectations of the people, to inflame and enrage them, before the contents of the letters were made publick. The words of the great Roman orator, though in a case not exactly similar, may be used with propriety on this occasion, ' *Quis enim unquam qui paulum modo bonorum consuetudinem nosset, literas ad se ab amico missas, offensione aliqua interposita in medium protulit, palamque recitavit? Quid est aliud tollere e vita vitæ societatem, tollere amicorum colloquia absentium? Quam multa joca solent esse in epistolis, quae prolata si sint, inepta divulganda.*'[1] . . .

" The great charge against him was his obstinate attachment to the prerogative of the Crown, and the authority of Parliament, etc. . . .

---

[1] What man even slightly acquainted with the decencies of life has ever brought forward and made public the private letters sent to him by friends, because there has been some occasion for offence? What else is this but to make impossible in life communication with one another, and the exchange of thoughts by friends? What pleasantries we put into our letters, which, if divulged, seem inept, and quite unfit to be spread abroad!

" Britain and its Colonies are alike dependent upon the supreme authority of the whole empire. The King, Lords, and Commons — this supreme authority appeared to him to be the sole bond which kept the several parts of the empire together. If any way could be found to give the subjects in the Colonies the same proportion or share in this authority, whether as members of one or other of the Houses of Parliament, or as Electors of the Representatives of the people, he has ever thought they had a fair claim to it. If their local circumstances made any distinction necessary, he thought they had, for that reason, a stronger claim to as great a share of legislative authority, within each Colony respectively, as can consist with the supreme authority of Parliament, which at all events must be maintained so far as is necessary for the purpose of preventing a separation, and preserving the peace and order of the whole. . . . It is a remark more ancient than any British Colony that ' Gubernatorum vituperatio populo placet ; ' and every Governor of Massachusetts Bay, for near a century past, has by experience found the truth of it." [1]

The evidence afforded by the " Diary and Letters," made up of the records kept by Hutchinson himself during his life in England, with passages penned also by his companions, Peter Oliver, the Chief Justice, who shared his exile, his son Elisha, and others, go to show that there is little foundation for the account written by John Adams to William Tudor : " Hardened as had been my heart against him, I assure you I was melted at the account I heard of his condition. . . . He was

[1] *Diary and Letters of Thomas Hutchinson*, vol. i., p. 576, etc.

ridiculed by the courtiers. They laughed at his manners at the levee, . . . and the King's turning away
from him with his nose up." [1] It may be presumed that
the company whom the ambassador of newly born America met in his English sojourn would not be likely to
give a flattering account of the impression made by the
old Tory chief. His reception by the King on his first
arrival has already been detailed. He often afterwards
was at Court, and never seems to have been treated
otherwise than with kindness by both King and Queen.
Through Dartmouth a baronetcy was offered him,
which he declined because of insufficient means to support the title, his fortune having been confiscated.[2]
He was, however, handsomely pensioned. He does
indeed write under date of February 16, 1776 : "We
Americans are plenty here and very cheap. Some of us,
at first coming, are apt to think ourselves of importance,
but others do not think so ; and few, if any of us, are
much consulted or inquired after." No doubt as time
wore on, and the intensity of the American resistance
exceeded far what the refugees had represented it would
be, discredit fell upon their judgment to some extent ;
but as far as the Governor was concerned, it led to
no unkindness or withdrawal of respect. May 29, of
this same year, he jots down : " At the King's levee.
He asked me if I did not think the weather very pleasing after so much raw disagreeable weather. I said I
was glad of the raw weather, as it was the effect of a
fair wind. But he said, ' You like a little mixture.'

---

[1] Tudor : *Life of Otis*, p. 431.
[2] *Diary and Letters*, vol. i., p. 221.

' Not whilst so important a service depended upon a
fair wind.' ' That was generous,' he said, ' but now you
wish to have a little news.' " Hutchinson is thinking
of ships on the way to America with reinforcements.[1]
Again, September 28, 1777 : " Mauduit called last evening and urged me against my inclination to go to court
to-day. The Queen asked me where I had been. I
told her I had been six months in the country with my
sick daughter. ' What ! she that used to be here ?
Why, she looked fine and healthy. I hope she will get
well again.' "[2]

The Governor in his letters and diaries is seldom pic-
turesque, any more than in his elaborate history. Peter
Oliver is a better painter. He was at Court with the
Governor, January 18, 1777, the Queen's birthday.

" I went to Court, and here appeared brilliancy in its
splendor. Before their Majesties appeared, 3 or 4 of
the young Princes were introduced. The Prince of
Wales exhibited an open, sensible, and active temper ;
Prince Frederick, the Bishop of Osnaburgh, is a fine
youth with a manly sensible behavior ; one of the
young Princes, abt 5 or 6 years old, behaved very gen-
teelly, and chatted a great deal with the foreign ambas-
sadors and others. Virgil's ' *Jam nova progenies*,'
recurred to the mind.

" Their Majesties soon entered ; the King was richly
dressed in honor to the Queen, and was very polite and
affable to the Company ; the Queen appeared in the
simplex munditiis, for she is not in high dress on her
Birthday, but on the King's Birthday she shines with

[1] *Diary and Letters*, vol. ii., p. 59.   [2] *Ibid.*, p. 158.

brilliance. Her Majesty walked round and conversed
with every lady ; and tho' she is not a perfect beauty as
a meer object, yet her sweet temper, her royal conde-
scension, and her engaging affability, rivalled the charms
of Venus. She is of so amiably a good temper, and
adorned with so much virtue, and meddles so little with
public affairs, that whenever scandal herself recollects
her Majesty, she at the same time recollects the *digito
compresse labellum.*"

Besides the royal personages, Hutchinson was on intimate terms throughout his years in England with
people of note, both noble and of lesser rank. The
Earls of Dartmouth and Hillsboro, with whom his
abundant correspondence had brought about a connection, received him into friendship; as did also the Archbishop of Canterbury, the Bishops of London and of
Oxford, Lord Mansfield, Lord Hardwick, Lord Loughborough, and Lord Townshend. To Dartmouth he was
especially drawn, from similarity of views both in politics and religion. Mansfield, too, has his full sympathy,
his humane views respecting negro slavery, in which
the great Chief Justice prefigured Wilberforce and
Clarkson, winning Hutchinson's especial approval.

"Feb. 2, 1778, at Lord Hillsborough's : his son,
Lord Fairford, at breakfast with him. Talked with
great freedom ; said he and I had always thought exactly alike ; asked what those members of Parlt. could
do at such a time, when they did not approve of particular measures, and yet, in general, approved the design
of the Ministry, in restoring America to the Empire ? —
the present Ministry, tho' feeble and irresolute, was

better than what would come in their room if there
should be a change ; and yet it was difficult to vote
for what was directly against their judgment ; asked
whether Ld. North ever consulted me ? I told him
No. He said he was a good man, but apt suddenly to
resolve on a thing, which upon second thoughts he repented of, and intimated that to be the case when he
promised to lay some plan, which he now found more
difficult than he expected. . . . Lord Loudoun asked
me yesterday at Court if I knew Gates ? and said,
when he was in America, he was the laughing stock
of the army, as an ignorant nonsensical fellow." [1]

Men illustrious in other ways than through birth seek
out the exile.

" Mar. 24. To my surprise Dr. Robertson of Edin-
burgh came in about noon. I had corresponded with
him in America, but never seen him before. An hour's
converse was very pleasing. He has laid aside his History of the English Colonies. He gave this reason —
that there was no knowing what would be the future
condition of them. I told him I thought, be it what it
may, it need make no odds in writing the History of
what is past, and I thought a true state of them ought
to be handed down to posterity.[2]

He mentions also dining with Gibbon.

Probably no distinction which Hutchinson ever attained was more valued by him than the reception of
the degree *Doctor Civilis Juris*, from the University of
Oxford ; and it is a coincidence worth noting that the
honor fell to him on the day when his country took

[1] *Diary and Letters*, vol. ii., p. 182.   [2] *Ibid.*, p. 194.

what seemed to him the irrevocable plunge toward destruction, July 4, 1776.

" Upon a message from the Vice Chancellor we attended at the publick schools at 11, and after putting on the Doctor's scarlet gown, band, and cap, were introduced by the Beadles into the Theatre, and received by Professor Vansittart who, after a Latin speech complimentary, presented separately to the Vice Chancellor, who conferred the degree of Doctor, *in Jure Civili, honoris causa*, and thereupon were placed in the Doctor's seats at the side of the Vice-Chancellor ; after which a Latin speech in verse was delivered by one of the Students in praise of the Spring; another in prose, elegant and much applauded, by Mr. Lowth, son to the Bishop of Oxford, upon Architecture ; and then a long Latin comemoration of Benefactors by Mr. Bandinelle, in a low voice and lifeless, being his first performance as University Orator. The whole ceremony was not over until two. A gentleman by the name of Paradis, born in Thessalonia, who had studied many years at Oxford, was admitted at the same time, and one other gentleman, whose name I have forgot, to Doctors' degrees." Peter Oliver received the degree at the same time ; he, too, describes the scene, telling of two thousand spectators, the ladies by themselves in brilliant order, the theatre a most noble building, with an accompaniment of music orchestral and vocal.[1]

When the Declaration of Independence reached England, Hutchinson reviewed it elaborately in a " Letter to a Noble Lord," which he took pains should come under

[1] *Diary and Letters*, vol. ii., p. 75, etc.

the eye of the King. The document (printed in Almon's "Remembrancer," vol. iv., p. 25, etc.), though unsigned, gives indisputable internal evidence of its authorship.[1] It is the work of a man thoroughly informed and able, whose strictures upon the generalities which have glittered so conspicuously from that day to this are often telling. No point is better made than the following: —

"I should be impertinent if I attempted to shew . . . in what sense all men are created equal; or how far life, liberty, and the pursuit of happiness may be said to be unalienable; only I could wish to ask the delegates of Maryland, Virginia, and the Carolinas how their constituents justify the depriving more than an hundred thousand Africans of their rights to liberty and the pursuit of happiness, and in some degree to their lives, if these rights are so absolutely unalienable." His active days were over, but this paper shows that his powers had undergone no decay, a fact still more conclusively attested by the third volume of the " History of Massachusetts Bay," in the preparation of which he was now engaged.

October 31, 1776, in company with Peter Oliver, again he visits the House of Lords, introduced by Lord Polworth. Oliver paints the scene : —

" This day I went to the House of Lords to hear the King deliver his speech to the Parliament. The procession was grand, his Majesty being in the elegant state-coach, which is glazed all around, and the body elegantly

---

[1] That Hutchinson was the author is also the opinion of Dr. George E. Ellis. See *Atlantic Monthly*, vol. lviii., p. 566.

gilt, with a gilt crown on the top, with other decorations, drawn by 8 dun horses, the finest I ever saw, and kept in such order that their skin and hair appeared like a rich velvet. The amazing string of coaches, and the vast crowd of spectators in the streets and in the windows of the houses, of ladies richly dressed, and the groups of figures from the first gentlemen to the lowest link-boy, was very picturesque, and was a true representation of the chequered state of mankind ; but the whole, united with the apparent joy of countenances, exhibited an idea of the grandeur and importance of a British Monarch.

"I entered the House of Lords under the umbrage of Lord Polworth. Without the Bar of the House it was much crowded, but within was a grand appearance of the nobility, and of ladies richly dressed. His Majesty was seated on his throne in the robes of royalty, with his rich crown upon his head. He then directed the attendance of the House of Commons, some of whom came, preceded by their Speaker, who also was preceded by his Mace Bearer, and followed by his Train Bearer : he was richly dressed in his gold-laced robes and made a magnificent appearance. His Majesty then delivered his speech, and with that dignity, propriety of accent and pronunciation that commanded attention and created esteem." [1]

It is quite possible that Hutchinson may have become, as John Adams represents, an object of ridicule to some members of the fine society of which he saw much ; but if so, it was for reasons discreditable rather to that

[1] *Diary and Letters*, vol. ii., p. 109.

society than to him. Though always genial and tolerant, as these pages have abundantly illustrated, he
was nevertheless gravely Puritan in all his tastes, and
while his condemnations have sometimes a touch of over-
severity, more frequently they are thoroughly merited
by the flippancy or vice which he is compelled to
encounter. Amusements in general have no attraction
for him. The opera, the races, the exhibitions of con-
jurers are tedious or offensive. As to assemblies, he
finds " his relish for such things entirely over, and I go
only to avoid being singular." He sees Garrick in the
" Beaux' Stratagem " of Farquhar at Drury Lane, with
frank dislike. " Either he is too old for such a character or I am too old to see the excellencies which draw
such crowds after him." Each Sunday finds him at
church, where, however, the Church of England minis-
trations are, to his mind, full of shortcomings. February 26, 1775, at the chapel of the Foundling Hospital, " Sir Charles Whitworth after the sermon during the
anthem, went into the pulpit to the Bishop [of Roches-
ter] and chatted with him for quarter of an hour, and did
not leave him till the anthem was over, and the Bishop
was standing up to give the blessing. Not very decent."[1]

June 16. " At the Temple Church, Mrs. Oliver [Sarah]
with me. Dr. Morill preached from Solomon's Song :
' The singing of birds is come,' &c. A florid description of the beauties of the spring, observing that
the perfection of Art was its approach to nature,
the imitation of which was necessary ; and among other
instances, mentioned the foliage in capitals of pillars

---

[1] *Diary and Letters*, vol. ii., p. 396.

— the festoons — without which they appeared naked; and the beauties of the roof over his head were owing to its resemblance of the branches of the trees of the forest; and he descended to the milkmaids, who would make no shew without a Garland. Less of religion could not well be in a sermon, the touches upon the wisdom of the Creator being slight." [1]

While the finer world is often distasteful to him, democracy is as hateful as it was in Faneuil Hall and the Old South. "February 26, 1776. Entered Guild hall with Wilkes' mob . . . as great blackguards as can well be conceived, and seemed ripe for a riot. . . . Never was so near Wilkes, to have so full a view since I have been in England." [2]

The Governor's diary, in fine, in England, is a profoundly pathetic record, that of a man broken-hearted by his expatriation and the wreck of the cause to which he is committed. His sons Thomas and Elisha, each with a wife and three children, his daughter Sarah with Dr. Peter Oliver, her husband, the younger daughter and son, "Peggy" and "Billy," were all dependent upon him, and still others, until his family numbered twenty-five. He is glad he has a home for them, when so many fellow-exiles are in want. His thoughts are constantly turning to the land which has cast him out. At Wimpole Hall, the handsome seat of Lord Hardwick, his exclamation is: "This is high life, but I would not have parted with my humble cottage at Milton for the sake of it." [3]

---

[1] *Diary and Letters*, vol. ii., pp. 69, 70.   [2] *Ibid.*, p. 21.
[3] *Ibid.*, p. 290.

" New England is wrote upon my heart in as strong
characters as ' Calais ' was upon Queen Mary's." [1]   He
cannot bear the thought that his own dust shall lie in
any other soil; his heart is always reaching out toward
the land and the people that have spurned him.

"LONDON, NEW BOND STREET, March 3, 1777.

" I have advantages here beyond most of the Americans, as I have a very extensive acquaintance with the
best people; but I prefer the *natale solum* to all other:
and it will give me great pleasure to hear you are peaceably settled at Brush Hill, and that I may as peaceably
settle at Unkity Hill.[2]   I hope to live to see not only
my Milton neighbors, but the people of the Province in
general, convinced that I have ever sincerely aimed at
their true interest ; and that if they had followed my
advice, they would have been free from all that distress
and misery which the envious, restless spirits of a few
designing men have brought upon them.   I have been
charged in America with false and unfavorable representations of the people there.   I am charged here with
neglecting to give advice of their intentions to revolt,
and representing the body of the people as disposed to
live quietly under the authority of Parliament, and to
take no exception to any other acts than those of taxation, which I ever endeavored to discourage.   General
Conway, in a speech last session, unexpectedly to me,
gave me credit for it ; and Almon has printed his
speech in one of the ' Remembrancers,' though he en-

---

[1] *Diary and Letters*, vol. i., p. 283.
[2] The Indian name of Milton Hill.

larged more than is printed on the subject in my favor. I send you one of the books (for I think it may be of service to have it known), and the extract in the papers. It will make me happier still if, when the Colonies come to be resettled, — as I hope they will, — I may be instrumental in securing every liberty, which, as British subjects, they are capable of enjoying." He goes on to speak of his farms at Conanicut and Milton. "At least £1100 was taken out of my house and off the farm (Milton) in movables. I know not how to obtain redress." He speaks of Elisha's coming to America, and Peggy's failing health. "I say nothing about public affairs, nor do I ever concern myself with them : nor am I ever inquired of or consulted about them ; and I am glad I am not. It is astonishing, considering the immense expense of this war and the stop put to the American trade, that nobody seems to feel it. Every merchant and every manufacturer, except a few who were factors for America, are as full of business as ever, and, in the manufacturing towns, they are fuller of business, from the increase of demand in other branches, than before the American war. With this amazing empire it is the unhappy case of my poor country to contend. May God Almighty in mercy put an end to this contest.

"Y^r faithful, humble servt,   T. H.

"James Murray, Esq., of Milton, in Mass. Bay. At Newport, R. I." [1]

March 12 : "Governor Pownal having lately buried his wife, I called upon him to-day. There has been no

[1] *Proceedings Mass. Hist. Soc.*, vol. v., pp. 363, 364.

visits passed for two years, which I think has not been my fault." [1]

May 8, as to Bristol : " I think, take in all circumstances, and I should prefer living there to any place in England. The manners and customs of the people are very like those of the people of New England, and you might pick out a set of Boston Selectmen from any of their churches." [2]

August 20 : " It is said everybody believes the news of Ticonderoga, and that New England would now be the object. I fear the destruction of poor Boston. What have those men to answer for who have brought on this destructive war ! " [3]

As this year advances, troubles both domestic and public thicken about him. His beloved youngest daughter, " Peggy," who captivated a few years before young Lord Fitzwilliam, so often in her father's confidence as the transcriber of his most important letters, dies of consumption, September 21. "Her breath grew shorter ; The last words she said were to Dr. Oliver, ' I am dying,' and continued speechless and but little, if at all, sensible until about half after ten P. M., when she expired."

The entries here are full of the heart-break, and in December comes in the news of Burgoyne's surrender, which produces terrible public discouragement. " Most of us expect to lay our bones here."

" Mar. 19, 1778. Called on Mr. Ellis.[4]   Laments

---

[1] *Diary and Letters*, vol. ii., p. 144.

[2] *Ibid.*, p. 148.   [3] *Ibid.*, p. 156.

[4] Welbore Ellis, Member of Parliament.

the universal despondency ; should not wonder if this afternoon the Americans were acknowledged Independent — a term they always avoided as a Religious distinction, but will always boast of as a civil character. After all, I shall never see that there were just grounds for this revolt. I see that the ways of Providence are mysterious, but I abhor the least thought that all is not perfect."

October 22, 1779, he notes great depression as to public affairs. Danger impends from the fleets of both France and Spain, with both which nations England is at war. The debt is becoming enormous ; Ireland is on the verge of revolt ; convulsions are impending in England.

He had hoped to be buried in his native land. In an affecting letter, soon after reaching England, he had written to his son Thomas, who did not leave Boston till the British evacuation, March, 1776, directing him to remove tenderly the remains of his wife, dead for twenty-one years, from Copp's Hill to the burying-ground in Milton. A tomb was to be arranged and the reinterment accomplished at night by a friendly sexton. The son was charged to see that room was left for his father. At last, however, this entry is encountered : —

"September 16, 1779. Stopped at Croydon, went into the church, and looked upon the grave of my dear child ; inquired whether there was room for me, and was informed there was."

He was indeed sinking fast. " Billy," too, always the hopeless one of the family, and for that very reason, perhaps, especially cherished, was nearing his end, and at the same time Sarah, Mrs. Oliver, was beginning to droop.

"Feb. 1. The prospect of returning to America and laying my bones in the land of my forefathers for four preceding generations and if I add the mother of W. H.[1] it will make five, is less than it has ever been. God grant me a composed mind submissive to his will; and may I be thankful that I am not reduced to those straits, which many others who are banished are, and have been."

"Billy" died on February 20. A child of Elisha's died on June 25; Sarah died on the 28th. The daughter and the grandchild, however, had been preceded. On the 3d of June death had come to the Governor. In the strangely smitten household the son Elisha writes as follows : —

"The Governor slept tolerably well, as he had done for several nights past; arose as usual at 8 o'clock shaved himself and eat his breakfast, and we all told him that his countenance had a more than healthy appearance, and if he was not better, we had no reason to conclude that he had lost ground. He conversed well and freely upon the riot in London the day before[2] and upon different subjects till the time for going out in the coach, at intervals however expressing his expectations of dying very soon, repeating texts of scripture, with short ejaculations to Heaven. He called for a shirt, telling Ryley, his servant, that he must die clean. I usually walked down the stairs before him, but he got up suddenly from his chair, and walked out

---

[1] William Hutchinson, his first American ancestor.
[2] The Gordon riots.

of the room, leaving the Doctor [Peter Oliver, Jr.] and I behind. We went into the room next the road; saw him whilst he was walking from the steps of the door to the coach (a few yds distance) hold out his hands to Ryley, and caught hold of him, to whom he said 'Help me!' and appeared to be fainting. I went down with the Doctor. The other servants had come to support him from falling, and had got him to the door of the house. They lifted him to a chair in the Servants' Hall or entrance hall into the house, but his head had fell, and his hands and f[eet?], his eyes diste[nded?] rolled up. The Doctor could feel no pulse; he applied volatiles to his nostrils, which seemed to have little or no effect; a be[d?] in the meantime was bro't, and put on the floor, on which he was laid, after which, with one or two gaspes, he resigned his soul to God who gave it."[1]

He was buried at Croydon on the 9th of June. It would scarcely be possible for a human life to close among circumstances of deeper gloom. He and his children, to be sure, were not in want; his balance at his banker's was £6387 15s. 3d. In every other way utter wreck had overtaken his family and himself. His daughters and his youngest son, dispirited, dropped prematurely at the same time with him into the grave. The prospects of the elder sons seemed quite blasted. In daily contact with him, a company of Loyalist exiles, once men of position and substance, now discredited and disheartened, were in danger of starvation. The country he had loved had nothing for him but con-

[1] *Diary and Letters,* vol. ii., pp. 353, 354.

tumely. To a man like Hutchinson public calamity would cause a deeper pang than private sorrows. No more threatening hour for England has probably ever struck than the hour when the soul of this man passed. It was becoming apparent that America was lost, a rending which easily might be fatal to the empire, and which her hereditary enemies were hastening to make the most of. To America herself the rending seemed to many certain to be fatal. While the members were thus being torn away, destruction seemed to impend at the heart. At the moment of the death, London was at the mercy of the mob in the Gordon riots. The city was on fire in many places ; a drunken multitude murdered right and left, laying hands even upon the noblest of the land. Mansfield, because he had recommended to the mercy of a jury a priest arrested for celebrating mass, saved his life with difficulty, his house with all his possessions going up in conflagration. The exile's funeral passed on its way through smoke and uproar that might easily have been regarded as the final crash of the social structure. No one foresaw then what was immediately to come : that England was to make good her loss twice over ; that America was to become the most powerful of nations; that the London disorders were on the surface merely and only transient. In Hutchinson's latest consciousness, every person, every spot, every institution dear to his heart, must have seemed to be overwhelmed in catastrophe. Such was the end of a life thoroughly dutiful and honorable !

APPENDIX A.

FURNITURE DESTROYED OR CARRIED FROM MY HOUSE AND
LOST THE NIGHT OF THE 26TH OF AUGUST, 1765.[1]

In the great room below.

	£	s.	d.
a teatable and burnt china set incompleat	5	10	
12 new walnut chairs all lost except some bottoms	11		
a large walnut table 3 10s ; a handsome couch 3 10s	7		
a bed and pillar for the couch & a dozen of cushions stuffed with feathers and covered with striped sattin	14		
2 large family pictures, gilt frames	20		
2 smaller size, my grandfather and mother	16		
4 large prints newly framed and glazed	6		
Andirons, shovel and tongs, brass	4		
large turkey-carpet	8		
In the closet 7½ doz. china plates	7	10	
a case of china handle knives & forks	4	3	
14 china dishes for table service	8		
blue and white tea set overplus cups & teapot with silver nose	5		
Decanters glasses mugs patty-pans & other glass-ware	5		
3 doz large hard metal plates 5 large dishes not in common use lost or bent up and spoilt	7		
2 glass sconces at ye side of the mantle-piece	3		
a large looking-glass cut down by a neighbor & saved	13	3	

In the Hall.

	£	s.	d.
2 large sconces with arms £12	12		
2 square mahogany tables 5 6 8 ; 2 smaller 4	9	6	8
3 painted oyl cloths 36s ; 2 large glazed prints 2 10	4	6	
7 glazed prints 2 10 ; 8 chairs morocco leather 9 10	11	10	
5 large luster (?) on the mantle-piece 10 sterl.	3	6	8

[1] *Mass. Archiv.* (*Colonial*, 1724–1776), vol. vi., pp. 301–320.

handsome andirons shovel & tongs 5

Dutch tea-kettle and stand & japanned tea-chest 2

In the buffett.

2 very large rich china bowls delft bowls & dishes china chocolate coffee and tea cups & plates at least in value 7

carpet cut and much damaged 2 10

In the little room.

6 walnut chairs turkey work bottoms & 1 great P (?) 9

small chairs 10s; very handsome table 48s 2 18

walnut desk & shelves & window cushion 7

round table 18s; polished andirons shovel &c. 4 4 18

a large sconce mahogany frame 6 13 4

a very good clock both clock & case broke to pieces & destroyed 12

a canvas floor cloth new-painted 3

In the Entry.

a dozen very good cane chairs & great chair 6

a large walnut table 30s; a large hanging lanthorn & small lanthorn 50s 4 10

In the great chamber.

a large looking glass japanned frame 12

a rich crimson damask bed, counterpin window curtains 8 chairs covered backs & seats with the same & outside covering part of the curtains only saved, lost more than 50

a rich India cabinet very little used with 3 stands of wax-work in glasses 38

a chamber fillegrain dressing glass large tortoise shell box small boxes, brushes &c. for a chamber table 5

furniture for another table of carved ivory very neat and curious 5

a japanned square table 3

a small table & toilet 1 10

bedside carpet 12

Andersons 30s; coat of arms glazed picture
&c. 70s 5; & glass sconce   120 2

In the hall chamber.

a very good glass   4
handsome case of draws & table   12
crimson boiled (?) camlet bed lined with silk   18
8 cane chairs & silk cushions   6
Andirons   1   41

In the back chamber.

Green harrateen (?) bed — part saved   3
6 chairs covered backs and seats wth camlet   2
old drawers   16

In my lodging chamber.

chintz bed part saved   3
buroa table new   2 13 4
small table   1
cane chairs & harrateen easy chair   3 10
Boxes for books & drawers   3 10
Scotch carpet   2   20 13

In the Kitchen Chamber.

blew and white camp bed part saved   1 10
a small sconce 15s; great chair camlet back
& seat 25   2   3 10

In the upper entry.

1 large table 20s; 1 Oval ditto 30s; 1 pin-
cerd (?) sideboard table 40s   4 10

In the chamber over great chamber.

Table press and draws; large turkey work
chairs   6

In the cellar.

12 pipes & 4 quarter cask wine 2 pipes only
saved & part of (?) lost
10 pipes very good Western Island wine
11 6 8   113 6 8
4 cask of sherry at 6£   24
In bottles Madeira Sherry claret Fortenac &
white wine with cyder & bottles none saved
value more than   20
1 cwt of Pork 8 hams about a dozen chaps (?)
of Bacon & other provisions at least   6 13 4 164

Articles not appropriated to any room.

a large new fashioned silver hilted sword gilt cost 6 guineas — blade & hilt broke to pieces damage	3		
a small silver hilted sword & 2 mourning swords lost	4	10	
a chased gold head of a cane & joint 4 guineas	5	12	
gold chain & hook of a watch cost 6 guineas	8	8	
microscope cost 3 guins. shaving apparatus 1 guin	4	4	
Telescope razors brush &c. 22s ; a set of plate buttons besides what are saved £4	6	2	
a rich cradle & basket with lining quilted sattin & set of laced linnen worth more than	14		
Eight feather beds (two or three only of the (?) saved) 8 bedsteads all broken to pieces two of them mahogany, bed cloaths, &c., a great part wholly destroyed cannot be replaced for more than	80		
a very large damask table cloth cut to pieces and other table linnen lost and destroyed I conclude	8		
leather & sealskin trunks damaged or destroyed	6		138 16
plate lost not recovered			
a dozen of silver handle knives & forks & shagreen case 4 or 5 only returned damaged	7		
a case of sweetmeat knives forks & spoons gilt one spoon only found	5	10	
Several silver spoons & tea spoons uncertain	6		
a Quart Tankard	10		
a stand of castors with silver tops	4		
a large handsome coffee pot top found beat up or as the mob term it stamped	16		
damage done to the other plate	16		164
about 20 bushels of split peas & 8 bags destroyed			13

I lost in money of which I am certain within
a few shillings I suppose —— (?) 170 10
I had received in my office deposited for the
   heirs of Richard Gooding which remained
   in my hands about 40 310 10
belonging to the province of the ship King
   George money uncertain the accounts being
   in the bag with the money suppose the amt
   about 100

I had in apparel
one camlet surtout one white cloth coat and
   breeches 1 suit of Pompadour cloth one
   lapelled corduroy waistcoat cost in London
   about £18 sterling very little worn 24
1 suit french grey button holes wrought with
   gold and gold basket buttons cost £13 sterling worn but a few times 17 6 8
1 suit mixed dark cloth gold holes cost about
   10 guineas half worn 7
1 black grey suit lined with ducape silk not
   much worn cost about 8 guineas 8 10
1 new black superfine cloth coat 7
2 black cloth waistcoats 2 10
1 laced crimson cloth waistcoat & breeches
   very little worn 7 10
1 velvet crimson waistcoat & breeches not
   half worn 5
1 padusoy coat & breeches half worn 6
1 superfine black grey coat & breeches ½ worn 5
1 Ratteen banyon (?) velvet cape little worn 3
2 pr black cloth 1 knit 1 cotton velvet breeches 4
2 white callicoe waistcoats 3
1 old coat gold holes much worn 1 10
1 scarlet Roquelaur 4 ; 1 scarlet Robe 8 12
1 black silk King's Council gown 3
3 hats £2 ; 1 wig 20s 3
6 pr kid gloves new ; other gloves caps ; 2 pr
   new shoes ; shoes in wear ; whips, &c.
   saddle bags portmanteau &c. 6

1 doz fine holland shirts new several not worn ruffled cost at least	20		
8 or 10 fine holland shirts more worn besides old shirts & some stocks handkerchiefs wig bags &c. &c.	8		
above a dozen pair of worsted stockings a dozen cotton silk & thredd	6		
Recovered of the above articles	159 6 8		
Camlet surtout £4 ; white breeches 40s	6		
Pompadour coat damaged	5		
grey suit worked with gold damaged	15		
waistcoat only of mixed dark cloth	2		
coat only of black grey suit	4 10		
new black coat 7 ; 1 black waistcoat 30s	8 10		
velvet breeches 30s ; padusoy & coat torn to pieces	3		
1 callico waistcoat 30s ; scarlet roqlaur	5 10		
scarlet robe £8	8		
about 10 shirts & stocks	10		
4 or 5 pr of hose	2	69 10	
remains lost		89 16 08	
		1225 6 8	
The loss in books & sets of books which are broke & spoiled & damage done to what are recovered cannot be estimated less than		50	
		£1275 6 8	

The following articles lost by my sister Miss Sanford
In gold received a day or two before of the

Treasurer £220 — & a years interest	233	
a gold chased watch chain & seal 21 guineas	29 8	
a spinnet 8 guineas £11 4 ; Burrow £3	14 4	
large sealskin trunk ; small ditto	2	
Paist necklace & earings cost 2 Johannes	4 16	
Topaz necklace & earings set in gold	5	
white stone earings French necklace & earings	2	
greenstone necklace & earings 2 french necklaces	2	

purple stone earings black necklac & earings	2	
Pair of stone shoe buckles 28s	1	8
new black full suit of best english padusoy	16	
a sack & petticoat of striped lustring	8	
a sack & petticoat of India padusoy	10	
a Brocade robe & petticoat	8	
a Red Genoa damask robe & petticoat	10	
a striped Lustring robe	6	
a Green damask robe	8	
a clouded gingham robe	4	
a chintz do & a worsted & silk ditto	4	
2 very handsome gauze suits compleat	6	
1 suit of Mecklenburgh lace	10	
3 gauze caps 30s ; 1 wide lace handkerchief 70s	5	
a fine laced handkerchief & single ruffles	4	
another handkerchief of ye same & double ruffles	6	
a muslin handkerchief & ruffles lawn ruffles	2	
a flowered lawn handkerchief & fine muslin apron	3	
a (?) stomacher & sleeve knots	2	
3 fine cambrick handkerchiefs 40s ; 1 embroidered apron	3	10
4 pair silk & fine thread mittens & gloves	1	10
5 ivory stick fans ribbands flowers &c.	4	
a white embroidered handkerchief & stomacher	3	
1 holland apron 10s ; 1 pr new silk hose 20s ; 2 pr cotton hose 12s	2	2
Dimity waistcoats 20s ; brocaded shoes 20s ; calam (?)	2	6
a scarlet cloth cloak head & body laced with silver entirely ruined	12	
2 silk cloaks with Ermine ; 1 velvet fringed	10	
1 purple sattin capuchin silver lace	8	
a silk tippet a cotton ditto	1	
a very fine camlet riding hood	4	
	459	4

besides many small articles of apparel not enumerated.

1734	9 8

My two daughters lost the following articles

one striped lustring robe & petticoat	6 10	
a brocaded robe & petticoat lined with silk	7 10	
a rich brocade petticoat (the sack damaged)	8	riding dress
a fine black russet quilt new	3	
a scarlet riding hood laced & scarlet petticoat	12	
a fine camlet riding hood 4£ ; new satin cloak	8	
a crimson satin hat black satin jockey ruined	1 5	
a pr satin shoes silver lace 30s ; 7 Ivory stick fans	4 10	
Ribbands & stones (?) 40s ; 1 suit blond lace 5£	7	
1 pair treble ruffles ; mechlin lace & tucker	3	
3 laced fly caps 2£ ; 1 pr garnet earings & necklace	6	
1 necklace with earings set in 4 ; gold ruby stone	4	
1 pr white stone earings, 1 ditto	3	
1 doz strings french beads 10s ; Handkercfs & ruffles 20s	1 10	
Lawn handkerchiefs & 2 pr plain ruffles	2 10	
Laced muslin handkerchief 40s ; double ruffles 30s	3 10	
one corded gawze apron 16s ; 1 lawn do worth 36s	2 12	
dresden work for aprons 40s	2	
6 pair fine cotton stockings 32s ; umbrella 16s	2 8	
holland shifts £6 ; tweezer case 8s	6 8	
a striped lustring sack of youngest daughter	3 10	
a clouded burdet (?) petticoat 20s ; worsted hose 20s	2	
shoes 16s ; 1 pr white silk hose 20s ; stone shoe buckles 28s	3 4	
Girdle buckle stone 20s ; stone drops in gold 30s	2 10	
stone buttons in do 20s ; blue & white gown & petticoat 40s ; gingham gown 30s	4 10	
a pocket-book glas &c. cost ½ guinea ; do 10s	1 4	
their mother's head cloths ruffled & laced worth more than	12	
a muff & tippet cost 48s ; another muff 12s	3	116 11

My son Thomas gives the following account
of the loss he sustained

1 surtout coat, 2 13 4 ; 1 light colored cloth							
suit £6 13 4	9	6	8				
1 new corduroy waistcoat	2	13	4				
1 black padusoy do £1 15; 3 pr cloth							
breeches 2 10	4	5					
1 pr cotton velvet 20s ; 2 pr worsted 1 6 8	2	6	8				
1 doz holland shirts one half of them little worn	7						
1 pr Irish shirting 25 yards at 4s 4d	5	8	4				
6 pr worsted 3 pr cotton hose	2	16					
3 pr silk do £3 ; 5 pr Thred ditto 20s	4						
4 pr shoes ; 1 pr spatterdashes & whip	1	10					
1 pr silver shoebuckles 15s ; Gold rings 6 13 4	7	8	4				
2 silk hair bags, stocks, & gloves	1	10					
1 pr silk gloves not worn cost		12		48	16	4	
deduct black silk waistcoat returned				1	15		
				47	1	4	

Furniture in my so Thomas' chamber

1 walnut desk 5£ ; 1 japan table £2 10s	7	10		
1 walnut table 24s ; 8 cane chairs 2 gt chairs	3			
1 handsome sconce 5s ; Metzotinto pictures				
4 10 ; curtains valliants &c. 4	8	10		
andirons, shovel, & tongs		19		
	19	19		
money in his desk of which he is certain	146	18	19	
			166	17

My son Elisha Hutchinson lost

1 superfine cinamon col'd cloth suit little worn	8	
1 light coloured suit	5	
1 suit double Allapeen	6	
1 new corduroy wastcoat	2	10
1 ditto little worn	1	10
1 new cloth wastcoat	2	10
2 ditto little worn	1	15
1 pr cloth breeches		12
2 pr worsted patterns	1	

6 pr worsted hose	1	16				
2 pr silk ditto	1					
2 pr cotton 3 pr Thred ditto		19				
8 holland shirts little worn	6	13	4			
2 pr shoes 2 pr gloves stocks &c.		18				
3 gold rings	1	4				
1 black cloth coat new	6					
1 black walnut desk	6					
1 Table &c.	1					
money in his desk of wch he is certain	110			164	7	4

My young son William Sanford

a surtout coat 2 13 4; pr breeches 16s 8d	2	10			
3 pr new cotton hose 16s; 2 pr worsted 10s	1	6			
2 pr shoes		12		4	8

Rebekah Whitmore housekeeper lost

4 new shifts cost 40s; 1 new lawn apron 18s	2	18			
1 muslin apron & handkerchief 8s; 1 pr new shoes 6s		14			
1 muslin apron worn 6s; 2 holland shifts worn 6s 8d		12	8		
1 pr silver buckles 9s 4d; 1 stone 3s; 1 red petticoat 6s 8d		19			
1 callico gown 16s; 1 poplin do 14s; 1 satin bonnet 9s 4d	1	19	4		
1 red cardinal 16s; 1 capuchin 16s; Velvet hood 8s	2				
2 pr kid gloves 3s 4d; 3 pr worsted hose 6s; 2 necklaces 4s		14			
3 fans 5s; 4 Ribbands 4s; Gloves & mits 13s 4d	1	2	8		
1 cambrick 1 gauze & several other handkerchiefs	1	1	4		
½ yd new holland 3s; a muff 6s; 1 dollor &c. 9s		18			
a black padusoy gown & petticoat part found	4	10		19	1

Susannah Townsend the maid's account

4 shifts 40s ; 1 plain lawn apron 13s 4d	2	13	4					
1 long lawn ditto 6s 8d ; 2 white 1 speckled do 9s		15	8					
1 pr new silk mits 6s ; 1 new hat cost 12s		18						
2 holland gowns 30s ; 1 Gold ring 12s	2	2						
a 13s 4d Calamanco shoes 6s		19	4					
Caps handkerchiefs 10s ; a muff 8s		18		8	6	4		

Moses Vose the coachman lost

one new striped wastcoat cost		17				
1 white shirt ; 3 pr stockings & 1 dollar	1	10		2	7	0

Mark negro

a new cloth coat 32s ; an old coat 18s ; shirt 10s				3	0	0

Mrs Walker a widow woman to whom I had allowed a living in the house several years lost

a feather bed 4s ; large glass		4				
Chintz gown 21s 4d ; walnut table 18s	1	19				
chamber table 18s ; [rest illegible ; comes in a worn fold]						
3 pr clogs 12s ; 1 pr do 5s 4d ; 1 mortar & pesttel	1	1				
3 chairs 9s ; 3 glazed pictures 4s		13				
a cambrick apron 13s 4d ; 4 holland shifts 40s	2	13	4			
1 muslin apron 10s ; 4 good handkercfs 20s	1	10				
2 pr silk hose 18s ; 2 pr cotton 6s	1	4				
3 pr worsted 6s ; 2 pr mits 2s		8				
5 aprons of Irish holland 20s ; 16 caps 13s 4d	1	13	4			
3 sheets 20s ; 3 pillowbeers 4s	1	4				
damage to a case of draws 6s ; chest 8s		14				
muff 6s 8d ; 3 Table cloths 8s		14	8			
4 pr cambrick ruffles 6s ; 1 coffee pot 2s 8d		8	8			
3 curtains		13	4	24	7	(?)

	£2290 16	6
Restored in money by persons unknown	72 15	0
	£2218 1	6

If any of the articles should appear to be too high rated others may be as low in proportion and upon the whole the same articles restored would be as valuable to me as the money. There are lost many articles which though singly too small to particularize yet when taken together amount to a large sum.

THO. HUTCHINSON.

[In a number of pages following are given what are apparently the rough drafts on which the foregoing inventory is based ; 1st, his own things, then "Apparel belonging to Miss Sanford," "Nurse's things," "Walker's things," "Sally's Cloathes & Peggy's," "Billy's," "Suoy's."]

[On scraps of paper the following entries :]

Books sets spoilt :

Universal History cost	5	
Mozzay's (?) Hist. of France	2	10
Harleian Miscellany	4	14
Cicero's Works	4	
Lewis 15 (?)		10
Magazines	3	4
	20	4
Middleton's Cicero		10

rich wrought satin child ~~bed blankets~~ sleeves & variety of child bed linen, satin cradle quilts & curtains — gawze handkerchief & apron embroidered with gold — a large octavo bible very richly bound & in an outside leather case — an inscription upon one leaf from Thomas Coram Esq. — several ancient english coins. If any of the above articles or any plate men's or women's apparel be offered to sale by any persons or seen in the possession of any persons of suspected characters it is desired notice may be given to either of ye L G's sons at their ware-houses in Boston — and whereas the history of ye prov- ince from the present charter to ye year 1750 ^{a manuscript} was among the spoil a part of which has been found if any of the remaining sheets should be discovered it is desired they may be sent together with any other of the L. G.'s papers or books to the Reverend Mr. Eliot.

APPENDIX B.

SPEECH OF THE GOVERNOR TO THE TWO HOUSES, JANUARY 6, 1773.[1]

Gentlemen of the Council, and Gentlemen of the House of Representatives,

I have nothing in special command from his Majesty to lay before you at this time ; I have general instructions to recommend to you, at all times, such measures as may tend to promote that peace and order, upon which your own happiness and prosperity, as well as his Majesty's service, very much depend. That the government is at present in a disturbed and disordered state, is a truth too evident to be denied. The cause of this disorder, appears to me equally evident. I wish I may be able to make it appear so to you, for then, I may not doubt that you will agree with me in the proper measures for the removal of it. I have pleased myself, for several years past, with hopes, that the cause would cease of itself, and the effect with it, but I am disappointed ; and I may not any longer, consistent with my duty to the King, and my regard to the interest of the province, delay communicating my sentiments to you upon a matter of so great importance. I shall be explicit, and treat the subject without reserve. I hope you will receive what I have to say upon it, with candor, and, if you shall not agree in sentiments with me, I promise you, with candor, likewise, to receive and consider what you may offer in answer.

When our predecessors first took possession of this plantation, or colony, under a grant and charter from the Crown of England, it was their sense, and it was the sense of the kingdom, that they were to remain subject to the supreme authority of Parliament. This appears from the charter itself, and from other irresistible evidence. This supreme authority has, from time to time, been exercised by Parliament, and submitted to by the colony, and hath been, in the most express terms, acknowledged by the Legislature, and, except about the time of the anarchy and confusion in England, which preceded the restoration of King Charles the Second, I have not discovered that it has been called in question, even by private or

---

[1] The text followed in these excerpts is that of the *Speeches of the Governors of Massachusetts from 1765 to 1775, with the Answers of the House of Representatives to the Same, etc.* Boston, Russell & Gardner, 1818 (sometimes referred to as Bradford's State Papers).

particular persons, until within seven or eight years last past. Our provincial or local laws have, in numerous instances, had relation to acts of Parliament, made to respect the plantations in general, and this colony in particular, and in our Executive Courts, both Juries and Judges have, to all intents and purposes, considered such acts as part of our rule of law. Such a constitution, in a plantation, is not peculiar to England, but agrees with the principles of the most celebrated writers upon the law of nations, that "when a nation takes possession of a distant country, and settles there, that country, though separated from the principal establishment, or mother country, naturally becomes a part of the state, equally with its ancient possessions."

So much, however, of the spirit of liberty breathes through all parts of the English constitution, that, although from the nature of government, there must be one supreme authority over the whole, yet this constitution will admit of subordinate powers with Legislative and Executive authority, greater or less, according to local and other circumstances. Thus we see a variety of corporations formed within the kingdom, with powers to make and execute such by-laws as are for their immediate use and benefit, the members of such corporations still remaining subject to the general laws of the kingdom. We see also governments established in the plantations, which, from their separate and remote situation, require more general and extensive powers of legislation within themselves, than those formed within the kingdom, but subject, nevertheless, to all such laws of the kingdom as immediately respect them, or are designed to extend to them ; and, accordingly, we, in this province have, from the first settlement of it, been left to the exercise of our Legislative and Executive powers, Parliament occasionally, though rarely, interposing, as in its wisdom has been judged necessary.

Under this constitution, for more than one hundred years, the laws both of the supreme and subordinate authority were in general, duly executed ; offenders against them have been brought to condign punishment, peace and order have been maintained, and the people of this province have experienced as largely the advantages of government, as, perhaps, any people upon the globe ; and they have, from time to time, in the most public manner expressed their sense of it, and, once in every year, have offered up their united thanksgivings to God for the enjoyment of these privileges, and as often, their united prayers for the continuance of them.

At length the constitution has been called in question, and the authority of the Parliament of Great Britain to make and establish laws for the inhabitants of this province has been, by many, denied. What was at first whispered with caution, was soon after openly asserted in print; and, of late, a number of inhabitants, in several of the principal towns in the province, having assembled together in their respective towns, and having assumed the name of legal town meetings, have passed resolves, which they have ordered to be placed upon their town records, and caused to be printed and published in pamphlets and newspapers. I am sorry that it is thus become impossible to conceal, what I could wish had never been made public. I will not particularize these resolves or votes, and shall only observe to you in general, that some of them deny the supreme authority of Parliament, and so are repugnant to the principles of the constitution, and that others speak of this supreme authority, of which the King is a constituent part, and to every act of which his assent is necessary, in such terms as have a direct tendency to alienate the affections of the people from their Sovereign, who has ever been most tender of their rights, and whose person, crown, and dignity, we are under every possible obligation to defend and support. In consequence of these resolves, committees of correspondence are formed in several of those towns, to maintain the principles upon which they are founded.

I know of no arguments, founded in reason, which will be sufficient to support these principles, or to justify the measures taken in consequence of them. It has been urged, that the sole power of making laws is granted, by charter, to a Legislature established in the province, consisting of the King, by his representative the Governor, the Council, and the House of Representatives; that, by this charter, there are likewise granted, or assured to the inhabitants of the province, all the liberties and immunities of free and natural subjects, to all intents, constructions and purposes whatsoever, as if they had been born within the realms of England; that it is part of the liberties of English subjects, which has its foundation in nature, to be governed by laws made by their consent in person, or by their representative; that the subjects in this province are not, and cannot be represented in the Parliament of Great Britain, and, consequently, the acts of that Parliament cannot be binding upon them.

I do not find, gentlemen, in the charter, such an expression as sole power, or any words which import it. The General Court has, by charter, full power to make such laws, as are not repugnant to the laws of England. A favorable construction has been put upon this clause, when it has been allowed to intend such laws of England only, as are expressly declared to respect us. Surely then this is, by charter, a reserve of power and authority to Parliament to bind us by such laws, at least, as are made expressly to refer to us, and consequently, is a limitation of the power given to the General Court. Nor can it be contended, that, by the limits of free and natural subjects, is to be understood an exemption from acts of Parliament, because not represented there, seeing it is provided by the same charter, that such acts shall be in force ; and if they that make the objection to such acts, will read the charter with attention, they must be convinced that this grant of liberties and immunities is nothing more than a declaration and assurance on the part of the Crown, that the place, to which their predecessors were about to remove, was, and would be considered as part of the dominions of the Crown of England, and, therefore, that the subjects of the Crown so removing, and those born there, or in their passage thither, or in their passage from thence, would not become aliens, but would, throughout all parts of the English dominions, wherever they might happen to be, as well as within the colony, retain the liberties and immunities of free and natural subjects, their removal from, or not being born within the realm notwithstanding. If the plantations be part of the dominions of the Crown, this clause in the charter does not confer or reserve any liberties, but what would have been enjoyed without it, and what the inhabitants of every other colony do enjoy where they are without a charter. If the plantations are not the dominions of the Crown, will not all that are born here, be considered as born out of the liegeance of the King of England, and, whenever they go into any parts of the dominions, will they not be deemed aliens to all intents and purposes, this grant in the charter notwithstanding?

They who claim exemption from acts of Parliament by virtue of their rights as Englishmen, should consider that it is impossible the rights of English subjects should be the same, in every respect, in all parts of the dominions. It is one of their rights as English subjects, to be governed by laws made by persons, in whose election they have, from time to time, a voice ; they remove from the kingdom, where, perhaps, they were in the full exercise of this right, to the plantations, where it cannot be exercised, or where the exercise of it would be of no benefit to them. Does it follow that the government, by their removal from one part of the dominions to another, loses its authority over that part to which they remove, and that they are freed from the subjection they were under before ; or do they expect that government should relinquish its authority because they cannot enjoy this particular right ? Will it not rather be said, that by this, their voluntary removal, they have relinquished for a time at least, one of the rights of an English subject, which they might, if they pleased, have continued to enjoy, and may again enjoy, whensoever they will return to the place where it can be exercised?

They who claim exemption, as part of their rights by nature, should consider that every restraint which men are laid under by a state of government, is a privation of part of their natural rights; and of all the different forms of government which exist, there can be no two of them in which the departure from natural rights is exactly the same. Even in case of representation by election, do they not give up part of their natural rights when they consent to be represented by such person as shall be chosen by the majority of the electors, although their own voices may be for some other person ? And is it not contrary to their natural rights to be obliged to submit to a representative for seven years, or even one year, after they are dissatisfied with his conduct, although they gave their voices for him when he was elected ? This must, therefore, be considered as an objection against a state of government, rather than against any particular form.

If what I have said shall not be sufficient to satisfy such as object to the supreme authority of Parliament over the plantations, there may something further be added to induce them to an acknowledgment of it, which, I think, will well deserve their consideration. I know of no line that can be drawn between the supreme authority of Parliament and the total independence of the colonies ; it is impossible there should be two independent Legislatures in one and the same state ; for, although there may be but one head, the King, yet the two Legislative bodies will make two governments as distinct as the kingdoms of England and Scotland before the union. If we might be suffered to be altogether independent of Great Britain, could we have any claim to the protection of that government, of which we are no longer a part? Without this protection, should we not become the prey of one or the other powers of Europe, such as should first seize upon us? Is there any thing which we have more reason to dread than independence? I hope it never will be our misfortune to know, by experience, the difference between the liberties of an English colonist, and those of the Spanish, French, or Dutch.

If, then, the supremacy of Parliament over the whole British dominions shall no longer be denied, it will follow that the mere exercise of its authority can be no matter of grievance. If it has been, or shall be exercised in such way and manner as shall appear to be grievous, still this cannot be sufficient ground for immediately denying or renouncing the authority, or refusing to submit to it. The acts and doings of authority, in the most perfect form of government, will not always be thought just and equitable by all the parts of which it consists; but it is the greatest absurdity to admit the several parts to be at liberty to obey, or disobey, according as the acts of such authority may be approved, or disapproved of by them, for this necessarily works a dissolution of the government. The manner, then, of obtaining redress, must be by representations and endeavors, in such ways and forms, as the established rules of the constitution prescribe or allow, in order to make any matters, alleged to be grievances, appear to be really such; but, I conceive it is rather the mere exercise of this authority, which is complained of as a grievance, than any heavy burdens which have been brought upon the people by means of it.

As contentment and order were the happy effects of a constitution, strengthened by universal assent and approbation, so discontent and disorder are now the deplorable effects of a constitution, enfeebled by contest and opposition. Besides divisions and animosities, which disturb the peace of towns and families, the law in some important cases cannot have its course; offenders ordered, by advice of his Majesty's Council, to be prosecuted, escape with impunity, and are supported and encouraged to go on offending; the authority of government is brought into contempt, and there are but small remains of that subordination, which was once very conspicuous in this colony, and which is essential to a well regulated state.

When the bands of government are thus weakened, it certainly behoves those with whom the powers of government are entrusted, to omit nothing which may tend to strengthen them.

I have disclosed my sentiments to you without reserve. Let me entreat you to consider them calmly, and not be too sudden in your determination. If my principles of government are right, let us adhere to them. With the same principles, our ancestors were easy and happy for a long course of years together, and I know of no reason to doubt of your being equally easy and happy. The people, influenced by you, will desist from their unconstitutional principles, and desist from their irregularities, which are the consequence of them; they will be convinced that every thing which is valuable to them, depend upon their connexion with their parent state; that this connexion cannot be carried in any other way, than such as will also continue their dependence upon the supreme authority of the British dominions; and that, notwithstanding this dependence, they will enjoy as great a proportion of those, to which they have a claim by nature, or as Englishmen, as can be enjoyed by a plantation or colony.

If I am wrong in my principles of government, or in the inferences which I have drawn from them, I wish to be convinced of my error. Independence, I may not allow myself to think that you can possibly have in contemplation. If you can conceive of any other constitutional dependence than what I have mentioned, if you are of opinion, that upon any other principles our connexion with the state from which we sprang, can be continued, communicate your sentiments to me with the same freedom and unreservedness, as I have communicated mine to you.

I have no desire, gentlemen, by any thing I have said, to preclude you from seeking relief, in a constitutional way, in any cases in which you have heretofore, or may hereafter suppose that you are aggrieved; and, although I should not concur with you in sentiment, I will, notwithstanding, do nothing to lessen the weight which your representations may deserve. I have laid before you what I think are the principles of your constitution; if you do not agree with me, I wish to know your objections; they may be convincing to me, or I may be able to satisfy you of the insufficiency of them. In either case, I hope we shall put an end to those irregularities, which ever will be the portion of a government where the supreme authority is controverted, and introduce that tranquillity, which seems to have taken place in most of the colonies upon the continent.

The ordinary business of the session, I will not now particularly point out to you. To the enacting of any new laws, which may be necessary for the more equal and effectual distribution of justice, or for giving further encouragement to our merchandize, fishery, and agriculture, which, through the divine favor, are already in a very flourishing state, or for promoting any measures, which may conduce to the general good of the province, I will readily give my assent or concurrence.   T. HUTCHINSON.

ANSWER OF THE COUNCIL TO THE SPEECH OF GOVERNOR HUTCHINSON OF JANUARY 6. JANUARY 25, 1773.

May it please your Excellency,

The Board have considered your Excellency's speech to both Houses, with the attention due to the object of it; and, we hope, with the candor you were pleased to recommend to them. We thank you for the promise, that, "if we shall not agree with you in sentiment, you will, with candor, likewise receive and consider what we may offer in answer."

Your speech informs the two Houses, that this government is at present in a disturbed and disordered state; that the cause of this disorder is the unconstitutional principles adopted by the people, in questioning the supreme authority of Parliament; and that the proper measure for removing the disorder, must be the substituting of contrary principles.

Our opinion on these heads, as well as on some others, proper to be noticed, will be obvious, in the course of the following observations.

With regard to the present disordered state of the government, it can have no reference to tumults or riots; from which this government is as free as any other, whatever. If your Excellency meant, only, that the province is discontented, and in a state of uneasiness, we should entirely agree with you; but you will permit us to say, that we are not so well agreed in the cause of it. The uneasiness, which was a general one, throughout the colonies, began when you inform us, the authority of Parliament was first called in question, viz. about seven or eight years ago. Your mentioning that particular time, might have suggested to your Excellency the true cause of the origin and continuance of that uneasiness.

At that time, the stamp act, then lately made, began to operate; which, with some preceding and succeeding acts of Parliament, subjecting the colonies to taxes, without their consent, was the original cause of all the uneasiness which has happened since; and has also occasioned an inquiry into the nature and extent of the authority, by which they were made. The late town meetings in several towns, are instances of both. These are mentioned by your Excellency, in proof of a disordered state. But, though we do not approve of some of their resolves, we think they had a clear right to instruct their Representatives in any subject they apprehended to be of sufficient importance to require it; which necessarily implies a previous consideration and expression of their minds on that subject, however mistaken they may be concerning it.

When a community, great or small, think their rights and privileges infringed, they will express their uneasiness in a variety of ways; some of which, may be highly improper and criminal. So far as any of an atrocious nature have taken place, we would express our abhorrence of them; and, as we have always done, hitherto, we shall continue to do every thing in our power, to discourage and suppress them. But it is in vain to hope that this can be done effectually, so long as the cause of the uneasiness exists. Your Excellency will perceive that the *cause* you assign, is, by us, supposed to be an *effect*, derived from the original cause, above mentioned; the removal of which, will remove its effects.

To obtain this removal, we agree with you in the method pointed out in your speech, where you say, "the manner of obtaining redress must be by representation, and endeavors, in such ways and forms as the constitution allows, in order to make any matters alleged to be grievances, appear to be really such.

This method has been pursued repeatedly. Petitions to Parliament have gone from the colonies, and from this colony in particular; but without success. Some of them, in a former Ministry, were previously shewn to the Minister, who, as we have been informed, advised the Agents to postpone presenting them to the House of Commons, till the first reading of the bill they referred to; when, being presented, a rule of the House against receiving petitions on money bills, was urged for rejecting them, and they were rejected, accordingly; and other petitions, for want of formality, or whatever was the reason, have had the same fate. This we mention, not by way of censure on that honorable House, but in some measure to account for the conduct of those persons, who, despairing of redress, in a constitutional way, have denied the just authority of Parliament; concerning which, we shall now give our own sentiments, intermixed with observations on those of your Excellency.

You are pleased to observe, that when our predecessors first took possession of this colony, under a grant and charter from the Crown of England, it was their sense, and the sense of the whole kingdom, that they were to remain subject to the supreme authority of Parliament ; and to prove that subjection, the greater part of your speech is employed.

In order to a right conception of this matter, it is necessary to guard against any improper idea of the term *supreme* authority. In your idea of it, your Excellency seems to include *unlimited* authority ; for, you are pleased to say, that you know of no line which can be drawn between the supreme authority of Parliament, and the real independence of the colonies. But if no such line can be drawn, a denial of that authority, in any instance whatever, implies and amounts to a declaration of total independence. But if supreme authority, includes unlimited authority, the subjects of it are emphatically slaves ; and equally so, whether residing in the colonies, or Great Britain. And, indeed, in this respect, all the nations on earth, among whom government exists in any of its forms, would be alike conditioned, excepting so far as the mere grace and favor of their Governors might make a difference, for from the nature of government there must be, as your Excellency has observed, one supreme authority over the whole.

We cannot think, that when our predecessors took possession of this colony, it was their sense, or the sense of the kingdom, that they were to remain subject to the supreme authority of Parliament in this idea of it. Nor can we find, that this appears from the charter ; or, that such authority has ever been exercised by Parliament, submitted to by the colony, or acknowledged by the Legislature.

Supreme, or unlimited authority, can with fitness, belong only to the Sovereign of the universe ; and that fitness is derived from the perfection of his nature. To such authority, directed by infinite wisdom and infinite goodness, is due both active and passive obedience ; which, as it constitutes the happiness of rational creatures, should, with cheerfulness, and from choice, be unlimitedly paid by them. But, this can be said with truth, of no other authority whatever. If, then, from the nature and end of government, the supreme authority of every government is limited, the supreme authority of Parliament must be limited ; and the inquiry will be, what are the limits of that authority, with regard to this colony ? To fix them with precision, to determine the exact lines of right and wrong in this case, as in some others, is difficult ; and we have not the presumption to attempt it. But we humbly hope, that, as we are personally and relatively, in our public and private capacities, for ourselves, for the whole province, and posterity, so deeply interested in this important subject, it will not be deemed arrogance to give some general sentiments upon it, especially as your Excellency's speech has made it absolutely necessary.

For this purpose, we shall recur to those records which contain the main principles on which the English constitution is founded ; and from them make such extracts as are pertinent to the subject.

Magna Charta declares, that no aid shall be imposed in the kingdom, unless by the Common Council of the kingdom, except to redeem the King's person, &c. And that all cities, boroughs, towns, and ports, shall have their liberties and free customs ; and shall have the Common Council of the kingdom, concerning the assessments of their aids, except in the cases aforesaid.

The statute of the 34th of Edward I. *de tallio non concedendo*, declares, that no tallage or aid should be laid or levied by the King or his heirs, in the realm, without the good will and assent of the Archbishops, Bishops, Earls, Barons, Knights, Burgesses, and others, the freemen of the commonalty of this realm. A statute of the 25th Edward III. enacts, that from thenceforth, no person shall be compelled to make any loans to the King, against his will, because such loans were against reason and the franchise of the land.

The petition of rights in the 3d of Charles I. in which are cited the two foregoing statutes, declares, that, by those statutes, and other good laws and statutes of the realm, his Majesty's subjects inherited this freedom, that they should not be compelled to contribute to any tax, tallage, aid, or other like charge, not set by common consent of Parliament.

And the statute of the 1st of William III. for declaring the rights and liberties of the subject, and settling the succession of the Crown, declares, that the levying of money for, or to the use of the Crown, by pretence of prerogative, without grant of Parliament for longer time, or in any other manner than the same is, or shall be granted, is illegal.

From these authorities, it appears an essential part of the English constitution, that no tallage, or aid, or tax, shall be laid or levied without the good will and assent of the freedom of the commonalty of the realm. If this could be done without their assent, their property would be in the highest degree precarious; or rather they could not, with fitness, be said to have any property at all. At best, they would be only the holders of it for the use of the Crown, and the Crown be the real proprietor. This would be vassalage in the extreme, from which the generous nature of Englishmen have been so abhorrent, that they have bled with freedom in defence of this part of their constitution, which has preserved them from it; and influenced by the same generosity, they can never view with disapprobation, any lawful measures taken by us for the defence of our own constitution, which entitles us to the same rights and privileges with themselves. These were derived to us from common law, which is the inheritance of all his Majesty's subjects; have been recognized by acts of Parliament, and confirmed by the province charter, which established its constitution; and which charter, has been recognized by acts of Parliament also. This act was made in the second year of the reign of his late Majesty George II. for the better preservation of his Majesty's woods in America, in which is recited the clause of the charter, reserving for the use of the royal navy, all trees suitable for masts; and on this charter is grounded the succeeding enacting clause of the act; and thus is the charter implicitly confirmed by act of Parliament. From all which it appears, that the inhabitants of this colony are clearly entitled to all the rights and privileges of free and natural subjects; which certainly must include that most essential one, that no aid or taxes be levied on them, without their own consent, signified by their Representatives.

But, from the clause in the charter, relative to the power granted to the General Court, to make laws not repugnant to the laws of England, your Excellency draws this inference, that surely this is, by charter, a reserve of power and authority to Parliament, to bind us by such laws, at least, as are made to refer to us, and consequently is a limitation of the power given to the General Court. If it be allowed, that, by that clause there was a reserve of power to Parliament, to bind the province, it was only by such laws as were in being at the time the charter was granted; for, by the charter, there is nothing appears to make it refer to any parliamentary laws, that should be afterwards made; and therefore, it will not support your Excellency's inference.

The grant of power to the General Court to make laws, runs

thus — " full power and authority, from time to time, to make and ordain, and establish, all manner of wholesome and reasonable laws, orders, statutes and ordinances, directions and instructions ; either with penalties or without, so as the same be not repugnant or contrary to the laws of this our realm of England, as they shall judge to be for the good and welfare of our said province." We humbly conceive an inference very different from your Excellency's, and a very just one too, may be drawn from this clause, if attention be given to the description of the orders and laws that were to be made. They were to be wholesome, reasonable, and for the good and welfare of the province ; and in order that they might be so, it is provided, that they be not repugnant or contrary to the laws of the realm, which were then in being ; by which proviso, all the liberties and immunities of free and natural subjects within the realm, were more effectually secured to the inhabitants of the province, agreeable to another clause in the charter, whereby those liberties and immunities are expressly granted to them ; and accordingly, the power of the General Court is so far limited, that they shall not make orders and laws to take away or diminish those liberties and immunities.

This construction appears to us a just one, and perhaps may appear so to your Excellency, if you will please to consider, that, by another part of the charter, effectual care was taken for preventing the General Assembly passing of orders and laws repugnant to, or that in any way might militate with acts of Parliament then or since made, or that might be exceptionable in any other respect whatever ; for the charter reserves to his Majesty the appointment of the Governor, whose assent is necessary in the passing of all orders and laws ; after which, they are to be sent to England, for the royal approbation or disallowance ; by which double control, effectual care is taken to prevent the establishment of any improper orders or laws, whatever. Besides, your Excellency is sensible that letters patent must be construed one part with another, and all the parts of them together, so as to make the whole harmonize and agree. But your Excellency's construction of the paragraph empowering the General Court to make orders and laws, does by no means harmonize and agree with the paragraph granting liberties and immunities ; and therefore, we humbly conceive, is not to be admitted : whereas on the other construction, there is a perfect harmony and agreement between them. But supposing your Excellency's inference just, that by said former paragraph, considered by itself, are reserved to Parliament, power and authority to bind us by laws made expressly to refer us, does it consist with justice and equity, that it should be considered a part, and urged against the people of this province, with all its force, and without limitation ; and at the same time, the other paragraph, which they thought secured to them the essential rights and privileges of free and natural subjects, be rendered of no validity ?

If the former paragraph (in this supposed case) be binding on this people, the latter must be binding on the Crown, which thereby became guarantee of those rights and privileges, or it must be supposed that one party is held by a compact, and the other not ; which supposition is against reason and against law ; and therefore, destroys the foundation of the inference. Supposing it well founded, however, it would not from thence follow, that the charter intended such laws as should subject the inhabitants of this province to taxes without their consent ; for (as it appears above) it grants to them all the rights and liberties of free and natural subjects ; of which, one of the most essential is, a freedom from all taxes not consented to by themselves. Nor could the parties, either grantor or grantees, intend such laws. The royal grantor could not, because his grant contradicts such intention, and because it is inconsistent with every idea of royalty and royal wisdom, to grant what it does not intend to grant. And it will be readily allowed, that the grantees could not intend such laws ; not only on account of their inconsistency with the grant, but because their acceptance of a charter, subjecting them to such laws, would be voluntary slavery.

Your Excellency next observes, " that it cannot be contended, that, by the liberties of free and natural subjects, is to be understood an exemption from acts of Parliament, because not represented there, seeing it is provided by the charter, that such acts shall be in force." If the observations we have made above, and our reasoning on them be just, it will appear, that no such provision is made in the charter ; and, therefore, that the deductions and inferences derived from the supposition of such provision, are not well founded. And with respect to representation in Parliament, as it is one of the essential liberties of free and natural subjects, and properly makes those who enjoy it, liable to parliamentary acts, so in reference to the inhabitants of this province, who are entitled to all the liberties of such subjects, the impossibility of their being duly represented in Parliament, does clearly exempt them from all such acts, at least, as have been or shall be made by Parliament, to tax them ; representation and taxation being, in our opinion, constitutionally inseparable.

This grant of liberties and immunities, your Excellency informs us, "is nothing more than a declaration and assurance on the part of the Crown, that the place to which our predecessors were about to remove, was, and would be considered, as part of the dominions of the Crown ; and, therefore, that the subjects, so removing, would not become aliens, but would, both without and within the colony, retain the liberties and immunities of free and natural subjects."

The dominion of·the Crown over this country, before the arrival of our predecessors, was merely ideal. Their removal hither, realized that dominion, and has made the country valuable both to the Crown and nation, without any cost to either of them, from that time to this. Even in the most distressed state of our predecessors, when they expected to be destroyed by a general conspiracy and incursion of the Indian natives, they had no assistance from them. This grant then of liberties, which is the only consideration they received from the Crown, for so valuable an acquisition to it, instead of being violated by military power, or explained away by nice inferences and distinctions, ought in justice, and with a generous openness and freedom, to be acknowledged by every Minister of the Crown, and preserved sacred from every species of violation.

"If the plantations be part of the dominions of the Crown, this clause in the charter, granting liberties and immunities, does not," your Excellency observes, "confer or reserve any liberties but what would have been enjoyed without it ; and what the inhabitants of every other colony do enjoy, where they are without a charter." Although the colonies, considered as part of the dominions of the Crown, are entitled to equal liberties, the inhabitants of this colony, think it a happiness, that those liberties are confirmed and secured to them by a charter ; whereby the honor and faith of the Crown are pledged, that those liberties shall not be violated. And for protection in them, we humbly look up to his present Majesty, our rightful and lawful Sovereign, as children to a father, able and disposed to assist and relieve them ; humbly imploring his Majesty, that his subjects of this province, ever faithful and loyal, and ever accounted such, till the stamp act existed, and who, in the late war, and upon all other occasions, have demonstrated that faithfulness and loyalty, by their vigorous and unexampled exertions in his service, may have their grievances redressed, and be restored to their just rights.

Your Excellency next observes, "that it is impossible the rights of English subjects should be the same in every respect, in all parts of the dominions," and instances in the right of " being governed by laws made by persons, in whose election they have a voice." When "they remove from the kingdom to the plantations, where it cannot be enjoyed," you ask, " will it not be said, by this voluntary removal, they have relinquished, for a time at least, one of the rights of an English subject, which they might, if they pleased, have continued to enjoy, and may again enjoy, whenever they will return to the place where it can be exercised ? "

When English subjects remove from the kingdom to the plantations, with their property, they not only relinquish that right *de facto*, but it ought to cease in the kingdom *de jure*. But it does not from thence follow, that they relinquish that right in reference to the plantation or colony, to which they remove. On the contrary, having become inhabitants of that colony, and qualified according to the laws of it, they can exercise that right, equally with the other inhabitants of it. And their right, on like conditions, will travel with them through all the colonies, wherein a Legislature, similar to that of the kingdom, is established. And therefore, in this respect, and, we suppose, in all other essential respects, it is not impossible the rights of English subjects should be the same in all parts of the dominions, under a like form of Legislature.

This right of representation, is so essential and indisputable, in regard of all laws for levying taxes, that a people under any form of government, destitute of it, is destitute of freedom : of that degree of freedom, for the preservation of which, government was instituted ; and without which, government degenerates into despotism. It cannot, therefore, be given up, or taken away, without making a breach in the essential rights of nature.

But your Excellency is pleased to say, " that they who claim exemption as part of their rights by nature, should consider that every restraint which men are laid under by a state of government, is a privation of part of their natural rights. Even in case of representation by election, do they not give up part of their natural rights, when they consent to be represented by such persons as shall be chosen by the majority of the electors, although their own voices may be for some other person ? And is it not

contrary to their natural rights, to be obliged to submit to a representation for seven years, or even one year, after they are dissatisfied with his conduct, although they gave their voices for him, when
he was elected? This must, therefore, be considered as an objection against a state of government, rather than against any particular form."

Your Excellency's premises are true, but we do not think your
conclusion follows from them. It is true, that every restraint of
government is a privation of natural right; and the two cases you
have been pleased to mention, may be instances of that privation.
But, as they arise from the nature of society and government; and
as government is necessary to secure other natural rights, infinitely
more valuable, they cannot, therefore, be considered as an objection,
either against a state government, or against any particular form
of it.

Life, liberty, property, and the disposal of that property, with
our own consent, are natural rights. Will any one put the other in
competition with these ; or infer, that, because those others must be
given up in a state of government, these must be given up also?
The preservation of these rights, is the great end of government.
But is it probable, they will be effectually secured by a government,
which the proprietors of them, have no part in the direction of, and
over which, they have no power or influence, whatever? Hence, is
deducible representation, which being necessary to preserve these
invaluable rights of nature, is itself, for that reason, a natural right,
coinciding with, and running into that great law of nature, self preservation.

Thus have we considered the most material parts of your Excellency's speech, and, agreeable to your desire, disclosed to you our
sentiments on the subject of it. " Independence," as you have
rightly judged, " we have not in contemplation." We cannot, however, adopt your principles of government, or acquiesce in all the
inferences you have drawn from them.

We have the highest respect for that august body, the Parliament, and do not presume to prescribe the exact limits of its
authority ; yet, with the deference which is due to it, we are
humbly of opinion, that, as all human authority is, in the nature of
it, and ought to be, limited, it cannot, constitutionally, extend, for
the reasons we have suggested, to the levying of taxes, in any form,
on his Majesty's subjects in this province.

In such principles as these, our predecessors were easy and happy, and in the due operation of such, their descendants, the present inhabitants of this province, have been easy and happy : but they are not so now. Their uneasiness and unhappiness are occasioned by acts of Parliament, and regulations of government, which lately, and within a few years past, have been made. And this uneasiness and unhappiness, both in the cause and effects of them, though your Excellency seems, and can only seem, to be of a different opinion, have extended, and continue to extend, to all the colonies, throughout the continent.

It would give us the highest satisfaction, to see happiness and tranquillity restored to the colonies, and, especially to see, between Great Britain and them, an union established on such an equitable basis, as neither of them shall ever wish to destroy. We humbly supplicate the sovereign arbiter and superintendent of human affairs, for these happy events.

[Hon. J. Bowdoin, H. Gray, J. Otis, and S. Hall, were the committee of Council, who prepared the above.]

ANSWER OF THE HOUSE OF REPRESENTATIVES TO THE SPEECH OF THE GOVERNOR, OF SIXTH JANUARY. . . . JANUARY 26, 1773.

May it please your Excellency,

Your Excellency's speech to the General Assembly, at the opening of this session, has been read with great attention in this House.

We fully agree with your Excellency, that our own happiness, as well as his Majesty's service, very much depends upon peace and order ; and we shall at all times take such measures as are consistent with our constitution, and the rights of the people, to promote and maintain them. That the government at present is in a very disturbed state, is apparent. But we cannot ascribe it to the people's having adopted unconstitutional principles, which seems to be the cause assigned for it by your Excellency. It appears to us, to have been occasioned rather by the British House of Commons assuming and exercising a power inconsistent with the freedom of the constitution, to give and grant the property of the colonists, and appropriate the same without their consent.

It is needless for us to inquire what were the principles that induced the councils of the nation to so new and unprecedented a measure. But, when the Parliament, by an act of their own, expressly declared, that the King, Lords, and Commons, of the nation "have, and of right ought to have full power and authority to make laws and statutes of sufficient force and validity, to bind the colonies and people of America, subjects of the Crown of Great Britain, in all cases whatever," and in consequence hereof, another revenue act was made, the minds of the people were filled with anxiety, and they were justly alarmed with apprehensions of the total extinction of their liberties.

The result of the free inquiries of many persons, into the right of the Parliament to exercise such a power over the colonies, seems, in your Excellency's opinion, to be the cause, of what you are pleased to call the present "disturbed state of the government;" upon which, you "may not any longer, consistent with your duty to the King, and your regard to the interest of the province, delay communicating your sentiments." But that the principles adopted in consequence hereof, are unconstitutional, is a subject of inquiry. We know of no such disorders arising therefrom, as are mentioned by your Excellency. If Grand Jurors have not, on their oaths, found such offences, as your Excellency, with the advice of his Majesty's Council, have ordered to be prosecuted, it is to be presumed, they have followed the dictates of good conscience. They are the constitutional judges of these matters, and it is not to be supposed, that moved from corrupt principles, they have suffered offenders to escape a prosecution, and thus supported and encouraged them to go on offending. If any part of authority shall, in an unconstitutional manner, interpose in any matter, it will be no wonder if it be brought into contempt; to the lessening or confounding of that subordination, which is necessary to a well regulated state. Your Excellency's representation that the bands of government are weakened, we humbly conceive to be without good grounds; though we must own, the heavy burdens unconstitutionally brought upon the people, have been, and still are universally, and very justly complained of, as a grievance.

You are pleased to say, that, "when our predecessors first took possession of this plantation, or colony, under a grant and charter from the Crown of England, it was their sense, and it was the sense of the kingdom, that they were to remain subject to the supreme authority of Parliament;" whereby we understand your

Excellency to mean, in the sense of the declaratory act of Parliament afore mentioned, in all cases whatever. And, indeed, it is difficult, if possible, to draw a line of distinction between the universal authority of Parliament over the colonies, and no authority at all. It is, therefore, necessary for us to inquire how it appears, for your Excellency has not shown it to us, that when, or at the time that our predecessors took possession of this plantation, or colony, under a grant and charter from the Crown of England, it was their sense, and the sense of the kingdom, that they were to remain subject to the authority of Parliament. In making this inquiry, we shall, according to your Excellency's recommendation, treat the subject with calmness and candor, and also with a due regard to truth.

Previous to a direct consideration of the charter granted to the province or colony, and the better to elucidate the true sense and meaning of it, we would take a view of the state of the English North American continent at the time, when, and after possession was first taken of any part of it, by the Europeans. It was then possessed by heathen and barbarous people, who had, nevertheless, all that right to the soil, and sovereignty in and over the lands they possessed, which God had originally given to man. Whether their being heathen, inferred any right or authority to Christian princes, a right which had long been assumed by the Pope, to dispose of their lands to others, we will leave to your Excellency, or any one of understanding and impartial judgment, to consider. It is certain, they had in no other sense, forfeited them to any power in Europe. Should the doctrine be admitted, that the discovery of lands owned and possessed by pagan people, gives to any Christian prince a right and title to the dominion and property, still it is vested in the Crown alone. It was an acquisition of foreign territory, not annexed to the realm of England, and, therefore, at the absolute disposal of the Crown. For we take it to be a settled point, that the King has a constitutional prerogative, to dispose of and alienate, any part of his territories not annexed to the realm. In the exercise of this prerogative, Queen Elizabeth granted the first American charter ; and, claiming a right by virtue of discovery, then supposed to be valid, to the lands which are now possessed by the colony of Virginia, she conveyed to Sir Walter Rawleigh, the property, dominion, and sovereignty thereof, to be held of the Crown, by homage, and a certain render, without any reservation to herself, of any share in the Legislative and Executive authority.   After the attainder of Sir Walter, King James the I. created two Virginian companies, to be governed each by laws, transmitted to them by his Majesty, and not by the Parliament, with power to establish, and cause to be made, a coin to pass current among them ; and vested with all liberties, franchises and immunities, within any of his other dominions, to all intents and purposes, as if they had been abiding and born within the realm. A declaration similar to this, is contained in the first charter of this colony, and in those of other American colonies, which shows that the colonies were not intended, or considered to be within the realm of England, though within the allegiance of the English Crown. After this, another charter was granted by the same King James, to the Treasurer and Company of Virginia, vesting them with full power and authority, to make, ordain, and establish, all manner of orders, laws, directions, instructions, forms and ceremonies of governments, and magistracy, fit and necessary, and the same to abrogate, &c. without any reservation for securing their subjection to the Parliament, and future laws of England. A third charter was afterwards granted by the same King, to the Treasurer and Company of Virginia, vesting them with power and authority to make laws, with an addition of this clause, " so, always, that the same be not contrary to the laws and statutes of this our realm of England." The same clause was afterwards copied into the charter of this and other colonies, with certain variations, such as, that these laws should be " consonant to reason," " not repugnant to the laws of England," " as nearly as conveniently may be to the laws, statutes and rights of England," &c.   These modes of expression, convey the same meaning, and serve to show an intention, that the laws of the colonies should be as much as possible, conformable in the spirit of them, to the principles and fundamental laws of the English constitution, its rights and statutes then in being, and by no means to bind the colonies to a subjection to the supreme authority of the English Parliament. And that this is the true intention, we think it further evident from this consideration, that no acts of any colony Legislative, are ever brought into Parliament for inspection there, though the laws made in some of them, like the acts of the British Parliament, are laid before the King for his dissent or allowance.

We have brought the first American charters into view, and the state of the country when they were granted, to show, that the right of disposing of the lands was, in the opinion of those times, vested solely in the Crown; that the several charters conveyed to the grantees, who should settle upon the territories therein granted, all the powers necessary to constitute them free and distinct states; and that the fundamental laws of the English constitution should be the certain and established rule of legislation, to which, the laws to be made in the several colonies, were to be, as nearly as conveniently might be, conformable, or similar, which was the true intent and import of the words, " not repugnant to the laws of England," " consonant to reason," and other variant expressions in the different charters. And we would add, that the King, in some of the charters, reserves the right to judge of the consonance and similarity of their laws with the English constitution, to himself, and not to the Parliament; and, in consequence thereof, to affirm, or within a limited time, disallow them.

These charters, as well as that afterwards granted to Lord Baltimore, and other charters, are repugnant to the idea of Parliamentary authority; and, to suppose a Parliamentary authority over the colonies, under such charters, would necessarily induce that solecism in politics, *imperium in imperio*. And the King's repeatedly exercising the prerogative of disposing of the American territory by such charters, together with the silence of the nation thereupon, is an evidence that it was an acknowledged prerogative.

But, further to show the sense of the English Crown and nation, that the American colonists, and our predecessors in particular, when they first took possession of this country, by a grant and charter from the Crown, did not remain subject to the supreme authority of Parliament, we beg leave to observe, that when a bill was offered by the two Houses of Parliament to King Charles the I. granting to the subjects of England, the free liberty of fishing on the coast of America, he refused his royal assent, declaring as a reason, that " the colonies were without the realm and jurisdiction of Parliament."

In like manner, his predecessor, James the I. had before declared, upon a similar occasion, that " America was not annexed to the realm, and it was not fitting that Parliament should make laws for those countries." This reason was, not secretly, but openly declared in Parliament. If, then, the colonies were not annexed to the realm, at the time when their charters were granted, they never could be afterwards, without their own special consent, which has

never since been had, or even asked. If they are not now annexed
to the realm, they are not a part of the kingdom, and consequently
not subject to the Legislative authority of the kingdom. For no
country, by the common law, was subject to the laws or to the Parliament, but the realm of England.

We would, if your Excellency pleases, subjoin an instance of conduct in King Charles the II. singular indeed, but important to our
purpose, who, in 1679, framed an act for a permanent revenue for
the support of Virginia, and sent it there by Lord Culpepper, the
Governor of that colony, which was afterwards passed into a law,
and "enacted by the King's most excellent Majesty, by, and with
the consent of the General Assembly of Virginia." If the King had
judged that colony to be a part of the realm, he would not, nor
could he, consistently with Magna Charta, have placed himself at
the head of, and joined with any Legislative body in making a law
to tax the people there, other than the Lords and Commons of
England.

Having taken a view of the several charters of the first colony in
America, if we look into the old charter of this colony, we shall
find it to be grounded on the same principle ; that the right of disposing the territory granted therein, was vested in the Crown, as
being that Christian Sovereign who first discovered it, when in the
possession of heathens ; and that it was considered as being not
within the realm, but being only within the Fee and Seignory of the
King. As, therefore, it was without the realm of England, must
not the King, if he had designed that the Parliament should have
had any authority over it, have made a special reservation for that
purpose, which was not done ?

Your Excellency says, "it appears from the charter itself, to
have been the sense of our predecessors, who first took possession
of this plantation, or colony, that they were to remain subject to the
authority of Parliament." You have not been pleased to point out
to us, how this appears from the charter, unless it be in the observation you make on the above mentioned clause, viz. : " that a favorable construction has been put upon this clause, when it has been
allowed to intend such laws of England only, as are expressly made
to respect us," which you say, "is by charter, a reserve of power
and authority to Parliament, to bind us by such laws, at least, as
are made expressly to refer to us, and consequently is a limitation
of the power given to the General Court." But, we would still re-

cur to the charter itself, and ask your Excellency, how this appears, from thence, to have been the sense of our predecessors ? Is any reservation of power and authority to Parliament thus to bind us, expressed or implied in the charter ? It is evident, that King Charles the I. the very Prince who granted it, as well as his predecessor, had no such idea of the supreme authority of Parliament over the colony, from their declarations before recited. Your Excellency will then allow us, further to ask, by what authority, in reason or equity, the Parliament can enforce a construction so unfavorable to us. *Quod ab initio injustum est, nullum potest habere juris effectum,* said Grotius. Which, with submission to your Excellency, may be rendered thus : whatever is originally in its nature wrong, can never be *sanctified,* or made right by *repetition* and use.

In solemn agreements, subsequent restrictions ought never to be allowed. The celebrated author, whom your Excellency has quoted, tells us, that, " neither the one or the other of the interested, or contracting powers, hath a right to interpret at pleasure." This we mention, to show, even upon a supposition, that the Parliament had been a party to the contract, the invalidity of any of its subsequent acts, to explain any clause in the charter ; more especially to restrict or make void any clause granted therein to the General Court. An agreement ought to be interpreted " in such a manner as that it may have its effect." But, if your Excellency's interpretation of this clause is just, " that it is a reserve of power and authority to Parliament to bind us by such laws as are made expressly to refer to us," it is not only " a limitation of the power given to the General Court " to legislate, but it may, whenever the Parliament shall think fit, render it of no effect ; for it puts it in the power of Parliament, to bind us by as many laws as they please, and even to restrain us from making any laws at all. If your Excellency's assertions in this, and the next succeeding part of your speech, were well grounded, the conclusion would be undeniable, that the charter, even in this clause, " does not confer or reserve any liberties," worth enjoying, " but what would have been enjoyed without it ; " saving that, within any of his Majesty's dominions, we are to be considered barely as not aliens. You are pleased to say, it cannot " be contended, that by the liberties of free and natural subjects," (which are expressly granted in the charter, to all intents, purposes and constructions, whatever) " is to be understood, an exemption from acts of Parliament, because not represented there ; seeing it is provided by the same charter, that such acts shall be in force." If, says an eminent lawyer, " the King grants to the town of D. the same liberties which London has, this shall be intended the like liberties." A grant of the liberties of free and natural subjects, is equivalent to a grant of the same liberties. And the King, in the first charter to this colony, expressly grants, that it "shall be construed, reputed and adjudged in all cases, most favorably on the behalf and for the benefit and behoof of the said Governor and Company, and their successors — any matter, cause or thing, whatsoever, to the contrary notwithstanding." It is one of the liberties of free and natural subjects, born and abiding within the realm, to be governed, as your Excellency observes, " by laws made by persons, in whose elections they, from time to time, have a voice." This is an essential right. For nothing is more evident, than, that any people, who are subject to the unlimited power of another, must be in a state of abject slavery. It was easily and plainly foreseen, that the right of representation in the English Parliament, could not be exercised by the people of this colony. It would be impracticable, if consistent with the English constitution. And for this reason, that this colony might have and enjoy all the liberties and immunities of free and natural subjects within the realm, as stipulated in the charter, it was necessary, and a Legislative was accordingly constituted within the colony ; one branch of which, consists of Representatives chosen by the people, to make all laws, statutes, ordinances, &c. for the well ordering and governing the same, not repugnant to the laws of England, or, as nearly as conveniently might be, agreeable to the fundamental laws of the English constitution. We are, therefore, still at a loss to conceive, where your Excellency finds it " provided in the same charter, that such acts," viz. acts of Parliament, made expressly to refer to us, "shall be in force " in this province. There is nothing to this purpose, expressed in the charter, or in our opinion, even implied in it. And surely it would be very absurd, that a charter, which is evidently formed upon a supposition and intention, that a colony is and should be considered as not within the realm ; and declared by the very Prince who granted it, to be not within the jurisdiction of Parliament, should yet provide, that the laws which the same Parliament should make, expressly to refer to that colony, should be in force therein. Your Excellency is pleased to ask, " does it follow, that the government, by their (our ancestors) removal from one part of the dominions to another, loses its authority over that part to which they remove; and that they are freed from the subjection they were under before?" We answer, if that part of the King's dominions, to which they removed, was not then a part of the realm, and was never annexed to it, the Parliament lost no authority over it, having never had such authority; and the emigrations were consequently freed from the subjection they were under before their removal. The power and authority of Parliament, being constitutionally confined within the limits of the realm, and the nation collectively, of which alone it is the representing and Legislative Assembly. Your Excellency further asks, "will it not rather be said, that by this, their voluntary removal, they have relinquished, for a time, at least, one of the rights of an English subject, which they might, if they pleased, have continued to enjoy, and may again enjoy, whenever they return to the place where it can be exercised?" To which we answer; they never did relinquish the right to be governed by laws, made by persons in whose election they had a voice. The King stipulated with them, that they should have and enjoy all the liberties of free and natural subjects, born within the realm, to all intents, purposes and constructions, whatsoever; that is, that they should be as free as those, who were to abide within the realm: consequently, he stipulated with them, that they should enjoy and exercise this most essential right, which discriminates freemen from vassals, uninterruptedly, in its full sense and meaning; and they did, and ought still to exercise it, without the necessity of returning, for the sake of exercising it, to the nation or state of England.

We cannot help observing, that your Excellency's manner of reasoning on this point, seems to us, to render the most valuable clauses in our charter unintelligible: as if persons going from the realm of England, to inhabit in America, should hold and exercise there a certain right of English subjects; but, in order to exercise it in such manner as to be of any benefit to them, they must *not inhabit* there, but return to the place where alone it can be exercised. By such construction, the words of the charter can have no sense or meaning. We forbear remarking upon the absurdity of a grant to persons born within the realm, of the same liberties which would have belonged to them, if they had been born without the realm.

Your Excellency is disposed to compare this government to the variety of corporations, formed within the kingdom, with power to make and execute by-laws, &c.; and, because they remain subject

to the supreme authority of Parliament, to infer, that this colony is
also subject to the same authority : this reasoning appears to us
not just. The members of those corporations are resident within
the kingdom ; and residence subjects them to the authority of Parliament, in which they are also represented ; whereas the people of
this colony are not resident within the realm. The charter was
granted, with the express purpose to induce them to reside without
the realm ; consequently, they are not represented in Parliament
there. But, we would ask your Excellency, are any of the corporations, formed within the kingdom, vested with the power of
erecting other subordinate corporations ? of enacting and determining what crimes shall be capital ? and constituting courts of common
law, with all their officers, for the hearing, trying and punishing
capital offenders with death ? These and many other powers vested
in this government, plainly show, that it is to be considered as a corporation, in no other light, than as every state is a corporation.
Besides, appeals from the courts of law here, are not brought before
the House of Lords ; which shows, that the peers of the realm, are
not the peers of America : but all such appeals are brought before
the King in council, which is a further evidence, that we are not
within the realm.

We conceive enough has been said, to convince your Excellency,
that, " when our predecessors first took possession of this plantation,
or colony, by a grant and charter from the Crown of England, it *was
not*, and never had been the sense of the kingdom, that they were to
remain subject to the supreme authority of Parliament." We will
now, with your Excellency's leave, inquire what *was* the sense of
our ancestors, of this very important matter.

And, as your Excellency has been pleased to tell us, you have not
discovered, that the supreme authority of Parliament has been called
in question, even by private and particular persons, until within
seven or eight years past ; except about the time of the anarchy
and confusion in England, which preceded the restoration of King
Charles the II. we beg leave to remind your Excellency of some
parts of your own history of Massachusetts Bay. Therein we are
informed of the sentiments of " persons of influence," after the restoration ; from which, the historian tells us, some parts of their
conduct, that is, of the General Assembly, " may be pretty well accounted for." By the history, it appears to have been the opinion
of those persons of influence, " that the subjects of any prince or

state, had a natural right to remove to any other state, or to another quarter of the world, unless the state was weakened or exposed by such remove ; and, even in that case, if they were deprived of the right of all mankind, liberty of conscience, it would justify a separation, and upon their removal, their subjection determined and ceased." That "the country to which they had removed, was claimed and possessed by independent princes, whose right to the lordship and sovereignty thereof had been acknowledged by the Kings of England," an instance of which is quoted in the margin. "That they themselves had actually purchased, for valuable consideration, not only the soil, but the dominion, the lordship and sovereignty of those princes ; " without which purchase, "in the sight of God and men, they had no right or title to what they possessed." They had received a charter of incorporation from the King, from whence arose a new kind of subjection, namely, "a voluntary, civil subjection ; " and by this compact, "they were to be governed by laws made by themselves." Thus it appears to have been the sentiments of private persons, though persons by whose sentiments the public conduct was influenced, that their removal was a justifiable separation from the mother state, upon which, their subjection to that state, determined and ceased. The supreme authority of Parliament, if it had then ever been asserted, must surely have been called in question, by men who had advanced such principles as these.

The first act of Parliament, made expressly to refer to the colonies, was after the restoration. In the reign of King Charles the II. several such acts passed. And the same history informs us, there was a difficulty in conforming to them ; and the reason of this difficulty is explained in a letter of the General Assembly to their Agent, quoted in the following words ; "they apprehended them to be an invasion of the rights, liberties and properties of the subjects of his Majesty, in the colony, they not being represented in Parliament, and according to the usual sayings of the learned in the law, the laws of England were bounded within the four seas, and did not reach America : However, as his Majesty had signified his pleasure, that those acts should be observed in the Massachusetts, they had made provision, by a law of the colony, that they should be strictly attended." Which provision, by a law of their own, would have been superfluous, if they had admitted the supreme authority of Parliament. In short, by the same history it appears, that those acts of Parliament, as such, were disregarded; and the following reason is given for it : " It seems to have been a general opinion, that acts of Parliament had 'no other force, than what they derived from acts made by the General Court, to establish and confirm them."

But, still further to show the sense of our ancestors, respecting this matter, we beg leave to recite some parts of a narrative, presented to the Lords of Privy Council, by Edward Randolph, in the year 1676, which we find in your Excellency's collection of papers lately published. Therein it is declared to be the sense of the colony, " that no law is in force or esteem there, but such as are made by the General Court; and, therefore, it is accounted a breach of their privileges, and a betraying of the liberties of their commonwealth, to urge the observation of the laws of England." And, further, " that no oath shall be urged, or required to be taken by any person, but such oath as the General Court hath considered, allowed and required." And, further, " there is no notice taken of the act of navigation, plantation or any other laws, made in England for the regulation of trade." " That the government would make the world believe, they are a free state, and do act in all matters accordingly." Again, " these magistrates ever reserve to themselves, a power to alter, evade and disannul any law or command, not agreeing with their humor, or the absolute authority of their government, acknowledging no superior." And, further, " he (the Governor) freely declared to me, that the laws made by your Majesty and your Parliament, obligeth them in nothing, but what consists with the interests of that colony ; that the Legislative power and authority is, and abides in them solely." And in the same Mr. Randolph's letter to the Bishop of London, July 14, 1682, he says, " this independency in government is claimed and daily practised." And your Excellency being then sensible, that this was the sense of our ancestors, in a marginal note, in the same collection of papers, observes, that, " this, viz. the provision made for observing the acts of trade, is very extraordinary, for this provision was an act of the colony, declaring the acts of trade shall be in force there." Although Mr. Randolph was very unfriendly to the colony, yet, as his declarations are concurrent with those recited from your Excellency's history, we think they may be admitted, for the purpose for which they are now brought.

Thus we see, from your Excellency's history and publications, the sense our ancestors had of the jurisdiction of Parliament, under the first charter. Very different from that, which your Excellency in your speech, apprehends it to have been.

It appears by Mr. Neal's History of New England, that the agents, who had been employed by the colony to transact its affairs in England, at the time when the present charter was granted, among other reasons, gave the following for their acceptance of it, viz. "The General Court has, with the King's approbation, as much power in New England, as the King and Parliament have in England; they have all English privileges, and can be touched by no law, and by no tax but of their own making." This is the earliest testimony that can be given of the sense our predecessors had of the supreme authority of Parliament, under the present charter. And it plainly shows, that they, who having been freely conversant with those who framed the charter, must have well understood the design and meaning of it, supposed that the terms in our charter, "full power and authority," intended and were considered as a sole and exclusive power, and that there was no "reserve in the charter, to the authority of Parliament, to bind the colony" by any acts whatever.

Soon after the arrival of the charter, viz. in 1692, your Excellency's history informs us, "the first act" of this Legislative, was a sort of Magna Charta, asserting and setting forth their general privileges, and this clause was among the rest; "no aid, tax, tallage, assessment, custom, loan, benevolence, or imposition whatever, shall be laid, assessed, imposed, or levied on any of their Majesty's subjects, or their estates, on any pretence whatever, but by the act and consent of the Governor, Council, and Representatives of the people assembled in General Court." And though this act was disallowed, it serves to show the sense which the General Assembly, contemporary with the granting the charter, had of their sole and exclusive right to legislate for the colony. The history says, "the other parts of the act were copied from Magna Charta;" by which we may conclude that the Assembly then construed the words, "not repugnant to the laws," to mean, conformable to the fundamental principles of the English constitution. And it is observable, that the Lords of Privy Council, so lately as in the reign of Queen Anne, when several laws enacted by the General Assembly were laid before her Majesty for her allowance, interpreted the words in this charter, "not repugnant to the laws of England," by the words, "as nearly as conveniently may be agreeable to the laws and statutes of England." And her Majesty was pleased to disallow those acts, not because they were repugnant to any law or statute of England, made expressly to refer to the colony, but because divers persons, by virtue thereof, were punished, without being tried by their peers in the ordinary "courts of law," and "by the ordinary rules and known methods of justice," contrary to the express terms of Magna Charta, which was a statute in force at the time of granting the charter, and declaratory of the rights and liberties of the subjects within the realm.

You are pleased to say, that "our provincial or local laws have, in numerous instances, had relation to acts of Parliament, made to respect the plantations, and this colony in particular." The authority of the Legislature, says the same author who is quoted by your Excellency, "does not extend so far as the fundamentals of the constitution. They ought to consider the fundamental laws as sacred, if the nation has not in very express terms, given them the power to change them. For the constitution of the state ought to be fixed ; and since that was first established by the nation, which afterwards trusted certain persons with the Legislative power, the fundamental laws are excepted from their commission." Now the fundamentals of the constitution of this province, are stipulated in the charter; the reasoning, therefore, in this case, holds equally good. Much less, then, ought any acts or doings of the General Assembly, however numerous, to neither of which your Excellency has pointed us, which barely relate to acts of Parliament made to respect the plantations in general, or this colony in particular, to be taken as an acknowledgment of this people, or even of the Assembly, which inadvertently passed those acts, that we are subject to the supreme authority of Parliament; and with still less reason are the decisions in the executive courts to determine this point. If they have adopted that "as part of the rule of law," which, in fact, is not, it must be imputed to inattention or error in judgment, and cannot justly be urged as an alteration or restriction of the Legislative authority of the province.

Before we leave this part of your Excellency's speech, we would observe, that the great design of our ancestors, in leaving the kingdom of England, was to be freed from a subjection to its spiritual laws and courts, and to worship God according to the dictates of their consciences. Your Excellency, in your history observes, that their design was " to obtain for themselves and their posterity, the liberty of worshipping God in such manner as appeared to them most agreeable to the sacred scriptures." And the General Court themselves declared in 1651, that "seeing just cause to fear the persecution of the then Bishop, and high commission for not conforming to the ceremonies of those under their power, they thought it their safest course, to get to this outside of the world, out of their view, and beyond their reach." But, if it had been their sense, that they were still to be subject to the supreme authority of Parliament, they must have known that their design might, and probably would be frustrated ; that the Parliament, especially considering the temper of those times, might make what ecclesiastical laws they pleased, expressly to refer to them, and place them in the same circumstances with respect to religious matters, to be relieved from which, was the design of their removal ; and we would add, that if your Excellency's construction of the clause in our present charter is just, another clause therein, which provides for liberty of conscience for all christians, except papists, may be rendered void by an act of Parliament made to refer to us, requiring a conformity to the rites and mode of worship in the church of England, or any other.

Thus we have endeavored to show the sense of the people of this colony under both charters ; and, if there have been in any late instances a submission to acts of Parliament, it has been, in our opinion, rather from inconsideration, or a reluctance at the idea of contending with the parent state, than from a conviction or acknowledgment of the Supreme Legislative authority of Parliament.

Your Excellency tells us, "you know of no line that can be drawn between the supreme authority of Parliament and the total independence of the colonies." If there be no such line, the consequence is, either that the colonies are the vassals of the Parliament, or that they are totally independent. As it cannot be supposed to have been the intention of the parties in the compact, that we should be reduced to a state of vassalage, the conclusion is, that it was their sense, that we were thus independent. "It is impossible," your Excellency says, "that there should be two independent Legislatures in one and the same state." May we not then further conclude, that it was their sense, that the colonies were, by their charters, made distinct states from the mother country ? Your Excellency adds, "for although there may be but one head, the King, yet the two Legislative bodies will make two governments as distinct as the kingdoms of England and Scotland, before the union."

Very true, may it please your Excellency ; and if they interfere not with each other, what hinders, but that being united in one head and common Sovereign, they may live happily in that connection, and mutually support and protect each other ? Notwithstanding all the terrors which your Excellency has pictured to us as the effects of a total independence, there is more reason to dread the consequences of absolute uncontroled power, whether of a nation or a monarch, than those of a total independence. It would be a misfortune " to know by experience, the difference between the liberties of an English colonist and those of the Spanish, French, and Dutch : " and since the British Parliament has passed an act, which is executed even with rigor, though not voluntarily submitted to, for raising a revenue, and appropriating the same, without the consent of the people who pay it, and have claimed a power of making such laws as they please, to order and govern us, your Excellency will excuse us in asking, whether you do not think we already experience too much of such a difference, and have not reason to fear we shall soon be reduced to a worse situation than that of the colonies of France, Spain, or Holland ?

If your Excellency expects to have the line of distinction between the supreme authority of Parliament, and the total independence of the colonies drawn by us, we would say it would be an arduous undertaking, and of very great importance to all the other colonies ; and therefore, could we conceive of such a line, we should be unwilling to propose it, without their consent in Congress.

To conclude, these are great and profound questions. It is the grief of this House, that, by the ill policy of a late injudicious administration, America has been driven into the contemplation of them. And we cannot but express our concern, that your Excellency, by your speech, has reduced us to the unhappy alternative, either of appearing by our silence to acquiesce in your Excellency's sentiments, or of thus freely discussing this point.

After all that we have said, we would be far from being understood to have in the least abated that just sense of allegiance which we owe to the King of Great Britain, our rightful Sovereign ; and should the people of this province be left to the free and full exercise of all the liberties and immunities granted to them by charter, there would be no danger of an independence on the Crown. Our charters reserve great power to the Crown in its Representative, fully sufficient to balance, analogous to the English constitution, all the liberties and privileges granted to the people. All this your Excellency knows full well; and whoever considers the power and influence, in all their branches, reserved by our charter, to the Crown, will be far from thinking that the Commons of this province are too independent.

[This answer was reported by Mr. S. Adams, Mr. Hancock, Maj. Hawley, Col. Bowers, Mr. Hobson, Maj. Foster, Mr. Phillips, and Col. Thayer.]

No doubt Hutchinson was agitated, but he by no means lost his head. His rejoinder to Council and House came promptly, and drove effectively at the positions of his adversaries.

SPEECH OF THE GOVERNOR TO BOTH HOUSES, FEBRUARY 16, 1773.

Gentlemen of the Council, and Gentlemen of the House of Representatives,

The proceedings of such of the inhabitants of the town of Boston, as assembled together, and passed and published their resolves or votes, as the act of the town, at a legal town meeting, denying, in the most express terms, the supremacy of Parliament, and inviting every other town and district in the province, to adopt the same principle, and to establish committees of correspondence, to consult upon proper measures to maintain it, and the proceedings of divers other towns, in consequence of this invitation, appeared to me to be so unwarrantable, and of such a dangerous nature and tendency, that I thought myself bound to call upon you in my speech at opening the session, to join with me in discountenancing and bearing a proper testimony against such irregularities and innovations.

I stated to you fairly and truly, as I conceived, the constitution of the kingdom and of the province, so far as relates to the dependence of the former upon the latter; and I desired you, if you differed from me in sentiments, to show me, with candor, my own errors, and to give your reasons in support of your opinions, so far as you might differ from me. I hoped that you would have considered my speech by your joint committees, and have given me a joint answer; but, as the House of Representatives have declined that mode of proceeding, and as your principles in government are very different, I am obliged to make separate and distinct replies. I shall first apply myself to you,

Gentlemen of the Council.

The two first parts of your answer, which respect the disorders occasioned by the stamp act, and the general nature of supreme authority, do not appear to me to have a tendency to invalidate any thing which I have said in my speech; for, however the stamp act may have been the immediate occasion of any disorders, the authority of Parliament was, notwithstanding, denied, in order to justify or excuse them. And, for the nature of the supreme authority of Parliament, I have never given you any reason to suppose, that I intended a more absolute power in Parliament, or a greater degree of active or passive obedience in the people, than what is founded in the nature of government, let the form of it be what it may. I shall, therefore, pass over those parts of your answer, without any other remark. I would also have saved you the trouble of all those authorities which you have brought to show, that all taxes upon English subjects, must be levied by virtue of the act, not of the King alone, but in conjunction with the Lords and Commons, for I should very readily have allowed it; and I should as readily have allowed, that all other acts of legislation must be passed by the same joint authority, and not by the King alone.

Indeed, I am not willing to continue a controversy with you, upon any other parts of your answer. I am glad to find, that independence is not what you have in contemplation, and that you will not presume to prescribe the exact limits of the authority of Parliament, only, as with due deference to it, you are humbly of opinion, that, as all human authority in the nature of it is, and ought to be limited, it cannot constitutionally extend, for the reasons you have suggested, to the levying of taxes, in any form, on his Majesty's subjects of this province.

I will only observe, that your attempts to draw a line as the limits of the supreme authority in government, by distinguishing some natural rights, as more peculiarly exempt from such authority than the rest, rather tend to evince the impracticability of drawing such a line; and, that some parts of your answer seem to infer a supremacy in the province, at the same time that you acknowledge the supremacy of Parliament; for otherwise, the rights of the subjects cannot be the same in all essential respects, as you suppose them to be, in all parts of the dominions, "under a like form of Legislature."

From these, therefore, and other considerations, I cannot help flattering myself, that, upon more mature deliberation, and in order to a more consistent plan of government, you will choose rather to doubt of the expediency of Parliament's exercising its authority in cases that may happen, than to limit the authority itself, especially, as you agree with me in the proper method of obtaining a redress of grievances by constitutional representations, which cannot well consist with a denial of the authority to which the representations are made ; and from the best information I have been able to obtain, the denial of the authority of Parliament, expressly, or by implication, in those petitions to which you refer, was the cause of their not being admitted, and not any advice given by the Minister to the Agents of the colonies. I must enlarge, and be more particular in my reply to you,

Gentlemen of the House of Representatives.

I shall take no notice of that part of your answer, which attributes the disorders of the province, to an undue exercise of the power of Parliament; because you take for granted, what can by no means be admitted, that Parliament had exercised its power without just authority. The sum of your answer, so far as it is pertinent to my speech, is this.

You allege that the colonies were an acquisition of foreign territory, not annexed to the realm of England; and, therefore, at the absolute disposal of the Crown; the King having, as you take it, a constitutional right to dispose of, and alienate any part of his territories, not annexed to the realm ; that Queen Elizabeth accordingly conveyed the property, dominion, and sovereignty of Virginia, to Sir Walter Raleigh, to be held of the Crown by homage and a certain render, without reserving any share in the legislative and executive authority; that the subsequent grants of America were similar in this respect ; that they were without any reservation for securing the subjection of the colonists to the Parliament, and future laws of England; that this was the sense of the English Crown, the nation, and our predecessors, when they first took possession of this country ; that if the colonies were not then annexed to the realm, they cannot have been annexed since that time ; that if they are not now annexed to the realm, they are not part of the kingdom ; and, consequently, not subject to the legislative authority of the kingdom ; for no country, by the common law, was subject to the laws or to the Parliament, but the realm of England.

Now, if this foundation shall fail you in every part of it, as I think it will, the fabric which you have raised upon it must certainly fall.

Let me then observe to you, that as English subjects, and agreeable to the doctrine of feudal tenure, all our lands and tenements are held mediately, or. immediately of the Crown, and although the possession and use, or profits, be in the subject, there still remains a dominion in the Crown. When any new countries are discovered by English subjects, according to the general law and usage of nations, they become part of the state, and, according to the feudal system, the lordship or dominion, is in the Crown; and a right accrues of disposing of such territories, under such tenure, or for such services to be performed, as the Crown shall judge proper; and whensoever any part of such territories, by grant from the Crown, becomes the possession or property of private persons, such persons, thus holding, under the Crown of England, remain, or become subjects of England, to all intents and purposes, as fully, as if any of the royal manors, forests, or other territory, within the realm, had been granted to them upon the like tenure. But, that it is now, or was, when the plantations were first granted, the prerogative of the Kings of England to alienate such territories from the Crown, or to constitute a number of new governments, altogether independent of the sovereign legislative authority of the English empire, I can by no means concede to you. I have never seen any better authority to support such an opinion, than an anonymous pamphlet, by which, I fear, you have too easily been misled; for I shall presently show you, that the declarations of King James the I. and of King Charles the I. admitting they are truly related by the author of this pamphlet, ought to have no weight with you; nor does the cession or restoration, upon a treaty of peace, of countries which have been lost or acquired in war, militate with these principles; nor may any particular act of power of a prince, in selling, or delivering up any part of his dominions to a foreign prince or state, against the general sense of the nation, be urged to invalidate them; and, upon examination, it will appear, that all the grants which have been made of America, are founded upon them, and are made to conform to them, even those which you have adduced in support of very different principles.

You do not recollect, that, prior to what you call the first grant by Queen Elizabeth to Sir Walter Raleigh, a grant had been made by the same Princess, to Sir Humphrey Gilbert, of all such coun-

tries as he should discover, which were to be of the allegiance of
her, her heirs and successors ; but he dying in the prosecution
of his voyage, a second grant was made to Sir Walter Raleigh,
which, you say, conveyed the dominion and sovereignty, without
any reserve of legislative or executive authority, being held by
homage and a render. To hold by homage, which implies fealty,
and a render, is descriptive of soccage tenure as fully, as if it had
been said to hold as of our manor of East Greenwich, the words in
your charter. Now, this alone was a reserve of dominion and sovereignty in the Queen, her heirs and successors ; and, besides this,
the grant is made upon this express condition, which you pass over,
that the people remain subject to the Crown of England, the head
of that legislative authority, which, by the English constitution, is
equally extensive with the authority of the Crown, throughout every
part of the dominions. Now, if we could suppose the Queen to
have acquired, separate from her relation to her subjects, or in her
natural capacity, which she could not do, a title to a country discovered by her subjects, and then to grant the same country to
English subjects, in her public capacity as Queen of England, still,
by this grant, she annexed it to the Crown. Thus by not distinguishing between the Crown of England, and the Kings and
Queens of England, in their personal or natural capacities, you have
been led into a fundamental error, which must prove fatal to your
system. It is not material, whether Virginia reverted to the Crown
by Sir Walter's attainder, or whether he never took any benefit
from his grant, though the latter is most probable, seeing he ceased
from all attempts to take possession of the country after a few years
trial. There were, undoubtedly, divers grants made by King James
the I. of the continent of America, in the beginning of the seventeenth century, and similar to the grant of Queen Elizabeth, in this
respect, that they were dependent on the Crown. The charter to
the Council at Plymouth, in Devon, dated November 3, 1620, more
immediately respects us, and of that we have the most authentic
remains.

By this charter, upon the petition of Sir Ferdinando Gorges, a
corporation was constituted, to be, and continue by succession, forever in the town of Plymouth aforesaid, to which corporation, that
part of the American continent, which lies between 40 and 48 degrees of latitude, was granted, to be held of the King, his heirs and
successors, as of the manor of East Greenwich, with powers to con-

stitute subordinate governments in America, and to make laws for
such governments, not repugnant to the laws and statutes of England. From this corporation, your predecessors obtained a grant of
the soil of the colony of Massachusetts Bay, in 1627, and in 1628,
they obtained a charter from King Charles the I. making them a
distinct corporation, also within the realm, and giving them full
powers within the limits of their patent, very like to those of the
Council of Plymouth, throughout their more extensive territory.

We will now consider what must have been the sense of the
King, of the nation, and of the patentees, at the time of granting
these patents. From the year 1602, the banks and sea coasts of New
England had been frequented by English subjects, for catching and
drying cod fish. When an exclusive right to the fishery was
claimed, by virtue of the patent of 1620, the House of Commons
was alarmed, and a bill was brought in for allowing a free fishery;
and, it was upon this occasion, that one of the Secretaries of State
declared, perhaps, as his own opinion, that the plantations were not
annexed to the Crown, and so were not within the jurisdiction of
Parliament. Sir Edwin Sandys, who was one of the Virginia Company, and an eminent lawyer, declared, that he knew Virginia had
been annexed, and was held of the Crown, as of the manor of East
Greenwich, and he believed New England was so also; and so it
most certainly was. This declaration, made by one of the King's
servants, you say, shewed the sense of the Crown, and, being not
secretly, but openly declared in Parliament, you would make it the
sense of the nation also, notwithstanding your own assertion, that
the Lords and Commons passed a bill, that shewed their sense to be
directly the contrary. But if there had been full evidence of express declarations made by King James the I. and King Charles the
I. they were declarations contrary to their own grants, which declare
this country to be held of the Crown, and, consequently, it must
have been annexed to it. And may not such declarations be accounted for by other actions of those princes, who, when they were
soliciting the Parliament to grant the duties of tonnage and pound-
age, with other aids, and were, in this way, acknowledging the rights
of Parliament, at the same time were requiring the payment of those
duties, with ship money, &c. by virtue of their prerogative?

But to remove all doubts of the sense of the nation, and of the
patentees of this patent, or charter, in 1620, I need only refer you
to the account published by Sir Ferdinando Gorges himself, of the

proceedings in Parliament upon this occasion. As he was the most active Member of the Council of Plymouth, and, as he relates what came within his own knowledge and observation, his narrative, which has all the appearance of truth and sincerity, must carry conviction with it. He says, that soon after the patent was passed, and whilst it lay in the Crown Office, he was summoned to appear in Parliament, to answer what was to be objected against it ; and the House being in a committee, and Sir Edward Coke, that great oracle of the law, in the chair, he was called to the bar, and was told by Sir Edward, that the House understood that a patent had been granted to the said Ferdinando, and divers other noble persons, for establishing a colony in New England, that this was deemed a grievance of the Commonwealth, contrary to the laws, and to the privileges of the subject, that it was a monopoly, &c. and he required the delivery of the patent into the House. Sir Ferdinando Gorges made no doubt of the authority of the House, but submitted to their disposal of the patent, as, in their wisdom, they thought good ; "not knowing, under favor, how any action of that kind could be a grievance to the public, seeing it was undertaken for the advancement of religion, the enlargement of the bounds of our nation, &c. He was willing, however, to submit the whole to their honorable censures." After divers attendances, he imagined he had satisfied the House, that the planting a colony, was of much more consequence, than a simple disorderly course of fishing. He was, notwithstanding, disappointed ; and, when the public grievances of the kingdom were presented by the two Houses, that of the patent for New England was the first. I do not know how the Parliament could have shewn more fully the sense they then had of their authority over this new acquired territory ; nor can we expect better evidence of the sense which the patentees had of it, for I know of no historical fact, of which we have less reason to doubt.

And now, gentlemen, I will shew you how it appears from our charter itself, which you say, I have not yet been pleased to point out to you, except from that clause, which restrains us from making laws repugnant to the laws of England ; that it was the sense of our predecessors, at the time when the charter was granted, that they were to remain subject to the supreme authority of Parliament.

Besides this clause, which I shall have occasion further to remark upon, before I finish, you will find, that, by the charter, a grant was made, of exemption from all taxes and impositions upon any goods imported into New England, or exported from thence into England, for the space of twenty-one years, except the custom of five per cent. upon such goods, as, after the expiration of seven years, should be brought into England. Nothing can be more plain, than that the charter, as well as the patent to the Council of Plymouth, constitutes a corporation in England, with powers to create a subordinate government or governments within the plantation, so that there would always be subjects of taxes and impositions both in the kingdom and in the plantation. An exemption for twenty-one years, implies a right of imposition after the expiration of the term, and there is no distinction between the kingdom and the plantation. By what authority then, in the understanding of the parties, were those impositions to be laid? If any, to support a system, should say by the King, rather than to acknowledge the authority of Parliament, yet this could not be the sense of one of our principal patentees, Mr. Samuel Vassal, who, at that instant, 1628, the date of the charter, was suffering the loss of his goods, rather than submit to an imposition laid by the King, without the authority of Parliament; and to prove, that a few years after, it could not be the sense of the rest, I need only to refer you to your own records for the year 1642, where you will find an order of the House of Commons, conceived in such terms, as discover a plain reference to this part of the charter, after fourteen years of the twenty-one were expired. By this order, the House of Commons declare, that all goods and merchandize exported to New England, or imported from thence, shall be free from all taxes and impositions, both in the kingdom and New England, until the House shall take further order therein to the contrary. The sense which our predecessors had of the benefit which they took from this order, evidently appears from the vote of the General Court, acknowledging their humble thankfulness, and preserving a grateful remembrance of the honorable respect from that high court, and resolving, that the order sent unto them, under the hand of the Clerk of the honorable House of Commons, shall be entered among their public records, to remain there unto posterity. And, in an address to Parliament, nine years after, they acknowledge, among other undeserved favors, that of taking off the customs from them.

I am at a loss to know what your ideas could be, when you say, that if the plantations are not part of the realm, they are not part of the kingdom, seeing the two words can properly convey but one idea, and they have one and the same signification in the different languages from whence they are derived. I do not charge you with any design; but the equivocal use of the word realm, in several parts of your answer, makes them perplexed and obscure. Sometimes you must intend the whole dominion, which is subject to the authority of Parliament; sometimes only strictly the territorial realm to which other dominions are, or may be annexed. If you mean that no countries, but the ancient territorial realm, can, constitutionally, be subject to the supreme authority of England, which you have very incautiously said, is a rule of the common law of England; this is a doctrine which you will never be able to support. That the common law should be controled and changed by statutes, every day's experience teaches, but that the common law prescribes limits to the extent of the Legislative power, I believe has never been said upon any other occasion. That acts of Parliaments, for several hundred years past, have respected countries, which are not strictly within the realm, you might easily have discovered by the statute books. You will find acts for regulating the affairs of Ireland, though a separate and distinct kingdom. Wales and Calais, whilst they sent no Representatives to Parliament, were subject to the like regulations; so are Guernsey, Jersey, Alderney, &c. which send no Members to this day. These countries are not more properly a part of the ancient realm, than the plantations, nor do I know they can more properly be said to be annexed to the realm, unless the declaring that acts of Parliament shall extend to Wales, though not particularly named, shall make it so, which I conceive it does not, in the sense you intend.

Thus, I think, I have made it appear that the plantations, though not strictly within the realm, have, from the beginning, been constitutionally subject to the supreme authority of the realm, and are so far annexed to it, as to be, with the realm and the other dependencies upon it, one entire dominion; and that the plantation, or colony of Massachusetts Bay in particular, is holden as feudatory of the imperial Crown of England. Deem it to be no part of the realm, it is immaterial; for, to use the words of a very great authority in a case, in some respects analogous, " being feudatory, the conclusion necessarily follows, that it is under the government of the King's laws and the King's courts, in cases proper for them to interpose, though (like Counties Palatine) it has peculiar laws and customs, *jura regalia*, and complete jurisdiction at home."

Your remark upon, and construction of the words, not repugnant to the laws of England, are much the same with those of the Council; but, can any reason be assigned, why the laws of England, as they stood just at that period, should be pitched upon as the standard, more than at any other period? If so, why was it not recurred to, when the second charter was granted, more than sixty years after the first? It is not improbable, that the original intention might be a repugnancy in general, and *a fortiori*, such laws as were made more immediately to respect us, but the statute of 7th and 8th of King William and Queen Mary, soon after the second charter, favors the latter construction only; and the province agent, Mr. Dummer, in his much applauded defence of the charter, says, that, then a law in the plantations may be said to be repugnant to a law made in Great Britain, when it flatly contradicts it, so far, as the law made there, mentions and relates to the plantations. But, gentlemen, there is another clause, both in the first and second charter, which, I think, will serve to explain this, or to render all dispute upon the construction of it unnecessary. You are enabled to impose such oaths only, as are warrantable by, or not repugnant to the laws and statutes of the realm. I believe you will not contend, that these clauses must mean such oaths only, as were warrantable at the respective times when the charters were granted. It has often been found necessary, since the date of the charters, to alter the forms of the oaths to the government by acts of Parliament, and such alterations have always been conformed to in the plantations.

Lest you should think that I admit the authority of King Charles the II. in giving his assent to an act of the Assembly of Virginia, which you subjoin to the authorities of James the I. and Charles the I. to have any weight, I must observe to you, that I do not see any greater inconsistency with Magna Charta, in the King's giving his assent to an act of a subordinate Legislature immediately, or in person, than when he does it mediately by his Governor or Substitute; but, if it could be admitted, that such an assent discovered the King's judgment that Virginia was independent, would you lay any stress upon it, when the same King was, from time to time, giving his assent to acts of Parliament, which inferred the dependence of all the colonies, and had by one of those acts, declared the plantations to be inhabited and peopled by his Majesty's subjects of England?

I gave you no reason to remark upon the absurdity of grant to persons born without the realm, of the same liberties which would have belonged to them, if they had been born within the realm; but rather guarded against it, by considering such grant as declaratory only, and in the nature of an assurance, that the plantations would be considered as the dominions of England. But is there no absurdity in a grant from the King of England, of the liberties and immunities of Englishmen to persons born in, and who are to inhabit other territories than the dominions of England; and would such grant, whether by charter, or other letters patent, be sufficient to make them inheritable, or to entitle them to the other liberties and immunities of Englishmen, in any part of the English dominions?

As I am willing to rest the point between us, upon the plantations having been, from their first discovery and settlement under the Crown, a part of the dominions of England, I shall not take up any time in remarking upon your arguments, to show, that since that time, they cannot have been made a part of those dominions.

The remaining parts of your answer, are principally intended to prove, that under both charters, it hath been the sense of the people, that they were not subject to the jurisdiction of Parliament, and, for this purpose, you have made large extracts from the history of the colony. Whilst you are doing honor to the book, by laying any stress upon its authority, it would have been no more than justice to the author, if you had cited some other passages, which would have tended to reconcile the passage in my speech, to the history. I have said, that except about the time of the anarchy, which preceded the restoration of King Charles the II. I have not discovered that the authority of Parliament had been called in question, even by particular persons. It was, as I take it, from the principles imbibed in those times of anarchy, that the persons of influence, mentioned in the history, disputed the authority of Parliament, but the government would not venture to dispute it. On the contrary, in four or five years after the restoration, the government declared to the King's commissioners, that the act of navigation had been for some years observed here, that they knew not of its being greatly violated, and that such laws as appeared to be against it, were repealed. It is not strange, that these persons of influence, should prevail upon a great part of the people to fall in, for a time, with their opinions, and to suppose acts of the colony necessary to give force to acts of Parliament. The government, however, several years before the charter was vacated, more explicitly acknowledged the authority of

Parliament, and voted that their Governor should take the oath required of him, faithfully to do, and perform all matters and things, enjoined him by the acts of trade. I have not recited in my speech, all these particulars, nor had I them all in my mind ; but, I think, I have said nothing inconsistent with them. My principles in government, are still the same, with what they appear to be in the book, you refer to ; nor am I conscious, that by any part of my conduct, I have given cause to suggest the contrary.

Inasmuch, as you say, that I have not particularly pointed out to you the acts and doings of the General Assembly, which relate to acts of Parliament ; I will do it now, and demonstrate to you, that such acts have been acknowledged by the Assembly, or submitted to by the people.

From your predecessors removal to America, until the year 1640, there was no session of Parliament ; and the first short session, of a few days only, in 1640, and the whole of the next session, until the withdraw of the King, being taken up in the disputes between the King and the Parliament, there could be no room for plantation affairs. Soon after the King's withdraw, the House of Commons passed the memorable order of 1642 ; and, from that time to the restoration, this plantation seems to have been distinguished from the rest ; and the several acts and ordinances, which respected the other plantations, were never enforced here ; and, possibly, under color of the exemption, in 1642, it might not be intended they should be executed.

For fifteen or sixteen years after the restoration, there was no officer of the customs in the colony, except the Governor, annually elected by the people, and the acts of trade were but little regarded ; nor did the Governor take the oath required of Governors, by the act of the 12th of King Charles the II. until the time which I have mentioned. Upon the revolution, the force of an act of Parliament was evident, in a case of as great importance, as any which could happen to the colony. King William and Queen Mary were proclaimed in the colony, King and Queen of England, France, and Ireland, and the dominions thereunto belonging, in the room of King James ; and this, not by virtue of an act of the colony, for no such act ever passed, but by force of an act of Parliament, which altered the succession to the Crown, and for which, the people waited several weeks, with anxious concern. By force of another act of Parliament, and that only, such officers of the colony as had taken the oaths of allegiance to King James, deemed themselves at liberty to take, and accordingly did take, the oaths to King William and Queen Mary. And that I may mention other acts of the like nature together, it is by force of an act of Parliament, that the illustrious house of Hanover succeeded to the throne of Britain and its dominions, and by several other acts, the forms of the oaths have, from time to time, been altered ; and, by a late act, that form was established which every one of us has complied with, as the charter, in express words, requires, and makes our duty. Shall we now dispute, whether acts of Parliament have been submitted to, when we find them submitted to, in points which are of the very essence of our constitution ? If you should disown that authority, which has power even to change the succession to the Crown, are you in no danger of denying the authority of our most gracious Sovereign, which I am sure none of you can have in your thoughts ?

I think I have before shewn you, gentlemen, what must have been the sense of our predecessors, at the time of the first charter ; let us now, whilst we are upon the acts and doings of the Assembly, consider what it must have been at the time of the second charter. Upon the first advice of the revolution, in England, the authority which assumed the government, instructed their agents to petition Parliament to restore the first charter, and a bill for that purpose, passed the House of Commons, but went no further. Was not this owning the authority of Parliament ? By an act of Parliament, passed in the first year of King William and Queen Mary, a form of oaths was established, to be taken by those Princes, and by all succeeding Kings and Queens of England, at their coronation ; the first of which is, that they will govern the people of the kingdom, and the dominions thereunto belonging, according to the statutes in Parliament agreed on, and the laws and customs of the same. When the colony directed their agents to make their humble application to King William, to grant the second charter, they could have no other pretence, than, as they were inhabitants of part of the dominions of England ; and they also knew the oath the King had taken, to govern them according to the statutes in Parliament. Surely, then, at the time of this charter, also, it was the sense of our predecessors, as well as of the King and of the nation, that there was, and would remain, a supremacy in the Parliament. About the same time, they acknowledge, in an address to the King, that they have no power to make laws repugnant to the laws of England.

And, immediately after the assumption of the powers of government, by virtue of the new charter, an act was passed to revive, for a limited time, all the local laws of the colonies of Massachusetts Bay and New Plymouth, respectively, not repugnant to the laws of England. And, at the same session, an act passed, establishing naval officers, in several ports of the province, for which, this reason is given; that all undue trading, contrary to an act of Parliament, made in the 15th year of King Charles the II. may be prevented in this, their Majesty's province. The act of this province, passed so long ago as the second year of King George the I. for stating the fees of the custom house officers, must have relation to the acts of Parliament, by which they are constituted; and the provision made in that act of the province, for extending the port of Boston to all the roads, as far as Cape Cod, could be for no other purpose, than for the more effectual carrying the acts of trade into execution. And, to come nearer to the present time, when an act of Parliament had passed, in 1771, for putting an end to certain unwarrantable schemes, in this province, did the authority of government, or those persons more immediately affected by it, ever dispute the validity of it? On the contrary, have not a number of acts been passed in the province, that the burdens to which such persons were subjected, might be equally apportioned; and have not all those acts of the province been very carefully framed, to prevent their militating with the act of Parliament? I will mention, also, an act of Parliament, made in the first year of Queen Anne, although the proceedings upon it, more immediately respected the Council. By this act, no office, civil or military, shall be void, by the death of the King, but shall continue six months, unless suspended, or made void, by the next successor. By force of this act, Governor Dudley continued in the administration six months from the demise of Queen Anne, and immediately after, the Council assumed the administration, and continued it, until a proclamation arrived from King George, by virtue of which, Governor Dudley reassumed the government. It would be tedious to enumerate the addresses, votes and messages, of both the Council and House of Representatives, to the same purpose. I have said enough to shew that this government has submitted to Parliament, from a conviction of its constitutional supremacy, and this not from inconsideration, nor merely from reluctance at the idea of contending with the parent state.

If, then, I have made it appear, that both by the first and second charters, we hold our lands, and the authority of government, not of the King, but of the Crown of England, that being a dominion of the Crown of England, we are consequently subject to the supreme authority of England. That this hath been the sense of this plantation, except in those few years when the principles of anarchy, which had prevailed in the kingdom, had not lost their influence here; and if, upon a review of your principles, they shall appear to you to have been delusive and erroneous, as I think they must, or, if you shall only be in doubt of them, you certainly will not draw that conclusion, which otherwise you might do, and which I am glad you have hitherto avoided; especially when you consider the obvious and inevitable distress and misery of independence upon our mother country, if such independence could be allowed or maintained, and the probability of much greater distress, which we are not able to foresee.

You ask me, if we have not reason to fear we shall soon be reduced to a worse situation than that of the colonies of France, Spain, or Holland. I may safely affirm that we have not; that we have no reason to fear any evils from a submission to the authority of Parliament, equal to what we must feel from its authority being disputed, from an uncertain rule of law and government. For more than seventy years together, the supremacy of Parliament was acknowledged, without complaints of grievance. The effect of every measure cannot be foreseen by human wisdom. What can be expected more, from any authority, than, when the unfitness of a measure is discovered, to make it void? When, upon the united representations and complaints of the American colonies, any acts have appeared to Parliament, to be unsalutary, have there not been repeated instances of the repeal of such acts? We cannot expect these instances should be carried so far, as to be equivalent to a disavowal, or relinquishment of the right itself. Why, then, shall we fear for ourselves, and our posterity, greater rigor of government for seventy years to come, than what we, and our predecessors have felt, in the seventy years past?

You must give me leave, gentlemen, in a few words, to vindicate myself from a charge, in one part of your answer, of having, by my speech, reduced you to the unhappy alternative of appearing, by your silence, to acquiesce in my sentiments, or of freely discussing this point of the supremacy of Parliament. I saw, as I have before observed, the capital town of the province, without being reduced to such an alternative, voluntarily, not only discussing but determining this point, and inviting every other town and district in the province to do the like. I saw that many of the principal towns had followed the example, and that there was imminent danger of a compliance in most, if not all the rest, in order to avoid being distinguished. Was not I reduced to the alternative of rendering myself justly obnoxious to the displeasure of my Sovereign, by acquiescing in such irregularities, or of calling upon you to join with me in suppressing them ? Might I not rather have expected from you an expression of your concern, that any persons should project and prosecute a plan of measures, which would lay me under the necessity of bringing this point before you? It was so far from being my inclination, that nothing short of a sense of my duty to the King, and the obligations I am under to consult your true interest, could have compelled me to it.

Gentlemen of the Council, and
Gentlemen of the House of Representatives,

We all profess to be the loyal and dutiful subjects of the King of Great Britain. His Majesty considers the British empire as one entire dominion, subject to one supreme legislative power ; a due submission to which, is essential to the maintenance of the rights, liberties, and privileges of the several parts of this dominion. We have abundant evidence of his Majesty's tender and impartial regard to the rights of his subjects ; and I am authorized to say, that " his Majesty will most graciously approve of every constitutional measure that may contribute to the peace, the happiness, and prosperity of his colony of Massachusetts Bay, and which may have the effect to shew to the world, that he has no wish beyond that of reigning in the hearts and affections of his people."

T. HUTCHINSON.

ANSWER OF THE COUNCIL TO THE SPEECH OF GOVERNOR HUTCHINSON, OF FEBRUARY SIXTEENTH . . . . FEBRUARY 25, 1773.

May it please your Excellency,

As a small part only of your Excellency's last speech to both Houses, is addressed to the Board, there are but a few clauses on which we shall remark.

With regard to the disorders that have arisen, your Excellency and the Board, have assigned different causes. The cause you are pleased to assign, together with the disorders themselves, we suppose to be effects, arising from the stamp act, and certain other acts of Parliament. If we were not mistaken in this, which you do not assert, it so far seems to invalidate what is said in your speech, on that head.

We have taken notice of this only, because it stands connected with another matter, on which we would make a few further observations. What we refer to, is the general nature of supreme authority. We have already offered reasons, in which your Excellency seem to acquiesce, to shew that, though the term *supreme*, sometimes carries with it the idea of *unlimited* authority, it cannot, in that sense, be applied to that which is human. What is usually denominated the supreme authority of a nation, must nevertheless be limited in its acts to the objects that are properly or constitutionally cognizable by it. To illustrate our meaning, we beg leave to quote a passage from your speech, at the opening of the session, where your Excellency says, "so much of the spirit of liberty breathes through all parts of the English constitution, that, although from the nature of government, there must be one supreme authority over the whole, yet, this constitution will admit of subordinate powers, with legislative and executive authority, greater or less, according to local and other circumstances." This is very true, and implies that the legislative and executive authority granted to the subordinate powers, should extend and operate, as far as the grant allows; and that, if it does not exceed the limits prescribed to it, and no forfeiture be incurred, the supreme power has no rightful authority to take away or diminish it, or to substitute its own acts, in cases wherein the acts of the subordinate power can, according to its constitution, operate. To suppose the contrary, is to suppose, that it has no property in the privileges granted to it; for, if it holds them at the will of the supreme power, which it must do, by the above supposition, it can have no property in them. Upon which principle, which involves the contradiction, that what is granted, is, in reality, not granted, no subordinate power can exist. But, as in fact, the two powers are not incompatible, and do subsist together, each restraining its acts to their constitutional objects, can we not from hence, see how the supreme power may supervise, regulate, and make general laws for the kingdom, without interfering with the privileges of the subordinate powers within it ? And also, see how it may extend its care and protection to its colonies, without injuring their constitutional rights ? What has been here said, concerning supreme authority, has no reference to the manner in which it has been, in fact, exercised ; but is wholly confined to its general nature. And, if it conveys any just idea of it, the inferences that have been, at any time, deduced from it, injurious to the rights of the colonists, are not well founded ; and have, probably, arisen from a misconception of the nature of that authority.

Your Excellency represents us, as introducing a number of authorities, merely to shew, that " all taxes upon English subjects, must be levied by virtue of the act, not of the King alone, but in conjunction with the Lords and Commons ; " and, are pleased to add, that " you should very readily have allowed it ; and you should as readily have allowed, that all other acts of legislation, must be passed by the same joint authority, and not by the King alone." Your Excellency " would have saved us the trouble of all those authorities ; " and, on our part, we should have been as willing to have saved your Excellency the trouble of dismembering our argument, and from thence, taking occasion to represent it in a disadvantageous light, or rather, totally destroying it.

In justice to ourselves, it is necessary to recapitulate that argument, adduced to prove the inhabitants of this province are not, constitutionally, subject to Parliamentary taxation. In order thereto, we recurred to Magna Charta, and other authorities. And the argument abridged, stands thus : that, from those authorities, it appears an essential part of the English constitution, " that no tallage, or aid, or tax, shall be laid or levied, without the good will and assent of the freemen of the commonalty of the realm." That, from common law, and the province charter, the inhabitants of this province are clearly entitled to all the rights of free and natural subjects, within the realm. That, among those rights, must be included the essential one just mentioned, concerning aids and taxes ; and therefore, that no aids or taxes can be levied on us, constitutionally, without our own consent, signified by our representatives. From whence, the conclusion is clear, that therefore, the inhabitants of this province are not, constitutionally, subject to Parliamentary taxation.

We did not bring those authorities to shew the tax acts, or any other acts of Parliament, in order to their validity, must have the concurrence of King, Lords, and Commons ; but to shew, that it has been, at least from the time of Magna Charta, an essential right of free subjects within the realm, to be free from all taxes, but such as were laid with their own consent. And it was proper to shew this, as the rights and liberties, granted by the province charter, were to be equally extensive, to all intents and purposes, with those enjoyed by free and natural subjects within the realm. Therefore, to shew our own right in relation to taxes, it was necessary to shew the rights of freemen within the realm, in relation to them; and for this purpose, those authorities were brought, and not impertinently, as we humbly apprehend. Nor have we seen reason to change our sentiments with respect to this matter, or any other contained in our answer to your Excellency's speech.

In the last clause of your speech, your Excellency informs the two Houses, "you are authorized to say, that his Majesty will most graciously approve of every constitutional measure, that may contribute to the peace, the happiness, and prosperity of his colony of Massachusetts Bay." We have the highest sense of his Majesty's goodness in his gracious disposition to approve of such measures, which, as it includes his approbation of the constitutional rights of his subjects of this colony, manifests his inclination to protect them in those rights; and to remove the incroachments that have been made upon them. Of this act of royal goodness, they are not wholly unworthy, as in regard to loyalty, duty, and affection to his Majesty, they stand among the foremost of his faithful subjects.

[The committee who prepared this answer, were, Mr. Bowdoin, Col. Otis, Mr. Dexter, Col. Ward, and Mr. Spooner.]

ANSWER OF THE HOUSE OF REPRESENTATIVES TO THE SPEECH OF THE GOVERNOR, OF FEBRUARY SIXTEENTH. . . . MARCH 2, 1773.

May it please your Excellency,

In your speech, at the opening of the present session, your Excellency expressed your displeasure, at some late proceedings of the town of Boston, and other principal towns in the province. And, in another speech to both Houses, we have your repeated exceptions at the same proceedings, as being "unwarrantable," and of a dangerous nature and tendency; "against which, you thought yourself bound to call upon us to join with you in bearing a proper testimony." This House have not discovered any principles advanced by the town of Boston, that are unwarrantable by the constitution;

nor does it appear to us, that they have "invited every other town and distrinct in the province, to adopt their principles." We are fully convinced, that it is our duty to bear our testimony against "innovations, of a dangerous nature and tendency;" but, it is clearly our opinion, that it is the indisputable right of all, or any of his Majesty's subjects, in this province, regularly and orderly to meet together, to state the grievances they labor under; and, to propose, and unite in such constitutional measures, as they shall judge necessary or proper, to obtain redress. This right has been frequently exercised by his Majesty's subjects within the realm; and, we do not recollect an instance, since the happy revolution, when the two Houses of Parliament have been called upon to discountenance, or bear their testimony against it, in a speech from the throne.

Your Excellency is pleased to take notice of some things, which we "allege," in our answer to your first speech; and, the observation you make, we must confess, is as natural, and undeniably true, as any one that could have been made; that, "if our foundation shall fail us in every part of it, the fabric we have raised upon it, must certainly fall." You think this foundation will fail us; but, we wish your Excellency had condescended to a consideration of what we have "adduced in support of our principles." We might then, perhaps, have had some things offered for our conviction, more than bare affirmations; which, we must beg to be excused, if we say, are far from being sufficient, though they came with your Excellency's authority, for which, however, we have a due regard.

Your Excellency says, that, "as English subjects, and agreeable to the doctrine of the feudal tenure, all our lands are held mediately, or immediately, of the Crown." We trust, your Excellency does not mean to introduce the feudal system in its perfection; which, to use the words of one of our greatest historians, was "a state of perpetual war, anarchy, and confusion, calculated solely for defense against the assaults of any foreign power; but, in its provision for the interior order and tranquillity of society, extremely defective. A constitution, so contradictory to all the principles that govern mankind, could never be brought about, but by foreign conquest or native usurpation." And, a very celebrated writer calls it, "that most iniquitous and absurd form of government, by which human nature was so shamefully degraded." This system of iniquity, by a strange kind of fatality, "though originally formed for an encampment, and for military purposes only, spread over a great part of Europe;" and, to serve the purposes of oppression and tyranny, "was adopted by princes, and wrought into their civil constitutions;" and, aided by the canon law, calculated by the Roman Pontiff, to exalt himself above all that is called God, it prevailed to the almost utter extinction of knowledge, virtue, religion, and liberty from that part of the earth. But, from the time of the reformation, in proportion as knowledge, which then darted its rays upon the benighted world, increased, and spread among the people, they grew impatient under this heavy yoke; and the most virtuous and sensible among them, to whose steadfastness, we, in this distant age and climate, are greatly indebted, were determined to get rid of it; and, though they have in a great measure subdued its power and influence in England, they have never yet totally eradicated its principles.

Upon these principles, the King claimed an absolute right to, and a perfect estate, in all the lands within his dominions; but, how he came by this absolute right and perfect estate, is a mystery which we have never seen unravelled, nor is it our business or design, at present, to inquire. He granted parts or parcels of it to his friends, the great men, and they granted lesser parcels to their tenants. All, therefore, derived their right and held their lands, upon these principles, mediately or immediately of the King; which Mr. Blackstone, however, calls, "in reality, a mere fiction of our English tenures."

By what right, in nature and reason, the christian princes in Europe, claimed the lands of heathen people, upon a discovery made by any of their subjects, is equally mysterious. Such, however, was the doctrine universally prevailing, when the lands in America were discovered; but, as the people of England, upon those principles, held all the lands they possessed, by grants from the King, and the King had never granted the lands in America to them, it is certain they could have no sort of claim to them. Upon the principles advanced, the lordship and dominion, like that of the lands in England, was in the King solely; and a right from thence accrued to him, of disposing such territories, under such tenure, and for such services to be performed, as the King or Lord thought proper. But how the grantees became subjects of England, that is, the supreme authority of the Parliament, your Excellency has not explained to us.

We conceive that upon the feudal principles, all power is in the King; they afford us no idea of Parliament. "The Lord was in early times, the Legislator and Judge over all his feudatories," says Judge Blackstone. By the struggle for liberty in England, from the days of King John, to the last happy revolution, the constitution has been gradually changing for the better; and upon the more rational principles, that all men, by nature, are in a state of equality in respect of jurisdiction and dominion, power in England has been more equally divided. And thus, also, in America, though we hold our lands agreeably to the feudal principles of the King; yet our predecessors wisely took care to enter into compact with the King, that power here should also be equally divided, agreeable to the original fundamental principles of the English constitution, declared in Magna Charta, and other laws and statutes of England, made to confirm them.

Your Excellency says, " you can by no means concede to us that it is now, or was, when the plantations were first granted, the prerogative of the Kings of England, to constitute a number of new governments, altogether independent of the sovereign authority of the English empire." By the feudal principles, upon which you say " all the grants which have been made of America, are founded, the constitutions of the Empire, have the force of law." If our government be considered as merely feudatory, we are subject to the King's absolute will, and there is no authority of Parliament, as the sovereign authority of the British empire. Upon these principles, what could hinder the King's constituting a number of independent governments in America? That King Charles the I. did actually set up a government in this colony, conceding to it powers of making and executing laws, without any reservation to the English Parliament, of authority to make future laws binding therein, is a fact which your Excellency has not disproved, if you have denied it. Nor have you shewn that the Parliament or nation objected to it; from whence we have inferred that it was an acknowledged right. And we cannot conceive, why the King has not the same right to alienate and dispose of countries acquired by the discovery of his subjects, as he has to " restore, upon a treaty of peace, countries which have been acquired in war," carried on at the charge of the nation; or to " sell and deliver up any part of the dominions to a foreign Prince or state, against the general sense of the nation; " which is " an act of power," or prerogative, which your Excellency allows. You tell us, that, "when any new countries are discovered by English subjects, according to the general law and usage of nations, they become part of the state." The law of nations is, or ought to be, founded on the law of reason. It was the saying of Sir Edwin Sandis, in the great case of the union of the realm of Scotland with England, which is applicable to our present purpose, that "there being no precedent for this case in the law, the law is deficient; and the law being deficient, recourse is to be had to custom; and custom being insufficient, we must recur to natural reason;" the greatest of all authorities, which, he adds, "is the law of nations." The opinions, therefore, and determinations of the greatest Sages and Judges of the law in the Exchequer Chamber, ought not to be considered as decisive or binding, in our present controversy with your Excellency, any further, than they are consonant to natural reason. If, however, we were to recur to such opinions and determinations, we should find very great authorities in our favor, to show, that the statutes of England are not binding on those who are not represented in Parliament there. The opinion of Lord Coke, that Ireland was bound by statutes of England, wherein they were named, if compared with his other writings, appears manifestly to be grounded upon a supposition, that Ireland had, by an act of their own, in the reign of King John, consented to be thus bound; and, upon any other supposition, this opinion would be against reason; for consent only gives human laws their force. We beg leave, upon what your Excellency has observed of the colony becoming a part of the state, to subjoin the opinions of several learned civilians, as quoted by a very able lawyer in this country. "Colonies," says Puffendorf, "are settled in different methods; for, either the colony continues a part of the Commonwealth it was set out from, or else is obliged to pay a dutiful regard to the mother Commonwealth, and to be in readiness to defend and vindicate its honor, and so is united by a sort of unequal confederacy; or, lastly, is erected into a separate Commonwealth, and assumes the same rights, with the state it descended from." And, King Tullius, as quoted by the same learned author, from Grotius, says, "we look upon it to be neither truth nor justice, that mother cities, ought, of necessity, and by the law of nature, to rule over the colonies."

Your Excellency has misinterpreted what we have said, "that no country, by the common law, was subject to the laws or the Parliament, but the realm of England;" and, are pleased to tell us, "that we have expressed ourselves incautiously." We beg leave to recite the words of the Judges of England, in the before mentioned case, to our purpose. "If a King go out of England with a company of his servants, allegiance remaineth among his subjects and servants, although he be out of his realm, whereto his laws are confined." We did not mean to say, as your Excellency would suppose, that "the common law prescribes limits to the extent of the Legislative power," though, we shall always affirm it to be true, of the law of reason and natural equity. Your Excellency thinks, you have made it appear, that the "colony of Massachusetts Bay is holden as feudatory of the imperial Crown of England ;" and, therefore, you say, "to use the words of a very great authority in a case, in some respects analogous to it," being feudatory, it necessarily follows, that "it is under the government of the King's laws." Your Excellency has not named this authority ; but, we conceive his meaning must be, that being feudatory, it is under the government of the King's laws absolutely, for, as we have before said, the feudal system admits of no idea of the authority of Parliament; and this would have been the case of the colony, but for the compact with the King in the charter.

Your Excellency says, that "persons thus holding under the Crown of England, remain, or become subjects of England," by which, we suppose your Excellency to mean, subject to the supreme authority of Parliament, "to all intents and purposes, as fully, as if any of the royal manors, &c. within the realm, had been granted to them upon the like tenure." We apprehend, with submission, your Excellency is mistaken in supposing that our allegiance is due to the Crown of England. Every man swears allegiance for himself, to his own King, in his natural person. "Every subject is presumed by law to be sworn to the King, which is to his natural person," says Lord Coke. Rep. on Calvin's case. "The allegiance is due to his natural body ; " and, he says, "in the reign of Edward II. the Spencers, the father and the son, to cover the treason hatched in their hearts, invented this damnable and damned opinion, that homage and oath of allegiance was more by reason of the King's Crown, that is, of his politic capacity, than by reason of the person of the King ; upon which opinion, they inferred execrable and detestable consequents." The Judges of England, all but one, in the case of the union between Scotland and England, declared, that " allegiance followeth the natural person, not the politic ; " and, "to prove the allegiance to be tied to the body natural of the King, and not to the body politic, the Lord Coke cited the phrases of divers statutes, mentioning our natural liege Sovereign." If, then, the homage and allegiance is not to the body politic of the King, then it is not to him as the head, or any part of that Legislative authority, which your Excellency says, " is equally extensive with the authority of the Crown throughout every part of the dominion ; " and your Excellency's observations thereupon, must fail. The same Judges mention the allegiance of a subject to the Kings of England, who is out of the reach and extent of the laws of England, which is perfectly reconcileable with the principles of our ancestors, quoted before from your Excellency's history, but, upon your Excellency's principles, appears to us to be an absurdity. The Judges, speaking of a subject, say, " although his birth was out of the bounds of the kingdom of England, and out of the reach and extent of the laws of England, yet, if it were within the allegiance of the King of England, &c. Normandy, Aquitain, Gascoign, and other places, within the limits of France, and, consequently, out of the realm or bounds of the kingdom of England, were in subjection to the Kings of England." And the Judges say, " *Rex et Regnum,* be not so relatives, as a King can be King but of one kingdom, which clearly holdeth not, but that his kingly power extending to divers nations and kingdoms, all owe him equal subjection, and are equally born to the benefit of his protection ; and, although he is to govern them by their distinct laws, yet any one of the people coming into the other, is to have the benefits of the laws, wheresoever he cometh." So they are not to be deemed aliens, as your Excellency in your speech supposes, in any of the dominions, all which accords with the principles our ancestors held. " And he is to bear the burden of taxes of the place where he cometh, but living in one, or for his livelihood in one, he is not be taxed in the other, because laws ordain taxes, impositions, and charges, as a discipline of subjection particularized to every particular nation." Nothing, we think, can be more clear to our purpose than this decision of Judges, perhaps as learned, as ever adorned the English nation, or in favor of America, in her present controversy with the mother state.

Your Excellency says, that, by " our not distinguishing between the Crown of England, and the Kings and Queens of England, in their personal or natural capacities, we have been led into a fundamental error." Upon this very distinction we have availed ourselves.

We have said, that our ancestors considered the land, which they took possession of in America, as out of the bounds of the kingdom of England, and out of the reach and extent of the laws of England; and, that the King also, even in the act of granting the charter, considered the territory as not within the realm; that the King had an absolute right in himself to dispose of the lands, and that this was not disputed by the nation; nor could the lands, on any solid grounds, be claimed by the nation; and, therefore, our ancestors received the lands, by grant, from the King; and, at the same time, compacted with him, and promised him homage and allegiance, not in his public or politic, but natural capacity only. If it be difficult for us to show how the King acquired a title to this country in his natural capacity, or separate from his relation to his subjects, which we confess, yet we conceive it will be equally difficult for your Excellency to show how the body politic and nation of England acquired it. Our ancestors supposed it was acquired by neither; and, therefore, they declared, as we have before quoted from your history, that saving their actual purchase from the natives, of the soil, the dominion, the lordship, and sovereignty, they had in the sight of God and man, no right and title to what they possessed. How much clearer then, in natural reason and equity, must our title be, who hold estates dearly purchased at the expense of our own, as well as our ancestors labor, and defended by them with treasure and blood.

Your Excellency has been pleased to confirm, rather than deny or confute, a piece of history, which, you say, we took from an anonymous pamphlet, and by which you "fear we have been too easily misled." It may be gathered from your own declaration, and other authorities, besides the anonymous pamphlet, that the House of Commons took exception, not at the King's having made an absolute grant of the territory, but at the claim of an exclusive right to the fishery on the banks and sea coast, by virtue of the patent. At this you say, "the House of Commons was alarmed, and a bill was brought in for allowing a free fishery." And, upon this occasion, your Excellency allows, that "one of the Secretaries of State declared, that the plantations were not annexed to the Crown, and so were not within the jurisdiction of Parliament." If we should concede to what your Excellency supposes might possibly, or, "perhaps," be the case, that the Secretary made this declaration, "as his own opinion," the event showed that it was the opinion of the King too; for it is not to be accounted for upon any other principle, that he would have denied his royal assent to a bill, formed for no other purpose, but to grant his subjects in England, the privilege of fishing on the sea coasts in America. The account published by Sir Ferdinando Gorges himself, of the proceedings of Parliament on this occasion, your Excellency thinks, will remove all doubt, of the sense of the nation, and of the patentees of this patent or charter, in 1620. "This narrative," you say, " has all the appearance of truth and sincerity," which we do not deny ; and, to us, it carries this conviction with it, that " what was objected " in Parliament, was the exclusive claim of fishing only. His imagining that he had satisfied the House, after divers attendances, that the planting a colony was of much more consequence than a simple disorderly course of fishing, is sufficient for our conviction. We know that the nation was at that time alarmed with apprehensions of monopolies ; and, if the patent of New England was presented by the two Houses as a grievance, it did not show, as your Excellency supposes, " the sense they then had of their authority over this new acquired territory," but only their sense of the grievance of a monopoly of the sea.

We are happy to hear your Excellency say, that " our remarks upon, and construction of the words, not repugnant to the laws of England, are much the same with those of the Council." It serves to confirm us in our opinion, in what we take to be the most important matter of difference between your Excellency and the two Houses. After saying, that the statute of 7th and 8th of William and Mary favors the construction of the words, as intending such laws of England as are made more immediately to respect us, you tell us, that " the province Agent, Mr. Dummer, in his much applauded defence, says, that, then a law of the plantations may be said to be repugnant to a law made in Great Britain, when it flatly contradicts it, so far as the law made there, mentions and relates to the plantations." This is plain and obvious to common sense, and, therefore, cannot be denied. But, if your Excellency would read a page or two further in that excellent defence, you will see that he mentions this as the sense of the phrase, as taken from an act of Parliament, rather than as the sense he would choose himself to put upon it ; and, he expressly designs to show, in vindication of the charter, that, in that sense of the words, there never was a law made in the plantations repugnant to the laws of Great Britain. He gives another construction, much more likely to be the true intent of the words, namely, " that the patentees shall not presume, under color of their particular charters, to make any laws inconsistent with the great charter, and other laws of England, by which the lives, liberties, and properties of Englishmen are secured." This is the sense in which our ancestors understood the words; and, therefore, they are unwilling to conform to the acts of trade, and disregarded them till they made provision to give them force in the colony, by a law of their own; saying, that "the laws of England did not reach America; and those acts were an invasion of their rights, liberties, and properties," because they were not "represented in Parliament." The right of being governed by laws, which were made by persons, in whose election they had a voice, they looked upon as the foundation of English liberties. By the compact with the King, in the charter, they were to be as free in America, as they would have been if they had remained within the realm; and, therefore, they freely asserted, that they " were to be governed by laws made by themselves, and by officers chosen by themselves." Mr. Dummer says, " it seems reasonable enough to think that the Crown," and, he might have added, our ancestors, " intended by this injunction to provide for all its subjects, that they might not be oppressed by arbitrary power; but being still subjects, they should be protected by the same mild laws, and enjoy the same happy government, as if they continued within the realm." And, considering the words of the charter in this light, he looks upon them as designed to be a fence against oppression and despotic power. But the construction which your Excellency puts upon the words, reduces us to a state of vassalage, and exposes us to oppression and despotic power, whenever a Parliament shall see fit to make laws for that purpose, and put them in execution.

We flatter ourselves, that, from the large extracts we have made from your Excellency's history of the colony, it appears evidently, that under both charters, it hath been the sense of the people and of the government, that they were not under the jurisdiction of Parliament. We pray you again to turn to those quotations, and our observations upon them; and we wish to have your Excellency's judicious remarks. When we adduced that history, to prove that the sentiments of private persons of influence, four or five years after the restoration, were very different from what your Excellency apprehended them to be, when you delivered your speech, you seem to concede to it, by telling us, " it was, as you take it, from the principles imbibed in those times of anarchy, (preceding the restoration,) that they disputed the authority of Parliament;" but, you add, "the government would not venture to dispute it." We find in the same history, a quotation from a letter of Mr. Stoughton, dated seventeen years after the restoration, mentioning "the country's not taking notice of the acts of navigation, to observe them." And it was, as we take it, after that time, that the government declared, in a letter to their Agents, that they had not submitted to them; and they ventured to "dispute" the jurisdiction, asserting, that they apprehended the acts to be an invasion of the rights, liberties, and properties of the subjects of his Majesty in the colony, they not being represented in Parliament, and that "the laws of England did not reach America." It very little avails in proof, that they conceded to the supreme authority of Parliament, their telling the Commissioners, "that the act of navigation had for some years before, been observed here; that they knew not of its being greatly violated; and that, such laws as appeared to be against it, were repealed." It may as truly be said now, that the revenue acts are observed by some of the people of this province; but it cannot be said that the government and people of this province have conceded, that the Parliament had authority to make such acts to be observed here. Neither does their declaration to the Commissioners, that such laws as appeared to be against the act of navigation, were repealed, prove their concession of the authority of Parliament by any means, so much as their making provision for giving force to an act of Parliament within this province, by a deliberate and solemn act or law of their own, proves the contrary.

You tell us, that "the government, four or five years before the charter was vacated, more explicitly," that is, than by a conversation with the Commissioners, "acknowledged the authority of Parliament, and voted, that their Governor should take the oath required of him, faithfully to do and perform all matters and things enjoined him by the acts of trade." But does this, may it please your Excellency, show their explicit acknowledgment of the authority of Parliament? Does it not rather show directly the contrary? For, what could there be for their vote, or authority, to require him to take the oath already required of him, by the act of Parliament, unless both he, and they, judged that an act of Parliament was not of force sufficient to bind him to take such oath? We do not deny, but, on the contrary, are fully persuaded, that your Excellency's principles in governments are still of the same with what they appear to be in the history; for, you there say, that "the passing this law, plainly shows the wrong sense they had of the relation they 'stood in to England." But we are from hence convinced, that your Excellency, when you wrote the history, was of our mind in this respect, that our ancestors, in passing the law, discovered their opinion, that they were without the jurisdiction of Parliament; for it was upon this principle alone, they shewed the wrong sense they had in your Excellency's opinion, of the relation they stood in to England.

Your Excellency, in your second speech, condescends to point out to us the acts and doings of the General Assembly, which relates to acts of Parliament, which, you think, " demonstrates that they have been acknowledged by the Assembly, or submitted to by the people ; " neither of which, in our opinion, shows that it was the sense of the nation, and our predecessors, when they first took possession of this plantation, or colony, by a grant and charter from the Crown, that they were to remain subject to the supreme authority of the English Parliament.

Your Excellency seems chiefly to rely upon our ancestors, after the revolution, " proclaiming King William and Queen Mary, in the room of King James," and taking the oaths to them, " the alteration of the form of oaths, from time to time," and finally, " the establishment of the form, which every one of us has complied with, as the charter, in express terms requires, and makes our duty." We do not know that it has ever been a point in dispute, whether the Kings of England were *ipso facto* Kings in, and over, this colony, or province. The compact was made between King Charles the I. his heirs and successors, and the Governor and company, their heirs and successors. It is easy, upon this principle, to account for the acknowledgment of, and submission to King William and Queen Mary, as successors of Charles the I. in the room of King James besides, it is to be considered, that the people in the colony, as wel as in England, had suffered under the tyrant James, by which, h had alike forfeited his right to reign over both. There had been ; revolution here, as well as in England. The eyes of the people here, were upon William and Mary ; and the news of their being proclaimed in England, was, as your Excellency's history tells us, "the most joyful news ever received in New England." And, if they were not proclaimed here, "by virtue of an act of the colony," it was, as we think, may be concluded from the tenor of your history with the general or universal consent of the people, as apparently, as if "such act had passed." It is consent alone, that makes any human laws binding; and as a learned author observes, a purely voluntary submission to an act, because it is highly in our favor and for our benefit, is in all equity and justice, to be deemed as not at all proceeding from the right we include in the Legislators, that they, thereby obtain an authority over us, and that ever hereafter, we must obey them of duty. We would observe, that one of the first acts of the General Assembly of this province, since the present charter, was an act, requiring the taking the oaths mentioned in an act of Parliament, to which you refer us. For what purpose was this act of the Assembly passed, if it was the sense of the Legislators that the act of Parliament was in force in the province? And, at the same time, another act was made for the establishment of other oaths necessary to be taken; both which acts have the royal sanction, and are now in force. Your Excellency says, that when the colony applied to King William for a second charter, they knew the oath the King had taken, which was to govern them according to the statutes in Parliament, and (which your Excellency here omits,) the laws and customs of the same. By the laws and customs of Parliament, the people of England freely debate and consent to such statutes as are made by themselves, or their chosen Representatives. This is a law, or custom, which all mankind may justly challenge as their inherent right. According to this law, the King has an undoubted right to govern us. Your Excellency, upon recollection, surely will not infer from hence, that it was the sense of our predecessors that there was to remain a supremacy in the English Parliament, or a full power and authority to make laws binding upon us, in all cases whatever, in that Parliament where we cannot debate and deliberate upon the necessity or expediency of any law, and, consequently, without our consent; and, as it may probably happen, destructive of the first law of society, the good of the whole. You tell us, that "after the assumption of all the powers of government, by virtue of the new charter, an act passed for the reviving, for a limited time, all the local laws of the Massachusetts Bay and New Plymouth respectively, not repugnant to the laws of England. And, at the same session, an act passed establishing naval officers, that all undue trading, contrary to an act of Parliament, may be prevented." Among the acts that were then revived, we may reasonably suppose, was that, whereby provision was made to give force to this act of Parliament, in the province. The establishment, therefore, of the naval officers, was to aid the execution of an act of Parliament, for the observance of which, within the colony, the Assembly had before made provision, after free debates, with their own consent, and by their own act.

The act of Parliament, passed in 1741, for putting an end to several unwarrantable schemes, mentioned by your Excellency, was designed for the general good; and, if the validity of it was not disputed, it cannot be urged as a concession of the supreme authority, to make laws binding on us in all cases whatever. But, if the design of it was for the general benefit of the province, it was, in one respect, at least greatly complained of, by the persons more immediately affected by it; and to remedy the inconvenience, the Legislative of this province, passed an act, directly militating with it; which is the strongest evidence, that although they may have submitted, *sub silentio*, to some acts of Parliament, that they conceived might operate for their benefit, they did not conceive themselves bound by any of its acts, which, they judged, would operate to the injury even of individuals.

Your Excellency has not thought proper, to attempt to confute the reasoning of a learned writer on the laws of nature and nations, quoted by us, on this occasion, to shew that the authority of the Legislature does not extend so far as the fundamentals of the constitution. We are unhappy in not having your remarks upon the reasoning of that great man; and, until it is confuted, we shall remain of the opinion, that the fundamentals of the constitution being excepted from the commission of the Legislators, none of the acts or doings of the General Assembly, however deliberate and solemn, could avail to change them, if the people have not, in very express terms, given them the power to do it; and, that much less ought their acts and doings, however numerous, which barely refer to acts of Parliament made expressly to relate to us, to be taken as an acknowledgment, that we are subject to the supreme authority of Parliament.

We shall sum up our own sentiments in the words of that learned writer, Mr. Hooker, in his Ecclesiastical Policy, as quoted by Mr. Locke. "The lawful power of making laws to command whole political societies of men, belonging so properly to the same entire societies, that for any prince or potentate of what kind soever, to exercise the same of himself, and not from express commission, immediately and personally received from God, is no better than

mere tyranny. Laws, therefore, they are not, which public approbation hath not made so; for laws human, of what kind soever, are
available by consent." "Since men, naturally, have no full and
perfect power to command whole politic multitudes of men, therefore,
utterly without our consent, we could in such sort, be at no man's
commandment living. And to be commanded, we do not consent,
when that society, whereof we be a party, hath at any time before
consented." We think your Excellency has not proved, either that
the colony is a part of the politic society of England, or that it has
ever consented that the Parliament of England or Great Britain,
should make laws binding upon us, in all cases, whether made
expressly to refer to us or not.

We cannot help, before we conclude, expressing our great concern,
that your Excellency has thus repeatedly, in a manner, insisted upon
our free sentiments on matters of so delicate a nature and weighty
importance. The question appears to us, to be no other, than,
whether we are the subjects of absolute unlimited power, or of a
free government, formed on the principles of the English constitution. If your Excellency's doctrine be true, the people of this province hold their lands of the Crown and people of England; and their
lives, liberties, and properties, are at their disposal, and that, even
by compact and their own consent. They were subject to the King
as the head *alterius populi* of another people, in whose Legislative
they have no voice or interest. They are, indeed, said to have a
constitution and a Legislative of their own; but your Excellency
has explained it into a mere phantom; limited, controled, superseded,
and nullified, at the will of another. Is this the constitution which
so charmed our ancestors, that, as your Excellency has informed us,
they kept a day of solemn thanksgiving to Almighty God when they
received it? And were they men of so little discernment, such
children in understanding, as to please themselves with the imagination, that they were blessed with the same rights and liberties which
natural born subjects in England enjoyed, when, at the same time,
they had fully consented to be ruled and ordered by a Legislative,
a thousand leagues distant from them, which cannot be supposed to
be sufficiently acquainted with their circumstances, if concerned for
their interest, and in which, they cannot be in any sense represented?

[The committee who reported the above, were, Mr. Cushing, (the
Speaker,) Mr. S. Adams, Mr. Hancock, Mr. Phillips, Maj. Foster,
Col. Bowers, Mr. Hobson, Col. Thayer, and Mr. Denny.]

APPENDIX C.

COPY OF LETTERS

Sent to *Great Britain*, by his Excellency *Thomas Hutchinson*, the Hon. *Andrew Oliver*, and several other persons, BORN AND EDUCATED AMONG US. Which original Letters have been returned to *America*, and laid before the honorable House of Representatives ·of this Province.

In which (*notwithstanding his Excellency's Declaration to the House, that the Tendency and Design of them was not to subvert the Constitution, but rather to preserve it entire*) the judicious Reader will discover the fatal Source of the Confusion and Bloodshed in which this Province especially has been involved, and which threatened total Destruction to the Liberties of all *America*.

BOSTON:

Printed by EDES and GILL, in Queen Street.

1773.[1]

BOSTON, 18th June, 1768.

SIR, — As you allow me the honour of your correspondence, I may not omit acquainting you with so remarkable an event as the withdraw of the commissioners of the customs and most of the other officers under them from the town on board the Romney, with an intent to remove from thence to the Castle.

In the evening of the 10th a sloop belonging to Mr. Hancock, a representative for Boston, and a wealthy merchant of great influence over the populace, was seized by the collector and comptroller for a very notorious breach of the acts of trade, and after seizure, taken into custody by the officer of the Romney man of war, and removed under command of her guns. It is pretended that the removal and not the seizure incensed the people. It seems not very material which it was. A mob was immediately rais'd, the officers insulted, bruis'd, and much hurt, and the windows of some of their houses broke ; a boat belonging to the collector burnt in triumph, and many threats utter'd against the Commissioners and their officers : no notice being taken of their extravagance, in the time of it, nor any endeavours by any authority except the governor, the next day to

---

[1] Title-page of the pamphlet published by the legislature. The letters follow with care the pamphlet text.

discover and punish the offenders ; and there being a rumour of a higher mob intended monday (the 13th) in the evening the Commissioners, *four of them*, thought themselves altogether unsafe, being destitute of protection, and removed with their families to the Romney, and there remain and hold their board, and next week intend to do the same, and also open the custom-house at the Castle. The governor press'd the council to assist him with their advice, but they declin'd and evaded, calling it a brush or small disturbance by boys and negroes, not considering *how much it must be resented* in England that the officers of the Crown should think themselves obliged to quit the place of their residence and go on board a King's ship for safety, and all the internal authority of the province take no notice of it. The town of Boston have had repeated meetings, and by their votes declared the Commissioners and their officers a great grievance, and yesterday instructed their representatives to endeavor that enquiry should be made by the assembly whether any person by writing or in any other way had encouraged the sending troops here, there being some alarming reports that troops are expected, but have not taken any measures to discountenance the promoters of the late proceedings ; but on the contrary appointed one or more of the actors or abettors on a Committee appointed to wait on the Governor and to desire him to order the man of war out of the harbour.

Ignorant as they be, yet the heads of a Boston town-meeting influences all public measures.

It is not possible this anarchy should last always. Mr Hallowell who will be the bearer of this tells me he has the honour of being personally known to you. I beg leave to refer you to him for a more full account.

> I am with great esteem,
> > Sir, your most humble and obedient servant,
> > > THO. HUTCHINSON.

BOSTON, August 1768.

SIR, — It is very necessary other information should be had in England of the present state of the commissioners of the customs than what common fame will bring to you or what you will receive from most of the letters which go from hence, people in general being prejudiced by many false reports and misrepresentations concerning them. Seven eighths of the people of the country suppose the board itself to be unconstitutional and cannot be undeceived and brought to believe that a board has existed in England all this century, and that the board established here has no new powers given to it. Our incendiaries know it, but they industriously and very wickedly publish the contrary. As much pains has been taken to prejudice the country against the persons of the commissioners and their characters have been misrepresented and cruelly treated especially since their confinement at the castle where they are not so likely to hear what is said of them and are not so able to confute it.

It is now pretended they need not to have withdrawn, that Mr. Williams had stood his ground without any injury although the mob beset his house, &c. There never was that spirit raised against the under officers as against the commissioners. *I mean four of them.* They had a public affront offered them by the town of Boston who refused to give the use of their hall for a public dinner unless it was stipulated that the commissioners should not be invited. An affront of the same nature at the motion of Mr Hancock was offered by a company of cadets. Soon after a vessel of Mr Hancock's being seized the officers were mobb'd and the commissioners were informed they were threatned. I own I was in pain for them. I do not believe if the mob had seized them, there was any authority able and willing to have rescued them. After they had withdrawn the town signified to the governor by a message that it was expected or desired they should not return. It was then the general voice that it would not be safe for them to return. After all this the sons of liberty say they deserted or abdicated.

The other officers of the customs in general either did not leave the town or soon returned to it. Some of them seem to be discontented with the commissioners. Great pains have been taken to increase the discontent. Their office by these means is rendered extremely burdensome. Everything they do is found fault with, and yet no particular illegality or even irregularity mentioned. There is too much hauteur some of their officers say in the treatment they receive. They say they treat their officers as the commissioners treat their officers in England, and require no greater deference. After all it is not the persons but the office of the commissioners which has raised this spirit, and the distinction made between the commissioners is because it has been given out that four of them were in favor of the new establishment and the *fifth was not.* If Mr Hallowell arrived safe he can inform you many circumstances relative to this distinction which I very willingly excuse myself from mentioning.

I know of no burden brought upon the fair trader by the new establishment. The illicit trade finds the risque greater than it used to be, especially in the port where the board is constantly held. Another circumstance which increases the prejudice is this; the new duties happened to take place just about the time the commissioners arrived. People have absurdly connected the duties and board of commissioners, and suppose we should have had no additional duties if there had been no board to have the charge of collecting them. With all the aid you can give to the officers of the Crown they will have enough to do to maintain the authority of government and to carry the taxes into execution. If they are discountenanced, neglected or fail of support from you, they must submit to everything the present opposers of government think fit to require of them.

There is no officer under greater discouragement than that of the commissioners. Some of my friends recommended me to the ministry. I think myself very happy that I am not one. Indeed it would have been incompatible with my post as chief-justice, and I must have declined it, and I should do it although no greater salary had been affixed to the chief-justices place than the small pittance allowed by the province.

From my acquaintance with the commissioners I have received a personal esteem for them, but my chief inducement to make this representation to you is a regard to the public interest which I am sure will suffer if the opposition carry their point against them.

I am with great esteem,

Sir, your most obedient humble servant,

THO. HUTCHINSON.

August 10. Yesterday at a meeting of the merchants it was agreed by all present to give no more orders for goods from England, nor receive any on commission untill the late acts are repealed. And it is said all except sixteen in the town have subscribed an engagement of that tenor. I hope the subscription will be printed that I may transmit it to you.

BOSTON, 4th October 1768.

DEAR SIR, — I was absent upon one of our circuits when Mr Byles arrived. Since my return I have received from him your obliging letter of 31st July. I never dared to think what the resentment of the nation would be upon Hallowell's arrival. It is not strange that measures should be immediately taken to reduce the colonies to their former state of government and order, but that the national funds should be affected by it is to me a little mysterious and surprising. Principles of government absurd enough spread thro' all the colonies ; but I cannot think that in any colony, people of any consideration have ever been so mad as to think of a revolt. Many of the common people have been in a frenzy, and talked of dying in defence of their liberties, and have spoke and printed what is highly criminal, and too many of rank above the vulgar, and some *in public posts* have countenanced and encouraged them untill they increased so much in their numbers and in their opinion of their importance as to submit to government no further than they thought proper. The legislative powers have been influenced by them, and the executive powers intirely lost their force. There has been continual danger of mobs and insurrections, but they would have spent all their force within themselves, the officers of the Crown and some of the few friends who dared to stand by them possibly might have been knock'd in the head, and some such fatal event would probably have brought the people to their senses. For four or five weeks past, the distemper has been growing, and I confess I have not been without some apprehensions for myself, but my friends have had more for me, and I have had repeated and frequent notices from them from different quarters, *one of the last I will inclose to you*.[1] In this state of things there was no security but quitting my post, which nothing but the last extremity would justify. As chief justice for two years after our first disorders I kept the grand juries tolerably well to their duty. The last spring there had been several riots, and a most infamous libel had been published in one of the papers, which I enlarged upon, and the grand jury had determined to make presentments, but the attorney general not attending them the first day, Otis and his creatures who were alarmed and frightened exerted themselves the next day and prevailed upon so many of the jury to change their voices, that there was not a sufficient number left to find a bill. They have been ever since more enraged against me than ever. At the desire of the governor I committed to writing the charge while it lay in my memory, and as I have no further use for it I will inclose it as it may give you some idea of our judicatories.

[1] See the following letters.

Whilst we were in this state, news came of two regiments being ordered from Halifax, and soon after two more from Ireland. The minds of people were more and more agitated, broad hints were given that the troops should never land, a barrel of tar was placed upon the bacon, in the night to be fired to bring in the country when the troops appeared, and all the authority of the government was not strong enough to remove it. The town of Boston met and passed a number of weak but very criminal votes; and as the governor declined calling an assembly they sent circular letters to all the towns and districts to send a person each that there might be a general consultation at so extraordinary a crisis. They met and spent a week, made themselves ridiculous, and then dissolv'd themselves after a message or two to the governor which he refused to receive; a petition to the King which I dare say *their agent* will never be allowed to present, and a result which they have published ill-natured and impotent.

In this confusion the troops from Halifax arrived. I never was much afraid of the people's taking arms, but I was apprehensive of violence from the mob, it being their last chance before the troops could land. As the prospect of revenge became more certain their courage abated in proportion. Two regiments are landed, but a new grievance is now raised. The troops are by act of parliament to be quartered no where else but in the barracks untill they are full. There are barracks enough at the castle to hold both regiments. It is therefore against the act to bring them into town. This was started by the council in their answer to the governor, which to make themselves popular, they in an unprecedented way published and have alarmed all the province; for although none but the most contracted minds could put such a construction upon the act, yet after this declaration of the council nine tenths of the people suppose it just. I wish the act had been better express'd, but it is absurd to suppose the parliament intended to take from the King the direction of his forces by confining them to a place where any of the colonies might think fit to build barracks. It is besides ungrateful, for it is known to many that this provision was brought into the bill after it had been framed without it, from meer favor to the colonies. I hear the commander in chief has provided barracks or quarters, but a doubt still remains with some of the council, whether they are to furnish the articles required, unless the men are in the province barracks, and they are to determine upon it to-day.

The government has been so long in the hands of the populace that it must come out of them by degrees, at least it will be a work of time to bring the people back to just notions of the nature of government.

Mr. Pepperell, a young gentleman of good character, and grandson and principal heir to the late Sir William Pepperell being bound to London, I shall deliver this letter to him, as it will be too bulky for postage, and desire him to wait upon you with it.

I am with very great esteem,

Sir, your most humble and most obedient servant,

THO. HUTCHINSON.

BOSTON, 10th December 1768.

DEAR SIR, — I am just now informed that a number of the council, perhaps 8 or 10, who live in and near this town, have met together and agreed upon a long address or petition to parliament, and that it will be sent by their ship to Mr. Bollan to be presented. Mr. Danforth who is president of the council told the governor upon enquiry, that it was sent to him to sign, and he supposed the rest of the council who had met together would sign after him in order, but he had since found that they had wrote over his name *by order of council*, which makes it appear to be an act of council. This may be a low piece of cunning in him, but be it as it may, it's proper it should be known that the whole is no more than the doings of a part of the council only, although even that is not very material, since, if they had all been present without the governor's summons the meeting would have been irregular and unconstitutional, and ought to be discountenanced and censured. I suppose there is no instance of the Privy Council's meeting and doing business without the King's presence or special direction, except in committees upon such business as by his majesty's order has been referred to them by an act of council, and I have known no instance here without the governor until within three or four months past.

I thought it very necessary the circumstances of this proceeding should be known, tho' if there be no necessity for it, I think it would be best it should not be known that the intelligence comes from me. I am with very great regard, Sir,

Your most humble and most obedient servant,

THO. HUTCHINSON.

BOSTON, 20th January 1769.

DEAR SIR, — You have laid me under very great obligations by the very clear and full account of proceedings in parliament, which I received from you by Capt. Scott. You have also done much service to the people of the province. For a day or two after the ship arrived, the enemies of government gave out that their friends in parliament were increasing, and all things would be soon on the old footing; in other words that all acts imposing duties would be repealed, the commissioners' board dissolved, the customs put on the old footing, and *illicit* trade carried on with little or no hazard. It was very fortunate that I had it in my power to prevent such a false representation from spreading through the province. I have been very cautious of using your name, but I have been very free in publishing abroad the substance of your letter, and declaring that I had my intelligence from the best authority, and have in a great measure defeated the ill design in raising and attempting to spread so groundless a report. What marks of resentment the parliament will show whether they will be upon the province in general or particular persons, is extremely uncertain, but that they will be placed somewhere is most certain, and I add because *I think it ought to be so*, that those who have been most steady in preserving the constitution and opposing the licentiousness of such as call themselves sons of liberty will certainly meet with favor and encouragement.

This is most certainly a crisis. I really wish that there may not have been the least degree of severity beyond what is absolutely necessary to maintain, I think I may say to you the *dependance* which a colony ought to have upon the parent state; but if no measures shall have been taken to secure this dependance, or nothing more than some declaratory acts or resolves, *it is all over with us.* The friends of government will be utterly disheartened, and the friends of anarchy will be afraid of nothing be it ever so extravagant.

The last vessel from London had a quick passage. We expect to be in suspense for the three or four next weeks and then to hear our fate. I never think of the measures necessary for the peace and good order of the colonies without pain. There must be an abridgment of what are called English liberties. I relieve myself by considering that in a remove from the state of nature to the most perfect state of government there must be a great restraint of natural liberty. I doubt whether it is possible to project a system of government in which a colony 3000 miles distant from the parent state shall enjoy all the liberty of the parent state. I am certain I have never yet seen the projection. I wish the good of the colony when I wish to see some further restraint of liberty rather than the connexion with the parent state should be broken; for I am sure such a breach must prove the ruin of the colony. Pardon me this excursion, it really proceeds from the state of mind into which our perplexed affairs often throws me.

I have the honor to be with very great esteem,

Sir, your most humble and most obedient servant,

THO. HUTCHINSON.

BOSTON, 20th October, 1769.

DEAR SIR, — I thank you for your last favor of July 18th. I fancy in my last to you about two months ago I have answered the greatest part of it.

My opinion upon the combination of the merchants, I gave you very fully. How long they will be able to continue them if parliament should not interpose is uncertain. In most articles they may another year, and you run the risque of their substituting when they are put to their shifts something of their own in the place of what they used to have from you, and which they will never return to you for. But it is not possible that provision for dissolving these combinations and subjecting all who do not renounce them to penalties adequate to the offence should not be made the first week the parliament meets. Certainly all parties will unite in so extraordinary case if they never do in any other. So much has been said upon the repeal of the duties laid by the last act, that it will render it very difficult to keep people's minds quiet if that should be refused them. They deserve punishment you will say, but laying or continuing taxes upon all cannot be thought equal, seeing many will be punished who are not offenders. *Penalties of another kind seem better adapted.*

I have been tolerably treated since the governor's departure, no other charge being made against me in our scandalous news-papers except my bad principles in matters of government, and this charge has had little effect, and a great many friends promise me support.

I must beg the favor of you to keep secret everything I write, untill we are in a more settled state, for the party here either by their *agent, or* by some of their emissaries in London, have sent them every report or rumor of the contents of letters wrote from hence. I hope we shall see better times both here and in England.

I am with great esteem,

Sir, your most obedient servant,

THO. HUTCHINSON.

[These Resolves were circulated, it must be remembered, before the Letters, as if to prepare the minds of the people for them.]

RESOLVES OF THE HOUSE OF REPRESENTATIVES, RESPECTING THE LETTERS OF THE GOVERNOR, LIEUTENANT GOVERNOR, AND OTHERS, JUNE 16, 1773.

Resolved, That the letters, signed Thomas Hutchinson, and those signed Andrew Oliver, now under the consideration of this House, appear to be the genuine letters of the present Governor and Lieutenant Governor of this province, whose hand writing and signatures are well known to many of the Members of this House; and, that they contain aggravated accounts of facts, and misrepresentations; and, that one manifest design of them, was, to represent the matters they treat of, in a light, highly injurious to this province, and the persons against whom they were wrote.

Resolved, That, though the letters aforesaid, signed Thomas Hutchinson, are said, by the Governor, in his message to this House, of June 9th, to be " private letters, wrote to a gentleman in London, since deceased;" and "that all, except the last, were wrote many months before he came to the chair; yet, they were wrote by the present Governor, when he was Lieutenant Governor and Chief Justice of this province, who has been represented abroad, as eminent for his abilities, as for his exalted station; and was under no official obligation to transmit intelligence of such matters as are contained in said letters; and, that they, therefore, must be considered, by the person to whom they were sent, as documents of solid intelligence; and, that this gentleman in London, to whom they were wrote, was then a Member of the British Parliament, and one who was very active in American affairs; and therefore, that these letters, however secretly wrote, must naturally be supposed to have, and really had, a public operation.

Resolved, That these " private letters," being wrote " with express confidence of secrecy," was only to prevent the contents of them being known here, as appears by said letters; and this rendered them the more injurious in their tendency, and really insidious.

Resolved, That the letters, signed Thomas Hutchinson, considering the person by whom they were wrote, the matters they expressly contain, the express reference in some of them, for "full intelligence," to Mr. Hallowell, a person deeply interested in the measures so much complained of, and recommendatory notices of divers other persons, whose emoluments arising from our public burdens, might excite them to unfavorable representations of us, the measures they suggest, the temper in which they were wrote, the manner in which they were sent, and the person to whom they were addressed; had a natural and efficacious tendency to interrupt and alienate the affections of our most gracious Sovereign, King George the III. from this, his loyal and affectionate province; to destroy that harmony and good will between Great Britain and this colony, which every friend to either, would wish to establish; to excite the resentment of the British administration against this province; to defeat the endeavors of our agents and friends to serve us, by a fair representation of our state of grievances; to prevent our humble and repeated petitions from reaching the royal ear of our common Sovereign; and to produce the severe and destructive measures which have been taken against this province, and others still more so, which have been threatened.

Resolved, That the letters, signed Andrew Oliver, considering the person by whom they were wrote, the matters they expressly contain, the measures they suggest, the temper in which they were wrote, the manner in which they were sent, and the person to whom they were addressed, had a natural and efficacious tendency to interrupt and alienate the affections of our most gracious Sovereign, King George the III. from this, his loyal and affectionate province; to destroy that harmony and good will between Great Britain and this colony, which every friend to either, would wish to establish; to excite the resentment of the British administration against this province; to defeat the endeavors of our agents and friends to serve us, by a fair representation of our state of grievances; to prevent our humble and repeated petitions from having the desired effect; and to produce the severe and destructive measures which have been taken against this province, and others still more so, which have been threatened.

Resolved, As the opinion of this House, that it clearly appears from the letters aforesaid, signed Thomas Hutchinson, and Andrew Oliver, that it was the desire and endeavor of the writers of them, that certain acts of the British Parliament, for raising a revenue in America, might be carried into effect by military force; and by introducing a fleet and army into his Majesty's loyal province, to intimidate the minds of his subjects here, and prevent every constitutional measure to obtain the repeal of those acts, so justly esteemed a grievance to us, and to suppress the very spirit of freedom.

Resolved, That it is the opinion of this House, that, as the salaries lately appointed for the Governor, Lieutenant Governor, and Judges of this province, directly repugnant to the charter, and subversive of justice, are founded on this revenue; and, as those letters were wrote with a design, and had a tendency to promote and support that revenue, therefore, there is great reason to suppose the writers of those letters, were well knowing to, suggested, and promoted the enacting said revenue acts, and the establishments founded on the same.

Resolved, That while the writer of these letters, signed Thomas Hutchinson, has been thus exerting himself, by his "secret confidential correspondence," to introduce measures, destructive of our constitutional liberty, he has been practising every method among the people of this province, to fix in their minds an exalted opinion of his warmest affection for them, and his unremitted endeavors to promote their best interest at the Court of Great Britain.

Resolved, As the opinion of this House, that by comparing these letters, signed Thomas Hutchinson, with those, signed Andrew Oliver, Charles Paxton, and Nathan Rogers, and, considering what has since, in fact taken place, conformable thereto, that it is manifest, there has been, for many years past, measures contemplated, and a plan formed, by a set of men, born and educated among us, to raise their own fortunes, and advance themselves to posts of honor and profit, not only to the destruction of the charter and constitution of this province, but at the expense of the rights and liberties of the American colonies. And, it is further the opinion of this House, that the said persons have been some of the chief instruments in the introduction of a military force into the province, to carry their plans into execution; and, therefore, they have been, not only greatly instrumental of disturbing the peace and harmony of the government, and causing, and promoting great discord and animosities, but are justly chargeable with the great corruption of morals, and all that confusion, misery and bloodshed, which have been the natural effects of the introduction of troops.

Whereas, for many years past, measures have been taken by the British administration, very grievous to the good people of this province, which this House have now reason to suppose, were promoted, if not originally suggested, by the writers of these letters; and many efforts have been made, by the people, to obtain the redress of their grievances:

Resolved, That it appears to this House, that the writers of these letters, have availed themselves of disorders, that naturally arise in a free government, under such oppressions, as arguments to prove, that it was, originally, necessary such measures should have been taken, and that they should now be continued and increased.

Whereas, in the letter, signed Charles Paxton, dated Boston Harbor, June 20, 1768, it is expressly declared, that, " unless we have immediately two or three regiments, it is the opinion of all the friends of government, that Boston will be in open rebellion: "

Resolved, That this is a most wicked and injurious representation, designed to inflame the minds of his Majesty's Ministers and the nation, and to excite in the breast of our Sovereign, a jealousy of his loyal subjects of said town, without the least grounds therefor, as enemies of his Majesty's person and government.

Whereas certain letters, signed by two private persons, viz.: Thomas Moffat, and George Rome, have been laid before the House, which letters contain many matters, highly injurious to government and to the national peace:

Resolved, That it has been the misfortune of this government, from the earliest period of it, from time to time, to be secretly traduced, and maliciously represented to the British Ministry, by persons, who were neither friendly to this colony, nor to the English constitution:

Resolved, That the House have just reason to complain of it, as a very great grievance, that the humble petitions and remonstrances of the Commons of this province, are not allowed to reach the hand of our most gracious Sovereign, merely because they are presented by an agent, to whose appointment, the Governor, with whom our chief dispute may subsist, doth not consent; while the partial and inflammatory letters of individuals, who are greatly interested in the revenue acts, and the measures taken to carry them into execution, have been laid before administration, attended to, and determined upon, not only to the injury of the reputation of the people, but to the depriving them of their invaluable rights and liberties.

Whereas, this House are humbly of opinion, that his Majesty will judge it to be incompatible with the interest of his Crown, and the peace and safety of the good people of this, his loyal province, that persons should be continued in places of high trust and authority in it, who are known to have, with great industry, though secretly, endeavored to undermine, alter, and overthrow the constitution of the province : therefore,

Resolved, That this House is bound, in duty to the King and their constituents, humbly to remonstrate to his Majesty, the conduct of his Excellency Thomas Hutchinson, Esquire, Governor, and the Honorable Andrew Oliver, Esquire, Lieutenant Governor of this province ; and to pray that his Majesty would be pleased to remove them forever from the government thereof.

APPENDIX D.

HUTCHINSON'S CONFISCATED MASSACHUSETTS ESTATE.

From the Records in the Suffolk Registry of Deeds.[1]

Land and dwelling-house in Boston, Fish St. W. ; land purchased by Thomas Stephenson N. ; passageway E. ; heirs of William Graves S.

Land, 43 A. 2 qr. 34 r., in Milton, a back lane E. ; Mr. Ivers and Milton River N. ; Stephen Badcock and a brook N. W. ; lane to Stephen Badcock S. W. ; road to Milton meeting-house S. E. —— Land, 33 A. 1 r., mansion house and barn in Milton, road to Braintree E. ; heirs of William Badcock S. E. and S. W. ; road to Milton meeting-house N. W. —— 14 A. 3 qr. 3 r. in Milton, road to Braintree S. W. ; Robert Williams S. E. ; heirs of William Badcock N. ; Milton River N. E. —— Woodland, 48 A. 1 qr. 9 r., in Milton, road by Moses Glover's N. W. ; Braintree town line S. E. ; John Bois S. W. ; John Sprague N. E. —— Tillage land, 17 A. 2 qr. 27 r., and salt marsh, 16 A. 14 r. adjoining, in Dorchester, lower road from Milton bridge to Dorchester meeting-house W. ; Hopestill Leeds N. E. ; John Capen and others E. ; Amariah Blake and the river N. ; Ebenezer Swift, Daniel Vose and a creek S. —— Salt marsh, 2 A. 3 qr. 9 r., near the Hum-

---

[1] See " Confiscated Estates of Boston Loyalists." a valuable paper by John T. Hassam, Esq., *Proceedings Mass. Hist. Society*, May, 1895.

mucks in DORCHESTER, Levi Rounsavel N.; Robert Swan and Madam Belcher S.; the river W. —— Salt marsh, 7 A., in DORCHESTER, Billings Creek S. and W.; Robert Spurr N.; Henry Leadbetter S. E. and E. —— One undivided third of 8 A. salt marsh in DORCHESTER, held in common with Timothy Tucker and Joseph Tucker, Billings Creek S.; Nathan Ford W. —— Woodland, 33½ A. 9 r., in BRAINTREE.

Land and dwelling-house in BOSTON, Fish St. W.; land purchased by Parsons and Sargeant N.; passageways E. and S.

Land and dwelling-house in BOSTON, Fish St. W.; passageways N. and E.; land purchased by Thomas Stephenson S. —— Land and dwelling-house, Fish St. W.; land purchased by John Hancock N.; Thomas Hutchinson E.; land purchased by John Hotty S. —— Land, store, block-maker's shop, and other work places near the above, passageways S.; W. and E.; Thomas Hutchinson N. —— Flats, dock, wharf and stores near the above, passage W.; dock N.; sea E.; dock S. —— Flats, dock and wharf adjoining the above-described wharf, John Brick S.; passageways W. and N.; dock N.; the sea E.

Land and dwelling-houses in BOSTON, Fish St. W.; land purchased by said Parsons and Sargeant S.; passage N.; passage E.; land purchased by said Parsons and Sargeant S.; passage W.; then running W. and S.

Land and dwelling-house in BOSTON, Fish St. W.; land purchased by Parsons and Sargeant N.; passage E.; land purchased by Joseph Veasey S.

Land and brick dwelling-house in BOSTON, Middle St. W.; Fleet St. N.; street from Clark's Square to Fleet St. E.; Lady Franklin S.

INDEX.

ACADIANS, deportation of, 40.

Adams, Charles Francis, 1st, on the controversy of 1773, 252.

Adams, Charles Francis, 2d, on the Braintree village school, 14.

Adams, John, on Hutchinson as a financier, on his merit in general, Introduction, xv, etc.; describes the case of the Writs of Assistance, 55, etc.; begins his public career, 107; on the disease of James Otis, 150, etc.; counsel for Preston and the soldiers after the Massacre, 165; in the legislature, 1770, 175; his prominence, 181; his manliness at the trial of the soldiers, 185; describes the controversy over Parliamentary authority, 252; claims large credit for himself, 255; his mistaken account of Hutchinson's treatment in England, 333.

Adams, Samuel, on Hutchinson as an aristocrat, Introduction, xix; his father a director of the Land Bank, 32; opposes representation of the Colonies in Parliament, 80; instructs the Boston seat in 1764, 82; begins to supersede James Otis, 83; in the legislature, 99; opposes Colonial representation in Parliament, 100; writes for the Assembly the letter to Deberdt, 129; and the "Circular Letter," 131; becomes leader of the opposition to Government, 156; his bearing at the Boston Massacre, 163; as a working member of the Assembly, 174; his relations with Hancock, 176; his bold manifestoes, 177, etc.; his prominence in 1770, 181; sets on foot a Committee of Correspondence, 184; his bad conduct before the trial of the soldiers, 186; denounces Hutchinson, 192; denounced by Hutchinson, 193; objects to Governor's salary coming from a royal grant, 209; almost alone in the struggle in 1771, 211; his relations with Hancock, 213; his firmness of spirit when apparently overwhelmed, 214; revulsion in his favor, 215; characterized by Hutchinson, 216; denounces Hutchinson for obeying royal instructions, 217; dawn of the great Committee of Correspondence, 219; on parliamentary authority, 220; his struggle against Tory writers in the Boston Gazette, 223; his quarrel with Hancock, 224; barely successful in 1771 in opposing the removal of the legislature to Cambridge, 225; his final triumph, 227; the Committee of Correspondence made potent through him, 236; justifies the Town-Meeting, 244, etc.; his views compared with those of Hutchinson, 246, etc.; excessive devotion to Town-Meeting methods, 247; appreciates the inconsistency of the Whig position in 1773, 259; his conduct in the affair of the Letters, 268, 270, 277; "Master of the Puppets," 286; characterized by Hutchinson, 290, etc.; chief figure in the Tea-Party tumult, 297, 304; manœuvres with Bowdoin to lay aside the Governor, 311; directions from England for his seizure, 315; Hutchinson describes him to George III., 327.

Albany, Convention at, in 1764, 38.

Ames, Fisher, compares Democracy to a raft, Introduction, xvii.

Anglo-Saxon race, the schism in not a calamity, Introduction, xviii.

Appleton, Rev. Daniel, on the sufferings of the people through paper money, 19.

Assembly, Second House in Massachusetts Bay, 6; Hutchinson a member, 16; its course in the paper-money troubles, 21, 23; won over for